Macromedia®
Dreamweaver® MX

Ruth Guthrie
Louise Soe

THOMSON

COURSE TECHNOLOGY

Australia • Canada • Mexico • Singapore • Spain • United Kingdom • United States

THOMSON

★

COURSE TECHNOLOGY

Macromedia® Dreamweaver® MX
by Ruth Guthrie and Louise Soe

Product Manager:
Tricia Boyle

Executive Editor:
Jennifer Locke

Acquisitions Editor:
Bill Larkin

Development Editor:
Jill Batistick

Associate Product Marketing Manager:
Angela Laughlin

Associate Product Manager
Janet Aras

Editorial Assistant:
Christy Urban

Production Editor:
Danielle Power

Cover Designer:
Joseph Lee, Black Fish Design

Compositor:
GEX Publishing Services

Manufacturing Coordinator:
Laura Burns

Contents

TABLE OF
Contents

Preface

Macromedia Dreamweaver MX and Fireworks MX are part of an integrated Web development environment, Macromedia Studio MX, which helps you develop exciting, integrated, and interactive Web sites. Web development has moved rapidly beyond the coding of simple HTML coded pages with flat text to the creation of animated, multimedia, and graphically enhanced products. With these advances, the use of technologies such as JavaScript, Flash, optimized graphics, digital movies, and MP3 has become common on the Internet. Dreamweaver helps you integrate these technologies by providing a suite of tools that enable you to easily embed them into Web pages, while generating the code, whether HTML or JavaScript, for you. Dreamweaver also provides design elements such as templates and styles that provide consistency, easier maintenance, and error checking and prevention features.

In this book, you learn how to create, modify, and optimize graphics in Fireworks MX, and conceptualize, design, and develop Web sites using Dreamweaver MX. You also learn how to use the Dreamweaver site management tools (both during development and when you upload your Web site to a server). You discover different layout methods, including frames, layers, Cascading Style Sheets (CSSs), and tables and cells. You learn how to develop an interactive form and provide feedback to the viewer from the client side because server-side programming is not covered in this book. You learn how to use behaviors and styles in Dreamweaver to make your site more dynamic, consistent, and easier to maintain.

Dreamweaver MX integrates two applications that were formerly separate: Dreamweaver 4 and UltraDev. This text covers the client-side aspects of Dreamweaver MX, which were part of Dreamweaver 4. It does not cover the functions in Dreamweaver MX that deal with server-side programming and datadase updates, which were part of UltraDev. Course Technology is publishing a text that will cover those features (Spring 2003). Please visit *www.course.com* for more information on this title.

The Intended Audience

Macromedia Dreamweaver MX is intended for the individual who wants to create Web sites using the integrated productivity tools of Macromedia Dreamweaver MX and Fireworks MX. The book not only discusses how to use these tools, but also shows you how to conceptualize, visualize, and produce an exciting, integrated Web site for a real business, La Bonne Cuisine. To successfully accomplish the task-based learning in this book, you must be familiar with the Windows operating system, have a basic understanding of Hypertext Markup Language (HTML), and have a basic understanding of how to use the Internet. No prior experience with graphics editors is assumed. Throughout the book, there is an emphasis not only on skill building, but also on concepts that are important in Web site development in the real world: navigation issues, optimization of graphics, layout and design of the Web site, attentiveness to the intended audience, and consideration of the customer's requirements.

The Approach

To facilitate the learning process, this book presents content and theory integrated with sample exercises that help you conceptualize and build a Web site. Each chapter includes references to additional resources on the Internet that are relevant to that chapter. Each chapter includes a summary and review questions that highlight and reinforce major concepts that were presented. The step-by-step tutorials within each chapter lead you through the development of a Web site for a real consulting business. These tutorials build on one another throughout the chapters, although it is possible to skip individual tutorials after you have created the Web site in Chapter 4.

You copy the data files you need for the tutorials in each chapter, even if you have copied them into the Web site in previous chapters. However, you may need to create placeholder pages if you want to ensure that your hyperlinks work, a task for which Dreamweaver provides site management tools to discover and fix dead links.

The Hands-on Projects are guided activities that let you practice and reinforce the techniques and skills you learn within the chapter and build on the techniques and skills you learned in previous chapters. These Hands-on Projects are independent of the La Bonne Cuisine Web site and independent of the Hands-on Projects in previous chapters. They enhance your learning experience by providing additional ways to apply your knowledge in new situations.

At the end of each chapter, there are Case Projects that allow you to use the skills that you have learned in the chapter to solve real world problems and invite you to explore Web sites on the Internet to look for examples of the concepts and methods you learned within the chapter.

The entire La Bonne Cuisine Web site is integrated. You need to complete the Chapter 4 tutorials in which you set up that Web site before you can complete the chapter tutorials for the La Bonne Cuisine Web site in subsequent chapters. However, you should be able to skip individual tutorials in which you develop content for the La Bonne Cuisine Web site in chapters after Chapter 4, as long as you are prepared to handle the dead links where content is missing (you learn how to do this in Chapter 4).

Note that the Hands-on Projects at the end of each chapter are independent of the La Bonne Cuisine Web site. Although they build on skills and knowledge from previous chapters, you should be able to complete the Hands-on Projects in any chapter while still reviewing content that was presented in a previous chapter. In some chapters, all Hands-on Projects are independent of one another. Occasionally, they build on a previous Hands-on Project within the same chapter, but such cases are always noted.

Overview of This Book

The examples, steps, projects, and cases in this book will help you achieve the following objectives:

- Gain an in depth understanding of Dreamweaver MX from building basic Web pages to building integrated Web sites

- Achieve a basic understanding of Fireworks MX and the benefits of an integrated development environment

- Learn by doing while creating the La Bonne Cuisine Web site throughout this book

- Master the intricacies of the advanced capabilities of Dreamweaver MX, including styles, animation, and the integration of multimedia

- Learn to apply productivity features that Dreamweaver MX offers for building professional Web sites

In **Chapter 1**, you learn about the new integrated workspace. You begin working in the Dreamweaver MX Document window and begin to understand the characteristics of tools that are used in creating and configuring HTML elements, such as tables and text. **Chapter 2** introduces you to the basic editing tools of Fireworks MX and shows you how to draw and edit images, work with layers, and optimize images for the Web. **Chapter 3** helps you learn how to develop more advanced graphics in Fireworks, including image maps, buttons, and animated graphics. **Chapter 4** leads you through the process of designing and developing a Web site for a small food-consulting firm in Southern California called La Bonne Cuisine. You learn how to analyze requirements, create a site management strategy, and then use Dreamweaver site management tools to set up a Web site that you continue to develop throughout the rest of the book. Different methods of navigation and navigation strategies are also emphasized. In **Chapter 5**, you learn how to accomplish layout in HTML using Dreamweaver's layout tools and functions. The Document Object Model that sets HTML standards offers only limited Web site layout options, but Dreamweaver has tools that make it easier for you to lay out Web pages in the way you want them to look. **Chapter 6** discusses uploading the Web site you developed in Chapter 4 to a Web server. In addition to learning how to set up a Web site and select a server, you learn to use the FTP utility provided by Dreamweaver MX. **Chapter 7** covers forms and form processing, features that add interactivity to your Web site. You use Dreamweaver tools that make it easy for you to develop forms with different types of form objects. You also learn how to use Dreamweaver tools to develop client-side responses to forms that viewers complete and submit. In **Chapter 8**, you return to the multimedia concepts and tools you learned in Chapters 2 and 3 and add other types of multimedia, including audio, movies, and Flash movies. Dreamweaver MX also makes it possible to create Flash buttons and Flash text, which add excitement and interactivity to your Web site. **Chapter 9** introduces you to style sheets and other techniques for achieving a consistent design, look, and feel for your Web sites. In **Chapter 10** you learn to create more interactive Web features using layers, timelines, and behaviors. Finally, in **Chapter 11**, you learn how to use Dreamweaver productivity tools (libraries and templates) to quickly develop and modify multiple pages that contain the same content and have the same look-and-feel on your

Web site. You also learn how to use Dreamweaver tools to edit HTML and JavaScript code, to make your Web site accessible to individuals with disabilities, to test and validate HTML code, and to check compatibility with different browsers.

Each chapter includes the following elements to enhance the learning experience:

- **Chapter Objectives:** Each chapter in this book begins with a list of the important concepts to be mastered within the chapter. This list provides you with a quick reference to the contents of the chapter. It is also a useful study aid.

- **Step-By-Step Methodology:** As new concepts are presented in each chapter, tutorials are used to provide step-by-step instructions that allow you to actively apply the concepts you are learning. Throughout this book, you build content and pages within the chapter tutorials for a Web site for La Bonne Cuisine, a small food consulting company located in Southern California.

- **Tips:** Chapters contain Tips designed to provide you with practical advice and proven strategies related to the concept being discussed. Tips also provide suggestions for resolving problems you might encounter while proceeding through the chapter tutorials.

- **Chapter Summaries:** Each chapter's text is followed by a summary of chapter concepts. These summaries provide a helpful way to recap and revisit the ideas covered in each chapter.

- **Review Questions:** End-of-chapter assessment begins with a set of approximately 20 review questions that reinforce the main ideas introduced in each chapter. These questions ensure that you have mastered the concepts and understand the information you have learned.

Hands-on Projects: Along with conceptual explanations and step-by-step tutorials, each chapter provides Hands-on Projects related to each major topic. They are designed to provide you with practical experience. Some of the Hands-on Projects provide detailed instructions; as the book progresses, others provide less detailed instructions that require you to apply the materials presented in the current chapter with less guidance.

Case Projects: Several cases are presented at the end of each chapter. These cases are designed to help you apply what you have learned in the chapter to real-world situations. They give you the opportunity to independently synthesize and evaluate information, examine potential solutions, and make recommendations, much as you would in an actual business situation. They also provide you with opportunities to search the Internet for examples of Web development techniques you learned in the chapter, so that you can analyze how these principles and techniques are applied in the real world.

Teaching Tools

The following supplemental materials are available when this book is used in a classroom setting. All of the teaching tools available with this book are provided to the instructor on a single CD-ROM.

Electronic Instructor's Manual. This contains additional instructional material to assist in class preparation, including suggestions for lecture topics. It is critical for the instructor to be able to help the students understand how to use the help resources and how to identify problems. The Instructor's Manual helps identify areas that are more difficult to teach and provides ideas on how to present the material in an easier fashion.

ExamView®. This textbook is accompanied by ExamView, a powerful testing software package that allows instructors to create and administer printed, computer (LAN-based), and Internet exams. ExamView includes hundreds of questions that correspond to the topics covered in this text, enabling students to generate detailed study guides that include page references for further review. The computer-based and Internet testing components allow students to take exams at their computers, and it also saves the instructor time by grading each exam automatically.

PowerPoint Presentations. This book comes with Microsoft PowerPoint slides for each chapter. These are included as a teaching aid for classroom presentation, to make available to students on the network for chapter review, or to be printed for classroom distribution. Instructors can add their own slides for additional topics they introduce to the class.

Data Files. These files, containing all the data necessary for steps within the chapters and the Hands-On Projects, are provided through the Course Technology Web site at *www.course.com*, and they are also available on the Teaching Tools CD-ROM.

Solution Files. Solutions to end-of chapter review questions, exercises, and Hands-on Projects are provided on the Teaching Tools CD-ROM and may also be found on the Course Technology Web site at *www.course.com*. The solutions are password-protected.

Distance Learning. Course Technology is proud to present online test banks in WebCT and Blackboard, as well as MyCourse 2.0, Course Technology's own course enhancement tool, to provide the most complete and dynamic learning experience possible. Instructors are encouraged to make the most of the course, both online and offline. For more information on how to access the online test bank, contact your local Course Technology sales representative.

ACKNOWLEDGMENTS

The authors wish to thank the production and editorial staff of Course Technology, including Tricia Boyle, Bill Larkin, Jill Batistick, Janet Aras, Danielle Power, and Laura Burns, for their diligent, coordinated efforts in bringing this book to press in a timely manner. The authors would also like to thank Iain MacDonald, who had the foresight and wisdom to involve us in this project.

In addition, we would like to thank the following reviewers for their time and expertise: Sue Casey, Ph.D., Weatherford College; Tamra S. Davis, Tulsa Community College - West; Robert Robertson, Southern Utah University; Deborah Stockbridge, Quincy College; Zac Van Note, University of New Mexico; and June West, Spartanburg Technical College. We would like to extend a special thanks to Julie Hallstrom, of Macromedia, for her technical review of the material.

We are grateful to Margaret Dennis for sharing her company name and logo, La Bonne Cuisine, for the Web site that students build in the chapter tutorials. She also supplied us with information about the food business, photographs, and graphics, and she enthusiastically led us on ethnic food tours in Southern California. Numerous ethnic grocery stores and restaurants both in Southern California and Japan require thanks for allowing us to photograph and videotape their displays of food. We thank the musicians of BonBon Meltdown (Debbie Richard and Deirdre McGrail, together with Andrew Weiss, and Nils Soe) for the use of the clip from their recording of "Country Roads" (available on the CD *Peppermint Swirl* from BBMD, 22 Zion Road, Hopewell, NJ 08525).

The authors thank our life partners (David Overoye and Christian Soe) and our children (Sage, Acacia, Jack, Rowena, Nils, and Erik) for always encouraging us to finish and for not complaining when we sat with our eyes glued to the computer monitor. We also thank our many students and colleagues in the Computer Information Systems Department at Cal Poly Pomona for encouraging us to be good teachers, for putting up with our collective obsession with Dreamweaver, and for helping us have fun at work. We also wish to thank our mothers, Judy Guthrie and Lillian Hedenblad, who have always inspired us to do our best. Louise Soe especially wants to thank Ruth Guthrie for her good humor, motivating words, and for being such a good colleague.

Read This Before You Begin

You can use a computer in your school lab or your own computer to complete the tutorials, Hands-on Projects, and Case Projects in this book. To use your own computer, you will need the following:

- **Dreamweaver MX and Fireworks MX.** Both can be purchased as part of a bundle called Macromedia Studio MX. You can download a free 30-day trial version of this software from *www.macromedia.com/downloads/* or purchase educational versions of the software for a reduced price at your bookstore or from academic distributors online. The authors wish to note that whenever you work with an application that automates part of the work (as both these applications do), you experience great productivity gains, but you also may have difficulty figuring out how to change the finished product, should you make an error or leave out a step. What we have learned from working with our own students is that it is often quicker to go back to the beginning and start the exercise over than it is to try to repair an error. Dreamweaver also offers a new user some help with different advanced features, often in the form of dialog boxes that include a "Don't show me this message again" check box. The exercises in this book indicate when these message dialog boxes appear, but if you check this check box, you obviously will not see the dialog boxes again.

- **Microsoft Windows 95, Windows 98, Windows NT Workstation, or Windows 2000 Professional.** The file naming convention used in this book predominantly uses lowercase letters for the filenames and extensions and .htm as the extension for the Web pages (not .html). This was done to avoid the necessity of remembering upper and lowercase letters when creating hyperlinks and integrating graphics. Case is important if you upload your work to a UNIX server, because UNIX views a "C" as a different character than a "c". On a UNIX server, you must make sure that the capitalization used in file names in HTML tags is the same as the actual file names. If you use Dreamweaver site management, and if you use the Browse-for-File or Point-to-File icons in the Property inspector to set up your hyperlinks, Dreamweaver inserts the correct pathname and capitalization for your files and they should work on a UNIX-based Web server.

- **Connection to the Internet.** You use this if you want to upload your files to a server and test your work online.

- **Microsoft Internet Explorer 5.0 or above.** You can download a copy of Internet Explorer for free at the Microsoft Web site (*www.microsoft.com/*).

- **Netscape Navigator 4.7 or above.** You can download a copy of Netscape Navigator for free at the Netscape Web site (*www.netscape.com/*).

- **FTP Program.** Often your computer will already have an FTP program installed. You can use Dreamweaver's FTP facility or your own. We recommend downloading WS_FTP or Cute_FTP from *www.downloads.com*.

- **Apple QuickTime Player 5.0 or above.** This should be installed as a plugin for both Microsoft Explorer and Netscape Navigator.

- **Flash Player 5.0 or above.** This should be installed as a plugin for both Microsoft Explorer and Netscape Navigator. Flash player is preinstalled in recent browsers, but you may need to upgrade to the most recent version.

- **Source Data Directories.** The data files for each chapter come in a folder or directory labeled "Chapter," followed by the chapter number (as in "Chapter1," "Chapter2," "Chapter3," ... "Chapter11").
  - HTML pages are stored within each Chapter folder.
  - For all chapters except Chapter 8, images are stored in a subfolder or subdirectory named images (Chapter1\images, Chapter 2\images, etc.)
  - Chapter 8, which concerns multimedia content, has a subdirectory called assets, which has three subdirectories, one for images, one for sounds, and one for movies.

- **Solution Directories.** In each chapter, you create HTML pages containing different types of content as you proceed through the tutorials, Hands-On Projects, and Case Projects. These pages are stored inside a Sites directory on your working drive on your computer. There are different subdirectories within this Sites directory:
  - Each chapter has a directory for Hands-On Projects (which are independent from in-chapter tutorials) within the Sites directory, which gives a structure such as Sites\ch1practice, Sites\ch2practice, etc. These directories frequently have a subdirectory for image files that you copy in to use in your work, with a file structure such as Sites\ch5practice\images.
  - In Chapter 4, you configure a Web site for the in-chapter tutorial work that you create for the La Bonne Cuisine consulting firm that continues throughout remainder of the book. The directory structure of this Web site is Sites\lbc\ with several nested subdirectories: one for assets, with subdirectories for images, movies, and sounds, and others to hold Web pages for different functions of the business (for example, training, consulting, etc.). In each chapter, you are asked to copy the data files you use in developing the La Bonne Cuisine Web site into the appropriate directory or folder.

- **The La Bonne Cuisine Web site.** After you create the La Bonne Cuisine Web site and begin to develop it in Chapter 4, Dreamweaver assumes that all the content you develop belongs within that the Sites\lbc directory. Because the Hands-on Projects, the Case Projects, and a few of the in-chapter tutorials are not part of the La Bonne Cuisine Web site, you will not save all your work within that Web site. However, after you have a Web site set up, Dreamweaver may assume that you are working within that site and prompt you to save your work within it (especially multimedia content that you insert on a page). To avoid problems, you should save pages in the correct practice directory (e.g., ch3practice and ch4practice) early in the exercise. Otherwise Dreamweaver will continue to prompt you with questions about saving content to the Sites\lbc directory.

Visit Our World Wide Web Site

Additional materials designed especially for you might be available for your course on the World Wide Web. Go to *www.course.com* and periodically search this site for more details.

1

INTRODUCTION TO DREAMWEAVER MX

How to Use Dreamweaver MX's Editing Features

In this chapter, you will:

- ◆ Learn about the evolution of Web authoring tools
- ◆ Learn about the capabilities of Dreamweaver MX and how they can assist you in Web development
- ◆ Refresh your knowledge of HTML
- ◆ Learn about the Dreamweaver MX workspace and how to create and save Web pages
- ◆ Learn to use text and page properties to compose a Web page
- ◆ Insert hyperlinks and links to electronic mail
- ◆ Learn to use the Common tab of the Insert bar to insert images, tables, rules, and rollovers

---

Dreamweaver MX is a powerful Web authoring tool that enables you to develop professional Web sites quickly and easily. Dreamweaver MX's feature integration with other products makes it possible to work in one environment, developing graphics, site layout, content, and interactivity so that you can author full, interactive Web applications. Dreamweaver MX lets you develop client side Web pages, giving you special code generating features, layout, and style assistance.

In this chapter, you learn how Web authoring tools have evolved from simple text editors to advanced code generators like Dreamweaver MX. You also become familiar with Dreamweaver MX by creating simple pages with graphics, text, hyperlinks, and rollovers.

This book assumes that you already have a basic understanding of **Hypertext Markup Language (HTML)**, the markup language that uses tags to define the layout and appearance of Web documents. However, this chapter does include a brief review of HTML tags and document structure.

THE EVOLUTION OF WEB DEVELOPMENT TOOLS

Not too long ago, Web developers used word processors to create HTML files, which they uploaded to the Web and then tested to make sure the links worked and the layout of the page was as expected. Tables and frames, while simple to code, were incredibly tedious to lay out and manipulate because visualizing the finished product when mired in HTML code was a difficult task.

As with all application software, "What you see is what you get" (also known as WYSIWYG) tools quickly emerged and made text manipulation, the use of color, and layout formatting much more visual tasks. These HTML generating tools were easy to use and affordable. However, as the Web evolved, the early tools soon proved unable to implement more advanced features of HTML. Developers wanted to code rollovers, menus, and active elements into their Web pages. They also needed tools that would generate code compatible with multiple versions of Web browsers. Ultimately, the goal was to develop tools that would enhance productivity by means of the use of reusable templates and styles that could be applied to entire sites, not just single pages.

As Web content evolved, more advanced sites incorporated graphics, forms, layers, and **JavaScript** to incorporate active elements. JavaScript is an object-oriented programming language that is the default for the Netscape Navigator and Internet Explorer browsers. These browsers run JavaScript programs on the local computer rather than the remote server. This can improve the performance of active elements on a Web site. Tools such as Dreamweaver MX that generate JavaScript allow developers to create animations and behaviors and to make Web pages more visually and textually interactive.

It may be helpful to think of Web development tools as having gone through a series of evolutionary changes. The first tools were text editors in which developers typed HTML tags before loading them to the Web or viewing them in Web browsers. The next generation of tools were simple applications that generated simple HTML code, such as hexadecimal codes to define color or tags used to define complex tables. Developers could create Web pages visually, format layout and images through graphical drag-and-drop manipulation, and have code generated for them. Next came tools with advanced features and the capacity to apply libraries of styles and templates to entire Web sites, which gave developers control over layout, look and feel, and consistency of design. Today, tools such as Dreamweaver MX enable developers to integrate Web site development, graphics, and site management features to implement interactive database applications within one Web development environment.

Macromedia Dreamweaver MX Overview

There are many different software tools available to create Web pages. You can easily code a simple page in HTML using Notepad or Simple Text, and then upload it to the Web. Many people have used features of Microsoft Word and Excel that allow them to save Word documents, Excel spreadsheets, and PowerPoint presentations in HTML format, thereby generating pages of code that work beautifully on the Web, with operational hyperlinks and photographs.

For a Web developer, the task of creating Web pages is more complex. A large commercial Web site is generally considerably more intricate than a few linked pages and often has functionality such as database retrievals or interactive forms. For this reason, Web developers need tools that do more than build Web pages. They need tools that generate code, troubleshoot errors, and offer Web site management utilities. Just as Microsoft Word generates a page, Macromedia Dreamweaver MX produces and manages a Web site.

Generating Code

Macromedia Dreamweaver MX is a WYSIWYG HTML and JavaScript code generator. These functions alone are a great boost to a Web developer's productivity. Instead of spending hours writing HTML tags to code a complex table, the developer can build the table, resize it, and preview it in a Web browser in a matter of minutes. Because the developer works visually, there is no chance that a tag will be omitted or that table cells will be the wrong size. Dreamweaver MX generates the correct code for the table. Similarly, Dreamweaver MX generates code for rollovers, image maps, style sheets, and Flash-animated buttons and text. Without a tool like Dreamweaver MX, coding these elements is a time consuming, detailed task.

Both Netscape Navigator and Internet Explorer can interpret the code created by Dreamweaver MX. Beginning HTML programmers commonly complain that their pages load in Internet Explorer and not Netscape Navigator or that their pages look different in the two browsers. Usually, this is due to a coding error or to code that is incompatible with certain browser versions. Dreamweaver MX removes the uncertainty by creating pages that load in both browsers. It also provides functions that test for browser compatibility with current and old versions of Web browsers.

In addition, Dreamweaver MX offers site management features that allow you to manage site files, generate a site map, and transmit files or an entire site to the Internet using **File Transfer Protocol (FTP)**, a transmission protocol used to transfer files from local computers to the Internet.

Dreamweaver MX is a comprehensive Web authoring tool that:

- Generates HTML and JavaScript source code while providing the user with an intuitive, powerful WYSIWYG interface

- Provides error checking capabilities to eliminate many mistakes in Web authoring
- Allows the user to perform site management functions such as shared development logs, site maps, and FTP
- Offers a comprehensive development environment in that it integrates with other Web development tools such as:
  - Macromedia Fireworks MX for development of Web graphics (Dreamweaver MX and Fireworks MX are more closely integrated than previous versions of the applications, and now offer Visual Roundtrip Editing, which lets you launch, edit, and optimize graphics files)
  - Macromedia Flash MX for Web animation (Dreamweaver MX allows developers to launch and edit Flash MX files, and to generate animated, rollover Flash buttons from a variety of preset button images and styles without the use of the Flash application)

Working with Macromedia Fireworks MX

Just as important as the technical underpinnings of a Web site is the visual appeal of its interface. Macromedia Fireworks MX is a graphics tool that greatly complements the Web development features of Dreamweaver MX. Fireworks MX allows users to create and manipulate graphics using a Web safe color palette.

Note that many developers use Adobe Photoshop to create Web images. You can use Fireworks MX to integrate these Photoshop images into your Dreamweaver MX Web pages, while retaining many attributes of the original graphics file. Furthermore, you can generate the JavaScript code that enables rollovers and other behaviors in Fireworks MX and directly incorporate them into a Dreamweaver MX Web site. This becomes useful, for example, when you are generating menus for use in Dreamweaver MX.

 Fireworks was specifically designed to create and optimize Web graphics. As such, Fireworks lets you preview a graphic so that you can optimize its size and appearance for the Web prior to inserting it into a Web page.

A BRIEF OVERVIEW OF HTML

Although you can easily create a Web page in Dreamweaver MX without understanding HTML, familiarity with HTML code helps you understand how Dreamweaver MX works. It is also vital when you need to edit or debug Web pages that you create in Dreamweaver MX.

HTML is a very simple language for formatting Web pages. Commands, called tags, tell the Web browser how to interpret and format segments of text. The tags are easy and intuitive. Most HTML tags are container tags. This means that a segment of text will be contained within two tags, such as the format: <tag> text </tag>. Note the / before the second tag, indicating the end of that tag. For example, if you want text to appear bold in the browser window, the <b> tag creates bold text. When you want the bold text to end, you use a </b> tag to indicate that bold text has ended.

Some examples of other intuitive and commonly used tags are:

- <em> to begin italicized text; </em> to end italicized text

- <center> to center text on the page; </center> to stop centering text

- <h1> to indicate the beginning of a Heading 1 (a top-level heading); </h1> to return to normal text

- <p> to indicate the beginning of a paragraph; </p> to end the paragraph

Even if you do not know all the HTML codes, interpreting an HTML document is generally easy because it is hierarchical and you can observe the results of the tags by viewing them in a Web browser.

The Structure of an HTML Document

All HTML documents adhere to the same structure. Tags get more complex and can contain a wide variety of attributes, but the content of an HTML document follows the structure shown in Figure 1-1.

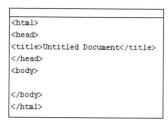

```
<html>
<head>
<title>Untitled Document</title>
</head>
<body>

</body>
</html>
```

Figure 1-1   Structure of an HTML document

The first tag on every HTML document is <html>. This tag indicates to the browser that an HTML document follows. Notice that </html> is the last tag in the document, indicating that the end of the page has been reached.

The second set of tags, the <head> and </head> tag set, is the HTML header. This tag set contains information about the document that is not displayed in the main browser window. In the HTML header, you can include JavaScript programming functions, or meta tags containing keywords that will be used by search engines.

Within the <head> tags, you also place a <title> and </title> tag set. The text within the <title></title> tags will be displayed by the browser window, telling the user what Web page he or she is accessing. It is very important to include a title for bookmarking and search engine purposes.

The <title> tags are always nested within the <head> tags.

After the close of the header information comes the body of the HTML document—that is, the material you actually see when you look at the Web page—indicated by <body>. The end of the body of text is indicated by </body>, followed by </html>, indicating the end of the HTML document.

In both Netscape Navigator and Internet Explorer, it is possible to view HTML code from any HTML document you access on the Internet. When viewing a Web page, click View from the menu bar and then Source (Internet Explorer) or View and Page Source (Netscape Navigator) to display the HTML source code used to program that page. Sometimes Web developers look at the source code to learn how a specific effect or feature was implemented on a Web site.

Inserting Images

The powerful feature of HTML is the ease with which you can insert hyperlinks and images into your document. Many people feel that the allure of the World Wide Web lies in its visual appeal. Instead of looking at giant streams of text, the Web can display colors, photographs, and graphics that make the content look more attractive. To insert an image into an HTML document, either of the following command formats could be used:

```
<img src="filename.gif"> <img src="directory/filename.gif">
```

The src attribute, whose value is set with the equal sign, points the browser to where the desired image is located. If the image is located in a subdirectory, you need to list the subdirectory name, followed by a slash and then the filename. It is wise to pay attention to filenames and case sensitivity. Only .gif and .jpg are acceptable image file formats for Internet Explorer and Netscape Navigator.

Using Hyperlinks

There are two types of hyperlink, absolute and relative. **Absolute hyperlinks** give the entire address of the Web site to be linked to. That is, it is an absolute address because it explicitly lists the entire URL by name. A **relative hyperlink** gives a portion of the address relative to the page that is currently showing in the browser window. If your Web site had two pages in the same directory named food.htm and drink.htm, you could link these two pages using only the names food.htm and drink.htm (instead of http://www.yoursite.com/food.htm, etc.) because they are relative to each other—in other words, they are located in the same directory structure.

Absolute Hyperlinks

To create an absolute hyperlink in an HTML document, the command format is as follows:

```
<a href="http://www.domainname.ext/filename.htm">hyperlink
text</a>
```

An absolute hyperlink is shown in the following code:

```
<a href="http://www.coke.com">Coke</a>
```

The tag <a> is called the anchor. The anchor contains the address of the hyperlink in quotation marks. The text that appears in the browser as underlined, linkable text is located between the beginning and ending anchors of the code. In the example above, the text "Coke" would appear with a blue underline in the browser window, and clicking the blue underlined text, which is a link, would open the Coke Web site, *http://www.coke.com*, in the browser window. The following code is also a hyperlink to the Coke home page:

```
<a href="http://www.coke.com/index.html">Coke</a>
```

This hyperlink is different because it calls a specific file, index.html. Often, index.html is the default file the browser opens from a directory. Thus, the result of both hyperlinks is the same: the opening of the Coke home page.

Filenames coded in HTML can end with .htm or .html. Both work because, in the past, Windows could have only a three-letter extension name for files. Note that although both extension names will open Web pages, "food.htm" and "food.html" are different files. You should choose a convention and stick to it so that you do not get confused as to the names of your files.

Relative Hyperlinks

You can create a relative hyperlink to a file contained on the same Web site as the file you are editing. To do this, you need only indicate the pathname and filename, not the entire URL. The hyperlink will be created relative to where your page is located on the Website. For example:

```
<a href="filename.htm">hyperlink text</a>
```

or

```
<a href="directory/filename.htm">hyperlink text</a>
```

Viewing a Simple Web Page

Figure 1-2 shows a very simple Web page for a site that you will develop throughout this book. The page consists of a graphic, text containing the title of the site, a bulleted list of three items, and a hyperlink to another page of the Web site centered at the bottom of the page. Figure 1-3 shows the HTML source code, with tags identified, that generated the Web page shown in Figure 1-2.

Figure 1-2   Simple Web page for La Bonne Cuisine in Web browser

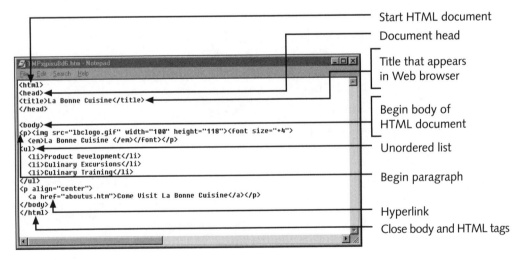

Figure 1-3   Source code for Figure 1-2

You can nest and combine many HTML tags to create beautifully laid-out Web pages. HTML is a very forgiving language in that if you do not nest tags logically, it is likely your code will still load in a Web browser, though perhaps not as you expect. For instance, if you drop the closing container tags, your errors will be obvious from your loaded pages. If you formatted text at the top of the page as Heading 1 (<h1>) and forgot to close the tag (/h1>), all the text on the page would be of Heading 1 format. In addition, if you fail to end documents with </body> and </html> tags, your document may not load at all, especially in Netscape Navigator. Fortunately, using a tool like Dreamweaver MX ensures that your tags nest logically and that you do not drop important formatting tags.

Table 1-1 lists common HTML tags to help refresh your knowledge of HTML.

Table 1-1   Overview of Common HTML Tags

Tag Name	Description	Code
Paragraph	Indicates a beginning of a new paragraph on a new line of text; you can change the default alignment of left to right or center	<p> <p align="right"> </p>
Break	Moves to the next line of text without skipping a line	
Blockquote	Indents blocks of text; for greater indenting, you can nest the blockquotes	<blockquote>*indented group of text*</blockquote>
Italic	Creates text in italic	<em>*italic text*</em>
Bold	Creates text in boldface	<b>*bold text*</b>
Strike	Creates strike through text	<strike>*strike through text*</strike>
Font attributes for color and absolute size	Controls font characteristics where n is a number from 1 to 7 indicating absolute size, and #rrggbb is a color	<font size="n" color="#rrggbb">*absolute control of font characteristics*</font>
Font attributes for relative size	Enlarges or reduces the font from its default size by using –1 to –7 or +1 to +7 as size modifiers	<font size=+"n">*relative control of font characteristics*</font>
Heading	Creates various headings in the document from h1, the largest, to h6, the smallest	<h1>*heading1*</h1> <h2>*heading2*</h2> <h3>*heading3*</h3> <h4>*heading4*</h4> <h5>*heading5*</h5> <h6>*heading6*</h6>
Center	Centers segments of text or other content	<center>*centered text*</center>

Table 1-1   Overview of Common HTML Tags (continued)

Tag Name	Description	Code
Preformatted text	Displays text just as you type it in the source code; highly useful if you wish to create more than one blank space between words	`<pre>`*text as is*`</pre>`

Ordered list	Creates a list of numbered items; you can nest lists	`<ol>`
		`<li>`*list item 1*`</li>`
		`<li>`*list item 2*`</li>`
		`</ol>`

Unordered or bulleted list	Creates a list of bulleted items; you can nest lists	`<ul>`
		`<li>`*list item 1*`</li>`
		`<li>`*list item 2*`</li>`
		`</ul>`

Horizontal rule	Inserts a horizontal line across the Web page	`<hr>`

Hyperlink	Inserts a hyperlink to another Web page	Absolute:
		`<a href="http://www.domain name.extension/filename.type">`*whatever text you like*`</a>`
		Relative:
		`<a href="`*path/filename.type*`">`*whatever text you like*`</a>`

Image	Inserts a graphic into a Web page; to align images use `<img src="file.jpg" ALIGN="left">` or right, center, top, or bottom	`<img src="`*path/filename.type*`">` where *type* is jpg or gif.
Body background color	Changes the background color of the page; #ffffff is white and #000000 is black	`<body bgcolor="#rrggbb">`
Body background image	Creates a wallpaper background on the Web page	`<body background="`*path/image.gif*`">`
Body tag text attributes	Changes the colors of the links, visited links, and active links; defaults are blue, purple, and red, respectively	`<body link="#rrggbb" vlink="#rrggbb" alink="#rrggbb">`

THE DREAMWEAVER MX WORKSPACE

When you first start Dreamweaver MX after installing it, you may be prompted as a new user to select Design, Code, or Development. This chapter describes the basic editing tools for creating Web pages in Design view. Pick this view when given the opportunity to do so.

1

If you are already familiar and comfortable with Dreamweaver 4.0, you can customize Dreamweaver MX to look like it, if you wish. Dreamweaver 4.0 has floating panels, while Dreamweaver MX provides navigation through panels via tabs at the top of the workspace. To use Dreamweaver MX in Dreamweaver 4.0 style, you can click Edit in the menu bar and Preferences. (You'll use the General category of the Preferences dialog box.) Click the Change Workspace button in the middle of the dialog box and click the Dreamweaver 4.0 Workspace option button. Click OK twice to change the preferences to display Dreamweaver MX in a manner that mimics Dreamweaver 4.0.

The Workspace in General

Dreamweaver MX provides a WYSIWYG workspace, called Design view, for building a Web site. Design view enables you to create a Web page that looks, for the most part, identical to the page that later appears in a browser.

Figure 1-4 shows the workspace that is installed by default in Dreamweaver MX. The screen displays an Insert bar, a Document toolbar, a Document window, and panel groups on the right. The Property inspector and Tag selector are displayed on the bottom of the workspace. The Insert bar and the Property inspector are the tools you will use most often to edit your Web page. You will learn about these and other tools throughout this book. Panels in the workspace can easily be shrunk and expanded by clicking the white expander arrows next to each panel's name.

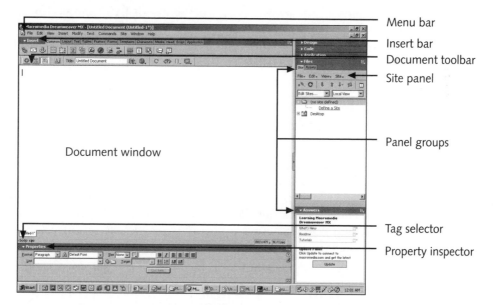

Figure 1-4   Dreamweaver MX workspace

Features of the Dreamweaver MX workspace shown in Figure 1-4 are described in the following list:

- The Menu bar contains drop-down menus to perform file commands and control site features. Many of the commands are duplicates of those available in specific panels. From the Window pull-down menu, you can access all of the panels. The Menu bar options are described in detail later in this section.

- When you are developing HTML pages, the Insert bar contains 12 panels. The Common category allows you to insert objects, such as images, tables, rollovers, and e-mail links in a Web page. Other panels in the Insert bar allow you to insert frames, forms, meta tags, media, and scripts. These panels will be discussed in future chapters.

- The Document toolbar lets you name your document and view it in Design view, Code view, or a combination of both. From this toolbar, you can also preview your document in your default Web browser.

- The Document window is where you can type and insert the content of your Web document.

- Panel groups (Design, Code, Application, Files, Answers) combine related panels that can be accessed by clicking the expander arrow next to each. You can undock panel groups by dragging them by the gripper 🗄 on the upper left of the panel.

- The Property inspector displays the attributes that you can set for objects on the Web page. For text formatting, the attributes are similar to those found in word processing and desktop publishing applications. For tables, images, and rollovers, the property attributes will change.

- The Tag selector lets you select precisely which tag you are trying to edit while you are working in Design view.

- The Site panel displays and lets you manage the files and assets related to the Web site you are developing.

In developing most of your pages in Dreamweaver MX, you work in what is known as Standard view. If you create a document layout in this view, you insert a table via a dialog box, entering a desired number of rows and columns. You need to resize the table to get the correct layout. Under the Layout tab of the Insert bar, there is also an option to work in Layout view. Using Layout view, you can draw tables directly on the documents, visually creating the desired layout for your page. In Chapter 4, you learn to use Layout view.

The Insert bar and the Property inspector open by default when you start Dreamweaver MX. You can open any of these windows or panels by clicking Window on the menu bar. The Insert bar, Property inspector, and Answers panel are the first three commands on the Window menu. Note the corresponding shortcut keys in Figure 1-5. As you become more familiar with Dreamweaver MX, you can save time with shortcut keys.

1

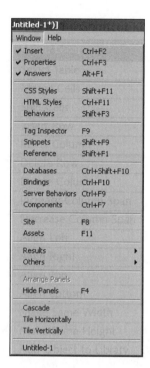

Figure 1-5   Window menu commands and shortcut keys

Shortcut keys are function keys or a series of keystrokes that perform certain actions on the page. For example, in Dreamweaver MX and many other applications, the sequence Ctrl+O opens a file and Ctrl+S saves it. In application software, shortcut keys allow experienced users to avoid navigating lengthy menu structures to complete simple actions.

The menu bar at the top of the Dreamweaver MX workspace contains the following menu options:

- File contains commands that allow you to create a new file, open an existing file, save work, export a file to the Web, or preview a file in a Web browser.

- Edit contains commands that allow you to cut, paste, select, and search text. This menu also contains default preference settings.

- View contains commands that help you manage and view Design view, including the display of frames, borders, tables, and gridlines.

- Insert contains commands that allow you to insert layers, form objects, tables, rollovers, and images. The Insert menu is much like the Insert bar Common tab, which is described later in this chapter.

- Modify contains commands that allow you to set the properties of a Web page, such as title, background attributes, and defaults for text properties. This menu also allows you to modify frames, tables, layers, and hotspots.

- Text contains commands that allow you to change text attributes, including styles.

- Commands contains commands that allow you to record command sequences for batch processing, clean up code, and apply predefined color schemes.

- Site contains commands that allow you to access site management capabilities.

- Window contains commands that allow you to select various windows and panels to help in the creation of frames, styles, behaviors, timelines, and so on.

- Help contains information about Dreamweaver MX support.

 Many commands on the drop-down menus duplicate options available on the Property inspector and the Insert bar. The menu commands offer another means of performing the same operations.

At the bottom of the workspace, you see the Tag selector, document tab, window size, and estimated download time as shown in Figure 1-6. The Tag selector gives you more control in selecting specific code elements while working in Design view. Clicking the document tabs is productive when you are working on multiple pages, because you can easily navigate between documents by clicking the tabs. The window size and download estimate give you an indicator of page performance before you publish the page to the Web.

You can relocate panel groups in the workspace by clicking and holding the gripper located at the upper left of the panel and then dragging the window to the desired place on the page. You can minimize and expand panels by clicking the expander arrow ▼ to the right of the gripper. At the far right of each panel group, you can select Close Panel Group from the list box to remove the panel from view. This is useful if you want a larger screen area to work in. To reopen the panel group, click Window on the menu bar, and then click the appropriate panel name.

 The workspace displays the main menu bar. As you work with panels, you will also see that some of them have specialized menu bars. This can be confusing sometimes if you are looking on the main menu bar for an operation that only exists in the panel menu bar. Keep this in mind as you work in later chapters with Dreamweaver MX.

Figure 1-6   Work area detail

Opening, Previewing, and Saving a Document

When you start Dreamweaver MX, a new, blank document will be shown in the work-space. If you want to create a new document, click File on the menu bar, and then New. The New Document dialog box will open as shown in Figure 1-7. From this dialog box, you can select pages and templates. Under the General tab, several page categories are shown, assisting you in setting up various, more advanced page types. You will explore some of these in later chapters. For this chapter, you will use the Basic Page Category under the General tab, and you will select HTML under Basic Page.

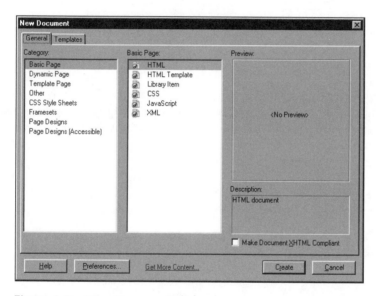

Figure 1-7   New Document dialog box

To save your Dreamweaver MX files, click File on the menu bar, and then click Save or Save As, just as you would in most desktop applications. A dialog box will open, where you can enter your filename, as shown in Figure 1-8. You should save your file as an HTM or HTML file type to indicate it is an HTML document. Several other file types are available for saving Active Server Pages, Cascading Style Sheets, Java programs, and many other Web related files. This book concentrates on building pages with HTML and JavaScript.

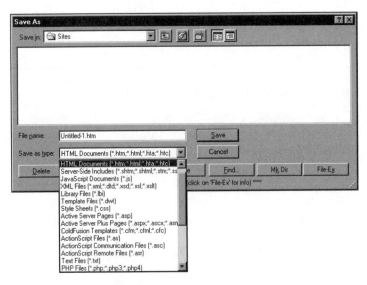

Figure 1-8   Save As dialog box

To see how your Dreamweaver MX Web pages will look in a Web browser, you can use the Preview in Browser command, which is found by clicking File on the menu bar, clicking Preview in Browser, and then clicking the Web browser you like. Alternatively, you can press the F12 key or click the icon for Preview in the Document toolbar, as shown in Figure 1-9.

Figure 1-9   Selecting a browser

 Save all your pages in the appropriate location before you do a lot of editing. When Dreamweaver MX inserts images and hyperlinks for you, it needs to know where your current page is located with respect to the files you are inserting or linking to. Saving your document tells Dreamweaver MX how to build the paths to these other files.

Design and Code Views

When you start Dreamweaver MX, you see a workspace similar to Figure 1-4. This view shows Design view. You can also work in Code view, which displays the HTML source code rather than the WYSIWYG design, by clicking the icon for Show Code View on the Document toolbar.

In addition, you can work in Code and Design views at one time, as shown in Figure 1-10, by clicking the icon for Show Code and Design views on the Document toolbar ⬚. In this view, the design and the code can be edited simultaneously. As you move the cursor through the design, it moves dynamically to the same location in the source code. This view enables you to control exactly what you are editing and see the result. To return to Design view only, you can click the Show Design View icon ⬚ on the Document toolbar.

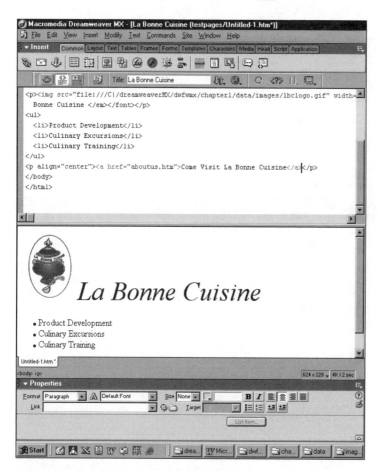

Figure 1-10   Design and Code views

The Property Inspector

The Property inspector is the primary tool for formatting text and controlling attributes of objects in Dreamweaver MX. With it, you can also create and manage hyperlinks, and control the size of images and tables. It is easy to understand and use, because several of its icons are commonly used in word processors.

The attributes displayed in the Property inspector change according to the content selected. For example, Figure 1-11 shows the editable attributes for text. If instead you select an image, the attributes in the Property inspector will allow you to change image size, name, and alternate text. Similarly, the Property inspector for a table lets you manipulate cell size, color, and borders. If you wanted to create a bulleted or numbered list, you would click the list icons in the Property inspector and type your list elements. Alternatively, you could select text elements on the page and then click the list buttons.

Figure 1-11   Property inspector for text

Table 1-2 describes the attributes of the Property inspector for text.

Table 1-2   Attributes of the Property Inspector for Text

Element	Description
Format	Inserts basic HTML tags for paragraphs, headers, and preformatted text
Font	Changes the font type face; for example, Arial, Helvetica, Sans-serif
Size	Changes the absolute or relative size of text using an exact number between 1 and 7 or a relative number between −7 and −1 or +1 and +7
Color	Modifies text color via the color picker or hexadecimal color code entered in the text box
Bold	Makes text bold
Italic	Makes text italic
Alignment	Aligns text left, center, right, and justified
Link	Defines the hyperlink to a Web site; you can type the address or add it using the Point to File or Browse for File icons
Point to File	Allows you to point to the file to insert a hyperlink
Browse for File	Allows you to browse for the file to insert a hyperlink, using a dialog box
Target	Controls whether a hyperlinked file opens in an existing browser window or in a new browser window
Unordered List	Creates a bulleted list
Ordered List	Creates a numbered list

Table 1-2 Attributes of the Property Inspector for Text (continued)

Element	Description
Text Outdent	Moves blocks of text left, positioning them on the page as you direct
Text Indent	Moves blocks of text right, positioning them on the page as you direct
Help	Accesses context-sensitive help
Quick Tag Editor	Inserts HTML tags manually; makes a lengthy list of HTML tags available from a pop-up menu
Expand/Contract	Expands or contracts the view of the Property inspector

Using the Property Inspector

In the following steps, you learn to examine attributes of page elements by looking at the properties of each object. You also learn to use Design and Code views.

To use the Property inspector:

1. Using Windows Explorer, create a new folder on the drive where you store your work for this chapter. Label the folder **Sites**. Create a nested folder **ch1practice** inside the Sites folder to store the practice pages you create in this chapter.

2. Create a second nested folder called **images**, inside the ch1practice folder, to store the images. Copy the file lbc.htm from your Chapter1 data folder into the ch1practice folder and the file logo.gif from your Chapter1\images folder into the images folder on your working drive.

3. Start Dreamweaver MX. If you are prompted to select Design, Code, or Development as a new user, select **Design**. You should see a blank Web page open in Design view, and the Property inspector should be displayed at the bottom of the workspace. If you are prompted to define a Web site, simply click **Cancel** and you will be able to edit a stand-alone page. Open the page lbc.htm that you copied into the ch1practice folder. A simple home page will appear.

4. In the Title text box on the Document toolbar, observe that you see **LBCuisine Home Page**. The title is always visible.

5. On the Document toolbar, notice the icons for changing the view. Click the Show Code View icon ◀▶ to the far left of the Document toolbar. Your screen shows the code used to build this simple page.

6. Click the Show Code and Design views icon ▤. Now you see the design along with the source code simultaneously. Click your mouse on the blank line under the table and above the e-mail address in Design view.

7. Type the text **Welcome to the La Bonne Cuisine Web site** into the document. Notice that as you type the text, the code is added to the code window.

8. Select the text **Welcome to the La Bonne Cuisine Web site** with your mouse. In the Property inspector, set the text properties to **Format: Heading 2**. Click the color picker and select **blue** (#0000FF). If you cannot find blue on the palette, you can type it into the text box next to the color box. As you do this, observe the changes in the source code.

9. Click the icon for Show Design View ▣ to return to the WYSIWYG view of the page.

10. Click the logo at the top of the page. Black handles will appear around the image. In the Image Property inspector, you can see the name of the file (logo.gif) and the size of the image, 518 × 80 pixels.

11. Click the corner of the table next to "About Us" to select the entire table. Notice that Table properties are now present in the Property inspector. The table is 500 pixels wide, with one row and four columns. It is aligned to center.

12. Click **About Us** in the first table cell. The Property inspector now reflects the attributes of the hyperlink (contact/aboutus.htm) and the table cell (red in color). Clicking **Consulting** shows that the hyperlink and the background color for the cell are different. Click **Tours** and observe that an absolute hyperlink to *http://www.tours.com* is present in the Property inspector.

13. Save the file as **ch1practice0.htm**, in the Sites\ch1practice folder on your working drive. Preview the file by clicking the **Preview** icon or by pressing the **F12** key. Observe that your browser starts and the page appears with the title "LBCuisine Home Page" in the top of the browser window.

The Insert Bar Common Tab

The Insert bar has several categories, as shown in Figure 1-12. Clicking the tabs on the Insert bar reveals different sets of icons that you use to edit Web pages. When developing HTML the Insert bar categories are Common, Layout, Text, Tables, Frames, Forms, Templates, Characters, Media, Head, Script, and Application. You will learn more about these panels in later chapters of this book.

Figure 1-12   Insert bar

The Common tab of the Insert bar is the default when you begin using Dreamweaver MX. It contains different icons, as shown in Figure 1-13, that allow you to insert commonly used elements in Web pages. For instance, from the Common tab, you insert graphics, tables, and layers. You can also incorporate active elements on the Web page, such as rollovers, and Flash buttons and text.

Figure 1-13 Insert bar Common tab

The Common tab contains the icons shown in Table 1-3.

Table 1-3 Elements of the Insert bar Common Tab

Element	Icon	Description
Hyperlink		Inserts a hyperlink
Email Link		Inserts a link to an electronic mail address
Named Anchor		Inserts a named anchor in a page
Insert Table		Inserts a table on a Web page
Draw Layer		Inserts layers on top of the Dreamweaver MX workspace
Image		Inserts an image on a Web page
Image Placeholder		Creates an image placeholder
Fireworks HTML		Incorporates Fireworks HTML code into the Dreamweaver MX HTML source code
Flash		Inserts a Flash movie; Flash movies are vector-based animations exported as .swf files
Rollover Image		Generates JavaScript for a rollover by prompting you for images and links to create the rollover image
Navigation Bar		Generates JavaScript for a navigation bar by prompting you for images and links to create the navigation bar
Horizontal Rule		Inserts a horizontal rule across a Web page
Date		Inserts a date into the workspace by prompting you for a specific date format
Tabular Data		Inserts delimited data from a spreadsheet or database
Comment		Inserts a comment into source code
Tag Chooser		Enables you to select tags from HTML or a variety of other languages that work on the Web, such as ASP, PHP, or JSP

Panel Groups

In addition to the Insert bar, you can use panel groups to control design, code, and files for your Web site. Five major panel groups, shown earlier in Figure 1-4, are provided: Design, Code, Application, Files, and Answers. They can be expanded and contracted using their respective expander arrows. They can be moved as floating panel groups by dragging them by their gripper.

Note the following facts about panel groups:

- The Design panel group consists of the CSS Styles, HTML Styles, and Behaviors panels. You can control page and site design and attach behaviors to pages, buttons, and layers.

- The Code panel group consists of the Tag inspector, Snippets, and Reference panels. The Tag inspector lets you edit tags from your page in a property sheet. The Snippets panel provides useful, preformatted code segments as if in a library. You can store your own preformatted snippets for use in several pages. The Reference panel gives interactive help from several reference guides.

- The Application panel group consists of the Database, Bindings, Server Behaviors, and Components panels. These panels allow you to set up database connectivity on your Web site.

- The Files panel group consists of the Site and Assets panels. The Site panel displays all the files associated with the Web site on which you are working. From it, you can view listings or a site map and create links by dragging. The Assets panel lists assets (images, sound, and video) associated with your site.

- The Answers panel group consists of a variety of resources for help.

TEXT AND PAGE PROPERTIES

Adding and editing text in Dreamweaver MX is much like using a word processor. For instance, the Property inspector contains several icons that may be familiar to you, and entering text is simply a matter of typing it in the blank workspace. To alter text, you click and drag to select it. Then you change its format by clicking icons in the Property inspector.

As you will see in the following sections of this chapter, adding and manipulating text in Dreamweaver MX's WYSIWYG interface is intuitive and easy.

Modifying Page Properties

You can modify page properties using the Page Properties dialog box. See Figure 1-14. To open this dialog box, click Modify on the menu bar, and then click Page Properties. **Page properties** are some of the elements defined in the head and body tags of the HTML code that change the look of the document, even though they do not actually display text or code in the browser window. For instance, in the body tag, you can indicate background color, text and link color, background image, or margin height and width.

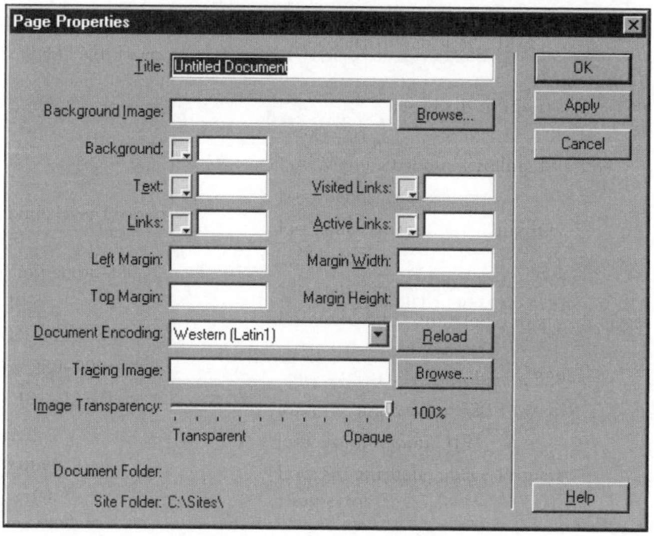

Figure 1-14   Page Properties dialog box

Making changes in the Page Properties dialog box affects the entire document. For example, if you change the property for hyperlink color to dark green in the body tag of the document, all hyperlinks on that page will appear as dark green underlined text. The Page Properties dialog box is useful in that it helps you create a consistent color scheme for your document.

In the Page Properties dialog box, you can set the page title, which will then appear at the top of the browser window when the page is loaded in a Web browser. (You can also do this in the Title text box on the Document toolbar. See Figure 1-4.)

If you do not enter a page title, the default text "Untitled Document" will appear in the top of the browser window. Setting the page title is very important because search engines often use this information to index pages. In addition, when users bookmark a page, the title appears in their bookmark list.

You can wallpaper the background of your page by browsing your hard drive for a background image. By selecting a tracing image, you can use an imported design layout to assist you in creating a new Web page layout. That is, if you have a mock-up of the layout you would like to use for your Web page in .gif, .jpg, or .png format, you can select it as a tracing image and then use it as a template to create the actual HTML layout. It is only a guide and will not show in your browser window.

Using Hexadecimal Color Codes

You may remember coding your first Web page and testing out different hexadecimal color codes. You probably used a hexadecimal color table to determine which colors to use. Remembering and changing the codes, viewing them, and then changing them again to find a pleasing color scheme was a tedious job.

Fortunately, Dreamweaver MX allows you to select colors from a palette instead of keying in hexadecimal codes; however, knowing the hexadecimal codes is important if you wish to match other colors on your Web site. The site you are working on may have a set color scheme that uses particular codes. Exact matching using the hexadecimal code is often more reliable than seeking the color in a palette.

Hexadecimal color codes are also important when using the Web safe color palette. The **Web safe color palette** contains 216 hexadecimal colors that display the same in both Netscape Navigator and Internet Explorer. Using these colors gives you control over what users see, no matter which browser they use.

 Less experienced Web developers commonly complain that their pages do not look the same when they open them on another computer. This difference occurs because they cannot control other users' settings or screen resolution. If another user's computer cannot display as many colors as the developer used in the original image, the machine uses dithering to produce like colors, effectively filling in the colors it cannot display. Thus, the design you see when you develop a page may not be exactly what the user sees depending upon their computer configuration. If you wish to control dithering, use the 216 colors in the Web safe color palette. This ensures a degree of image quality on the Web.

To reiterate, a hexadecimal code designates color on a Web page. For example, if you want red text, use the following command in the font tag, where #FF0000 is the hexadecimal code for pure red:

```
<font color="#FF0000">test</font>
```

A hexadecimal number is characterized by the integers 0, 1, 2, 3, 4, 5, 6, 7, 8, 9, and the letters A, B, C, D, E, and F. Recall that binary numbers are characterized by two digits, 0 and 1 (also known as base 2). Hexadecimal numbers are characterized by 16 digits (also known as base 16). Colors represented on the Web use hexadecimal numbers in each of

1

six spaces. The significance of the six characters is that the first two represent the amount of red, the second two represent the amount of blue, and the third two represent the amount of green. Thus, the hexadecimal number format #RRGGBB identifies a specific mixture of red, blue, and green colors. So, from the example, #FF0000 represents pure red. If the number for red, green, or blue is low, you can expect a darker color, while higher numbers display lighter colors. #000000 represents black, while #FFFFFF represents pure white.

Selecting a Color Scheme

Using the Property inspector, you can easily change the color scheme of text objects on a page. For a large Web site, changing the color scheme for the entire site might be more productive. Dreamweaver MX provides several set color schemes that enable you to select a predetermined set of colors for background, text, and links for your entire page. To apply a pre-set color scheme, click Commands on the menu bar, and then click Set Color Scheme. Figure 1-15 shows the Set Color Scheme Command dialog box.

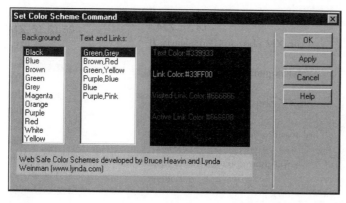

Figure 1-15   Set Color Scheme Command dialog box

Selecting background, text, and link colors from the three selection areas and applying them to the workspace is a fast and easy way to experiment with a variety of color schemes. These Dreamweaver MX color schemes use a Web safe color palette by default.

 Many businesses already have color schemes that are used throughout their printed materials. If this is the case, make sure the color scheme for the Web site matches.

Creating a Storefront Web Page

In this section, you will create a simple storefront for La Bonne Cuisine, a food consulting firm. To create this Web page, you must first enter text into the blank workspace in Dreamweaver MX, and then use the Property inspector to format it. Specifically, you will make the text stand out and look appealing by adding different heading styles, fonts, and colors to the text, and by centering it on the page. You will also add a page title and experiment with varied color schemes.

To use the workspace:

1. Start Dreamweaver MX. If you are prompted to select Design, Code, or Application as a new user, select **Design**. You should see a blank Web page open in Design view, and the Property inspector should be displayed at the bottom of the workspace. If you are prompted to define a Web site, simply click **Cancel** and you will be able to edit a stand-alone page.

2. In the Title text box on the Document toolbar, type **La Bonne Cuisine**.

3. At the top of the blank Web page, type **La Bonne Cuisine** and then select it.

4. In the Property inspector, click the **Format** list arrow, and then click **Heading 1**. Observe that the text size becomes larger.

5. Click the **Font** list arrow and click **Arial, Helvetica, sans-serif**.

6. Change the color of the selected text by clicking the **text color box** and selecting blue **(#0000FF)** from the colors listed in the column on the left of the color picker, as shown in Figure 1-16. The hexadecimal color code for the blue you select appears in the text box next to the color box.

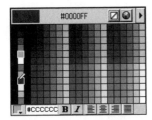

Figure 1-16 Select blue in the color picker

7. With the La Bonne Cuisine text still selected, click the **Align Center** button in the Property inspector. Deselect the text by clicking the end of the line, and then press the **Enter** key to go to a new line.

8. Type the following address for La Bonne Cuisine, pressing **Shift+Enter** at the end of each line of text:

2395 N. Lake St.

La Verne CA 91750

909 123-4567

9. Select the text you typed in Step 8. In the Property inspector, click **Heading 2** in the Format list box and set the font color to **black** on the color picker.

10. Save the file as **ch1practice1.htm**, in the Sites\ch1practice folder on your working drive. Preview the file by clicking the **Preview** button or by pressing the **F12** key. Observe that your browser starts and the page appears with the title "La Bonne Cuisine" in the top of the browser window.

This is a very basic start. Often storefront sites like this will list a mission, show a map of how to get to the store, and include pictures or the names of the owner(s) or employees. As we develop this storefront in this chapter, you add a logo for La Bonne Cuisine and hyperlinks to the various services offered by this company.

CREATING HYPERLINKS

Hyperlinks make the Web fun and easy to navigate. People familiar with the Web automatically know that blue underlined text is an invitation to click and visit another page for more information. The simple click navigation means that users need not remember addresses and commands to connect to other computers. They simply click the hyperlink and access Web sites all over the globe.

To implement hyperlinks in Dreamweaver MX, you type the address in the Link text box in the Property inspector. Every file on the Internet has a Universal Resource Locator (URL), a unique address consisting of a protocol, domain name, and extension, as shown in Figure 1-17. (In Chapter 6, you learn more about the components of a URL and how files are transmitted across the Internet.)

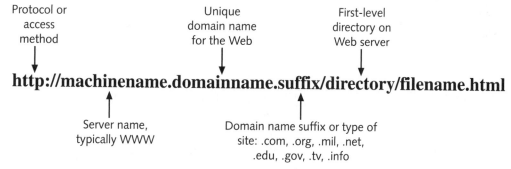

Figure 1-17   Components of a URL

If you wanted to create a link to the Coke Web site, you would select text in Design view, and then type the URL for the Coke Web site in the Link text box in the Property inspector, as shown in Figure 1-18. The selected text shows in your workspace as a blue, underlined hyperlink. Of course, you can change the color of the hyperlink using the Page Properties dialog box, as you learned earlier in this chapter. Recall also from earlier that this type of hyperlink is an absolute link; that is, you write the entire address to create the link.

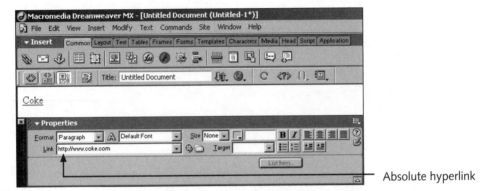

Absolute hyperlink

Figure 1-18   Adding an absolute link using the Property inspector

How Site Organization Affects Hyperlink Usage

When you create a large Web site containing many files, you must create a directory structure for the site so that you can find and maintain files easily. Figure 1-19 shows the directory structure of the LBCuisine.com Web site, which has four directories (about, consulting, tours, and training) and many files.

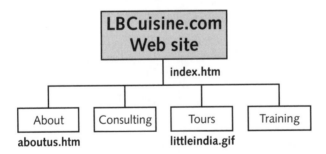

Figure 1-19   File structure for the LBCuisine.com Web site

In Figure 1-19, the index.html file is contained in the top level of the Web site. This is true for many sites because index.html represents a default file that loads automatically when someone accesses LBCuisine.com. That is, typing the address *http://www.lbcuisine.com* in a Web browser yields the same result as *http://www.lbcuisine.com/index.html*.

The four directories illustrated in Figure 1-19 are for about, consulting, tours, and training. A Web site is likely to have hyperlinks on the index.html Web page to the other directories in the Web site. In this case, you can use a relative address for the hyperlink because the folders are contained in the same directory structure. That is, instead of using *http://www.lbcuisine.com/about/aboutus.htm*, you can just use *about/aboutus.htm*. This address is relative to the index.html document. To create the link using Dreamweaver, simply enter the pathname and filename into the Link text box in the Property inspector, as shown in Figure 1-20.

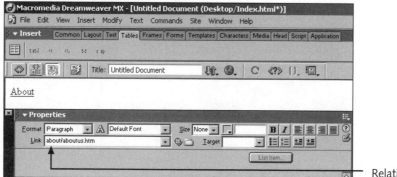

Relative hyperlink

Figure 1-20   A relative hyperlink to the aboutus.htm file

Dreamweaver MX lets you create hyperlinks by clicking the Point-to-File icon and dragging it to show the file you want to link to in the Site panel. Figure 1-21 shows a link being created using the Point-to-File method. You can also browse through your directory structure to find files by clicking the Browse for File icon.

To create a link to electronic mail, you can type mailto: LaBonneCuisine@lbcuisine.com in the Link text box in the Property inspector. Dreamweaver MX also has an Email Link button in the Insert bar Common tab shown in Figure 1-13 that prompts you for the e-mail text and address and creates the code for you. You can use either method to create a link to electronic mail. You learn more about hyperlinks and navigation strategy in Chapter 4.

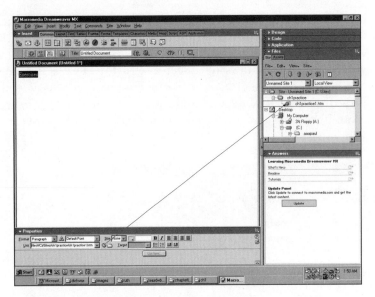

Figure 1-21   Creating a hyperlink using the Point-to-File method

Adding Hyperlinks to the Storefront Page

At the very least, a Web storefront should include contact information and an e-mail address so that potential or existing customers can make inquiries electronically. Simple storefronts also often display hyperlinks to allied or associated sites that might interest their customers. When creating a Web storefront, you should select these hyperlinks with care, because a business shouldn't send its customers to its competitors.

Next on your La Bonne Cuisine Web page, you are going to add hyperlinks to the various services offered by La Bonne Cuisine. These include relative links to pages describing the company, the consulting services, information about food tours to foreign countries, and information about the culinary training services offered by La Bonne Cuisine. Your storefront will also include an absolute hyperlink to the La Verne Chamber of Commerce *(http://www.lavernechamber.org)* and a link to La Bonne Cuisine's e-mail.

To add hyperlinks:

1. Open ch1practice1.htm in Dreamweaver MX if it is not already open. Save this file with a new name, **ch1practice2.htm**, in the same directory.

2. Edit the contact information so that it appears on one line of the page, with dashes to separate the blocks of information. Select this text, and then use the Property inspector to change the format of the address to **Heading 4**.

3. Click to the right of the address, and then press the **Enter** key to move to a blank line in the workspace. In the Format style list on the Property inspector, click **Paragraph** if it is not already selected.

4. The cursor should be centered in the line. If it is not, click the **Align Center** button in the Property inspector, to center it in the workspace.

5. Type the following text: **[about us] [food consulting] [culinary explorations] [culinary training]**. Select the text you just entered and set Format to **Heading 4** in the Property inspector. These are the services La Bonne Cuisine offers.

6. Select the text **about us**, then type the path and filename **contact/aboutlbc.htm** in the Link text box on the Property inspector. Press **Enter**. Observe that a relative hyperlink has been created for about us, indicated by the blue, underlined text. This folder and file do not exist yet, but will be developed in a later chapter.

7. Repeat Step 6 to create hyperlinks for food consulting (**consulting/consulting.htm**), culinary excursions (**tour/tour.htm**), and culinary training (**training/training.htm**).

8. Make sure the insertion point is at the end of the line, press **Enter** to move to the next line, then type **La Verne Chamber of Commerce.**

9. Select the text **La Verne Chamber of Commerce** and add the URL **http://www.lavernechamber.org** in the Link text box in the Property inspector. Press **Enter**. Observe that an absolute link has been created to the La Verne Chamber of Commerce.

10. Click to the right of the text La Verne Chamber of Commerce, press the **Enter** key twice, and type this centered text: **Contact La Bonne Cuisine**.

11. To create a link to the La Bonne Cuisine e-mail, select the text and type **mailto:LaBonneCuisine@lbcuisine.com** in the Link text box. Press **Enter**. Observe that the text appears as a hyperlink. (Of course, you would enter a real e-mail address for a valid site.)

12. Save the file, preview it in your Web browser by pressing **F12**, and observe the hyperlinks that you created. Your screen should resemble Figure 1-22. If you click the hyperlinks in brackets, you will get an error message because you haven't created the linked pages yet.

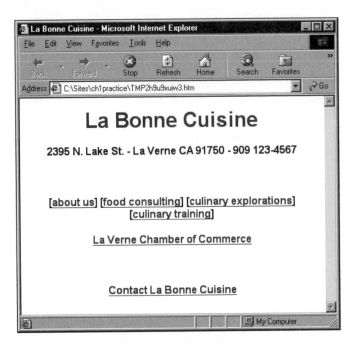

Figure 1-22   La Bonne Cuisine Web site with hyperlinks

USING THE INSERT BAR COMMON TAB TO INSERT IMAGES, TABLES, RULES, AND ROLLOVERS

This section introduces key options on the Insert bar Common tab. These options enable you to insert images, tables, and horizontal rules, and to create rollovers.

After you insert each element on the page, the Property inspector can be used to change the element's attributes. For example, if you choose to insert a horizontal rule across the center of a page, you can modify attributes such as its width and thickness. Dreamweaver MX generates the code necessary to implement these page elements and associated attributes. The Design view WYSIWYG workspace is especially useful when you work with images and tables. In addition to entering size attributes, you can select the image or table and drag your mouse to resize it. Sometimes, it is much more efficient to manipulate an object in the workspace where you can see the changes than to alter code, or even to change attributes in the Property inspector.

The following sections cover each of these Common tab options and give you practice using them.

Inserting Images

To insert images on a page, you can use the Image button 🖳 on the Common tab. You can also insert an image by selecting Image from the Insert menu or by using the short-cut key sequence, Ctrl+Alt+I. Each option allows you to browse your local drive and select an image via the Select Image Source dialog box, as shown in Figure 1-23. This helps avoid errors when you type file names and directory locations.

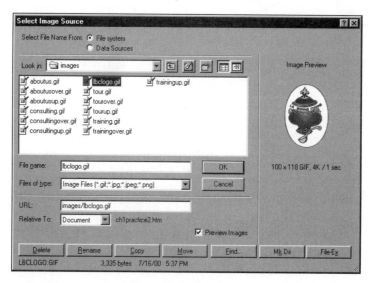

Figure 1-23   Select Image Source dialog box

A preview of the image appears on the right side of the dialog box to ensure that you select the correct file. In Figure 1-23, the filename is lbclogo.gif, located in the Sites\ch1practice\images folder.

As with hyperlinks, you can type in absolute or relative addresses for image files if you wish. An example of an absolute address for an image file would be *http://www.lbcuisine.com/ tour/littleindia.gif*. "lbcuisine.com" is the domain name, "tour" is the directory, and "littleindia.gif" is the filename. To insert this on a Web page, you could use this code:

```
<img src="http://www.lbcuisine.com/tour/littleindia.gif">
```

However, using a relative address when possible usually makes more sense. In the index.html file, you could use the following command to insert the littleindia.gif image:

```
<img src="tour/littleindia.gif">
```

Rather than having to type an address in manually, using the Insert Image option generates code that does this for you automatically. Once an image has been inserted, you can change attributes of the image in two ways. First, you can select the image by clicking it. Tiny black squares, called handles, will appear around the image, as shown in

Figure 1-24. You can resize the image by holding the mouse button down on the squares and dragging it to the desired size. The image skews (become tall and thin or short and wide) unless you hold down the Shift key. Holding the Shift key down allows you to resize the image and maintain its proportions.

Figure 1-24   Selected image and Property inspector for images

In the Property inspector, the image size is displayed in kilobytes (KB) and in terms of width and height. Use the blank text box under the image for adding a name identifier to the image, which is useful if you create an image map. (You learn more about image maps in Chapters 3 and 4.)

Table 1-4 lists the attributes of the Property inspector for images.

Table 1-4   Attributes of the Property Inspector for Images

Element	Description
Image	Image name and memory size; displays image thumbnail, defined variable name for scripting purposes, and memory size in kilobytes
W	Gives image dimensions in pixel width
H	Gives image dimensions in pixel height
Src	Identifies pathname (relative or absolute) to image source
Link	Identifies the URL to which the image links; you can type the address or add it using the Point-to-File or Browse for File icons
Point-to-File ⊕	Inserts a hyperlink using the Site panel
Alt	Identifies the text that appears in the browser when the pointer is over the image
External Editor [🖉 Edit]	Brings up the image in an external editor
Reset Size [Reset Size]	Resets image size to actual dimensions
Help [?]	Links to context-sensitive help

Table 1-4 Attributes of the Property Inspector for Images (continued)

Element	Description
Quick Tag Editor	Inserts HTML tag manually; a lengthy list of HTML tags is available from a pop-up menu
Map	Changes the image to an image map, gives it a variable name for scripting purposes, and defines image map shapes
V Space	Provides vertical pixel spacing to set the image apart from surrounding text or page content
H Space	Provides horizontal pixel spacing to set the image apart from surrounding text or page content
Target	Indicates the window in which the hyperlinked file is to open
Low Src	Identifies the smaller version (in memory) image file that appears until the image finishes downloading
Browse for File	Opens a Select File dialog box, where you can browse for and select a hyperlink file
Border	Establishes the width of the border around the image in pixels
Align	Provides a list of image alignment icons, and left, center, and right horizontal alignments
Expand/Contract button	Expands and contracts the view of the Property inspector

 Entering alternate text is really important when you use images on the Web. People with vision impairments use electronic readers to browse the Web by listening. If a picture has no alternate text, the person cannot hear what the picture is showing. Additionally, alternate text can assist a search engine in indexing and finding your page. Always include alternate text tags on all your images.

Another feature Dreamweaver MX offers is inserting an image placeholder. Perhaps you have created a page layout and wish to identify a specific portion of that page for various graphics. Clicking Insert on the menu bar and selecting Image Placeholder lets you create a space for the image via the Image Placeholder dialog box shown in Figure 1-25. The dialog box lets you designate a name, size, color, and alternate text for the image prior to inserting it. Later, when the image is available, it can replace the placeholder and fit the scale requirements already set by you in the placeholder image.

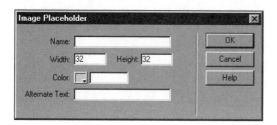

Figure 1-25 Image Placeholder dialog box

Creating Simple Tables

In this section, you learn to lay out tables in Standard view. (In Chapter 4, you learn to use Layout view.) Standard view is the default. To set up Standard view, click the Layout tab on the Insert bar and click Standard view. To insert tables on a Web page in Standard view, use the Insert Table button 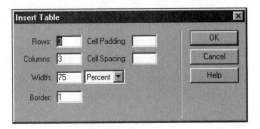 on the Common or Layout tab on the Insert bar. You can also insert a table by selecting the Table command from the Insert menu, or by using the shortcut key sequence Ctrl+Alt+T.

Each of these options allows you to create a table using the Insert Table dialog box, shown in Figure 1-26. In the dialog box, you are prompted to enter the number of rows and columns that your table will contain. The Cell Padding attribute controls the number of pixels between images and text in the cell and the edge of the cell. The Cell Spacing attribute controls the number of pixels between table cells. You can also indicate a width for the table as a percent of the Web browser window or as a number of pixels. The Border option allows you to set the thickness for the borders of your table. Using a large border gives a nice 3-D effect. A border of zero produces a table with invisible borders. This is useful when you want to align text and graphics neatly on the page but don't want a table to be visible. In HTML, you can often use tables to align page elements, creating a more appealing page layout.

Figure 1-26   Insert Table dialog box

Figure 1-27 shows a simple two-by-two table and the Property inspector that appears when you select the entire table. Just as when you select an image, you will see small handles appear on the table that allow you to resize the table visually. You may have resized table rows and columns in a word processor. Resizing Dreamweaver MX tables in Standard view is no different. By positioning your mouse between rows and columns, you can drag the lines dividing the cells to resize portions of the table.

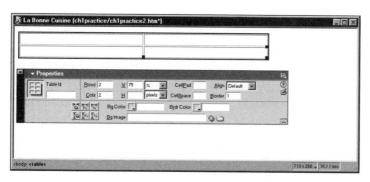

Figure 1-27   Selected table and its expanded Property inspector

Table 1-5 lists the attributes of the Property inspector for tables.

Table 1-5   Attributes of the Property Inspector for Tables

Element	Description
Table ID	Allows you to give the table a unique name identifier
Rows	Displays the number of rows the table contains
Cols	Displays the number of columns the table contains
W	Sets the table width, either in pixels or as a percentage of the browser window
H	Sets the table height in pixels or percent
CellPad	Controls the padding in pixels between the cell walls and text or images contained within the table cell
CellSpace	Controls the spacing between cells in the table
Align	Controls positioning of the table relative to the browser window
Border	Controls the border width in pixels; a border of 0 allows you to control page layout without displaying the table borders
Clear Column Widths	Clears present or modified column widths so that you can edit them
Clear Row Heights	Clears present or modified row heights so that you can edit them
Convert Table Widths to Pixels	Controls table width in absolute pixel size
Convert Table Heights to Pixels	Controls table height in absolute pixel size
Convert Table Width to Percent	Controls layout of table width as a percent
Convert Table Height to Percent	Controls layout of table height as a percent
Bg Color	Changes table cells to a designated background color
Bg Image	Inserts a background image shown in all table cells
Brdr Color	Changes the color of the table border

The Property inspector for a table is modified if you select a row, column, or single cell. The Property inspector for a cell is shown in Figure 1-28. This gives you greater control than modifying attributes for an entire table.

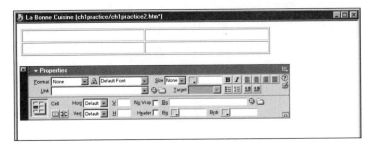

Figure 1-28   Property inspector for a table cell

Table 1-6 lists selected attributes of the Property inspector in Figure 1-27.

Table 1-6   Selected Attributes of the Property inspector for Cells, Rows, and Columns

Element	Description
Merge Cell	Merges selected table cells
Split Cell	Splits table cell into rows or columns
Horz	Controls the horizontal alignment of table cell data
Vert	Controls the vertical alignment of table cell data
W	Sets the cell width explicitly
H	Sets the cell height explicitly
No Wrap	Prevents wrapping, causing the table cell to resize if the content of the cell is larger than the cell's original size
Header	Creates a table header in the specified cell
Bg Image	Determines the source for a background image
Bg Color	Background color; changes the background color for a cell
Brdr	Changes the border color for a cell

Using Horizontal Rules

To insert horizontal rules on a Web page, you can use the Horizontal Rule button on the Common tab. You can also insert a rule using the Horizontal Rule command on the Insert menu. A horizontal rule is inserted automatically on the Web page at the insertion point. To change the attributes of the rule, click to select it, and then make changes, as shown in Figure 1-29.

Figure 1-29   Horizontal rule Property inspector

Unlike images and tables, rules cannot be resized by dragging your mouse. You must change the attributes in the Property inspector if you want the rule's appearance to differ from the default. The attributes you can control are the rule name, the width (either as a percentage of the browser window or in pixels), the height in pixels, rule alignment, and shading.

Horizontal rules are useful for dividing a Web page into logical areas, making it easier for the user to read. For example, if you post instructions for copying files onto a computer, you might list a title for the instructions, step-by-step instructions, and information on who to contact for help. You could divide these three portions of the page using horizontal rules, making it a more readable document.

Creating Rollovers

Rollovers are images (and sometimes text images) that change when the mouse crosses over the rollover image. They are actually composed of two images, controlled with JavaScript code that calls a hidden image when the mouse crosses over it. Typically, the image that loads first is called the up image and the image that displays with the mouse over is called the over image. Rollovers are important visual tools that help users operate Web pages. Having a rollover button that changes in appearance when the user crosses it with a mouse makes a Web page more responsive, telling the user that he or she can click the rollover to get more information on another Web page.

Dreamweaver MX assists you in creating rollovers by having you navigate through files to select the rollover images and then generating the JavaScript to operate the rollover. On the Common tab, clicking the Rollover Image button ⬚ opens the Insert Rollover Image dialog box shown in Figure 1-30. From the dialog box, you enter an image name, the original (the up image), the rollover (the over image), the alternate text, and a hyperlink where you would like the rollover to direct the user when clicked.

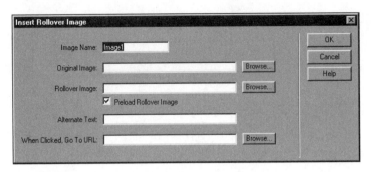

Figure 1-30   Insert Rollover Image dialog box

Working with the La Bonne Cuisine Web Page

In this section, you insert a company logo and rollover images that link to other portions of the La Bonne Cuisine Web page. To align everything properly and make an attractive page, you decide to insert graphics and text in a table with invisible borders.

To work with graphics and text:

1. Copy all the images (**lbclogo.gif**, **aboutusover.gif**, **aboutusup.gif**, **consultingover.gif**, **consultingup.gif**, **tourover.gif**, **tourup.gif**, **trainingover.gif**, and **trainingup.gif**) from the Chapter1\images folder on your Data Disk into the **ch1practice\images** folder in the Sites directory on your hard drive.

2. Open the ch1practice2.htm Web page from the previous exercise. Save the page as **ch1practice3.htm** in the same directory to prevent overwriting your previous work.

3. Place the insertion point to the left of the title "La Bonne Cuisine" on the page. On the Insert bar Common tab, click the **Image** button [img] select the image **lbclogo.gif** in the ch1practice\images folder, and then click **OK**. Observe that the image is displayed to the left of the title.

4. Place the insertion point in the blank line beneath the address for La Bonne Cuisine. Then click the **Insert Table** button [img] on the Insert bar. The Insert Table dialog box will open. Enter **1** row, **4** columns, **90%** for width, and a Border value of **0**. Leave Padding and Spacing blank. Click **OK**.

5. If necessary, check the Property inspector to ensure the table align attribute is set to **Center**.

6. Move the cursor to the first cell of the table and click the **Rollover Image** button [img] on the Common tab. The Insert Rollover Image dialog box will open. Leave the Image Name as the default setting. For Original Image, click **Browse**. Select the file **aboutusup.gif** from the Sites\ch1practice\images folder. Click **OK**. For Rollover Image, click **Browse**. Select the file **aboutusover.gif** from the Sites\ch1practice\images folder. Click **OK**. In the Alternate Text text box, type **Learn More About La Bonne Cuisine**. In the

1

When Clicked Go To URL: text box, type **contact/aboutlbc.htm**. The Preload Rollover Image checkbox will be checked by default. Selecting this ensures that your graphics for the rollover preload so that they operate more quickly on your Web page. Click **OK**. The table may resize.

7. Press **F12** to preview your rollover in your Web browser. Observe that the image rolls over as expected.

8. Repeat Step 6 for three more images on the Web site. The second table cell should use **consultingup.gif** for the original image and **consultingover.gif** for the rollover image with alternate text **Consulting Services** and URL **consulting/consulting.htm**.

   The third table cell should use **tourup.gif** for the original image and **tourover.gif** for the rollover image with alternate text **Culinary Explorations** and URL **tour/tour.htm**.

   The fourth table cell should use **trainingup.gif** for the original image and **trainingover.gif** for the rollover image with alternate text **Culinary Training** and URL **training/training.htm**.

9. Preview the page in your Web browser. Observe that it appears as shown in Figure 1-31 and that the graphics for the rollovers operate as expected.

10. Save the page.

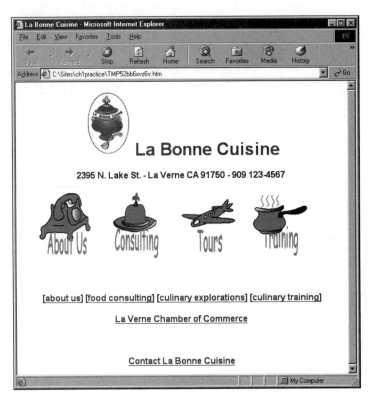

Figure 1-31   La Bonne Cuisine Web page with images and table layout

CHAPTER SUMMARY

- Dreamweaver MX is a WYSIWYG authoring tool that generates HTML and JavaScript code.

- The panels commonly used to develop a Web site are the Property inspector and the Insert bar. Other tools can be found on the Window menu on the menu bar.

- The Property inspector is used for basic text manipulation such as changing fonts, sizes, justification, and color of text. Using the Property inspector, you can also create hyperlinks to other Web pages. The shortcut key for displaying the Property inspector is Ctrl+F3.

- The Insert bar is used to insert various elements into a Web site. The Insert bar categories are Common, Layout, Text, Tables, Frames, Forms, Templates, Characters, Media, Head, Script, and Application. The shortcut key for displaying the Insert bar is Ctrl+F2.

1

❏ Using the Common tab in the Insert bar, you can insert images, rollovers, tables, and horizontal rules. You can also create a hyperlink to an e-mail address and insert Web page elements created by other applications.

❏ You insert a table in Dreamweaver MX using a dialog box, entering the number of rows and columns. After the table is created, you can resize and manipulate it by dragging it with your mouse or by changing the attributes in the Property inspector. Setting a table width to a percent causes the table to resize when the browser window is resized.

❏ To insert a rollover in Dreamweaver MX, you need two images. The first image is the one that appears when the page loads; the second image is the one that appears when the mouse is over the first image. Dreamweaver MX lets you browse through your files to select the two images needed to create a rollover.

❏ In Dreamweaver MX, you can choose a predefined color scheme for a page. You can also select hexadecimal color codes for background, text, links, visited links, and active links. The predefined schemes use the Web safe color palette, ensuring that your colors look the same in any browser.

❏ In Dreamweaver MX, you can create a space for an image that does not yet exist. This lets you control layout before you have all the images you need for your site.

REVIEW QUESTIONS

1. What does WYSIWYG mean?

2. What is a Web safe color?

3. What types of graphics can be used on the Web?

    a. gif and jpg

    b. html and htm

    c. png and psd

    d. all of the above

4. What do shortcut keys do?

5. Why might it be useful to look at the source code in Dreamweaver MX?

6. To add a title to a page in Dreamweaver MX, you can select and change which of the following:

    a. the title of the document in the source code

    b. the title of the document in the Property inspector

    c. the title of the document in the Page Properties dialog box

    d. both a and b

    e. both a and c

7. Dreamweaver MX is capable of generating HTML and JavaScript code. True or False?

8. In the hexadecimal color code format #RRGGBB, R, G, and B represent amounts of Red, Green, and Blue to create the color. True or False?

9. To change the absolute text size to 6, you will need to enter which code in the size text box in the Properties inspector:

   a. 6

   b. +6

   c. −6

   d. %6

10. Heading 1 in HTML code is smaller than Heading 6. True or False?

11. Which of the following statements is true about the Property inspector?

    a. Attributes of the Property inspector are used to format text.

    b. The Property inspector changes depending upon the page element selected.

    c. It allows you to make relative and absolute hyperlinks.

    d. all of the above

12. How can you resize an image?

    a. Edit the image size in the source code.

    b. Select the image and resize it with the mouse.

    c. Use the Property inspector to change the height and width of the image.

    d. all of the above

13. Inserted images in the Dreamweaver MX workspace must be in the .gif format. True or False?

14. It is impossible to change the blue underlined text for hyperlinks to another color. True or False?

15. Background images can be inserted in a Web page using the Page Properties dialog box to navigate to and select the image file. True or False?

16. What is the difference between a relative and an absolute hyperlink?

17. How can you absolutely control the size of a table cell?

    a. Represent the cell width in terms of pixel size.

    b. Represent the cell width in terms of percentage of a browser window.

    c. Set the cell border to 0.

    d. none of the above

18. A table width of 100% will not resize the browser window. True or False?

19. How can a table help you control the layout of a Web page?

20. When is it appropriate to use a horizontal rule?

HANDS-ON PROJECTS

Project 1-1

In this project, you create an HTML document that links to major soft drink companies. You also create a title for the page telling the user what the links are and place the links in a bulleted (unordered) list.

1. Start Dreamweaver MX and edit the blank page that appears. If you are already running Dreamweaver MX, click **New** under the File menu or use the keyboard shortcut **Ctrl+N**. Under the General Category select **Basic page** and **HTML**. Click **Create**.

2. In the Document toolbar, type **Soft Drink Links** in the Title text box.

3. Click the **Modify** menu in the menu bar and then click **Page Properties**. Type in the following colors for these page attributes:

   ❑ Background: **#FFCC99** (light orange)

   ❑ Text: **#330033** (dark purple)

   ❑ Links: **#3333FF** (blue)

   ❑ Visited Links: **#CC0033** (dark red)

   Click **OK** to close the Page Properties dialog box.

4. Your cursor should be at the top of the workspace. In the Property inspector, click the **Format** list arrow and click **Heading 1**. Type **Soft Drink Links**. Click the **Align Center** button on the Property inspector.

5. Press the **Enter** key twice to move down two lines, then click the **Unordered List** button in the Property inspector. If necessary, change the alignment to **Left Align** in the Property inspector.

6. Type the elements **Coke**, **Pepsi**, **Mountain Dew**, and **Sprite** on separate lines to create four bulleted items in the list. Click and drag to select the entire list and change the format to **Heading 2**.

7. Select the text **Coke**, and type *http://www.coke.com* in the **Link** text box in the Property inspector.

8. Repeat Step 7 for the other soft drinks: *http://www.pepsi.com*, *http://www.mountaindew.com*, and *http://www.sprite.com*.

9. Save the page as **drinkslinks.htm** in the ch1practice folder on your working drive.

10. Preview the page in your Web browser by pressing **F12**, and test to see if the links work.

11. Close the drinkslinks.htm file.

Project 1-2

In this project, you create a Web page that gives directions to a party using several aspects of text manipulation.

1. Start Dreamweaver MX and edit the blank page that appears. If you are already running Dreamweaver MX, click **New** under the File menu or use the keyboard shortcut **Ctrl+N**. Under the General Category, select **Basic page** and **HTML**. Click **Create**.

2. In the Document toolbar, type **Party Invitation** in the Title text box.

3. Click the **Modify** menu in the menu bar and then click **Page Properties**. Type in the following colors for these page attributes:

   - Background: **#FF6600** (bright orange)
   - Links: **#FFFF99** (yellow)
   - Visited Links: **#CC0000** (dark red)

   Click **OK** to close the Page Properties dialog box.

4. Enter text in the workspace to provide instructions for people wishing to attend a Halloween party. Type **INVITATION** at the top of the page. Drag your mouse to select **INVITATION**, and then, using the Property inspector, italicize and center the text and change its format to **Heading 1**. Deselect **Italicize**, if necessary.

5. Click to the right of the word INVITATION to deselect it, and then press **Enter** to move to the next line. In the Property inspector, change the format to **Heading 2**, type **TO A HALLOWEEN PARTY**. Press **Enter** to move to the next line in the workspace.

6. In the workspace type the following text on different lines:

   Location: Student Union

   Time: 12 midnight, October 31st

   Guests should bring their own drinks. Food provided.

   R.S.V.P to bob@notmail.edu

7. Select all four of the lines of text created in Step 6. In the Property inspector, set Format to **Heading 3** and Font to **Geneva, Arial, Helvetica**.

8. At the bottom of the page, select **R.S.V.P to bob@notmail.edu** by dragging your mouse over the text. Type **mailto:bob@notmail.edu** in the Link box in the Property inspector. Press **Enter**.

9. Save the page as **invite1.htm** in your ch1practice folder on your hard drive.

10. Preview your page in your Web browser by pressing **F12**.

11. Open the document invite1.htm in Dreamweaver MX, if it is not already open. Save the page as **invite2.htm** in your ch1practice folder.

12. Click the **Modify** menu in the menu bar and then click **Page Properties**. Type in the following colors for these page attributes:

- Background: **#000000** (black)

- Text: **#FFCC99** (light orange)

- Links: **#CCCCFF** (light blue)

- Visited Links: **#FFFF66** (light yellow)

Click **OK** to save the changes and return to the Dreamweaver MX editing window.

13. Select all of the text, and change the font to **Arial, Helvetica, sans-serif** in the Property inspector.

14. Select the lines of text that begin with the words **Location**, **Time**, and **Guests**, and change the Format in the Property inspector to **Paragraph** and the Size option to **+3**.

15. Save the page **invite2.htm** in your ch1practice folder and preview it in your Web browser by pressing **F12**.

16. Close the invite2.htm file.

Project 1-3

In this project, you create a page with a list of links to famous people's e-mail addresses.

1. Start Dreamweaver MX and edit the blank page that appears. If you are already running Dreamweaver MX, click **New** under the File menu or use the keyboard shortcut **Ctrl+N**. Under the General Category, select **Basic page** and **HTML**. Click **Create**.

2. In the Document toolbar, type **Famous People's E-mail Addresses** into the Title text box.

3. From the **Commands** menu on the menu bar, select **Set Color Scheme**. Under Background, choose **Purple**. Under Text and Links, choose **yellow, orange, and olive**, and then press **OK**.

4. At the top of the workspace, type the text **E-mail Addresses of the Rich and Famous**. Select the text you just typed and, using the Property inspector, center it and set the format to **Heading 1**. Click to the right of the text to deselect it. Press the **Enter** key to create a new blank line.

5. Left align the new line in the Property inspector by clicking the **Left align** icon.

6. Click the **Email Link** button on the Insert bar Common tab to insert a link to e-mail. Type **Bill Gates** in the text box and **billgates@notmail.edu** for the e-mail address. Click **OK**. Click to the right of the text to deselect it. Press **Enter** to start a new line.

7. Repeat Step 6, but type your own name and e-mail address.

8. Repeat Step 6 three more times for three more e-mail addresses: **Madonna** (**madonna@madonna.edu**); **Steven Spielberg** (**steve@dreamworks.edu**); and **Jesse Ventura** (**jesse@minnesota.edu**).

9. Select the five e-mail links you just created. Use the **Text Indent** button in the Property inspector to indent the line and change the format to **Heading 2**.

10. Save the page as **emaillinks.htm** in the ch1practice folder on your hard drive.

11. Preview your page in the Web browser by pressing **F12**. Click the link to your email to test it.

12. If necessary, open emaillinks.htm in Dreamweaver MX if it is not already open and save it as **emaillinks2.htm** in your ch1practice folder.

13. Change the heading at the top of the page so that it is split into two lines; the first line should contain "E-mail Addresses of the", and the second line should contain "Rich and Famous." You can make the split by using the Enter key.

14. From the Commands menu, select **Set Color Scheme**. Under Background, choose **Magenta**. Under Text and Links, choose **white, green, and blue**, and click **OK**.

15. Select the list of names.

16. Change the font to **Verdana, Arial, Helvetica**.

17. Click **Unordered List**.

18. Save the changes and preview the page in your Web browser.

19. Close the emaillinks2.htm file.

Project 1-4

In this project, you will integrate images and text into a table to create a Web page about pet adoption.

1. Copy three files (**dog.gif**, **bird.gif**, **cat.gif**) into the subdirectory in your ch1practice folder named images.

2. Open Dreamweaver MX if it is not already open. Click **File**, **New** to open a blank document. Click **Basic Page and HTML** on the General tab of the New Document window. Click **Create**. Save your blank document as **pets.htm** in your ch1practice folder.

3. On the Document toolbar, type **Adopt a Pet** in the Title text box.

4. Click in the workspace. In the Property inspector, set Format to **Heading 1** and text color to red (**#FF0000**). Type **Adopt a Pet Today** in the workspace. Press **Enter** to move to the next line.

5. On the Insert bar Common tab, click the **Insert Table** icon. In the Insert table dialog box, set Rows to **2**; Columns to **3**, Width to **400 pixels**, and Border to **0**. Click **OK**.

6. Click your mouse in the first column top table cell. Click the **Image** button on the Insert bar Common tab. Browse your directory structure and select **dog.gif**. Click **OK**. Click the **Align Center** button in the Property inspector.

7. Click your mouse in the first column bottom table cell. In the Property inspector, set Format to **Heading 3** and **Center**. Type **I'm adorable and good with kids**.

8. Click your mouse in the second column top table cell. Click the **Image** button on the Insert bar Common tab. Browse your directory structure and select **bird.gif**. Click **OK**. Click the **Align Center** button in the Property inspector.

9. Click your mouse in the second column bottom table cell. In the Property inspector, set Format to **Heading 3** and **Center**. Type **I sing show tunes and say hello**.

10. Click your mouse in the third column top table cell. Click the **Image** button on the Insert bar Common tab. Browse your directory structure and select **cat.gif**. Click **OK**. Click the **Align Center** button in the Property inspector.

11. Click your mouse in the third column bottom table cell. In the Property inspector, set Format to **Heading 3** and **Center**. Type **A companion that is already house broken**.

12. Save pets.htm. Press **F12** to preview this page in your Web browser.

13. Close the pets.htm file.

Project 1-5

In this project, you create a simple rollover of a person winking.

1. Copy the files **sageup.jpg** and **sageover.jpg** into the subdirectory in your ch1practice folder named images.

2. Open Dreamweaver MX if it is not already open. Click **File**, **New** to open a blank document. Click **Basic Page and HTML** on the General tab of the New Document window. Click **Create**. Save your blank document as **wink.htm** in the ch1practice folder.

3. In the Document toolbar, type **Winky** in the Title text box.

4. Click in the workspace. On the Insert bar Common tab, click the **Rollover Image** button. The Insert Rollover Image dialog box will open. Leave the Image name as the default setting. For Original Image, click **Browse**. Select the file **sageup.jpg** from the **images** folder. For Rollover Image, click **Browse**. Select the file **sageover.jpg** from the images folder. In the Alternate Text text box, enter **Find This**. In the When Clicked Go To URL: text box, type **http://www.google.com**. Make sure the **Preload Rollover Image** checkbox is selected. Click **OK**.

5. Press **F12** to preview your rollover in your Web browser. Observe that the image rolls over as expected.

6. Save the file in your ch1practice folder.

7. Close the wink.htm file.

CASE PROJECTS

Create a Web page that contains hyperlinks to your favorite Web sites in three categories: Movies, Music, and Hobbies. Put an appropriate title at the top of the page. Add a blank line and then add a table with three columns and seven rows. Place three category titles (Movies, Music, and Hobbies) in the first row. Use search engines to locate at least six Web sites for each category, and list them in the appropriate column under the category title. Use descriptive titles in the table cells, and create hyperlinks to each Web site. Add a title to the page and modify the page properties to a color scheme you like.

Develop a resume in Dreamweaver MX. Include information such as your name, phone number, e-mail address, homepage URL, desired position, education, experience, and technical skills. Insert hyperlinks into logical places in the resume. For example, if you list your school, create a hyperlink to the home page for that school. If you list Dreamweaver MX as a skill, create a link to the Macromedia Web site (*http://www. macromedia.com*). Enter a page title and modify the page properties by changing the color scheme to one you find appropriate for a resume.

Develop a storefront for a karate studio. Think about what kinds of information would be useful to customers visiting the page. Design the text and information on the page to emphasize important information. Use a search engine to find links to Web sites that sell karate clothes and equipment. At the bottom of your page, underneath your own karate studio information, add a table that contains at least four links to appropriate Web sites. Include a link to the karate studio owner's e-mail address. At the bottom of the page, include a credit that says "This page developed by *your name*." Make your name a hyperlink to your own e-mail address. Enter a page title and modify the page properties to a color scheme you find appropriate for a karate studio.

Develop a four-page Web site for a small business of your choice. Think about who your customers are and what kind of information they would seek on your Web site. As a minimum, your site should include a home page with a logo for the company with links to an about page where customers can contact the store, a products or services page where customers can see what your business offers, and a promotions page showing any special deals or coupons.

2

INTRODUCTION TO
FIREWORKS MX

Making It Graphic

In this chapter you will:

♦ Learn how to work with graphics using Fireworks MX
♦ Learn how to use the Tools panel
♦ Work with the Optimize, Layers, and Assets panels

Knowing how to build HTML Web pages is very important. Integrating graphics into your pages is just as important. Many say the Internet's expanding popularity in the early 1990s was due to the visual appeal and easy navigation made possible by Web pages using graphics. Graphics can make a Web site more visually appealing to look at, causing the user to visit a site for a longer period of time. Graphics can also help users to navigate a Web site by showing them how to navigate with icons rather than having them read links. Many student Web sites are developed with 'borrowed' graphics. If you are connected to the Internet and right-click on most images, a pop-up menu will allow you to save the image on your hard drive. However, the images posted on the Web are copyrighted, unless otherwise stated. Knowing how to create your own images is essential to becoming a professional Web developer. The following two chapters introduce you to Fireworks MX, a Macromedia graphics package designed specifically for developing Web graphics.

Fireworks MX enables you to integrate graphics seamlessly into your Dreamweaver MX Web pages. The HTML and JavaScript code that is created by Fireworks MX is fully compatible with Dreamweaver MX. This lets you work on graphics and Web design in an integrated development environment. Fireworks MX offers in a single package various tools for creating and working with many different kinds of graphics files. For example, Fireworks allows you to create both bitmapped and vector graphics, and to scan and edit graphics, photographs, and files from many other graphics applications.

In this chapter, you learn how to use the basic editing features of Fireworks and become familiar with the tools and effects that are available in Fireworks MX. In Chapter 3, you learn about the more advanced features of Fireworks MX.

FIREWORKS MX EDITING TOOLS AND FILE CREATION

When you first start Fireworks MX, you may be a little intimidated by the number of elements displayed in the workspace. However, if you have worked with another drawing tool, some of what you see may be familiar to you. For example, the Paint Bucket tool for filling a shape or area with a specific color is used in many applications. Figure 2-1 shows a Fireworks MX screen, as it appears when you first open a blank document in the Fireworks MX application.

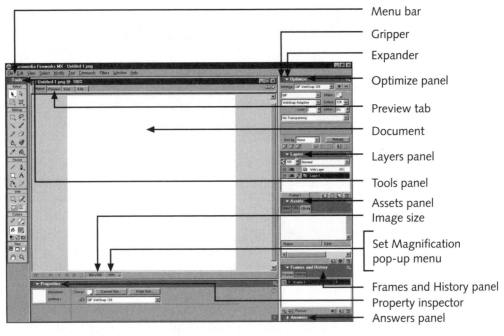

Figure 2-1   Fireworks MX work area

Most of the buttons on the screen offer rollover text to indicate what operation executes when you click the button. At the top of the screen, you see a menu bar. On the left side of the workspace, a two-column Tools panel shows several drawing tools to help you create and modify artwork. The blank, center area of the screen is your document or canvas.

At the top of the document, there are four tabs. The Original tab lets you view your original document, the Preview tab lets you see what your image will look like when loaded in a Web browser, and the other tabs help you to compare settings when you optimize a document for the Web. At the bottom of the document, the image size is listed and an option exists for you to change the magnification of the image. At the bottom of the Fireworks screen is the Property inspector. This is used to edit attributes of objects you are using in the canvas, such as size, color, and effects.

By default, the workspace contains five panels:

- The Optimize panel assists you with optimizing graphics for the Web, creating balance between file size and image quality.

- The Layers panel allows you to work in multiple layers, creating complex graphics, text, and effects.

- The Assets panel lets you use and manage styles, URLs, and library items for your Fireworks document.

- The Frames and History panel group lets you use the Frames tab to create rollovers and animations and use the History tab to reverse and repeat commands.

- The Answers panel gives links to online Help and tutorials.

You can navigate between the panels by clicking them or the tabs associated with them. You can minimize or expand the panels by clicking the expander ▼ to the left of the panel title. You can access any of the panels by clicking Window in the menu bar and selecting the desired panel from the menu.

The panels available from the Window menu are shown in Figure 2-2. Panels can be moved to other locations in the workspace by dragging them with the gripper ▊, located at the upper-left corner of the panel.

The menu bar at the top of the Fireworks screen contains ten options:

- File provides options for opening, scanning, previewing, saving, and exporting files. It also offers features for printing, preferences, HTML properties, and scripting.

- Edit provides standard cut, copy, and paste editing tools. It also offers features for inserting objects and using libraries.

- View contains controls for magnification, grids, edges, and rulers.

- Select allows you to control selection of areas of the workspace by defining attributes of the selection marquee and by shrinking and expanding the marquee. You can also select everything or deselect objects.

- Modify provides options for modifying canvas and image properties and also makes controls for transforming and aligning objects available.

- Text provides options for basic text formatting of font, size, style, and alignment.

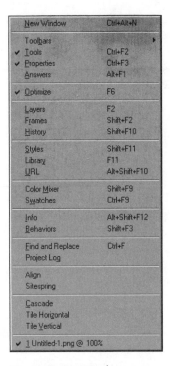

Figure 2-2   Window menu

- Commands allows you to create your own commands by recording scriptlets (which are similar to macros) or by using the History file to create a command script.

- Filters contains some effects that you can apply to selections or layers to make an image appear a specific way.

- Window allows you to open and close panels.

- Help provides online help, a tutorial, and access to the Fireworks Product Support Center and product Web site.

Previewing the Tools Panel

The Tools panel is divided into six categories: Select, Bitmap, Vector, Web, Colors, and View. The Tools panel and categories are shown in Figure 2-3. You learn more about these tools as you apply them throughout the chapter. If you have used other drawing applications, these tools may be familiar to you. To use a tool, you click it and then apply it to the document in the workspace. If you see a small triangle at the lower-right corner of the tool, holding your mouse button down while the pointer is over the tool will reveal more tool options. Note that some tools will be grayed out unless there is a shape drawn on the canvas.

2

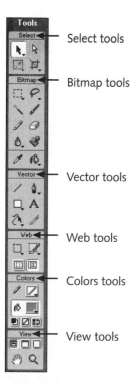

- Select tools
- Bitmap tools
- Vector tools
- Web tools
- Colors tools
- View tools

Figure 2-3 Tools panel categories

Table 2-1 gives a description of each tool in the Fireworks MX Tools panel.

Table 2-1 The Fireworks MX Tools Panel

Element	Icon	Description
Select Tools		
Pointer tool		Used to select objects and groups of objects by clicking or by clicking while holding down the Shift key
Select Behind tool		Used to select an object located behind another object in the workspace
Subselection tool		Used to select an object for the purpose of reshaping it; handles will appear so the object can be altered
Scale tool		Used to change an object's size and/or rotate the object
Skew tool		Used to stretch and/or rotate an object
Distort tool		Used to distort and/or rotate an object
Crop tool		Used to select only a portion of the document and discard the remainder
Export Area tool		Used to export a cropped area of a document

Table 2-1   The Fireworks MX Tools Panel (continued)

Element	Icon	Description
Bitmap Tools		
Marquee tool		Used to make a rectangular selection in the workspace
Oval Marquee tool		Used to make an oval selection in the workspace
Lasso tool		Used to make a free form selection by dragging the mouse
Polygon Lasso tool		Used to make a polygon selection by clicking and dragging the mouse
Magic Wand tool		Used to select areas of a document that are similar in color
Brush tool		Used to draw paint lines (paths) freehand in the workspace
Pencil tool		Used to draw lines (paths) freehand in the workspace
Eraser tool		Used to erase portions of a graphic
Blur tool		Used to blur a selected area of an image
Sharpen tool		Used to sharpen a selected layer or area of an image
Dodge tool		Used to lighten a selected area of an image
Burn tool		Used to darken a selected area of an image
Smudge tool		Used to smudge an image by dragging color out from a selected area
Rubber Stamp tool		Used to copy a portion of a graphic and reproduce it somewhere else in the workspace
Eyedropper tool		Used to select a color from a pixel in the graphic to be placed in the fill color box
Paint Bucket tool		Used to fill areas with specified colors
Gradient tool		Used to create fills and effects that gradually change from one color to another
Vector Tools		
Line tool		Used to draw a straight line (path)
Pen tool		Used to draw lines
Vector Path tool		Used to draw lines as a series of editable segments (paths)
Redraw Path tool		Used to reshape selected segments of a path
Rectangle tool		Used to draw rectangular shapes
Rounded Rectangle tool		Used to draw rectangular shapes with rounded edges by entering the desired corner angle
Ellipse tool		Used to draw elliptical shapes
Polygon tool		Used to draw polygons by indicating a number of sides and to draw stars by indicating a number of sides and an angle
Text tool	A	Used to type text onto a document
Freeform tool		Used to reshape a selected path by dragging points located on the path

Table 2-1   The Fireworks MX Tools Panel (continued)

Element	Icon	Description
Reshape Area tool		Used to reshape a selected area by dragging a selection circle located on the path
Path Scrubber tool Additive		Advanced tool for changing/adding speed and pressure-sensitive stroke effects
Path Scrubber tool Subtractive		Advanced tool for changing/removing speed and pressure-sensitive stroke effects
Knife tool		Used to slice lines (paths) into more segments
Web Tools and Buttons		
Rectangle Hotspot tool		Used to create rectangular shapes within a graphic that will link to URLs (hotspots) as part of the graphic; used to create an image map
Circle Hotspot tool		Used to create circular shapes within a graphic that will link to URLs (hotspots) as part of the graphic
Polygon Hotspot tool		Used to create polygons within a graphic that will link to URLs (hotspots) as part of the graphic
Slice tool		Used to create rectangular shaped slices of an image
Polygon Slice tool		Used to create polygon shaped slices of an image
Hide Slices and Hotspots button		Used to hide slices and hotspots of a graphic
Show Slices and Hotspots button		Used to show slices and hotspots of a graphic
Colors Tools, Boxes and Buttons		
Stroke Color box		Used to access the stroke color palette and select a line color
Fill Color box		Used to access the fill color palette and select a fill color
Set Default Stroke/ Fill Colors button		Used to set the fill and stroke colors to the default
No Stroke or Fill button		Used to set the fill and stroke colors to transparent
Swap Stroke/Fill Colors button		Used to trade the fill and stroke colors
View Tools and Buttons		
Standard Screen mode button		Default view of a Fireworks document
Full Screen with Menus mode button		Displays image with menus
Full Screen mode button		Minimizes menus so full image can be displayed
Hand tool		Used to move a document within the workspace for viewing
Zoom tool		Used to magnify and de-magnify a document

2

The Main and Modify Toolbars

From the Window menu, you can access two additional toolbars that contain shortcut buttons for frequently used functions. To access these two toolbars, you must click Toolbars on the Window menu and select either Main or Modify.

The Main toolbar, shown in Figure 2-4, is similar to that of many applications you may already use. Using this toolbar, you can create a new document or open an existing one, save a file, import or export a file, and print. Two arrow buttons located near the center of the toolbar indicate options for edit undo and redo. Buttons for cut, copy, and paste are also available. The Modify toolbar, shown in Figure 2-5, contains buttons that allow you to orient objects in the workspace with respect to one another.

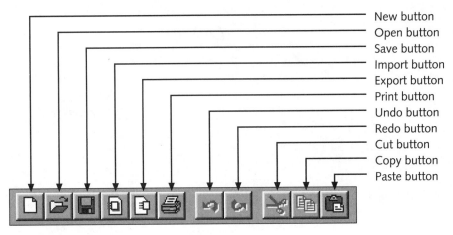

Figure 2-4   Main toolbar

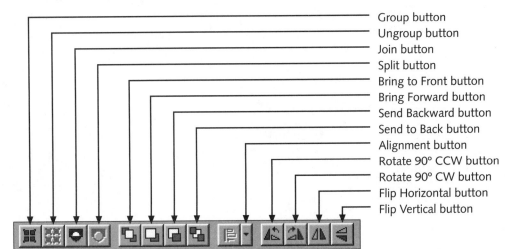

Figure 2-5   Modify toolbar

The Property Inspector

Every element you work with on the Fireworks canvas has properties associated with it. For example, if you draw a simple rectangle, it has width, height, color, and placement attributes that can all be defined and controlled. After you import or draw graphics and text on the canvas, you will see that the Property inspector, at the bottom of the workspace, changes depending upon which object on the canvas is selected. It is much easier to manipulate attributes of an object through the Property inspector than it is to search through panels. Every time you select an object on the canvas, all of its attributes are displayed in the Property inspector and are easily modified via text boxes and slider bars. Figure 2-6 shows the Property inspector for a rectangle.

Figure 2-6   Property inspector for a rectangle

Creating a New Document

To create a new document, simply select the New command on the File menu. Using the New Document dialog box in Figure 2-7, you must specify the canvas size and resolution, and select a canvas type. Most Web graphics are 72 dots per inch (dpi) because most monitors display graphics at this resolution. If you find working in inches or centimeters easier, you can click the list arrow next to the height and width text boxes.

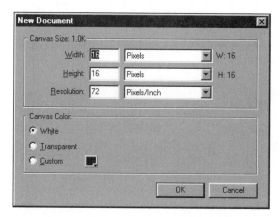

Figure 2-7   New Document dialog box

To determine the canvas size that you require, consider what you are trying to accomplish. Graphics for the Web come in many sizes; you need to consider who your user is and what you are trying to show:

- If you are designing individual rectangular buttons for a Web site, the pixel size of your canvas could be 100 pixels wide by 20 pixels high.

- If you are designing several buttons for a vertical navigation bar, then obviously the height of the canvas would need to be greater.

- If you are designing a page for users who are children, you may design large colorful buttons with graphics showing the button destination. In this case, the size of 100 pixels high by 100 pixels wide for an individual button may be more appropriate.

An image designed to be a banner across the top of a Web page can be 500 to 600 pixels wide and 100 to 200 pixels in height. You want to avoid images that are so large that they take too long to download or they distract the user from scrolling to see other information on the Web page. It is useful to create a mock-up page and gain feedback before committing to a specific design concept. Doing this gives you a better idea of what your image size requirements are. Remember that when using cropping, resizing, and scaling tools in Fireworks, you can modify the graphic size after it has been created.

Choosing a Canvas Color

You can choose one of three options for canvas color:

- White is the most popular background for a business Web page.

- Transparent displays a checkered background in the workspace that disappears (becomes transparent) when you save your graphics.

- Custom Background allows you to choose the background color from the Web safe 216-color palette.

Modifying Properties for Your New Document

After you create your workspace, you may decide that you need to modify the size of the canvas or image. To change any of these attributes, click Modify on the menu bar and then click Canvas. Figure 2-8 shows the options for editing the canvas attributes.

Selecting the options Image Size, Canvas Size, or Canvas Color lets you edit the original settings for your document. Trim Canvas lets you reduce the canvas to fit the content. Fit Canvas does this too; however, if your content exceeds the canvas area, Fit Canvas will increase the canvas size. This can eliminate unnecessary white space and create more efficient graphics by ensuring that extraneous white space is not saved with your drawing. The Canvas submenu also provides options for rotating the entire canvas by 180 degrees, 90 degrees clockwise, or 90 degrees counter-clockwise.

2

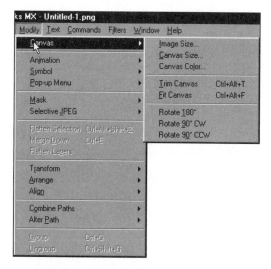

Figure 2-8   Options on the Canvas submenu

Working with Bitmap and Vector Graphics

Fireworks MX lets you edit bitmap and vector graphics. A **bitmap** graphic is an image created from individual pixels of color. A scanned-in photograph is a good example of a bitmap image. Photographs have complex variations of color. When digitized, a photograph is represented by a grid of pixels of these color variations, which together make up the image.

A **vector** graphic is one that uses mathematical formulas and vector paths to define shapes and figures. Because the image is defined mathematically, you do not see the pixel variations as you do with a bitmap image. Images created from scratch using tools such as those found in Fireworks are generally vector graphics. Fireworks MX lets you edit bitmap and vector images in one document.

Figures 2-10 and 2-11, shown later in this chapter, are examples of vector graphics.

Saving and Exporting Files

To save your work in Fireworks MX, click File on the menu bar, then click Save or Save As. Fireworks will automatically save your file in **Portable Network Graphic (PNG)** format. Many Web browsers do not support .png graphics without the use of a plug-in. Saving your graphics file in .png format maintains all the file's editable features as well as the layers created as part of the graphic, so that you may continue editing the file in detail. To save the file in .gif or .jpg format to be used with your Dreamweaver MX application, you must export the file.

Before exporting a file in a given format, Fireworks helps you preview and optimize it so you can see which format has optimal quality at minimal file size. You can use the 2-Up and 4-Up preview tabs to optimize your graphic. The 2-Up tab shows the original image and an additional panel in which you can alter the image characteristics to suit your needs. Similarly, the 4-Up tab will show you four different panels of your image. The first is the original image, the next three can be altered using the Optimize panel, and a direct comparison can be made between the different images.

After you've selected the optimized file, you can export the image or the image and the HTML code. To optimize a graphic means to obtain acceptable image quality with the smallest possible file size. Images in the 2-Up and 4-Up panels can be optimized individually using the Optimize panel at the upper-right of your screen. Comparing the same image with different optimization characteristics lets you make the trade-off visually between image size and image quality.

You can click Export Preview from the File menu to open the Export Preview dialog box, as shown in Figure 2-9. You use this dialog box to preview changes to the file format, palette, transparency, and other formatting features.

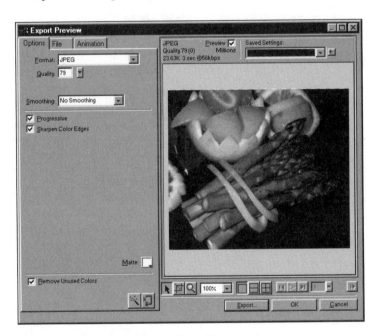

Figure 2-9   Export Preview dialog box

For a complete discussion of graphics formats, you may wish to read *Principles of Web Design, Second Edition* by Joel Sklar. Chapter 7 of Sklar's book discusses Web graphic formats in detail.

As mentioned, when you save an image for use on a Web page, it must be of .jpg or .gif format. The .gif format is better for line art and graphics with few colors. The .jpg format is better for photographs and complex pictures. The formats differ in the way that they compress image data. Thus, using .jpg for a photo will result in better quality and smaller file size than using .gif. Similarly, using .gif for text, a logo, or line art will result in a smaller file size than using .jpg.

In the following steps, you open, optimize, and save a Web graphic.

To work with a Web graphic:

1. Create a nested folder called **ch2practice** inside the Sites folder on your working drive to store the practice pages you create in this chapter. Create a second nested folder called **images** inside the ch2practice folder to store the images.

2. Start Fireworks. If this is the first time you start Fireworks, a dialog box appears, asking you to select Graphic Design, What's New, or Web Design. These options take you to tutorials that give you a quick overview of the Fireworks product. Close this Window to begin using Fireworks.

3. Copy the file **lbclogotext.png** from the Chapter2\images folder on your Data Disk into the ch2practice\images folder on your working drive. Click **File** on the menu bar, and then click **Open** to open an existing document that you will optimize. Navigate to and select the file **lbclogotext.png** from the ch2practice\images folder. Fireworks will open many file types, including .psd, .gif, .jpg and .tif.

4. Click the **2–Up** tab at the top of the document workspace. Two copies of your image appear, the original image and a preview image. If the Optimize panel is not open, open it now by selecting it from the Window menu in the menu bar or by pressing the **F6** key.

5. The image on the left is your original image. You can see that it is 100.38KB in size. Click the second image, at the right of the screen. You can see it is selected because an outline appears around it. This image shows a 13.26KB size with a 2 second download time for a 56kbps modem. Click the **Settings** pop-up menu at the very top of the Optimize panel and select **JPEG – Smaller File**. The file size is 11.71KB with a 1 second download time, but the image quality is highly degraded.

6. Click the **Settings** pop-up menu at the very top of the Optimize panel and select **GIF Web 216**. Now the file size is 11.53K with a 1 second download time, and the image quality is better.

7. Click the **Choose type of transparency** list arrow and click **Index Transparency** on the Optimize panel. A checkered grid should appear in the background of your image, indicating it has a transparent background.

8. Click the **File** menu and then click **Export**. Because the GIF file was selected in the Optimize panel, .gif file format is automatically set for you with the file. The Export dialog box will open. Type the filename **lbclogotext.gif**.

9. Click the **Save as type:** list arrow and click **HTML and Images** to save an HTML file and a .gif file from your Fireworks document.

10. In the Export dialog box, navigate to the ch2practice folder. The filename has changed to .htm file format, and **lbclogotext.htm** is the filename.

11. At the bottom of the Export dialog box, click the **Put Images in Subfolder** checkbox. The subfolder will default to images, and your .gif file will automatically be stored in ch2practice\images. Click **Save**. Your .gif and .htm files have been exported. Click **File** and **Save** to save your .png file.

12. Preview your Web page by opening lbclogotext.htm in your Web browser. To do this you can double-click the file, or you can click **File** and **Open** from the Web browser and navigate through your file structure to Sites\ch2practice\lbclogotext.htm.

13. Close the lbclogotext.png file.

USING THE TOOLS PANEL

The Tools panel is located to the far left of the Fireworks workspace. With it, you can create basic shapes, insert text, add color to shapes and text, and manipulate objects in the workspace. In this section, the major categories of the Tools panel are discussed.

Selection Tools

Selection tools are important for manipulating graphics and photographs in any graphics application. Being able to select shapes allows you to add colors to specific objects very precisely. Being able to select portions of drawings allows you to delete unneeded colors and backgrounds and to recolor photographs so that they fit any color scheme. Graphics applications usually give you several different ways to select elements of a drawing. The Fireworks tools that allow you to select objects and areas of the page are located at the top of the Tools panel (refer back to Figure 2-3).

Pointer and Subselection Tools

The Pointer tool actually has two options: the Pointer tool ▶ and the Select Behind tool ▶. Using the Pointer tool, you can select and reposition a shape any place on the canvas. A selected object has an outline around it. The Property inspector will display the attributes of that object for editing. To deselect an object, click elsewhere on the canvas, or click the object while holding the Shift key down.

Figure 2-10 shows a selected rectangle and a selected line as they would appear in your workspace. The Select Behind tool lets you perform the same action. However, if you have one object on top of another, it will enable you to select the object beneath by displaying red handles (dots) that outline that object. This is extremely useful for selecting and manipulating objects in a complex graphic.

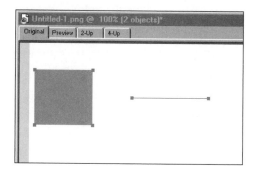

Figure 2-10   Selected rectangle and line

The Subselection tool [ ] is used to select an object for reshaping. When you select the tool and click an object you will see several small squares—called **Bezier points**—around the object. With your mouse, you can drag these points into new positions, and thus create new shapes. Figure 2-11 shows how a Bezier point looks on the screen. In this figure, a polygon is being reshaped by dragging one of its points to another position.

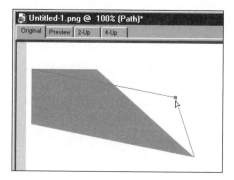

Figure 2-11   Reshaping a polygon using a Bezier point

Pointer selection tools are useful for vector graphics because you can select an entire object and manipulate it. However, if you are editing a photograph, the Pointer tools cannot select a single object in the photograph, because it is a bitmap image. For example, you cannot select someone's hair the same way that you would select a line or a rectangle. Clicking on a photograph reveals no selectable shape, just a canvas of single colors. To select areas of a bitmap image, you need to use bitmap tools like the Marquee, Magic Wand, and Lasso.

If you want to select multiple objects, hold the Shift key down and click on each object you want to select.

Scale Tools

The Scale tool  offers two additional tools in its pop-up menu: the Skew tool, and the Distort tool. The Scale tool lets you change the size of an object; the Skew tool lets you stretch a selection along its vertical or horizontal axis; and the Distort tool lets you stretch a selection by dragging its sides with the mouse.

All three tools let you rotate selections. To use these tools, you must select the shape you wish to transform. After you use the tool, the selected shape changes. Handles appear around the shape, including a small circle handle in the center of the transformation selection, as shown in Figure 2-12.

Figure 2-12 Handles shown during use of Scale tool

You can rotate a selected object when a curved arrow appears next to the selection, as shown in Figure 2-13. You can grab the shape by the handles and drag or rotate it into the desired form. You can also scale an object by using the Property inspector. The inspector displays width and height that you can modify precisely by entering pixel numbers in this panel.

Figure 2-13 Preparing to rotate an object

Cropping Tools

The Crop tool ⌗ is used to select a portion of the document you are working on and discard the remainder of the document. This is a quick way to select part of a photograph or graphic that you wish to use and immediately get rid of everything else. To use the Crop tool, drag the tool across the canvas to create a rectangular shape. Double-clicking the shape reduces the canvas size to the size of the selected, cropped area.

The Crop tool has one other option, the Export Area tool ▣. The Export Area tool allows you to select a smaller portion of your graphic by dragging your mouse over that area. Double-clicking that area opens the Export Preview dialog box, which you can use to export that portion of your graphic into another file.

Select Menu Options

More selection alternatives are available under Select in the menu bar. These options are useful in making selections or if you make a selection and then change it slightly to create a specific effect. For example, you may wish to select an entire image (including all the layers). Using the Select All option is much quicker than clicking each object in the workspace individually. Another example is if you have an image you want to select that is on top of an entirely white background. Clicking the white background with the magic wand and then using the Select Inverse option lets you select only the image of interest. Figure 2-14 shows how the Select Inverse option may look. It is much more accurate than using a lasso or marquee tool. Table 2-2 describes each option on the Select menu on the menu bar.

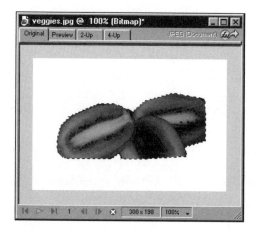

Figure 2-14   Using Select Inverse

Table 2-2   Options on the Select Menu

Selection Options	Description
Select All	Selects the entire document; shortcut Ctrl+A performs the same action
Deselect	Releases every element in the workspace from being selected
Superselect	Selects the larger group when working with grouped objects
Subselect	Selects a sub-member of a group when working with grouped objects
Select Similar	Selects all pixels of a similar color in the workspace
Select Inverse	Inverses a selection so that everything except the currently selected object is selected; this is useful if you want to edit an object out of a colored background (use the Lasso tool to select the object, apply Select Inverse, and then delete the background)
Feather...	Creates a feathered (blurred) effect on the edge of the marquee
Expand Marquee...	Creates a larger marquee by indicating a number of pixels; if you create a rectangular marquee of 10 pixels around an object and then expand it by 5 pixels, the new marquee will be 15 pixels
Contract Marquee...	Shrinks a marquee by the number of pixels you define
Border Marquee...	Creates a border (like a picture frame) that is a marquee around a selected area; you can define the width of the border
Smooth Marquee...	Smooths the edges of an already created marquee
Save Bitmap Selection	Saves a predefined marquee
Restore Bitmap Selection	Recalls a saved marquee

Using Selection Tools

In the following step sequence, you will modify a photograph of a decorative garnish using the Crop tool.

To modify a photograph:

1. Copy the file **garnish.png** from the Chapter2\images folder of your Data Disk to the ch2practice\images folder on your hard drive. Start Fireworks and open **garnish.png** from your ch2practice\images folder.

2. Click the **Crop tool** in the Tools panel. Place your mouse over the image. You see the Crop icon over the canvas. Drag the Crop tool over the asparagus garnish. In the Property inspector at the bottom of the workspace, enter the following values in the width, height, and coordinate boxes: W: **273**, H: **216**, X: **17**, and Y: **40**.

3. Double-click your mouse in the middle of the selection and see that the image has been cropped.

4. Click **File** and then click **Save As**. In the Save dialog box, navigate to the Sites\ch2practice\images folder and enter the filename **croppedgarnish.png**. Click **Save**.

5. Close the croppedgarnish.png file.

Bitmap Tools

As discussed, a grid of pixels defines bitmap images. Each pixel has a color assigned to it. The combination of all the pixel colors makes up the image. The Bitmap tools in the Tools panel are used to select and modify images based upon selections of areas or selections of colors. Each tool in the Bitmap area of the Tools panel is described in this section.

Marquee and Lasso Tools

The Marquee and Lasso tools allow you to select an area of the canvas by drawing a shape around it.

Using the Marquee tool ⊞, you can draw a fixed selection shape. The Marquee tool has one other option, an Oval Marquee tool ⊙, that you can view and select by holding down the mouse button over the tool.

Both the Rectangular Marquee and the Oval Marquee tools are used to draw a fixed shape over an area so that you can use or modify only the area selected. For example, if you wanted to copy the cherry on top of a photo of a sundae, you could drag the marquee tool over the cherry and then copy it into another layer or canvas to use for some other purpose (like making it a button). You can select an area of the canvas by dragging the marquee over the desired area. After a marquee is drawn, you can reposition it to select an area more accurately by dragging it on the canvas with your mouse. You can also resize it using the Property inspector. Figure 2-15 shows a rectangular marquee drawn on a photograph to select a portion of a photo.

Figure 2-15   Using the Rectangular Marquee tool to select an area

The Property inspector for the marquee lets you change attributes for width, height, X and Y location on the canvas, style, and edge. The Style setting lets you set constraints for the marquee if desired. For example, if you only wish to select images 100 by 100 pixels, you can set Style to Fixed Size. You can also select Fixed Ratio. Under the Edge option, Hard, Anti-Alias, and Feathered are the possible options. A hard edge creates a straight edge for the marquee as if you cut something with a pair of scissors. The Anti-Alias option lets you create an edge that blends into the canvas color. This sometimes helps to make images appear cleaner on a Web page, reducing jagged edges. The Feathered option allows you to create a fuzzy effect where the marquee line cuts.

Using the Lasso tool ⌜🄿⌟, you can draw a customized selection shape. To use the Lasso tool, simply drag the mouse around a desired area, holding the mouse button down. The Lasso tool allows you to draw freely around a shape.

The Lasso tool has one additional option, the Polygon Lasso tool ⌜🄿⌟. Using the Polygon Lasso tool, you can select part of an image by clicking points around the desired area. The Polygon Lasso tool thus lets you select a shape without having to drag the mouse around by hand.

Figure 2-16 shows an area selected using the Polygon Lasso. The Property inspector for the Lasso tool lets you change size and location options and Edge options just like the Marquee tool does.

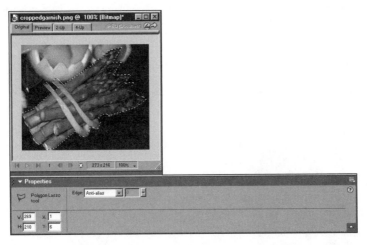

Figure 2-16   Selection made using the Polygon Lasso tool

The Magic Wand Tool

Using the Magic Wand tool ⌜🄦⌟, you can select areas of a document that are all the same color. For example, if your photograph has a blue sky and you want a pink sky, you could use the Magic Wand tool to select the blue area and recolor it to a shade of pink. Figure 2-17 shows how the Magic Wand selection will look in the workspace.

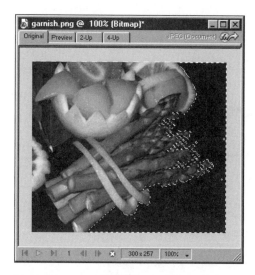

Figure 2-17   Selection made using the Magic Wand tool

In Figure 2-17, the dark area behind the garnish was clicked using the Magic Wand tool. Notice that not all of the dark area in the image was selected. This is because the dark area to the left of the garnish is physically separated from the dark area to the right of the garnish. To get all of the dark area, you can hold the shift key down and click the magic wand over the other dark areas. Additionally, in the Property inspector, you can set the tolerance of the magic wand to be more or less sensitive. As with previous selection tools, you can select an edge that is Hard, Anti-Alias, or Feathered.

Brush, Pencil, and Eraser Tools

The Brush tool 🔲, Pencil tool ✏️, and Eraser tool 🖋️ operate in a similar way. To use them, you simply click the tool in the Tools panel and begin drawing on the document. You can use the Brush and Pencil tools to draw lines freehand by dragging them across the canvas. If you wish to paint or draw a straight line, you can hold the Shift key down while dragging the brush or pencil in the desired direction.

The Property inspector for the Brush tool, shown in Figure 2-18, provides you with many options for changing the brush stroke. Using the Property inspector for the Brush tool, you can alter the brush color, the tip size of the brush, the stroke category, the brush edge, the texture of the stroke, and how strongly it is applied to the canvas. The Texture pop-up menu lets you pick a style (grain, parchment, or sand) so that your stroke appears as a pattern instead of a solid fill. You can also change the opacity of the brush application and control how it will blend into the canvas. The Preserve Transparency option only lets you draw paths over existing pixels and will not draw on transparent areas of the image.

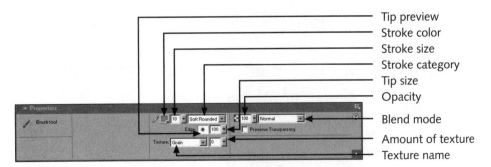

Figure 2-18   Property inspector for the Brush tool

You can use the Property inspector for the Pencil tool, shown in Figure 2-19, to control color, anti-aliasing, auto erase, opacity, and blends.

Figure 2-19   Property inspector for the Pencil tool

Checking the Anti-aliased checkbox will create a softer line that blends with the background color of the canvas. Figure 2-20 shows a close-up of two lines drawn with the Pencil tool, one normal and one anti-aliased. Notice the blurred appearance of the anti-aliased line.

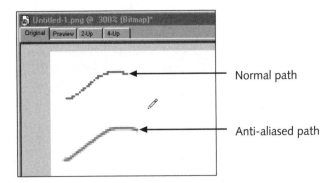

Figure 2-20   Standard and anti-aliased paths

With a specified fill color, the Auto Erase option lets you use the pencil in a manner that has the visual effect of erasing. The Preserve Transparency option only lets you draw paths over existing pixels. The Opacity option lets you control how transparent the line is, showing details of the image below the line. The Blend mode options let you control different blending options for a selection.

The Eraser tool allows you to erase portions of your document by dragging an eraser over the canvas. Using the Property inspector for the Eraser tool, you can control the size, edge, shape, and opacity of the eraser.

Blur Tools

The Blur tool can distort the focus of selected areas of an image. By holding the mouse down and dragging the tool over the canvas, areas of a bitmapped image become less defined, in effect blurred. Under the Blur tool, four other options exist: the Sharpen tool, the Dodge tool, the Burn tool, and the Smudge tool. The Property inspectors for this group of tools are highly similar, allowing you to change size, edge, and shape of the effect. These tools are used to touch-up small portions of bitmapped images.

Rubber Stamp and Eyedropper Tools

Using the Rubber Stamp tool, you can copy a portion of a graphic and duplicate it over another area of the canvas. For example, if your graphic is an orange tree with only two oranges on it, you can create a rubber stamp of one orange and stamp the image to create a tree full of oranges. When you select the Rubber Stamp tool, you see a small indicator on the canvas. Clicking sets the beginning position for the rubber stamp. After you click, a blue circle appears on the canvas. Place the circle over the area you want to copy and drag it to fill in as much of the stamped area as you choose. The Rubber Stamp tool pastes copies of the stamped area over the canvas.

In Figure 2-21, the Rubber Stamp tool was used to eliminate the price card from a tray of tarts. The Property inspector for the Rubber Stamp tool lets you modify size, edge, offset from cursor, source of pixels, opacity, and blend mode.

Figure 2-21   Using the Rubber Stamp tool

Sometimes when you edit a graphic or photograph, you want to use an exact color from one portion of the photo and apply it to another area. The Eyedropper tool 🖉 lets you change the fill color in the Fill tool color box 🔵 by clicking a pixel that contains the color you wish to use. After the color is copied into the color box, you can use it as a fill color on other selections (like the Brush or Pencil tools). It may be easier to match a color exactly using the eyedropper, rather than trying to select it from a palette.

Paint Bucket Tools

With the Paint Bucket tool 🪣, you can fill selections and areas with color. The Paint Bucket tool can be used in conjunction with the color box at the bottom of the Tools panel. When you click the Paint Bucket color box, a palette of colors is displayed. After a color is selected, it is displayed in the color box. To apply that color, you simply click the Paint Bucket tool over a selected area to fill it with color. The Paint Bucket tool Property inspector, shown in Figure 2-22, lets you change the tool's attributes, including edge, texture, tolerance, and opacity.

Figure 2-22   Property inspector for the Paint Bucket tool

Holding the mouse down over the Paint Bucket tool reveals another option, the Gradient tool 🔲. This tool enables you to fill selections with a gradient fill rather than a solid fill, as shown for a gradient filled rectangle in Figure 2-23. To apply the gradient, click the Gradient tool then click and drag your mouse in the fill area, in the direction you want the gradient to be applied. To edit the appearance of the gradient, click the color box in the Gradient Property inspector as shown in Figure 2-23. Dragging the color swatches lets you control how the gradient will appear; a preview is given so you can see if it is exactly the effect you want. The remaining items on the Property inspector are the same as with the Paint Bucket tool.

Using Bitmap Tools

In the following step sequence, you use the Rubber Stamp tool to edit a price card out of a photograph of tarts at a bakery. To do this, you will copy an image of an un-obscured tart and then stamp it over the tart with the price card.

To use the Bitmap tools:

1. Copy the file **tarts.jpg** from the Chapter2\images folder of your Data Disk to the ch2practice\images folder of your hard drive. Start Fireworks and open **tarts.jpg** from your ch2practice\images folder.

2. Click the Rubber Stamp tool 🖋 in the Tools panel. In the Property inspector for the Rubber Stamp tool, set Size as **100**, and Edge as **25**.

2

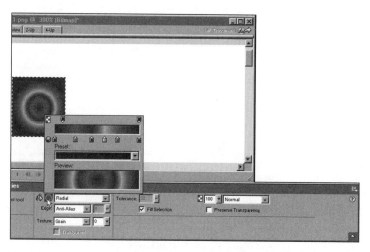

Figure 2-23 Property inspector for the Gradient tool

3. Place the crosshairs in the center of the tart just above the tart that is covered by the card. Click your mouse. A blue circle will appear. You have stamped the image of the tart that you want to use to cover the other tart.

4. Position the blue circle over the tart covered by the price card. You will stamp the copied tart image over the card. Click and hold your mouse, dragging it over the price card to replace the card with the new tart image. Use Edit and Undo if you have trouble covering the card. Some of the card will still show once you have applied the rubber stamp.

 To select another part of the image to copy, just press the Alt key while clicking the desired area of the image.

1. The tart to the right of the one you just stamped has part of the price card still showing. Repeat Step 4 to cover the price card on this tart too.

2. To cover the rest of the price card, we use the color from below the tarts and paint it onto the remaining card edges. Click the **Stroke** color box in the Tools panel in the Colors category to make sure it is selected. Click the eyedropper on part of the white cloth beneath the tarts. Notice that the color from the image appears in the Stroke color box in the Tools panel. Selecting the color right below the price card edge (#8C9A69) gives a nice result because it is closest to what you are trying to cover.

3. Click the **Brush** tool . Set the Brush Properties inspector to a Tip Size of **10**, a Stroke category of **Soft rounded**, and an Edge of **50**. Drag the Brush tool over the remaining price card to blend it into the photograph.

4. The image may not be perfect if you take a really close look. However, stamping, blurring, and filling elements of a photograph can give you images that more closely fit your design concept for the Web.

5. Click **File** and **Save As** to save this file as **tarts.png** in the ch2practice\images folder of your hard drive. The file should appear similar to Figure 2-21.

6. Close the tarts.png file.

Vector Tools

Vector images are defined by mathematical formulas and algorithms rather than by individual pixels. Codes that indicate color and scale, along with formulas for the shape or line, define the image. Vector lines and areas are often called paths and fills. This terminology reflects the fact that the images are defined mathematically. The Vector tools in the Tools panel are used to draw, select, and modify lines and shapes drawn on the canvas. Each shape consists of strokes and fills that can be solid or patterned colors. While the Property inspector will change for each object you create, some of the more common attributes of these objects are identified in Table 2-3.

Table 2-3   Vector Attributes from the Property Inspector

Attribute	Description
Object Name Box	A blank text box is available to name the object you draw
W	Width of the object
H	Height of the object
X	Position coordinate; the X coordinate is the number of pixels from the left of the canvas
Y	Position coordinate; the Y coordinate is the number of pixels from the top of the canvas
Fill Color	Defines the fill color of the object
Fill Options pop-up menu	Defines patterns, gradients, and effects for a filled object
Edge pop-up menu	Sets the fill edge to Hard, Anti-Alias, or Feathered
Edge Feather	Defines pixel amount of a feathered edge
Fill Texture pop-up menu	Provides a menu of various textures to apply to fills and strokes
Amount of Texture	Defines how intensely the fill or stroke texture will be applied to an object
Transparent Texture	Creates a transparent texture
Stroke Color	Sets the outline color of an object
Stroke Options	Provides a variety of stroke styles such as Crayon, Water Color, or Felt Tip
Edge Softness	Defines the softness of the stroke tip

Table 2-3 Vector Attributes from the Property Inspector (continued)

Attribute	Description
Opacity	Makes an object opaque or 'see through'; 100% makes the object solid and 0% makes it invisible
Blend Mode	Allows you to define the attributes of an object with respect to the canvas, thus controlling how an object blends with the document
Effects	Sets special effects on objects such as drop shadows, blurring, and beveling

You will see how these attributes are defined and modified in the sections that follow.

Line and Pen Tools

To use the Line tool, you simply click the button designated by a diagonal line $\boxed{/}$ and then click and drag the crosshairs over the canvas. You can constrain the angles of the lines to 45 degrees if you hold the Shift key down while you drag the mouse. You can alter the appearance of the line by changing its attributes in the Property inspector for the Line tool, shown in Figure 2-24.

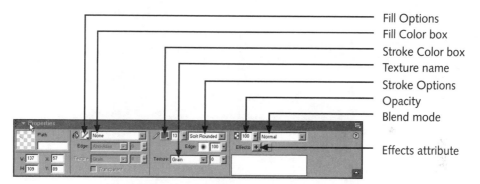

Fill Options
Fill Color box
Stroke Color box
Texture name
Stroke Options
Opacity
Blend mode
Effects attribute

Figure 2-24 Property inspector for the Line tool

The Pen tool $\boxed{\triangle}$ is a bit more complex to operate. Again, you create the line (or path) by dragging the mouse over the canvas. However, this tool lets you define a path using anchor points and segments. You can draw straight lines in a series of segments by clicking the mouse to create anchor points. You can also draw curved lines by creating an anchor point and then holding the mouse button down as you drag it to create the desired curve. It takes some practice to get used to drawing curves. The Property inspector for the Pen tool has identical options to those of the Property inspector for the Line tool.

Shape Tools

If you click and hold the solid rectangle in the Vector section of the Tools panel, you see a menu for four shapes: rectangle, rounded rectangle, ellipse, and polygon. You can change the Shape attribute of the polygon shape to draw a star. You can also change the Rectangle Roundedness attribute of a rounded rectangle to adjust the corners of the rectangle. To draw a rectangle, click the Rectangle tool ⬜, and then position the mouse over the canvas. Notice that crosshairs appear. Hold down the mouse button and drag the crosshairs until the rectangle is the size you desire, as shown in Figure 2-25. Releasing the mouse button draws the rectangle on the page. You can also draw from the center out by holding down the Alt key while you draw the rectangle.

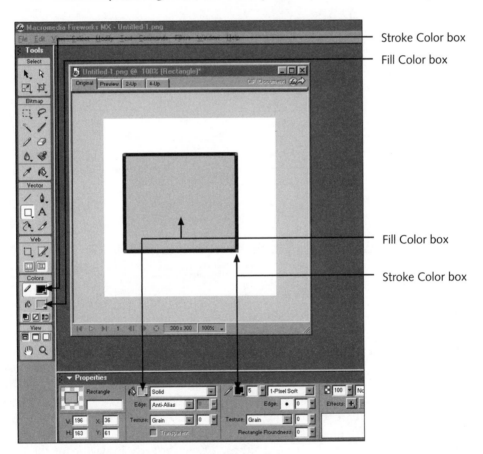

Figure 2-25   Drawing a rectangle

The object you draw will automatically apply the current color box selections. You can change stroke and fill colors in the Property inspector. Clicking the color box displays a palette of colors. You can use your mouse to select the color you want from the palette.

2

The Property inspector for the Rectangle tool is identical to the Property inspector for the Line Tool shown in Figure 2-24, with one additional attribute, Rectangle Roundness. You can either enter a number between 0 and 100, or you can use the pop-up slider to open a slider bar and slide to the desired number. At 0%, there is no angle on the corners, and at 100%, the maximum angle, the rectangle will appear as an oval on the canvas. Alternatively, you could hold your mouse down over the Rectangle tool and select the Rounded Rectangle tool ⌐Q. The default setting for Rectangle Roundness is 30. You can edit this in the Property inspector. Setting it to 0 will result in the object becoming a rectangle with straight edges.

 To draw a shape of equal height and width, hold down the Shift key as you drag the mouse over the canvas to create the shape.

Drawing an ellipse is a matter of selecting the Ellipse tool ⌐Q and then dragging the mouse across the canvas to form the shape. If you hold down the Shift key, you form a circle. The Property inspector for the Ellipse tool is identical to the Property inspector for the Line tool.

The last shape tool is the Polygon Shape tool ⌐Q. The Property inspector for the Polygon Shape tool is similar to that of the Line tool. However, an option is available to change the shape of the polygon to that of a star. If you select the Star shape, you can indicate the number of sides of the star and the angle of the points of the star.

Using the Basic Shape Drawing Tools

The steps that follow will guide you through the creation of the four basic shapes that you can create using the Shape tool.

To use the Shape tool:

1. Start Fireworks, click **File** on the menu bar, and then click **New** to create a new document. In the New Document dialog box, enter dimensions of **350 pixels** × **350 pixels**, and **72-pixel resolution**. Click the **White** option if it is not already selected. Click **OK**.

2. Click the **Rectangle** tool and drag the crosshairs to draw a rectangle in the center of the canvas. Releasing the mouse will draw the rectangle onto the canvas. In the Property inspector for the rectangle, enter the following values in the width, height, and coordinate boxes: W: **100**, H: **100**, X: **30**, and Y: **30**.

3. With the rectangle still selected, click the **Fill** color box in the Property inspector (See Figure 2-24) and enter **#FF00FF** (pink). Click the **Stroke** color box in the Property inspector and enter **#00FFFF** (blue). Enter **4** for Tip size.

4. Select the **Rounded Rectangle** tool by clicking and holding the **Rectangle** tool and selecting **Rounded Rectangle** from the pop-up menu.

5. Draw the rounded rectangle in the upper-right corner of your canvas by dragging your mouse on the workspace. Releasing the mouse draws the object. The object should have the same attributes you set for the previous object. In the Property inspector, enter the following values in the width, height, and coordinate boxes: W: **100**, H: **100**, X: **200**, and Y: **30**.

6. With the rounded rectangle still selected, click the **Fill** Options pop-up menu in the Property inspector (See Figure 2-24) and click **Pattern**. Click the **Fill** Color box (instead of a palette of colors, you are supplied with a list of patterns), click the list arrow, and click **Grass-Large**. Press **Enter**. Enter **50** for Rectangle Roundness.

7. Click and hold the **Rounded Rectangle** tool in the Tools panel, and then select the **Ellipse** tool from the pop-up menu.

8. Draw a circle in the lower-left corner of your canvas by dragging the mouse and simultaneously pressing the Shift key so that the height and width dimensions of the ellipse remain equal.

9. In the Property inspector, enter the following values in the width, height, and coordinate boxes: W: **100**, H: **100**, X: **30**, and Y: **200**.

10. Click and hold the **Ellipse** tool in the Tools panel, and then select **Polygon** tool from the pop-up menu.

11. Draw a polygon in the lower-right corner of your canvas by dragging the mouse over the workspace. Dragging will cause the polygon shape to form from the center outward.

12. In the Property inspector, enter the following values in the width, height, and coordinate boxes: W: **100**, H: **100**, X: **200**, and Y: **200**.

13. With the polygon still selected, click the **Stroke** Color box and select the **Transparent** button [☑]. Click the **Edge** pop-up menu under the Fill Color box and click **Feather**. Set Amount of Feather to **20** by clicking the list arrow or by entering 20 into the text box.

14. Save your image as **shapes.png** in your ch2practice\images folder on your hard drive. The results should appear as shown in Figure 2-26.

15. Close the shapes.png file.

Text Tool

The Text tool [A] is useful for adding labels and text to your graphics. For example, if you are creating buttons or rollovers, you may need to add text to indicate the link destinations. Click the Text tool and then click the canvas where you would like your text to appear. A blue rectangle will show on the canvas and display the text as you type it. If you want text to wrap horizontally as you type it on the canvas, you can draw a text area where you would like the text to display. The text area will grow vertically (not horizontally), wrapping the text. The Property inspector for the Text tool, shown in Figure 2-27, lets you modify the characteristics of the text.

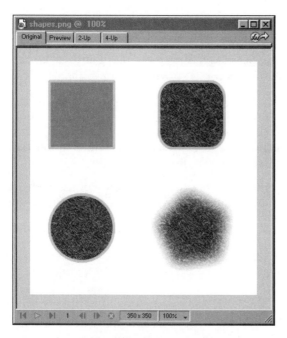

Figure 2-26   Results of using the tools

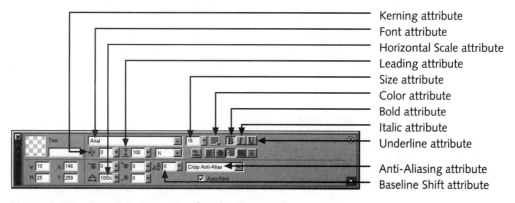

Figure 2-27   Property inspector for the Text tool

Attributes in the Property inspector for the Text tool allow you to change font type, size, color, and style. You can also control text alignment and flow. Many of these text tools are probably familiar to you. What you may not have seen before are the following:

- With the Kerning attribute, you can control the amount of space between the characters of the text. A negative kerning value brings the text closer together, while a positive value adds more space. You can control the kerning value by using the slider or by typing a value directly into the text box, or by selecting the Auto Kern checkbox.

- The Leading attribute allows you to control the amount of space between multiple lines of text.

- Changing the Horizontal Scale stretches or shrinks your text horizontally. A value of less than 100% shrinks the text, while values greater than 100% enlarge it.

- The Baseline Shift attribute is like superscript and subscript options you may have used in a word processor for creating a degree sign or an exponent. When text is placed on the page, it has a natural baseline. Using Baseline Shift moves the text either up or down from the natural baseline.

- The Anti-Aliasing attribute smoothes the edges between the path and the canvas. Without it, text and graphics can sometimes appear block-like. You can choose Crisp, Strong, Smooth, or Anti-Alias for this attribute.

Using the Text Tool

In the following step sequence, you will create stylized text with a drop shadow.

To use the Text tool:

1. Start Fireworks, click **File** on the menu bar, and then click **New** to create a new document. In the New Document dialog box, enter these dimensions: Width: **500**, Height: **100**, and **72-pixel resolution**. Click the **White** option if it is not already selected. Click **OK**.

2. Click the **Text** tool A .

3. In the Property inspector, enter the following options:

   - Font: **Comic Sans MS**
   - Size: **60**
   - Color: **#FF0000** (red)
   - Anti-aliasing level: **Crisp Anti-Alias**

4. Click your mouse in the center of the canvas. Type **Culinary Tours**. You may need to reposition your text if it doesn't fit on the canvas.

5. In the Property inspector for the Text object, enter the following values in the coordinate boxes: X: **10** and Y: **10**.

6. Click the **Pointer** tool. With the Text object still selected, click **Add effects or choose a preset** ⊞ , then **Shadow and Glow**, then click **Drop Shadow**. In the Drop Shadow dialog box, set the distance to **8**, the color to **#000068** (blue), opacity to **65%**, softness to **4**, and angle to **315** degrees. Press **Enter** to close the dialog box. Preview your image by pressing **F12**.

7. Close the preview. Save your image as **culinarytours.png** in your ch2practice\ images folder on your hard drive.

8. Close the culinarytours.png file.

Freeform and Knife Tools

The Freeform tool ⟨⟩ has three additional options in the pop-up menu: the Reshape Area tool ⟨⟩, the Pathscrubber tool-additive ⟨⟩, and the Path Scrubber tool-subtractive ⟨⟩.

You use the Freeform tool to reshape the selected line. When you select a path and use the Freeform tool, a small s-shaped pull pointer appears next to the pointer. It indicates that you can stretch the line freely in whatever direction you choose. You can drag the line by its Bezier points or by a smooth segment of the line, where a Bezier point will be inserted for you. The Reshape Area tool works like the Freeform tool, except that you drag a circled area, forcing portions of a path in a specific direction. Path Scrubber tools are advanced tools for working with vector drawings.

Using the Knife tool ⟨⟩, you can cut vector paths into more than one path. As you use the Knife tool on a path in Fireworks, Bezier points appear indicating where the new break is in the path. After the cut is made, the newly created paths can be moved and modified individually.

Web Tools

Fireworks MX lets you create hotspots and slices. **Hotspots** are areas defined on a graphic that a user can click like a hyperlink to go to another Web page. The three Hotspot tools (Rectangle ⟨⟩, Circle ⟨⟩, and Polygon ⟨⟩) help you create the shape on a graphic that you want.

The Slice tool and Polygon Slice tool let you cut a graphic into several smaller graphics or **slices** and arrange them in a table using HTML. Slices reduce the time needed to load a large graphic and let you attach different behaviors to specific areas of the table. Slices are also the most productive way to create rollovers. You will learn to use these tools in Chapter 3. The Hide Slices and Hotspots button ⟨⟩ lets you view your image free of hotspot or slice outlines. The Show Slices and Hotspots button ⟨⟩ displays hotspot or slice outlines for your image.

Colors Tools

In addition to being able to control stroke and fill color in the Property inspector, you can also set stroke and fill color using the Stroke Color box ⟨⟩ and the Fill Color box ⟨⟩ in the Tools panel. Figure 2-28 shows the Stroke Color pop-up window displayed when you click the Stroke Color box in the Tools panel. You can select a color by choosing a swatch on the Stroke Color pop-up window or by entering a hexadecimal color code in the text box. Clicking the Transparent button ⟨⟩ makes the path invisible.

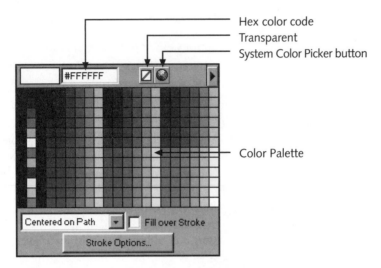

Hex color code
Transparent
System Color Picker button

Color Palette

Figure 2-28   Stroke Color pop-up window

Clicking the Sys Color Picker icon 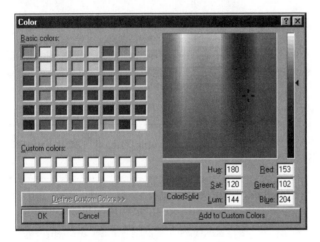 opens the System Color Picker palette, shown in Figure 2-29, where you can designate colors using another method.

Figure 2-29   System Color Picker palette

Clicking the list arrow on the right of the Stroke Color pop-up window lets you select other Color palettes available in Fireworks MX, as shown in Figure 2-30. At the bottom, you can set properties for the location of stroke relative to path as Inside Path, Centered on Path, or Outside Path in the Stroke Relative to Path pop-up menu. This lets you control exactly how lines are displayed on the canvas. Clicking the Fill over Stroke checkbox will cause the fill area to cover the stroke. Clicking the Stroke Options button opens a panel in which you can define attributes of the stroke, much like you did with the Property inspector for the Line tool earlier in the chapter.

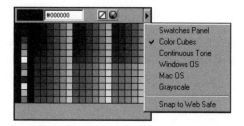

Figure 2-30   Available palette types

The Fill Color pop-up window looks and operates similarly to the Stroke Color pop-up window as shown in Figure 2-28. Clicking the Fill Options button allows you to change fill attributes such as Fill Category, Edge, and Texture.

Beneath these color boxes for strokes and fills are three small buttons. The first, a black square over a clear square, is Set Default Stroke/Fill Colors. Click it to set or restore default brush and fill colors. Next is the No Stroke or Fill option, which sets both color boxes to transparent, or no colors. Next is a double sided, curved arrow, the Swap Stroke/Fill Colors option, which lets you instantly swap the color values for stroke and fill.

 Use the Eyedropper tool in the Tools panel to sample a color from an existing graphic. The eyedropper sample will be added to the color box for your fill or stroke tool in the Tools panel.

View Tools

View tools are located at the very bottom of the Fireworks MX Tools panel. The first three options let you quickly set how you will view the screen: Standard Screen mode ▣ , Full Screen with Menus mode ▢ , or Full Screen mode ▢ . The Hand tool ✋ is used to move around the workspace to view specific portions of documents that are bigger than your display. The Zoom tool ⌕ is for magnifying a document. This helps you edit a graphic more accurately. You can zoom into a graphic and edit it at the pixel level to achieve a perfect effect for your artwork. You can also use the View menu on the menu bar to zoom into or out of a drawing. At the bottom of the canvas, clicking the Set Magnification pop-up menu, shown in Figure 2-1, will open a list of different sizes to view your document.

WORKING WITH PANELS

When you first open Fireworks MX, you see that several panels are available to assist you in editing your drawings. Figure 2-1 showed the panels available when you first open Fireworks MX and Figure 2-2 showed panels available from the Window menu in the menu bar. In the following sections the Optimize, Layers, and Assets panels are examined.

The Optimize Panel

The Optimize panel lets you select export settings for the file you are working with. Earlier in this chapter, you used the Optimize panel in conjunction with the 2-Up tab to change the settings and export a graphic. Recall that the original file you work with is saved as .png format.

In the Preview, 2-Up, and 4-Up tabs, you can change the settings in the Optimize panel to preview how your image will look and what the file size is at different settings. This is an effective way to experiment with different file settings. Your objective is to achieve the smallest possible file size with the highest acceptable image quality. As a rule, photographs compress well using JPEG format and line art or images with fewer colors work well as GIF format.

The Optimize panel for GIF and JPEG formats are different because of file characteristics. Figure 2-31 shows the Optimize panel for a GIF image. Selecting fewer colors or less dithering can decrease your file size.

Figure 2-31   Optimize panel for GIF

  Dithering is a technique that widens your color options by placing pixels of two colors together to give the appearance of a third color. This is similar to the way a color printer works. If you look closely at your printout, you will see areas of color where two colors form a pattern, having the effect of creating a third color. Dithering gives you a wider selection of colors but can also increase the file size of your graphic.

Figure 2-32 shows the Optimize panel for a JPEG image. In this panel, file size can be reduced by reducing the Quality value. As you alter the settings, it is important to examine how the image degrades as the file size changes. As an alternative to the Optimize panel, you can optimize your file using the Export Preview option available on the File menu. You can also select Export Wizard from the File menu to gain Fireworks suggestions for Export file type. After the Wizard is finished, the Export Preview dialog box opens.

2

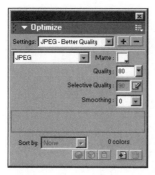

Figure 2-32 Optimize panel for JPEG

The Layers Panel

When you create a complex graphic, it is often necessary to work in layers. **Layers** are transparent canvases, stacked on top of one another. For example, an image that contains a boy with a ball playing in the grass, and some text, might have a background layer containing the grass and sky, another layer containing the boy and the ball, and a third layer containing the text. Fireworks MX creates multiple objects in one layer, allowing you to edit the boy and ball and the background while working in the same layer.

The graphic formats available on the Web (.gif and .jpg) do not display layers. When you complete your drawing, you must flatten the layers or export your document so that the layers are flattened for you. Flattened layers cannot be separated again. The .png format in which you work in Fireworks preserves your layers. Saving the .png file is a good idea in case you decide later to change the document and need to alter the layers within it.

Figure 2-33 shows the Layers panel for a food train graphic composed of several cropped images of various types of produce. Each object on the canvas occupies its own layer.

In the Layers panel, you can see each layer of the document (indicated by a folder) and the images that each layer contains. When an object is selected in the workspace, the layer is highlighted in the Layers panel. A pencil icon 🖊 indicates that the layer is ready for editing. If you click the pencil icon, a lock will appear indicating that the layer cannot be edited. Clicking the eye will turn on and off layers in your graphic. This is useful for uncluttering the workspace so you can focus on a specific part of a document.

To rename a layer, you must click twice on the layer name in the Layers panel to type in your own custom layer name. To reposition layers with respect to one another, you can drag them in the Layers panel to the desired position, below or above another layer. The small squares on the left side of the panel let you contract or expand the layer, hiding or showing the layer objects. A square with a plus sign will appear, showing that the layer is contracted. Clicking the Options menu of the Layers panel opens an editing menu, so you can add, delete, and perform other layer operations.

Figure 2-33   Layers panel

Working with the Layers Panel

In the following step sequence, you use layers to create a logo for a company named La Bonne Cuisine. To do this, you reposition layers in the workspace with respect to one another. You also add text to the file and create a drop shadow effect for the logo.

To create a logo:

1. Copy the file **layering.png** from the Chapter2\images subdirectory on your Data Disk into the ch2practice\images folder of your hard drive. Open this file in Fireworks.

2. If it is not already open, open the Layers panel by pressing **F2** key. In the layering.png file, the images in the layers are overlapping so you cannot see them all. You can see them in the Layers panel.

3. Use the Pointer tool to move the images to separate parts of the canvas so that you can see them all at once.

4. Click the **cabbage** image and observe that the corresponding layer in the Layers panel is highlighted. Double-click the text **Layer 2** in the Layers panel, and rename this layer **cabbage**. Rename the other layers the same way, calling them **orange**, **shrimp**, and **salad**.

5. Select the orange with the Pointer tool. Slide it around on the canvas and observe that it is located below the salad layer. (The Web layer at the top of the Layers panel is used for hotspots and sliced images.) Click and hold the **orange** layer name in the Layers panel and drag it to the top, above the Web layer. Drag the orange around the canvas to demonstrate that it now is on top of the shrimp and salad layers.

6. Click the **cabbage** object. In the Property inspector, enter the coordinates X: **4** and Y: **50**. Click the **salad** object. In the Property inspector, enter the coordinates X: **100** and Y: **4**. Click the **shrimp** object. In the Property inspector, enter the coordinates X: **10** and Y: **140**. Click the **orange** object. In the Property inspector, enter the coordinates X: **80** and Y: **115**.

7. Add a new layer to place text by clicking the **New/Duplicate Layer** button (a folder) at the bottom of the Layers panel.

8. Name the new layer **Text**.

9. Click the **Text** tool in the Tools panel, and position and click the mouse over the workspace. Create **#0000FF** (blue)**, bold** Text that is of size **50** and font **Arial** by changing the attributes in the Property inspector. Type **La Bonne Cuisine**. Enter position coordinates of X: **70** and Y: **100**.

10. Click the **Pointer** tool. Click **Select** from the menu bar and click **Select All**. Click the **Add Effects** button in the Property inspector, select **Shadow and Glow**, and **Drop Shadow**. Press **Enter**. A black shadow will appear beneath your image and you will see that the Drop Shadow effect is added to the Effects panel automatically. If you click twice on the Drop Shadow text in the Effects panel, you can edit the attributes of the effect, changing such things as the color, distance, and angle of the shadow.

11. Press **F12** to preview your image in your Web browser. It should look like Figure 2-34. Close the browser window.

12. Save this file as **lbclogo.png** in the ch2practice\images folder on your hard drive.

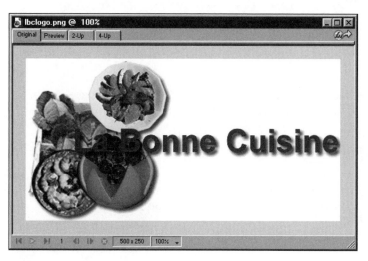

Figure 2-34   La Bonne Cuisine logo with drop shadow

The Assets Panel Group

The Assets panel group has three tabs: Styles, URLs, and Library. You will use these panels in Chapter 3. The Styles panel lets you define a style for objects on your page and store it so you can reuse it again on other objects. The URLs panel lets you create hyperlinks from images. In the Library panel, you can define symbols and then use them throughout your document.

 It can be overwhelming to work with so many options, and experimenting with them can be an unproductive way to approach your project. Often, it is better to plan your Web site's graphics in advance and to make modifications as you develop the site. Knowing what you are hoping to create ahead of time is much more effective than randomly seeking an effect that looks appealing to you or your client. For more discussion of graphics design, you may wish to read *Principles of Web Design, Second Edition* by Joel Sklar.

CHAPTER SUMMARY

❑ The Fireworks Tools panel allows you to create shapes and lines in a variety of colors, fills, and strokes.

❑ Selection tools include Pointer, Subselection, and Scale so that you can select, reshape, and resize images.

❑ You can apply a wide variety of strokes and fills to paths and objects using the Stroke and Fill options in the Property inspector for an object.

❑ Text tools are used to enter text on top of the canvas. You can alter text features, including font, size, color, and style. You can also adjust alignment, kerning, and anti-aliasing. You can add effects to apply effects to text and other objects. Effects such as drop shadows and embossing can create appealing headlines and titles on a Web page.

❑ Paths, or lines, can be manipulated using the Property inspector. A wide variety of strokes create different pen styles, pen tip widths, and textures.

❑ The Optimize panel can be used with the preview of your graphic to experiment with different optimization properties.

❑ Layers are independent, stacked canvases in one document. Using layers allows you to create a complex graphic with independent, editable objects on the different layers. The file you save in .png format will maintain layers. The file you export (for use on the Web) as a .gif or .jpg will not.

2

REVIEW QUESTIONS

1. What is the optimal resolution for a Web graphic?

    a. 72 dpi

    b. 100 dpi

    c. 200 dpi

    d. 350 dpi

2. What is the Fireworks source file type?

    a. .bmp

    b. .png

    c. .gif

    d. .jpg

3. Fireworks will only allow you to edit bitmapped graphics. True or False?

4. What is the difference between saving and exporting a file?

5. What does it mean to optimize an image for the Web?

6. You can _____ an object using the Scale tool.

    a. scale

    b. skew

    c. rotate

    d. distort

    e. All of the above

7. What shapes can you draw using the Shape tool?

    a. rectangle, rounded rectangle, ellipse, and star

    b. rectangle, rounded rectangle, ellipse, and polygon

    c. rectangle, rounded rectangle, circle, and triangle

    d. polygon and line

8. How do you draw a shape that maintains equal height and width?

9. Describe how you can create a rectangle with rounded edges.

10. Opaque refers to a fill texture for coloring an object. True or False?

11. What is a Bezier point?

12. Using the Magic Wand tool, you can _____.

    a. repeat functions you already performed located on the History panel

    b. copy and duplicate images

    c. select areas of similar color for editing

    d. undo mistakes quickly and easily

13. Bezier points are useful for reshaping marquees. True or False?

14. The Kerning option in the Property inspector for the Text tool allows you to control the amount of space displayed between different characters. True or False?

15. Anti-aliasing softens lines and edges by blurring the edge with the background. True or False?

16. Describe the difference between a stroke and a fill.

17. The .jpg file format does not preserve layers. True or False?

18. Which of the following statements is true of layers?

    a. They can be displayed on the Web.

    b. Layers place objects together so they cannot be separated.

    c. They let you edit elements in a graphic document separately.

    d. Each layer of a file can have a different graphic format.

19. Using fewer colors yields an optimized file. True or False?

20. A photograph is best saved as what file format for the Web?

    a. .gif

    b. .jpg

    c. .png

    d. .bmp

HANDS-ON PROJECTS

Project 2-1

In this project, you will open, optimize, and save a Web graphic.

1. Copy the file **soaplogo.png** from the Chapter2\images folder on your Data Disk into the ch2practice\images folder on your working drive. Click **File** on the menu bar, and then click **Open** to open an existing document that you will optimize. Navigate through the Find File dialog box and select the file **soaplogo.png** from the ch2practice\images folder.

2. Click the **2-Up** tab at the top of the document workspace. Two copies of your image appear, the original image and a preview image. If the Optimize panel is not open, open it now by selecting it from the Window menu or by pressing the **F6** key.

3. The image on the left is your original image. You can see that it is 81.50KB in size. Click the second image, at the right of the screen. You can see it is selected because an outline appears around it. This image shows 16.51KB size with a 2 second download time for a 56kbps modem. Click the **Settings** pop-up menu at the very top of the Optimize panel and select **JPEG – Smaller File**. The file size is 10.28KB with a 1 second download time, but the image quality is highly degraded.

4. Click the **Settings** pop-up menu at the very top of the Optimize panel and select **GIF Web 216**. Now the file size is 11.17KB with a 1 second download time and the image is much better quality.

5. Click the **No Transparency** pop-up menu on the Optimize panel and click **Alpha Transparency**. A checkered grid should appear in the background of your image, indicating that it has a transparent background.

6. Click the **File** menu and then click **Export**. Because the GIF file was selected, .gif file format is automatically set for you with the file. The Export dialog box will open. Type the filename **soaplogo.gif**.

7. Click the **Save as type:** list arrow and click **HTML and Images** to save an HTML file and a .gif file from your Fireworks document.

8. Navigate to the ch2practice folder. The filename has changed to .htm file format and soaplogo.htm is the filename.

9. At the bottom of the Export dialog box, click the **Put Images in subfolder** checkbox. The subfolder will default to images, and your .gif file will automatically be stored in ch2practice\images. Click **Save**. Your .gif and .htm files have been exported. Click **File** and **Save** to save your .png file.

10. Preview your Web page by opening soaplogo.htm in your Web browser. To do this, you can click **File** and **Open** from the Web browser and navigate through your file structure to Sites\ch2practice\soaplogo.htm.

11. Close the browser window. Close the soaplog.png file.

Project 2-2

In this project, you will use Fireworks to create a button.

1. Open a new document in Fireworks giving it the pixel dimensions of Width: **90** and Height: **50** and a transparent canvas.

2. Click the **Rounded Rectangle** tool in the Tools panel. Drag the mouse over the canvas to draw the rectangle.

3. In the Property inspector for the rectangle, enter the following values in the width, height, and coordinate boxes: W: **80**, H: **25**, X: **6**, and Y: **12**. Set the Fill color to **#0000FF** (blue) and the Stroke color to **Transparent**. Set Rectangle Roundness to **30** if it is not already set.

4. Add text on top of the rectangle you just created by clicking the **Text** tool in the Tools panel and clicking on the canvas. In the Property inspector, change the text color to **#FFFF00** (yellow), size **16**, **bold**, and font **Arial**. Type the text **Welcome**. Enter the position coordinates X: **6** and Y: **13**. Yellow text should appear on top of the blue rectangle.

5. Using the Pointer tool, select both the **rectangle** and the **text** by holding the mouse button down and dragging it from the upper-left of the canvas to the lower-right.

6. In the Property inspector, click **Add Effects** [+], click **Shadow and Glow**, and **Drop Shadow**. If necessary, change the Drop Shadow attributes to Distance: **7**, Color: **black**, Opacity: **65%**, Softness: **4**, and Angle: **315** degrees.

7. Save this file as **button.png** in the ch2practice\images folder of your working drive. (To use this button on a Web page, you would export it as a transparent .gif and insert it as an image using Dreamweaver MX. You will learn how to do this in Chapter 3.)

8. Close the button.png file.

Project 2-3

In this project, you will make a button out of a photograph.

1. Copy the image **veggies.jpg** from the Chapter2\images subdirectory of your Data Disk into the ch2practice\images subdirectory on your hard drive. Open the file **veggies.jpg** in Fireworks.

2. Using the Oval Marquee tool, draw an oval over the kiwi fruit. This selection becomes the button background.

3. Cut the selected area out of the veggies photograph by selecting **Cut** from the **Edit** menu, or by pressing **Ctrl+X**.

4. Open a new canvas using the default dimensions and paste the cut oval into the new workspace. Observe that the canvas is the size of the oval.

5. In the new canvas, select the oval image of the kiwi fruit using the Pointer tool. A blue rectangle will appear around the selected image. Click **Add Effects** [+] in the Property inspector, click **Bevel and Emboss**, and **Inner Bevel**.

   Observe that an inner bevel is created on the button.

6. Use the Text tool to insert the text **Healthy Diet** over the button. Use text color **#FF6633**, text size **24**, and an **Arial** font.

7. Save this file as **kiwibutton.png** in the ch2practice\images folder of your hard drive. (To use this button on a Web page, you would need to export it as a transparent GIF and insert it as an image using Dreamweaver MX. You will learn how to do this in Chapter 3.)

8. Close the veggies.jpg and kiwibutton.png files.

Project 2-4

In this project, you will create a textured background for a Web page.

1. Open a new document in Fireworks, giving it the pixel dimensions **500 × 500** and a **Transparent** canvas.

2. Draw a rectangular over the entire canvas.

3. Click the **Paint Bucket** tool in the Tools panel. Enter **#FF33FF** (pink) as the fill color and press **Enter**. Click the **Texture** list arrow and select **Parchment** texture, set **100%**, for your background. Click the canvas with the Paint Bucket tool to fill the marquee with the Parchment texture.

4. Save this file as **background.png** in the ch2practice\images folder of your hard drive. (To use this background on a Web page, you would set the Dreamweaver MX Page Properties to use this file as the background. The Parchment texture will then appear as a wallpaper background for the page.)

5. Close the background.png file.

Project 2-5

In this project, you will create an elliptical background for the side menu to appear over.

1. Open a new document in Fireworks, giving it the pixel dimensions Width: **500**, Height: **700**, and a **Transparent** canvas.

2. Draw an oval marquee that extends beyond the right side of the canvas, leaving a curved shape on the left side of the canvas.

   Your objective is to create a curved solid object on the left side of the workspace. Using this graphic as wallpaper for a Web page provides a nice background for menu buttons.

3. After you are satisfied with the appearance of the oval over the canvas, click **Select** on the menu bar, and then click **Select Inverse**.

4. Click the **Paint Bucket** tool, type the color **#0099FF** (blue), and press **Enter**. Click inside the marquee to apply the fill color.

5. Use the **Subselection** tool and double-click the shape you created to select it. In the Property inspector, click **Add Effects** ⊞, **Shadow and Glow**, and **Drop Shadow**. Change the Drop Shadow settings so that the distance is **20** and the softness is **16**. This will create the illusion that the swath of color is coming off the page.

6. Save this file as **background2.png** in the ch2practice\images folder of your working drive. (To use this background on a Web page, you would set the Dreamweaver MX Page Properties to indicate this file as the background.)

7. Close the background2.png file.

Project 2-6

In this project, you will crop a photograph and optimize a file, saving the HTML and image files when you export your work.

1. Copy the image **britishdairy.jpg** from the Chapter2\images subdirectory of your Data Disk into the ch2practice\images subdirectory on your hard drive. Open the file **britishdairy.jpg** from the ch2practice\images subdirectory for editing in Fireworks.

2. Using the Crop tool, select the woman behind the counter of the dairy by dragging your mouse over the woman in the photograph. In the Crop tool Property inspector, enter the following values in the width, height, and coordinate boxes: W: **80**, H: **130**, X: **175**, and Y: **119**. Double-click the selected area to crop the graphic.

3. Click **File** on the menu bar and click **Export Wizard**. Click **Continue** and click **Continue** again. Notice that Fireworks suggests either .gif or .jpg file types. Click **Exit**.

4. The Export dialog box opens with .jpg format selected. The .jpg file is 3.2K in size, very small. Click the **Export** button.

5. In the Export File dialog box, name this file **dairywoman.htm**. Under Save as Type: click **HTML and Images**. Click the **Put images in subfolder** checkbox. Click the **Save** image in subfolder text box. Store the file in the ch2practice folder and the image in the subfolder beneath it.

6. Open the file dairywoman.htm in your Web browser to view the result.

7. Close the **britishdairy.jpg** file.

CASE PROJECTS

The BuyMe.com Toy Company wants to create a Web site to market its products to children and their parents who shop online. They have asked you to create a button style for their site that uses primary colors and would be attractive to children. Use Shape, Fill, and Text tools to create three buttons titled Stop, Go, and Play for a children's Web page.

The BuyMe.com Toy Company hires you to create a logo for the company. Use Shape, Fill, and Text tools to create a logo for BuyMe.com, and export it as a .gif graphic. Insert it into a Dreamweaver MX Web page with a non-white background. Export and insert the buttons. Align them in the Dreamweaver MX workspace using a table.

Scan a photograph of yourself into Fireworks. Use selection tools to edit out the background, leaving a cleanly selected image of yourself on the canvas. Find a picture of someone famous that you would like to meet and paste the cropped image of yourself in the same photograph with this person. You probably need to adjust the scale of your image so it looks size-appropriate with the other person.

Find an image of a car you would like to own. Crop the image of yourself that you created in the first exercise, so that you will fit in the car and appear to be driving it. Using the Preview and Optimize panels, optimize and export this file for the Web.

The Sprinkles Cookies Company wants you to design a Web site. As part of their concept for the design, they would like several "cyber-cookies" used as images on their site. Use the Shape tools to create rectangles, circles, and polygons for the Web site. Make sure to decorate the cookies. Create four basic cookies, and then use the drawing tools to create a cookie that looks like a gingerbread man.

3

ADVANCED FIREWORKS MX

Creating Image Maps, Buttons, and Animations

In this chapter, you will:
- Create image maps to produce linkable hotspots on top of images
- Slice and optimize an image for the Web
- Create buttons and rollovers

Fireworks MX is a powerful graphics tool that takes time and practice to master. Entire courses and texts are needed to cover the entire Fireworks MX application. The two chapters in this book are to introduce you to Fireworks MX with the expectation that you will investigate further on your own. In Chapter 2, you learned to use Fireworks MX tools to edit and manipulate images. In this chapter you use these skills to create image maps, buttons and rollovers, and animations, all of which can greatly enhance the visual appeal of a Web page and make it easier for users to navigate. Storing the buttons you create in a document's Library panel in Fireworks can also enhance your productivity, because you can reuse the buttons and all their defined states. You can also import graphics created in other applications—such as FreeHand, Corel Draw, Adobe Illustrator, and Photoshop—into Fireworks MX to create a button, navigation bar, or animation for use in Dreamweaver.

HOTSPOTS AND LINKS

In Chapter 1, you learned how to create a hyperlink by using the Property inspector to associate a URL with a segment of text. Another method for creating hyperlinks, briefly introduced in Chapter 2, is to create several different links, or hotspots, on top of an image. These hotspots work well if the links on the image form a intuitive mapping to the operations the user performs on the page. An image with several clickable links is called an **image map**. You can see good use of hotspots on many real estate Web pages, where clicking a portion of a map brings you to a particular area. (If, for example, you wanted to look for New York real estate, you could click the image of the state of New York on the map of the United States.) You can also use image maps to set up a navigational strategy by creating one image with several meaningful links. If you design a Web site for a classroom, for example, you can create an image map of the class picture and define each student's face as a linkable hotspot that takes the visitor to that student's home page. You can also create a simple rectangular picture that contains all of your linked text as part of an image. By placing several hotspots over the text on the rectangle, you create a simple navigation bar and place it as one image on all pages of your site. (Note that this kind of navigation bar is somewhat restrictive, because you cannot create rollovers or edit links individually without editing the entire image map.)

Creating an Image Map

To create an image map, you place shapes on top of an existing image, in the areas where you want to define the links. These shapes can be rectangles, circles, or polygons. In the Tools panel, shown in Figure 3-1, is the Rectangle Hotspot tool ▣, which works like the Rectangle tool. That is, you select the tool, place the crosshairs on top of the image, and drag the crosshairs until you have the desired shape.

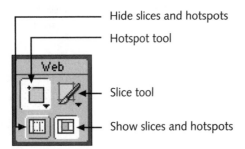

Figure 3-1 Web tools in the Tools panel

Pressing and holding the mouse button on the Rectangle Hotspot tool reveals the two other hotspot shape options, a circle ⊙ and a polygon ⊻. Note that the Polygon Hotspot tool creates a freely drawn polygon. Buttons available at the bottom of the Tools panel hide or show image hotspots. You might use these buttons to hide the hotspots when editing graphics to make the image more visible.

When you draw the hotspot on the workspace, a blue shape will appear over the canvas indicating the location of the hotspot. You can hide and show the hotspots using the Hide Slices and Hotspots icon 🔲 or Show Slices and Hotspots icon 🔳. These tools let you quickly change the view of your document to assist in editing.

Attributes of hotspots can be modified in the Property inspector. Figure 3-2 shows what a hotspot looks like over a photograph, including the Property inspector associated with that hotspot. From the Property inspector, you can change a hotspot's width, height, and location coordinates. You can also set the address of where you would like the hotspot to link. Entering text in the Alt text box causes alternative text to appear over the image. If you leave this option blank, no text appears and the user may not realize that the hotspot exists. Alternative text also provides the user with more information about where the link takes them before they actually click the hotspot, and can be used to help search engines index pages.

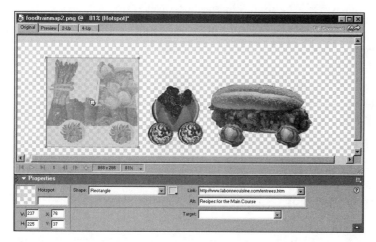

Figure 3-2   Hotspot and Hotspot Property inspector

You can define several targeting options on your image map. You may be familiar with these options from using frames in HTML. (You learn more about targeting options in Chapter 5.) Using targeting, you can control how a Web page opens. In the Property inspector, you specify targeting options in the Target list arrow. Entering None results in the link opening in the current browser window. That is, when the user clicks the hotspot, the page opens in the same browser window, replacing the current Web page. If you want the link to open in a new browser window, select the _blank target. Select _self to open the link in the same browser window. The _parent and _top options are useful only if you use frames on your Web site.

You use the Shape list box to modify the shapes of existing hotspots you drew on your image. Follow the steps below to create several hotspots on an image.

To create hotspots:

1. Create a nested folder called **ch3practice** inside the Sites folder on your working drive to store the practice pages you create in this chapter. Create a second nested folder called **images**, inside the ch3practice folder, to store the images. Copy the image **foodtrain.png** from the Chapter3\images subdirectory on your Data Disk to ch3practice\images on your working drive. Open this file in Fireworks, and save it as **foodtrainmap1.png** in ch3practice\images folder of your working drive.

2. Click the **Rectangle Hotspot** tool in the Tools panel to select it. Move the pointer over the canvas, and place the crosshair pointer above the image of the first train car. Click and hold down the mouse button while you drag the crosshairs over the image of the left-most train car.

   A shaded rectangle appears over the train (refer to Figure 3-2). This delineates the area that contains the active hyperlink.

3. In the Property inspector for the rectangle hotspot, enter the following values in the width, height, and coordinate boxes: W: **240**, H: **230**, X: **75**, and Y: **35**. Press **Enter**. In the Link text box, type **recipe1.htm**. In the Alt text box, type **Entree**. From the Target drop-down list, click **_blank**.

   This ensures that the recipe opens in a new browser window. You have created the hotspot.

4. Click and hold the **Rectangle Hotspot** tool in the Tools panel, point to the **Circle Hotspot** tool, and release the mouse to select the Circle Hotspot tool.

5. Drag the crosshairs over the image of the second train car to create a circular hotspot.

6. In the Property inspector for the circle hotspot, enter the following values in the width, height, and coordinate boxes: W: **180**, H: **180**, X: **320**, and Y: **100**. Press **Enter**. In the Link text box, type **http://www.salad.com.** In the Alt text box, type **A Simple Salad.** From the list arrow, click **_blank**.

7. In the Tools panel, click and hold the **Circle Hotspot** tool, then select the **Polygon Hotspot** tool.

8. To use the Polygon Hotspot tool, click the mouse around the edges of the image that you wish to create a hotspot over, instead of dragging the crosshairs over it. Click around the image of the third train car to create a fitted blue shaded area over the train car.

9. In the Property inspector, enter these values for the width, height, and coordinate text boxes: W: **260**, H: **160**, X: **500**, and Y: **100**. Type **recipe3.htm** in the Link text box, type **A Sandwich** as the alternative text, and make the target **_blank**.

10. To preview the hotspots, you need to export the graphic. From the File menu, select **Export**. In the Export dialog box, the filename **foodtrainmap1.htm** appears in the File Name box. (Make sure you select the ch3practice folder.)

11. At the bottom of the Export window, click the checkbox for **Put Images in Subfolder**. Click the **Browse** button, select **ch3practice\images** as the Save In folder. Click **Open** to select the folder and close the dialog box, and then click **Save**.

The HTML document that is created contains the code for the image map that corresponds to your graphic, foodtrainmap1.gif in the images folder. Later, you can import the image map code into Dreamweaver by selecting the HTML file.

12. Preview foodtrainmap1.htm by opening the file in your Web browser. Move your mouse over the three train cars to see that the recipe links are there and that the alternative text is activated. The train car named "A Simple Salad" is the only one created with an operating link. Click it to see that the link opens in a new browser window. Save the file **foodtrainmap1.png** in your ch3practice\images folder and close the file.

 When you create hotspots on an image, do not allow them to overlap. Overlapping the hotspots prevents the links from working properly. Also, note that very small hotspots or hotspots drawn too close together are very difficult for users to identify and click.

Creating Multiple Hotspots

In Fireworks MX, you can automatically create multiple hotspots using the Insert Hotspot option available on the Edit menu. Using this option, you can make multiple hotspots from components of a single image (similar to what you did in the previous exercise when you used the Hotspot tools), or from several images.

Selecting a path or object and having Fireworks draw the polygon for you is much quicker than drawing a free-form polygon yourself using the Hotspot tool. You may find that this saves a lot of time. If you select several objects on the page and use the Insert Hotspot command, a dialog box prompts you for single or multiple hotspots. Fireworks automatically creates appropriate shapes for each object you select. If you select the option for creating a single hotspot, Fireworks creates one hotspot for the image.

To create multiple hotspots:

1. Open the image **foodtrain.png** from the ch3practice\images folder on your working drive, and save it as **foodtrainmap2.png** in the same folder.

2. Holding down the **Shift** key, click each train car with the Pointer tool ⟨**⟨** to select them all.

3. Click **Edit** on the menu bar, click **Insert**, and then click **Hotspot**.

   A dialog box appears asking if you require single or multiple hotspots.

4. Click the **Multiple** button and observe that Fireworks creates three rectangular hotspots automatically.

5. Press **Ctrl+D** to deselect the train cars.

6. Type the following data for each hotspot by clicking each hotspot individually and entering the data in the Property inspector:

   Train car 1: Link = **recipe1.htm**, Alt text = **Entree**, target = **_blank**

   Train car 2: Link = **http://www.salad.com**, Alt text = **A Simple Salad**, target = **_blank**

   Train car 3: Link = **recipe3.htm**, Alt text = **A Sandwich**, target = **_blank**

7. Save the file **foodtrainmap2.png** in your ch3practice\images folder.

8. A shortcut to previewing the hotspots is pressing the F12 key. Press **F12**. Your Web browser will open automatically. Move your mouse over the train cars to see that the hotspots are present.

9. Close your browser and close the file **foodtrainmap2.png**.

When you export the image, you create the HTML code for the image map and hyperlinks for the polygons so that you can incorporate the code into Dreamweaver.

Exporting an Image Map to Dreamweaver MX

To use your Fireworks MX image in Dreamweaver, simply click File on the menu bar, and then click Export. As you saw in the previous exercise, this generates two files; one is the Web graphic itself, saved as a .gif file, and the other is an HTML file that contains all the code needed to set up the image map in Dreamweaver MX.

To incorporate your food train into an existing Web page using Dreamweaver:

1. Copy the graphic **lbclogo.gif** from the Chapter3\images folder on your Data Disk to the ch3practice\images folder on your working drive.

2. Create a new file in Dreamweaver, and save it as **dwimap.htm** in the ch3practice folder. Type **Food Map** in the Title text box on the Document toolbar. Click your mouse in the workspace.

3

3. In the Dreamweaver workspace, insert the image **lbclogo.gif** in the upper-left corner of the canvas by clicking the **Image** button on the Insert bar Common tab, and finding the file in the ch3practice\images folder. After inserting the image, click to the right of the image to deselect it.

4. In the Property inspector, select **Heading 1** as the Format and type **#0000FF** (blue) in the text box next to the color box. Click the workspace to the right of the image again. Type the text **La Bonne Cuisine**.

5. Press **Enter** to move to the next line.

   This is where you insert the Fireworks-generated image map that you created in a previous exercise.

6. Click the **Fireworks HTML** button on the Common tab to open the Insert Fireworks HTML dialog box. Click the **Browse** button, and then locate and select the **foodtrainmap1.htm** file in your ch3practice folder. Click **Open**. Click **OK** to close the Insert Fireworks HTML dialog box. An alert window that says "Some referenced files are outside the root folder of your site and may not be accessible when you publish your site. Copy these files into Site?" will open. This is because we have not defined a site to edit. We will learn how to do this in Chapter 4. Click **Cancel**. The image map will appear on the page.

> **Note**
> You must insert the HTML file to transfer the code to Dreamweaver. If you insert the .gif file, your page does not contain the code for the image map.

7. Preview and test your page in your Web browser by clicking **F12**.

8. Return to Dreamweaver and click the **Show Code View** button to view the source code for the image map. Observe that the image map is inserted and the polygons and hyperlinks are present.

9. Save the file **dwimap.htm** in the ch3practice folder on your working drive. Close the file.

SLICING IMAGES FOR THE WEB

Slicing is similar to creating an image map. However, instead of defining a map name with polygons, you define rectangular areas of a graphic and divide them into slices of a table. Each table cell holds a slice of the image. Like image maps, each slice can have a link to another Web page. Later in this chapter you learn that slicing is the technique used to produce cleanly aligned menu bars and rollovers. Using slicing in your Web applications offers several other advantages, among them:

- Sliced images load faster on a Web page. Instead of loading a giant file, you effectively break the image into several smaller files. Individual files load more quickly, letting the user see the image more quickly because slices fill in as the page loads.

■ You can optimize your Web page by using different export formats for individual slices. Suppose your graphic has several regions that might be saved more efficiently in .gif format and several that might be saved more efficiently in .jpg format. Slicing the image lets you fully optimize the graphic using appropriate formats for the different slices.

Fireworks offers two ways to create slices from images. With the first technique, you use guides to slice an image. This is useful if you want to optimize the image slices individually to improve performance. When you export the image, you must select Slice Along Guides to create the proper HTML code for the sliced image. The second technique allows you to draw the slices yourself using the Slice tool ▨ in the Tools panel. This technique sets up your slices so that you can associate a hyperlink with the slice. Exporting the file and specifying Export Slices in the Export dialog box generates HTML code that Dreamweaver uses.

Slicing an Image Using Guides

To slice an image using guides, you need to use the guide rulers in the workspace to create guidelines for slicing the image. To do this, click View on the menu bar, and then click Rulers, or press the Ctrl+Alt+R key combination. Once the rulers appear, you can draw guides by dragging them from the ruler to the desired place on the canvas, as shown in Figure 3-3. To generate the code for use in Dreamweaver, you must select Slice Along Guides from the Slices drop-down list in the Export dialog box shown in Figure 3-4. This export option generates code for an HTML table that includes a slice of the image for each cell of the table.

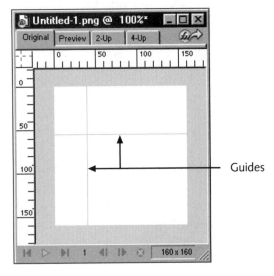

Figure 3-3   Guides

Figure 3-4   Export window for slicing an image using guides

To slice an image into a three-cell table:

1. Create a new folder in the ch3practice folder of your working drive named **slices**. Start Fireworks MX if it is not already running.

   You create the slices folder because when you slice an image, you generate many graphic files. Keeping them in a different subdirectory makes finding your files easier.

2. Open the image **foodtrain.png** (in the ch3practice\images folder), and save it as **slicedtrain.png** in the new ch3practice\slices folder.

3. Click **View** on the menu bar, and then click **Rulers**, or press the **Ctrl+Alt+R** key combination to display rulers in the workspace.

   Horizontal and vertical rulers appear on the top and left side of the workspace.

4. To insert a guide, click and hold the mouse button over the ruler, and then drag the mouse to the position where you want your guide placed. For slicedtrain.png, drag from the vertical ruler to the space between the first and second train cars, and then repeat for the space between the second and third train cars.

   A narrow green line identifies the edges of each slice. Your image should contain three slices, one for each train car. This generates a one-row by three-column table containing the three slices.

5. Click **File** on the menu bar, and then click **Export**. Export the file as **slicedtrain.htm** in the ch3practice\slices folder. In the Export window, from the Save as Type drop-down list, click **HTML and Images**. In the Slices drop-down list, click **Slice Along Guides**. Click **Save**.

You created four files: three graphics representing the sliced train and one HTML file containing the code to be imported into Dreamweaver. An empty folder named _notes is also created in the sliced folder. (The _notes folders created by Fireworks are used for collecting information about the file, such as who changed it last.)

6. Open the HTML file in your Web browser to see the image of the train. View the source code for the slices train, and you see that a three-column table has been created to display the image.

7. Return to Fireworks, click **View** on the menu bar, and then click **Rulers** to hide the rulers shown on the workspace. Save **slicedtrain.png** in your ch3practice\slices folder. Close the **slicedtrain.png** file.

Slicing an Image Using the Slice Tool

The Slice tool allows you to define sliced areas on your canvas either as rectangles or as polygons. The Slice tool is in the Web category of the Tools panel. Below the Hotspot and Slice tools are tools that allow you to show and hide hotspots and slices on your image. When you edit an image and need to see it uncluttered, the Hide Hotspots and Slices icon can help by making the slices transparent until you are ready to use them.

There are two reasons why you may find it beneficial to define slice objects using the Slice tool in Dreamweaver. First, using the Slice tool, you can attach behaviors to the slice. Individual slices can link to other Web pages using the options available in the Slice Property inspector shown in Figure 3-5. These options allow you to set type, links, alternative text, and targeting options, much like you did when you defined hotspots for an image map. You can also select slice filenames and coloring options for the slices. Moreover, you can set width and height attributes and position coordinates for each slice.

Figure 3-5   Slice Property inspector

The second reason you might use the Slice tool is to optimize slices individually. In other words, if you have a text slice and an image slice, the text slice can contain HTML code, while the image slice can be in .gif format. This is more efficient than defining both slices as .gif files. To optimize individual slices, you can use the Optimize panel (click Window on the menu bar and then click Optimize to open the panel if it is not already open). This panel allows you to change attributes of the individual slices to reduce file size.

When exporting an image sliced using the Slice tool for use in Dreamweaver, you must select Export Slices from the Slices drop-down list in the Export dialog box. Again, the code generated is an HTML table. Several image files are generated to fill the table with the individual slices. You may also see files named spacer.gif in your sliced image. These files are one-pixel image files put in the table as spacers to ensure that the image aligns properly.

To slice foodtrain.png using the Slice tool:

1. Start Fireworks MX if it is not already running. Open the original file **foodtrain.png** from the ch3practice\images folder on your working drive, and save it as **slicedtrain2.png** in the ch3practice\slices folder.

2. Click the **Slice** tool ✐ on the Tools panel. Move the pointer into the work-space to display the crosshairs, and then click and drag the crosshair pointer over the first train car.

   Notice that a shaded slice appears over the image and that horizontal and vertical red lines appear, positioning the slice.

3. In the Property inspector for the slice, enter the following values in the width, height, and coordinate boxes: W: **250**, H: **250**, X: **70**, and Y: **20**.

   Notice that the slice guides readjust as you position the slice.

4. In the Slice Property inspector, set the following attributes:

   Link: **recipe1.htm**

   Alt: **Entree**

   Target: **_blank**

5. To select the Polygon Slice tool, click and hold the **Slice** tool, point to the **Polygon Slice** tool ✐, and then release the mouse button. Draw a polygonal slice around the second train car by clicking around the image. Note that when you create a polygon slice, the slice will actually be rectangular with a polygon hotspot.

   The shaded area represents the slice. The size and coordinates of this slice will vary.

6. Define the attributes for this polygon in the Property inspector as follows:

   Link: **recipe2.htm**

   Alt: **A Simple Salad**

   Target: **_blank**

   Deselect the polygon by pressing **Ctrl+D**.

7. Draw a polygon over the third train car using the Polygon Slice tool ✐. Define the slice attributes as follows:

   Link: **recipe3.htm**

   Alt: **A Sandwich**

   Target: **_blank**

8. Click the **Hide Slices and Hotspots** icon ⊞ to make the slices transparent.

   Observe that your slices disappear. This can be very useful when you are editing an image, as working around the slices can become annoying.

9. Now click the **Show Slices and Hotspots** icon ⊞ so that you can see the slices again.

10. Click **File** on the menu bar, and then click **Export**. Export the file as **slicedtrain2.htm** in the ch3practice\slices folder. In the Export window, from the Save as Type drop-down list, click **HTML and Images**. From the Slices drop-down list, click **Export Slices**. Click **Save**.

    You created several files. The .gif files hold the graphics for the slices. A spacer file ensures correct spacing of the slices, and an HTML file contains the table code for Dreamweaver to insert the sliced image.

11. Open **slicedtrain2.htm** in your Web browser, and test the slices to see that the alternate text shows.

12. In Fireworks, save the file **slicedtrain2.png** in your ch3practice\slices folder. Close the **slicedtrain2.png** file.

BUTTONS AND ROLLOVERS

Using buttons instead of static, blue, underscored hyperlinks helps give your Web application a much more dynamic look and feel. Enhancing buttons using rollovers allows you to provide users with visual and audio feedback when they click the button, so that they know they've clicked it and begun whatever process the button executes. For example, if you design a Web site for a furniture company, and you want visitors to select a type of furniture easily, a button or icon with an image of a table that they can click makes the Web site more user friendly. After using the furniture site once, the user knows how to navigate through the site quickly and easily without reading text at all. Chapter 4 provides a more detailed discussion of navigation strategies.

Buttons in Fireworks MX are created by slicing images and then exporting HTML tables and JavaScript code for use in Dreamweaver. Buttons come in many forms. Some buttons are text on a geometrically shaped background with added 3-D effects—they look like users can physically push them. Some buttons use images and pictures that illustrate their purpose, and some combine graphics and text to tell users where the button takes them. Combining several buttons on a navigation bar allows you to give the user a high level view of the Web site without showing all its content. Designing rollovers so that the current page is highlighted in the navigation bar is a good way to indicate to users where they are and where they can go. Consistent style and navigation strategy are very important to the usability of your Web applications.

Having a potential user review your navigational buttons and graphics is a good idea. It helps to ensure that these elements are meaningful to your target audience. Once you incorporate graphics into your Web site, ask a group of people to perform a usability test. It may reveal hidden flaws in the way you designed your graphics for the site. It is important to do this before actually posting the site on the Internet.

Each Fireworks MX file you create has its own independent library associated with it. Opening a new canvas in Fireworks automatically creates a library for that file; you can use this library to store the objects and styles that you created while editing the file.

Libraries store three types of symbols: graphics, animations, and buttons. Once you create a symbol and Fireworks stores it in the library, you can reuse it, edit it, and drag it onto the canvas any time you choose. The symbol is an object, and dragging and dropping it on the canvas creates an instance of the object. If you want to use the symbols you created on one canvas on another canvas, you can export them from the library and import them into the new file.

Using symbols is important because you can store them in a library and reuse them as needed. If your library contains a button symbol that you want to reuse, you can duplicate it several times and change its text. This is an easy way to create consistent-looking buttons for your site. Once you create a button on your Fireworks canvas, code can be generated to create rollover buttons for use in Dreamweaver and Flash, enhancing the visual appeal of your Web page.

To insert a new button, click Edit then Insert on the menu bar, and then click New Button. The Button Editor opens, as shown in Figure 3-6. This window contains five tabs in which you can define the state of the button. As you click the various tabs, instructions defining each button state appear at the bottom of the Button Editor. The Property inspector works the same as when you work on your document, so you can use it to change the attributes of the graphics you define for your buttons.

This list describes button states and options:

- Up—The up state displays the normal (mouse off) state of the button as it appears on the Web page. A button named Import a Button, is at the lower-left corner of the Up tab of the Button Editor. Clicking this lets you browse the predefined buttons that come with the Fireworks MX application. The Import a Button option is available in the other button states as well.

- Over—The over state shows how the button looks when the user places the mouse over it. At the bottom right of the Over tab is a button labeled Copy Up Graphic. Clicking this button copies the graphic from the up state to the over state.

- Down—The down state is used when the button is included in a navigation bar. The button, once selected, appears as a pushed-in image in the navigation bar while a user visits a particular link. The fact that the Include Nav Bar Down state option at the top left of the Down tab is already checked tells you that the feature is activated. Again, a button for copying the graphic from the previous state is available.

- Over While Down—If you create a navigation bar and use the down option, the over while down state displays the defined button style when the mouse is over the pushed-in button. You must click the checkbox labeled Include Nav Bar Over While Down State to activate this button state. The checkbox, of the Over While Down tab is checked automatically as you define this button state.

- Active Area—This button state is not actually displayed. The active area, also known as the hit area, defines a button's clickable range. Sometimes, an active area is larger than the actual button so that the user need not be extremely accurate with his or her pointer. At the top of the Active Area panel, the Set Active Area Automatically checkbox is checked by default. If you want to define your own hit area for the button, you uncheck this checkbox.

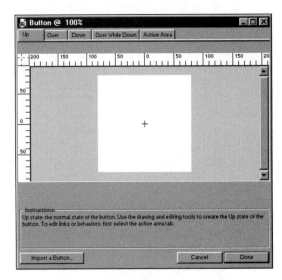

Figure 3-6   Button Editor

Suppose you want to create a black button with white text that blurs when the user moves the mouse over it. First, you create the button in the up state, a simple black rectangle with white text. Then, switch to the over state, copy the existing button, and blur the white text. Basically, you alter the original button graphic so the user sees a change when performing an operation. To create this rollover, you need two images, the original button and the blurred state. Fireworks generates the JavaScript to implement the rollover for you.

After creating a button, click Done. You can link the button to a Web page by using the Property inspector when the button is selected. The Button Property inspector is shown in Figure 3-7.

Figure 3-7 Button Property inspector

In the Property inspector, you can set text, export options (GIF or JPG), link, alternate text, and targeting options. You can also set effects such as embossing or a drop shadow. Being able to edit button text in the Property inspector is convenient when you want to change a button or recycle an already created button.

Letting Fireworks MX automatically name the states creates filenames that are extensions of the existing filename and that indicate rows and columns for the table being created. Figure 3-8 shows a button placed on the canvas, with the filenames for each slice. Notice that the slice containing the actual image, r2_c2, has four associated image files. Note that four images are actually created for one button, one for each state of the button. When you export the file, JavaScript code is generated that swaps the images for the various states of the button. To import the code into Dreamweaver, click the Fireworks MX button on the Dreamweaver Insert bar Common tab and select the .htm file generated by Fireworks MX.

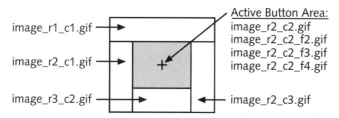

Figure 3-8 Naming conventions for image files created while exporting a button

Creating a Button

The following set of steps defines a simple button for the La Bonne Cuisine Web site. You define an initial state for the button, and then copy the graphic to define the other four states of the button. You create a button with yellow text, and a blue background that changes color when the rollover state is activated. Make sure you save this file, because you use it to create a menu bar later in this chapter.

To create a button:

1. In Fireworks, open a new document that is **500** pixels wide by **500** pixels high with a white canvas.

2. Click **Edit** on the menu bar, and then click **Insert** and then **New Button**.

   The Button Editor opens. You create your first drawing on the canvas of the Up tab.

3. Click the **Rectangle** tool ⬜ on the Tools panel and draw a rectangle over the crosshairs in the Button Editor workspace. In the Property inspector, enter the following values in the width, height, and coordinate boxes: W: **110**, H: **50**, X: **-55**, Y: **-25**. Click the fill color box and select blue (**#0000FF**). Click the stroke color box and select **Transparent**. (The Transparent button, represented by a white square with a red line through it, is located at the top of the color palette.)

4. Click the **Text** tool Ⓐ. In the Property inspector, make the text **Arial**, size **16**, color yellow (**#FFFF00**), bold, and centered. Click over the blue rectangle and type **Food**, press **Enter**, and then type **Consulting**. Enter the following values in the Property inspector X: **-45** and Y: **-21**. Press **Enter**. Alternatively, you can resize and reposition the text or the rectangle using the Scale and Pointer tools.

5. Click the **pointer** tool, hold down the **Shift** key, and click the text and button. Add a drop shadow effect to your text and button by clicking the **+** button in the Property inspector and selecting the effect **Shadow and Glow**, **Drop Shadow**. Set the attributes for this effect to a distance of **6**, color **black**, opacity **75%**, a **2**-pixel softness factor, and a **330**-degree angle. Click **Enter**.

   The shadow should appear beneath the text and button. The button state you just created determines how your button looks when your Web page first loads into the browser. Now you need to create a look for when the pointer moves over the button.

6. Click the **Over** tab in the Button Editor, and then click the **Copy Up Graphic** button. This copies your entire image onto the Over tab workspace. *Hint*: If you cannot see the Copy Up Graphic button, it may be hidden by the open panels. Maximize your workspace to make the button visible.

7. Using the Pointer tool ▶, select the blue rectangle. In the fill color box in the Property inspector for the rectangle, set the color to orange (**#FF6600**).

8. Click the **Active Area** tab, and make sure the checkbox for Set Active Area Automatically is selected.

   This ensures that the hit area for the button covers your entire button.

9. Click the **Done** button to return to your canvas with the button on it. On the Button Property inspector, for Button export options, choose **Gif Web 216**. In the Link text box, enter the Link **consulting/consulting.htm**. In the Alt text box, type **Consulting Services**.

10. Click the **Preview** tab (see Figure 2-1) and move your mouse over the button to see that it changes color.

11. Open the Library panel by clicking the **Window** menu and selecting **Library**, if it is not already open, to see that the library contains the button for this canvas.

12. Rename the button by double-clicking the text **Button** in the Name column in the Library panel and typing the name **Consulting** in the dialog box. Click **OK**.

13. Save this file in your ch3practice\images folder as **bluebutton.png**.

Creating a Menu Bar

Once you create a button, you can duplicate it to create several more buttons with the same style and the same button states. Since you have already created the up, over, down, and over while down states of the food consulting button, you can maintain consistency by copying these states and merely altering the text and links associated with each duplicated button. To do this, you duplicate and edit the button to create the three other buttons for the lbc site—About Us, Culinary Explorations, and Culinary Training—forming a menu bar.

To create the three new buttons:

1. Create a new folder named **menu** nested within your ch3practice folder. If necessary, open the file **bluebutton.png** that you created in the last exercise. It should be in your ch3practice\images folder.

2. Click **Window** on the menu bar, and then click **Library** to open the Library panel, if it is not already open. You see your Consulting button listed in the Library. Click the **Consulting** button to select it.

3. Click the **Options** menu in the upper-right corner of the Library panel, and then click **Duplicate**. This creates Consulting 1 and adds it to the bottom of the object list in the Library.

4. Double-click the **Consulting 1** button in the Library panel, and rename it **Excursions** in the Symbol Properties dialog box. Click **Edit** to open the Button Editor.

5. On the Up tab, double-click the button text with the Pointer tool and then drag your mouse over it to select it. Replace the Food Consulting text with **Culinary Explorations**, with "Explorations" appearing on the line below "Culinary". The text should be centered on the blue rectangle. If it is not, enter the following values in the coordinate boxes: X: **-52** and Y: **-21**. Click the white space outside the button. When prompted to update the text in the other button states, click **Yes**.

This changes the text to "Culinary Explorations" for all the button states.

6. Go through the other button states, clicking each tab, to ensure that the text appears as you wish. If the text alignment is off, adjust it using the Pointer tool. Then click the **Done** button at the bottom of the Active Area tab. Your button, Excursions, is now in your Library.

7. Make sure the Excursions button is selected in the Library by clicking it, and then drag it onto your canvas beneath the Consulting button. In the Property inspector for the Excursions button, enter **tour/tour.htm** in the Link text box, and the alternative text to **Come Dine with Us in Exotic Places**. Enter the following values in the width, height, and coordinate boxes: W: **124**, H: **58**, X: **195**, Y: **290**. Press **Enter**.

   You successfully created another button in the same style as your previous one.

8. Repeat Steps 2 through 6 to create two other buttons for Culinary Training and About Us. To do this, duplicate the Consulting button, and rename it **Training**. Type the text **Culinary**, press **Enter**, and then type **Training**. Duplicate the button for Consulting again, and rename it **About Us**. Type the text **About**, press **Enter**, and then type **Us**.

9. Click the **Training** button in the Library panel. Drag it onto the canvas beneath the button for Culinary Explorations. In the Property inspector, enter the link **training/training.htm**. Enter the alternative text **Learn to Prepare a Gala Event**. Enter the following values in the width, height, and coordinate boxes: W: **124**, H: **58**, X: **195**, Y: **355**. Press **Enter**.

10. Click the **About Us** button in the Library panel. Drag it onto the canvas above the button for Food Consulting. In the Property inspector change the link to **about/aboutlbc.htm**. Change the alternative text to **Learn About LBC**. Enter the following values in the width, height, and coordinate boxes: W: **124**, H: **58**, X: **195**, Y: **160**. Press **Enter**.

11. Click the **Options** menu in the upper-right corner of the Library panel, and click **Export Symbols**.

    The Export Symbols dialog box appears.

12. Click **Select All** to select all of the buttons you just created, click **Export**, and save the file as **symbolsformenu.png** in the ch3practice\menu folder. You saved all the symbols you selected as a .png file that you can import for use in other Fireworks graphics.

13. Save your current file as **bluebutton2.png** in your ch3practice\images folder. Close the **bluebutton2.png** file.

14. Open a new document in Fireworks that is **200** pixels wide and **300** pixels high with a white canvas.

3

15. In the Library panel, click the **Options** menu, and then click **Import Symbols**. Locate the file **symbolsformenu.png** in the ch3practice\menu folder. Click **Open**. Click **Select All** to insert every symbol from symbolsformenu.png. Click **Import**.

Observe that you imported all the buttons into the library for your current document.

16. To create the menu, select **Edit** from the menu bar and click **Insert**, and then click **New Symbol**. Name the new symbol **Menu**, and ensure that the Graphic option button is selected in the Symbol Properties dialog box. Click **OK**. Creating the menu as a symbol in the library makes reusing the menu easy and ensures a consistent appearance.

17. Select and drag each button from the Library preview area onto the symbol editing canvas you just opened. Drag them in the vertical order About Us, Consulting, Excursions, and Training. You may need to modify the canvas size so that all the buttons fit in the workspace.

Note that as you place the buttons on the canvas, slicing lines appear. To organize your buttons uniformly, you may want to select all four buttons and then use the Align option from the Modify menu in the menu bar to space them evenly and align them exactly.

18. Close the symbol editing canvas.

Observe that your menu appears in your document library and in your Fireworks canvas.

19. Click the **Preview** tab and test the menu to see that all of the rollovers work.

Now you can export the menu and preview it in your Web browser.

20. Select **Export Preview** from the **File** menu on the menu bar. Click the first eyedropper button (**Select transparent color**) to the left of the Export window. Move the eyedropper to the preview canvas, and click the white area on the menu. The white area around the buttons should become transparent. Click **Export** to export the menu, name it **mainmenu.htm**, and store it in the ch3practice\menu folder. Make sure that the Save as Type text box is set to **HTML and Images** and that the Slices text box is set to **Export Slices**. Click **Save**.

21. Save your current file as **mainmenu.png** in your ch3practice\menu folder. Close the **mainmenu.png** file.

22. Open the file **mainmenu.htm** in your Web browser.

The file should display the menu with the rollover buttons. (To incorporate this menu into Dreamweaver, you click the Fireworks MX button on the Dreamweaver Insert bar Common tab and browse the files until you find the file mainmenu.htm. Selecting the HTML file inserts the image and the JavaScript to operate the rollovers into your Dreamweaver file.)

This is an easy way to insert a menu bar, because you need not insert the rollovers in Dreamweaver. Exporting the code from Fireworks is less labor-intensive than navigating through the rollover states in Dreamweaver and inserting each individual button state.

Using Libraries and Styles

Fireworks MX comes with a library of symbols, including animations, bullets, buttons, and themes. To import a predefined Fireworks MX button, click Edit on the menu bar, then click Libraries, and then click which library you want to use (as shown in Figure 3-9). When you select the Buttons option, the Import Symbol dialog window appears, allowing you to navigate through and select a predefined button.

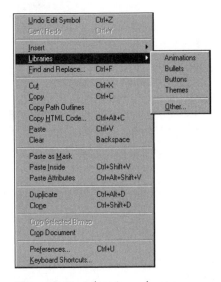

Figure 3-9 Libraries submenu

Four libraries (Animations.png, Bullets.png, Buttons.png, and Themes.png) are available. You can play a button to observe its various states by clicking the play arrow in the upper-right corner of the window, as shown in Figure 3-10. You can view the different button alternatives by highlighting each image. You can import buttons into the library of your current document, where you can then edit and use them as you wish.

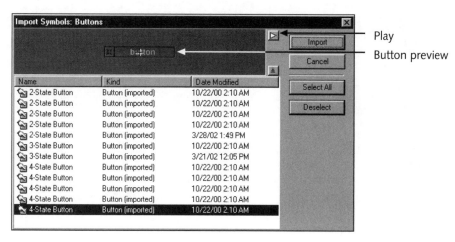

Play

Button preview

3

Figure 3-10   Import Symbols: Buttons window

The bullets and themes libraries work in a similar way. You import the pre-created graphic and then edit it as needed. The theme library contains graphics for page division and buttons that you can incorporate into the design of your Web site. On a large project, where many graphics repeat throughout the Web site, creating a site library enables all project members to use the same graphics. This is important because you want all the buttons, icons, and styles to create a consistent look and feel for your site.

Another way to achieve a consistent style on your page is to use a pre-defined style or to create, store, and reuse a style. A style refers to defined characteristics for an image. For a given image, you may define a specific color, stroke, fill, and effect that you want to reuse. After creating an image with the desired style, you can store the style in the Styles panel and reuse it for other images you produce. Click Window on the menu bar and then click Styles, or press the Shift+F11 key sequence, to open a short panel of styles that you can use for images that you create. Figure 3-11 shows this panel. To apply one of these styles, simply draw your shape on the canvas, and then click the style that you want to apply instantly to your image.

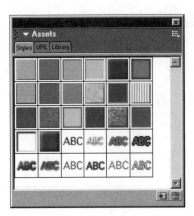

Figure 3-11 Styles panel

To define your own style, create an image in the style you prefer, click the Options menu on the right of the Styles panel, and then click New Style, as shown in Figure 3-12. The dialog box shown in Figure 3-13 opens, prompting you to name the style and to select the attributes for the style you create. The style becomes part of the collection of styles on the panel. Notice also that you can edit and delete styles, import and export styles from other documents, reset the Styles panel, or view the styles in a larger format to see more clearly what the style you select looks like.

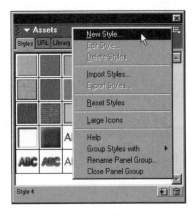

Figure 3-12 Defining a new style

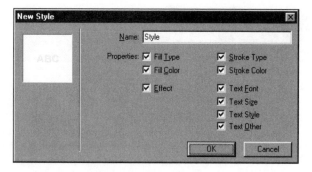

Figure 3-13   New Style dialog box

Creating a Pop-up Menu

On a Web site that has a large amount of information, sometimes it is useful to use pop-up menus. A pop-up menu lets a user see what information is available in specific content areas by moving his or her mouse over them. Users can examine their options before they actually visit a new page of the site.

Dreamweaver MX gives you a simple way to implement pop-up menus using slices. By right-clicking a slice, a menu appears giving you the option to add a pop-up menu, as shown in Figure 3-14.

Figure 3-14   Selecting Add Pop-up Menu

Figure 3-15 shows the Content tab on the Pop-up Menu Editor. Clicking the + and – buttons lets you add text, link, and targeting information for your pop-up menu.

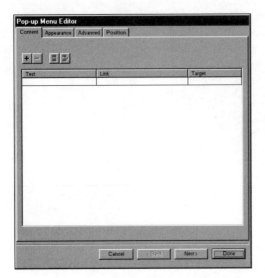

Figure 3-15   Content tab on Pop-up Menu Editor

The Appearance tab, shown in Figure 3-16, lets you interactively select and preview how your menu will appear. Using the Advanced tab, you control other attributes (like the dimensions) of your menu. The Position tab lets you choose the location of the pop-up menu relative to the slice.

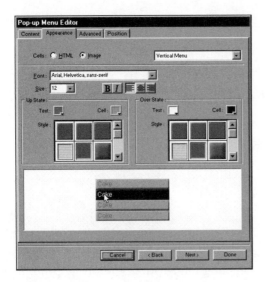

Figure 3-16   Appearance tab on Pop-up Menu Editor

To create a simple pop-up menu for soft drinks:

1. Open a new document in Fireworks that is **300** pixels wide and **300** pixels high with a white canvas.

2. Click the **Rectangle** tool ⬜ on the Tools panel and draw a rectangle on the canvas. In the Property inspector, enter the following values in the width, height, and coordinate boxes: W: **120**, H: **50**, X: **10**, Y: **10**. Click the fill color box and select blue (**#0000FF**). Click the stroke color box and select **Transparent**.

3. Click the **Text** tool Ⓐ. In the Property inspector, make the text **Arial**, size **16**, color yellow (**#FFFF00**). Click over the blue rectangle and type **Pick A Soda**. Enter the following values in the coordinate boxes: X: **18** and Y: **22**. Press **Enter**.

4. Click the **Slice** tool 🔲 and draw a slice over the rectangle. In the Slice Property inspector, enter the following values in the width, height, and coordinate boxes: W: **120**, H: **50**, X: **10**, Y: **10**. Press **Enter**.

5. Position the mouse over the slice, right-click and hold the mouse button down, and then click **Add Pop-up Menu**.

6. Double-click in the space below the Text column in the Pop-up Menu Editor. A blank text area will appear. Type **Coke**. Press **Tab**. Now you are below the Link column. Type **http://www.coke.com**. Press **Tab** twice to advance to the next line.

7. Type **Pepsi**. Press **Tab**. Now you are below the Link column again. Type **http://www.pepsi.com**. Press **Tab** twice to advance to the next line.

8. Type **Sprite**, press **Tab**, then type **http://www.sprite.com**.

9. Click the **Appearance** tab at the top of the Pop-up Menu Editor. The tab will now have a highlight across the top. Click the **Appearance** tab again to open the panel. Click the **Image** option (Vertical Menu should be selected already in the drop-down list to the right). Set the Font to **Arial, Helvetica, sans-serif**. In the Up State color boxes, set the text to red (**#FF0000**) and the cell to light blue (**#00FFFF**). Select the style from the upper-left corner of the Style list. Notice the preview of your button. In the Over State color boxes, set the text to white (**#FFFFFF**) and the cell to blue (**#000088**).

10. Click the **Position** tab at the top of the Pop-up Menu Editor to advance to the Position panel. Under Menu Position, click the fourth icon so that your menu pops out to the top and right of your button (see Figure 3-17). Click **Done**.

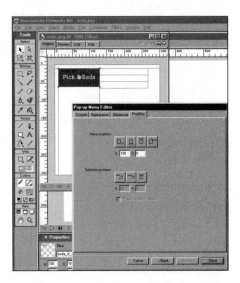

Figure 3-17   Positioning the pop-out menu

11. Press **F12** to preview the menu in your Web browser. Save this file as **soda.png** in your **ch3practice\images** folder on your working drive. Close the **soda.png** file.

FIREWORKS MX ANIMATION

You may have noticed small, animated graphics decorating many Web site pages. Animation can make a Web page more visually interesting and can persuade the user to perform a particular action. Perhaps you have seen banner advertisements that contain animation enticing you to click a box that, in fact, takes you to for another Web site offering a product or service. You may have also noticed flashing stars or icons telling you where to find new information or encouraging you to participate in a contest. Animation can draw a visitor's eye to an important section of the Web page.

Use animations appropriately on your Web site. Too many animations can detract from your design and distract the user from doing what you want. Don't use animations for animations' sake! Use animations that are appropriate and well integrated with the purpose of your site.

Creating animation on the Web is much like creating animation in cartoon strips. You draw frames for each consecutive cartoon image, changing characters and scenes slightly to create the appearance of motion. For example, to animate a blinking eye, you could create three frames. In frame 1, the eye appears open, in frame 2, it's half shut, and in frame 3, the eye is completely closed. To animate the frame, you loop frame 1, frame 2, frame 3, frame 2, and then frame 1 again continuously to make the eye look as if it were actually blinking.

3

There are several ways to create animation on the Web. You can create JavaScript code that rotates an array of images in a loop. For our eye example, the images loop so that the blinking eye effect occurs. On the other hand, you can create an animated .gif in which the images also loop. When you animate images as a .gif, however, the images that comprise the animation are all contained in a single file.

The Macromedia product Flash MX produces a third type of animation, using frames and tweening to create very complex movies playable on the Web. **Tweening** is a process whereby you define a beginning and an ending frame, and the software fills in the frames between them—in effect creating the animation for you. Without tweening, you need to define each individual frame.

Director 8.5.1 is a major product used to develop multimedia CD-ROMs. Although Fireworks MX can generate animations for use in the Flash MX program, in this chapter you use Fireworks to create animated .gifs that you can import into Dreamweaver MX.

Using Frames to Create Animation

In Fireworks, the term **frames** refers to animation frames, not the frames you are familiar with in HTML or Dreamweaver. To create frame-by-frame animation, you need to use the Layers panel and the Frames panel in unison to draw and distribute the animation as desired across the frames.

In the Layers panel shown in Figure 3-18, layers of your image can be associated with specific frames. If you want all frames to share a layer, that is, you want that layer to show throughout the animation, you need to double-click the layer in the Layers panel as if you were going to rename it. Under the name of the layer is a checkbox labeled Share Across Frames. Once you select this option, any changes you make to that layer are propagated across all of your frames.

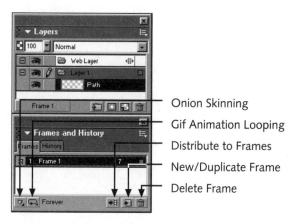

Onion Skinning
Gif Animation Looping
Distribute to Frames
New/Duplicate Frame
Delete Frame

Figure 3-18   Layers and Frames panels

The Frames panel, also shown in Figure 3-18, shows the frame number with a frame delay of .07 seconds, the default setting. Double-clicking the frame speed allows you to change the timing. You can also reorder frames by selecting them and dragging them to another position. Fireworks renumbers the frames and maintains the sequential order. At the bottom right of the Frames panel, three buttons provide shortcuts to frequently used operations:

- Distribute to Frames  distributes selected images over many frames. If you create all images for an animation in one frame or layer, selecting this option then creates a single frame for every selection and distributes the selections across the frames.

- New/Duplicate Frame creates a new blank frame or duplicates an existing one.

- Delete Frame deletes unnecessary frames.

Two buttons are at the bottom left of the Frames panel, Onion Skinning and GIF Animation Looping . Click and hold the GIF Animation Looping button to open a menu from which you can select various looping options, including No Looping, a number from 1 to 20, or Forever.

Figure 3-19 shows the Frame Panel Options menu in the upper-right corner of the Frames and History panel. Selecting the Add Frames option opens a dialog box in which you can indicate how many frames to insert and where to place them relative to the currently selected frame. You can also duplicate or delete an existing frame. Using the Copy to Frames option, you can select an object from a particular frame and copy it over all frames or specifically selected frames. (This is more productive than cutting and pasting the image into each frame individually.)

Figure 3-19   Frames Options menu

Once you create your animations, you can preview them before exporting them as animated .gifs. To do this, use the controls at the bottom of the workspace for your image, as shown in Figure 3-20. You are probably already familiar with the controls from playing media files on the Web, or from using your VCR or CD player. Using the controls, you can play and stop the animation, play it backward and forward, or advance frame-by-frame backward and forward.

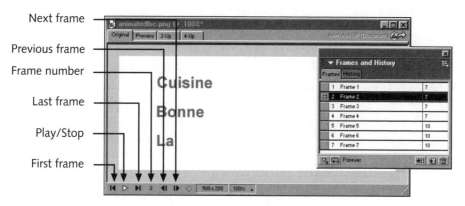

Figure 3-20   Detail of controls to preview an animation

If you are unfamiliar with working in frames, you may find it difficult at first. The following steps take you through the process of animating a simple string of text for the lbc Web site. During this exercise, you learn how to use layers and frames together, and how to apply a style to create an animated effect on text.

To create a simple text animation:

1. Open a new document in Fireworks that is **400** pixels wide by **400** pixels high with a white canvas. (The text will look small on the canvas, but you can crop it later if you wish.)

2. Select the **Text** tool A from the Tools panel. In the Property inspector, set the font to **Arial**, size to **28**, with the color red (**#FF0000**). Click the canvas and type the letter B.

3. Click the **Pointer** tool . Click the **B** and copy it (**Ctrl+C**). Paste (**Ctrl+V**) it onto your canvas four times. The Bs will be on top of each other so it may not look like 5 Bs until you move them.

   You must now separate each character so that you can alter each character individually.

4. Use your Pointer tool to position the Bs next to each other so they appear as a word. Press **Ctrl+A** to select all the Bs. Using the **Align** option on the Modify menu, distribute the Bs evenly on the canvas by clicking **Distribute Widths**. Then click the **Modify** menu, click **Align**, and then click **Top**. Space them close enough together so they still look like a single word rather than individual letters. Deselect the letters by clicking somewhere else on the canvas or by pressing **Ctrl+D**.

5. Double-click the second **B** so you can edit the text. Change the B to an **o**, leaving all the letter characteristics the same. Repeat this process for all duplicated Bs until you create the word **Bonne**.

Next, you create more frames that use this same image.

6. Click **Window** on the menu bar, and then click **Layers** to open the Layers panel if it is not already open. Double-click **Layer 1** to open the Layer Options dialog box. Make sure that the Share Across Frames option is *not* checked for Layer 1. Click **Layer 1** again to close the dialog box.

7. Click **Window** on the menu bar, and then click **Frames** to open the Frames panel, or click the **Frames** tab. In the Frames panel, click the **Options** menu in the upper-right corner, and then click **Duplicate Frame** to open the Duplicate Frame dialog box. Type **5** in the Number text box, and then click the **After current frame** option button to select it if it is not already selected. Click **OK**.

Note that the Frames panel now contains six frames, all identical. To create the animation, you need to edit each frame individually.

8. Click **Frame 1** in the Frames panel. Use the Pointer tool to click the **B** on the canvas. In the Property inspector, under **Effect**, click **+**. Under the drop-down list, point to **Shadow and Glow**, select the **Glow** effect, and color it yellow (**#FFFF00**).

9. Click **Window** on the menu bar, and then click **Styles** to open the Styles panel, if it is not already open. Select the letter **B** that you defined the glow effect for, click the **Panel Options** menu on the Styles panel, and click **New Style**. Name this style **Glow Effect** in the New Style dialog box. Leave all the Properties checked. Click **OK**.

Now you can easily apply the style to consecutive letters in other frames.

10. In the Frames panel, click **Frame 2**, select the letter **o**, and assign it the style you just created by selecting **Glow Effect** from the Styles panel.

11. In the Frames panel, click **Frame 3**, select the letter **n**, and assign it the style you just created by selecting **Glow Effect** from the Styles panel.

12. In the Frames panel, click **Frame 4**, select the letter **n**, and assign it the style you just created by selecting **Glow Effect** from the Styles panel.

13. In the Frames panel, click **Frame 5**, select the letter **e**, and assign it the style you just created by selecting **Glow Effect** from the Styles panel.

You are now ready to play the animation.

14. At the bottom of the workspace, press the **Play/Stop** button to activate the animation. Notice that the glow effect scrolls through the letters sequentially. Click the **Play/Stop** button again.

15. Save this file as **textglow.png** in the ch3practice\images folder. Close the **textglow.png** file. (To save this file as an animated .gif, use the Export Wizard and select the option Animated GIF.)

Using Symbol Tweening to Create Animation

Another way to create animated .gifs in Fireworks MX is to create instances of an image and have Fireworks fill in the animation in between (tweening) the first and last frames. You define a symbol in the symbols library for your document, and then drag that symbol onto the canvas, creating two or more instances of that symbol. To create an animation tween between the two images, you simply select the instances of that symbol, click Modify on the menu bar, point to Symbol, and then click Tween Instances. You are prompted for the number of frames you want to create between the two instances, as shown in Figure 3-21.

Figure 3-21   Tween Instances dialog box

Selecting 5 creates five frames between the two instances. That is, the animation then consists of a total of seven frames: the first and last frames contain the original image, and Fireworks generates the five in between. You can also distribute the tweened images directly to frames by selecting the Distribute to Frames checkbox in the Tween Instances dialog box. This has the effect of placing a slightly changed image in each frame of the animation. For example, if you start with a circle in the upper-left corner of the canvas for the first frame and the same circle in the lower-right corner of the last frame, tweening the image across five frames automatically fills the intermediate frames with the circle, so that the animation appears as a circle traveling downward and to the right.

Tweening is frequently used in the Macromedia application Flash. Working with instances and tweening, you can create complex, multi-object animations much more quickly than you can generate every frame individually.

To create a motion tween for three individual text symbols—La, Bonne, and Cuisine:

1. Open a new Fireworks document of dimensions **500** pixels wide by **200** pixels high with a white canvas.

   You need a wide canvas so that your animation can play across it.

2. Using the Text tool $\boxed{A}$, create the words **La**, **Bonne**, and **Cuisine** on the canvas individually with text attributes **Arial** font, size **28**, and the color red (**#FF0000**).

   You should have three separate text objects when you are finished.

3. Align the text on the left side of the canvas with Cuisine on top, Bonne in the center, and La on the bottom.

4. Double-click **Layer 1** in the Layers panel, and make sure your layer is *not* shared across frames. Click Layer 1 again to close the dialog box.

   Now you need to convert the text into symbols so that you can create instances of a symbol and activate tweening between the instances to create the animation.

5. Press **Ctrl+D** to deselect everything. Use the Pointer tool [🔍 to select the text **La** and press the **F8** key (Convert to Symbol). When the Symbol Properties dialog box appears, name the symbol **La** and make sure the **Graphic** option button is selected. Click **OK**.

6. Select the text **Bonne** and press the **F8** key. When the Symbol Properties dialog box appears, name the symbol **Bonne** and make sure the **Graphic** option button is selected. Click **OK**.

7. Select the text **Cuisine** and press the **F8** key. When the Symbol Properties dialog box appears, name the symbol **Cuisine** and make sure the **Graphic** option button is selected. Click **OK**.

8. Click **Window** on the menu bar, and then click **Library** if the Library panel is not already open.

   The library now contains the symbols that you just created.

9. Click **La** in the list at the bottom of the Library panel and observe that it appears in the Library preview window. Drag and drop the **La** symbol from the Library preview window onto the right side of the canvas, and place it at the top.

   You created a second instance of the La symbol on your canvas.

10. Drag and drop the **Bonne** symbol from the Library preview window onto the right side of the canvas and place it below the La symbol.

11. Drag and drop the **Cuisine** symbol from the Library preview window onto the right side of the canvas, placing it at the bottom.

    You may wish to align your symbols at the end of the animation as you want them to appear. Your canvas should now appear with the first set of instances in reverse order on the left and the second set of instances in correct order on the right. The animation you will add floats the text from the left to the right, placing it in the correct order.

12. Select both instances of **La** by holding down the Shift key as you click each one. Click **Modify** on the menu bar, point to **Symbol**, and then click **Tween Instances** to open the Tween Instances dialog box. Select the number **5**, which creates five images in between your instances for La. Click the **Distribute to Frames** checkbox to select it. Click **OK**.

    This creates an individual frame for each tweened instance. Now, the last frame of your animation disappears from the workspace, leaving only one La

3

on the canvas. Actually, only the first frame shows. The other frames exist but only show when active.

13. Repeat Step 12 for the instances of **Bonne** and **Cuisine**.

14. Play the animation using the controls in the lower-left corner of your workspace. In the Frames panel, hold the Shift key down, and click each frame with your mouse to select it. It should be a bit fast. Click the **Options** menu of the Frames panel to open the Frames menu and then click **Properties**. In the Frame Delay dialog box, type **20**. Test your animation.

The animation shows the text moving from left to right on the canvas.

15. Save this file as **animatedlbc.png** in the ch3practice\images folder.

Saving it as a .png file enables you to edit it in the future. To use this animation in Dreamweaver, you must export it as an animated .gif.

16. Click **File** on the menu bar, and then click **Export Preview**. On the Options tab, from the Format drop-down list, click **Animated GIF**. Click the **Export** button to open the Export dialog box. Select the option **Images Only** in the Save as Type: list box to export the .gif without creating an HTML file. Save this file as **animatedlbc.gif** in your ch3practice\images folder. Close the **animatedlbc.png** file.

17. Open your Web browser and preview the file **animatedlbc.gif** by opening it.

CHAPTER SUMMARY

❏ Using the advanced features of Fireworks MX, you can create image maps, buttons, navigation bars, and animations that you can easily import into Dreamweaver MX.

❏ An image map is a graphic that has hotspots defined over specific areas. A user can click a hotspot on a Web page and be taken to another Web page. Usually, you define multiple hotspots on one image. However, you can define an image with just one hotspot if you wish.

❏ Slicing is a technique used to cut a picture into segments and load the segments as individual graphics on a Web page. Individual slices are positioned in a table so that the graphic appears as one image, even though it may be sliced into several. Slicing an image is advantageous because you can optimize each slice to load quickly on the Web, thereby reducing the download time for a large graphic.

❏ You can slice images in two ways using Fireworks MX: you can use guides to divide an image and then export the slices along the guides, or you can define slice areas and export the slices using sliced objects.

❏ A button is a special symbol that you create on and associate with the canvas you are working on. The button symbols you create appear in the library, and you can export them for use in other documents. You create and edit buttons on a separate canvas from your primary images. To use a button, you must drag it from the library onto the primary canvas. To activate the button, you must configure link and targeting attributes in the Button Property inspector.

❏ Creating several buttons in one library enables you to generate a new graphic containing a navigation bar. Doing this can save you time, because you can duplicate buttons and button states to create consistent buttons across the application. Also, exporting a navigation bar for use in Dreamweaver is easier than importing individual buttons.

❏ A pop-up navigation menu can be created by inserting a slice and right-clicking to open the Pop-up Menu Editor. Fireworks MX generates all the JavaScript code to create the pop-up menu. The code can later be imported into Dreamweaver.

❏ You can create animated .gifs using Fireworks MX, either by creating a frame-by-frame animation or by tweening images over frames. Animated .gifs are like simple cartoons that play a series of frames in logical sequence.

REVIEW QUESTIONS

1. A hotspot is:

   a. a selected path on the canvas

   b. multiple selected paths on the canvas

   c. a rectangle, circle, or polygon shape laid over the canvas that links to a URL

   d. an image map

2. Image maps generated in Fireworks MX use JavaScript code to create hotspots that can be exported into Dreamweaver. True or False?

3. Targeting an image as _blank results in a new browser window opening for the link. True or False?

4. A slice is the same thing as a hotspot. True or False?

5. Slicing an image:

   a. refers to dividing an image into several smaller images

   b. is a technique for cropping an image

   c. is a technique for creating an image map

   d. converts segments of an image into symbols

6. What does it mean to optimize a slice?

7. What is the purpose of a spacer graphic?

8. Slicing an image allows you to:

    a. optimize individual slices of an image, creating a faster-loading graphic

    b. attach behaviors to slices individually

    c. provide the user with some image portions, or slices, while the remaining slices load to complete the full image

    d. all of the above

9. A sliced image is incorporated into Dreamweaver using a table. True or False?

10. Which list below represents possible button states created in Fireworks MX?

    a. up, over, down, and off

    b. up, over, down, and over while down

    c. up, over, off, and on

    d. off, over, down, and over while down

11. Why are buttons on Web pages useful?

12. Describe how you might copy an existing button to create a new one.

13. A navigation bar is defined as a button symbol in Fireworks MX. True or False?

14. When you implement a button or a navigation bar rollover in Dreamweaver, Fireworks MX generates JavaScript code. True or False?

15. Describe how you can reuse a specific style on a particular image.

16. What is an instance of a symbol?

17. Describe how an animated graphic works.

18. To share an animation to play on the Web, use the Export Preview option to export the image in which file format?

    a. .png

    b. animated .gif

    c. .gif

    d. .png and .gif

19. To tween images in Fireworks MX, you must define them as graphic symbols. True or False?

20. How do you create a symbol tween in Fireworks MX?

    a. Duplicate the frames containing the instance for the desired number of frames.

    b. Insert frames and then copy the image to all frames.

    c. Insert frames and then share the image across all frames.

    d. Create instances of the symbol on the canvas, and insert several frames that distribute the tweened image across them.

HANDS-ON PROJECTS

Project 3-1

In this hands-on project, you create an image map to serve as a navigation tool for a shopping Web site.

1. Copy the file **starmenu.gif**, located in the Chapter3\images folder on your Data Disk, into the ch3practice\images folder on your working drive. Open this file in Fireworks.

2. Using the **Circle Hotspot** tool, draw hotspots over the four navigation choices: **Home**, **email**, **Shop**, and **Exit**.

3. Select the hotspot over Home by clicking it, and enter the link **home.htm** in the Property inspector. Select the hotspot over email and enter the link **mailto:contactus@shop.edu** in the Property inspector. Select the hotspot over shop and enter the link **shop.htm**. Select the hotspot over exit and enter the link **exit.htm**.

4. Click **File** on the menu bar, and click **Export**. Export this file to the **ch3practice** folder on your working drive, naming the file **starmenu1.htm**. Make sure the Save as Type option is set to **HTML and Images**. At the bottom of the Export window, click the checkbox for **Put Images in Subfolder**, and select the **images** subfolder to ensure that the starmenu1.gif file is placed there. Click **Save**.

5. Open the file **starmenu.htm** in your Web browser, and observe that the hotspots are active. Close the **starmenu.gif** file in Fireworks but do not save the changes.

Project 3-2

In this project you create and test buttons in various states.

1. Open a new Fireworks document with dimensions **200 × 200** pixels with a white canvas.

2. Click **Edit** on the menu bar, and then click **Insert**, and then **New Button**.
   Observe that the Button Editor opens.

3. Click the **Polygon** tool. In the Property inspector for the Polygon tool, enter these values: Shape: **Star**, Sides: **5**, and Angle: **40**. Set the fill color box to gray (**#666666**). Draw the star in the Up tab of the Button Editor by dragging your mouse over the workspace. In the Property inspector, enter the following values for the width, height, and coordinate boxes: W: **142**, H: **130**, X: **-70**, Y: **-60**. Press **Enter**. Set the stroke color to **transparent**.

4. Click the **Text** tool and set Font to **Arial**, size to **28**, style **bold**, and color to red (**#FF0000**) in the Property Inspector. Click over the star and type the text **Welcome**. Set the coordinate boxes to X: **-70** and Y: **-7**. Press **Enter**.

5. Click the **Over** tab and click the button labeled **Copy Up Graphic**.

   This copies the button you created in the Up tab into the Over tab.

6. Select the **star** using the Pointer tool, and set the fill color box in the Property inspector to color the star blue (**#3300FF**). Set the stroke color to **transparent**. Click the **Down** tab and click the **Copy Over Graphic** button. Click the **Over While Down** tab and click the button labeled **Copy Down Graphic**. Click **Done**.

7. In the Link text box on the Property inspector, type the Link **http://www.shop.com**.

8. Click the **Preview** tab in the workspace, and place your mouse over the button to see that the rollover works. Open the **Library** panel in Fireworks and observe that your button is named Button. Rename the button by double-clicking the text **Button** and then typing **welcome**. Click **OK**.

9. Save the file as **starbutton.png** in the ch3practice\images folder on your working drive.

Project 3-3

In this project, you create a three-button menu by duplicating the button from the previous exercise.

1. Open the file **starbutton.png** in Fireworks. It should be in the ch3practice\images folder of your working drive. Make sure the original tab is selected.

2. Change the size so that more buttons can fit. Click **Modify** on the menu bar, and then click **Canvas**, and then **Canvas size**. Enter a Width of **500** and Height of **200**. Click **OK**. Resize the working window so that you can see the whole canvas.

3. Click the **welcome** button on the canvas. In the Property Inspector, set the coordinates to X: **20** and Y: **40**, moving it to the left side of the canvas.

4. Open the Library panel and observe the button you created in the previous exercise stored there.

   You need to duplicate this button to create a consistent style for a small menu bar.

5. Click the **Options** menu on the upper-right side of the Library panel, and click **Duplicate** to copy the button. Double-click the name **welcome 1** and rename it **shop now**. Click **Edit**.

   The Button Editor for the shop now button opens.

6. In the Up tab in the Button Editor, double-click the text to make it available to editing. Modify the button text to read **Shop Now**. Click off of the text. When prompted to update text in the other button states, click **Yes**. Click **Done**.

7. From the Library panel, drag your shop now button to the center of the canvas. In the Button Property inspector, modify the Link that the button opens to **http://www.shop.com/catalog.htm**. Set the coordinates to X: **170** and Y: **40**, aligning the Shop Now button with the Welcome button. Press **Enter**.

8. Repeat Steps 5 through 7 to create a third button for your menu bar, naming the button **bargains**, typing **Bargains** for the text, and using the link **http://www.shop.com/bargains.htm**. Set the coordinates to X: **320** and Y: **40**, moving it to the right side of the canvas. Press **Enter**.

9. Select the **Preview** panel to view the menu as it will appear on your Web page.

10. Click **File** on the menu bar, and click **Export**. Export this file to the ch3practice folder on your working drive, naming the file **simplemenu.htm**. Make sure the Save as Type option is set to **HTML and Images**. At the bottom of the Export window, click the checkbox for **Put Images in Subfolder**. Click the **Browse** button and in the Select Folder dialog box, create the subfolder **ch3practice\ simplemenuimages**. Double-click the **simplemenuimages** folder, and then click **Select simplemenuimages** button. Click **Open**. You return to the Export window. Click **Save**.

11. Open the file **simplemenu.htm** in your Web browser, and observe that the rollovers work.

12. Click **File**, and then click **Save As** to save the working file as **simplemenu.png** in the ch3practice\images folder. Close the **simplemenu.png** file.

Project 3-4

In this project, you make the background of your simple menu transparent. Doing this ensures that if your Web page has a colored background, the background shows through. Otherwise, the white space around your menu appears on top of the colored Web page.

1. Open the file **simplemenu.png** in Fireworks. It should be in your ch3practice\images folder on your working drive.

2. Click **File** on the menu bar, and then click **Export Preview**. In the Export Preview window, click the first eyedropper (**Select Transparent Color**) in the far left of the window. Click the eyedropper on the canvas, and observe that the white space changes to checkered, indicating it is transparent. Click **Export**.

3. Export this file to the ch3practice folder on your working drive, naming the file **simplemenu2.htm**. Make sure the Save as Type option is set to **HTML and Images**. At the bottom of the Export window, click the **Put Images in Subfolder** checkbox. The simplemenuimages subfolder should be selected. Click **Save**. Save the **simplemenu2.png** file, and then close it.

4. Open the file **simplemenu2.htm** in Dreamweaver and set the background color to green (**#66FFCC**) to contrast with your buttons. Save the changes, open it in your Web browser, and observe that the rollovers work and that the menu's white space is transparent.

3

Project 3-5

In this project, you create a pop-up menu for some technology companies.

1. Open a new document in Fireworks that is **300** pixels wide and **300** pixels high with a white canvas.

2. Click the **Rectangle** tool on the Tools panel and draw a rectangle in the workspace. In the Property inspector, enter the following values in the width, height, and coordinate boxes: W: **140**, H: **40**, X: **30**, Y: **30**. Click the fill color box and select red (**#FF0000**). Click the stroke color box and select **Transparent**.

3. Click the **Text** tool. In the Property inspector, make the text **Arial**, size **18**, color white (**#FFFFFF**). Click on the red rectangle and type **Technology**. Press **Enter**, and then type **Companies**. Enter the following values in the coordinate boxes: X: **42** and Y: **29**. Press **Enter**.

4. Click the Slice tool and draw a slice around the rectangle. In the Slice Property inspector, enter the following values in the width, height, and coordinate boxes: W: **140**, H: **40**, X: **30**, Y: **30**. Press **Enter**.

5. Right-click and hold over the slice, and then click **Add Pop-up Menu**.

6. Double-click in the space below the Text column. A blank text area will appear. Type **Microsoft**. Press **Tab**. Now you are below the Link column. Type **http://www.microsoft.com**. Press **Tab** twice to advance to the next line.

7. Type in **Apple**. Press **Tab**. Now you are below the Link column again. Type **http://www.apple.com**. Press **Tab** twice to advance to the next line.

8. Type in **Macromedia**, press **Tab**, then type **http://www.macromedia.com**.

9. Click the **Appearance** tab at the top of the Pop-up Menu Editor. The tab will now have a highlight across the top. Click the **Appearance** tab again to open the panel. Click the **Image** option button (Vertical Menu should be selected already). Set the Font to **Arial, Helvetica, sans-serif**. In the Up state color boxes, set the text to white (**#FFFFFF**) and the cell to red (**#FF0000**). Select the style from the upper-left corner of the menu. Notice the preview of your button. In the Over state color boxes, set the text to white (**#FFFFFF**) and the cell to blue (**#000088**).

10. Click the Position tab at the top of the Pop-up Menu Editor to advance to the Position panel. Under Menu Position, click the second icon so your menu pops out of the bottom of your button. Click **Done**.

11. Press **F12** to preview the menu in your Web browser. Save this file as **techmenu.png** in your **ch3practice\images** folder on your working drive. Close the **techmenu.png** file.

Project 3-6

In this project, you create an animation of a circle and some text that is first spaced apart and then comes together as the animation plays.

1. Open a new Fireworks canvas that is **500** pixels wide and **200** pixels high.

2. Using the **Text** tool, type the text **Hello** in the upper-left corner of the canvas, making its color **black** and its font **Arial**, size **28**. Set the coordinates to X: **20**, Y: **5** in the Property inspector. Press **Enter**.

3. Click the **Ellipse** tool and draw a **circle** in the lower-right corner of the canvas. In the Property inspector, set the fill color box to red (**#FF0000**). Set the following values in the width, height, and coordinate boxes: W: **60**, H: **60**, X: **425**, Y: **130**. Press **Enter**.

   This is the first frame of your animation.

4. Open the **Layers** panel and double-click the layer you just created. Make sure that your layer is *not* shared across frames.

5. Press **Ctrl+D** to deselect the objects on the canvas. Convert the circle and text to symbols by selecting them, one at a time, with the Pointer tool and pressing the **F8** key. Rename the symbols **text** and **circle** and be sure to choose the Type: **Graphic**. Open the Library panel and see your objects added to the library, with the names you gave them.

6. Drag the circle symbol from the Library preview window onto the center of the canvas. In the Property inspector, set the coordinates to X: **215** and Y: **70**. Press **Enter**. Drag the text symbol from the Library preview window onto the center of the canvas on top of the circle. Set the coordinates to X: **215** and Y: **87**. Press **Enter**.

   The animation should float the text and the shape together, ending with the text on top of the shape.

7. Select both instances of circles, click **Modify** on the menu bar, point to **Symbol**, and then click **Tween Instances**. When the Tween Instances dialog box opens, select the number **5**, to create five images in between your circle instances. Click the **Distribute to Frames** checkbox to select it. Repeat this step for the text instances.

8. Play the animation using the controls in the lower-left corner of the workspace. Save this file as **animatedtext.png** in the ch3practice\images folder of your working drive.

CASE PROJECTS

1. Using Fireworks MX, draw a simple floor plan for a small house. Create an Image Map that takes visitors to each room of the house when they click the hotspot on the floor plan.

2. Slice an image of yourself into three sections. Link the top to your resume. Link the middle section to your favorite restaurant, and link the remaining section to a Web site showing where you went on your last vacation.

3. The Green Party hires you to help with its Web site. On the site, they want a fast, visual way for a visitor to gain information about registering to vote. Design a button for the Green Party home page that a visitor can click to learn about registering.

4. Create a horizontal menu of buttons for Bart's Whale Watching. The menu should consist of five selections for the Web site. Export the menu as a transparent .gif so that the background of the HTML document shows through. Edit the HTML document in Dreamweaver, and give it a colored background.

5. Create an animated logo for Bart's Whale Watching. Export the logo as a transparent .gif to the ch3practice\images folder on your working drive. Use Dreamweaver to incorporate the logo in the Web page you created in the previous Case Project.

3

4

WEB SITE MANAGEMENT

Creating and Structuring Sites and Navigation Strategies

In this chapter, you will:

♦ Create a Web site using the Dreamweaver MX site tools and Site Definition Wizard

♦ Design and build a Web site structure

♦ Understand the use of the Site map

♦ Design a navigation strategy for your site that makes it easy for visitors to find the information they need

---

In this chapter, you learn how to initialize, design, build, and maintain the directory structure for a Web site, using the Dreamweaver MX site definition and maintenance tools. These tools help you create and design the Web site, and provide you with a visual image of the Web site you create. As you make changes to the Web site organization, Dreamweaver MX propagates the changes throughout the site. You also learn how to develop a navigation strategy for your Web site and how to use Dreamweaver MX to make certain that pathnames to the elements (for example, pages, images, and sounds) are correct. In Chapter 6, you learn how to transfer this Web site structure and its contents to a Web server.

This chapter covers some of the theoretical ideas for effective Web site design, but if you want more information, we recommend that you read *Principles of Web Design, Second Edition*, also published by Course Technology.

CREATING A WEB SITE IN DREAMWEAVER MX

In this section, you create a Web site from scratch, using the Dreamweaver MX Site panel and Site Definition Wizard. These tools help you design and organize your site by:

- Displaying a Site map to help you visualize your Web site structure and change it

- Providing a link checker that identifies broken links and unused elements, such as graphics

- Maintaining the relationship between elements on the Web site by updating the link pathnames when you drag-and-drop files to move their site location

- Allowing you to create links from the Design window using the Site panel

- Providing check-in and check-out functions to limit file updates to the remote version of the Web site to one developer at a time; these configuration management functions work just like a library system—when one Web developer checks out a page to update it, other Web developers involved in the same project cannot work on it until the first developer checks it back in, thus preventing developers from overwriting one another's changes to a file

Understanding the Uses of the Site Panel

The Site panel in Dreamweaver MX provides access to a complete set of site management functions both for the local site you develop in this book, and for a remote version of a site on a server you may develop later. Some of these functions are also available from the Site command on the Dreamweaver MX menu bar.

Figure 4-1 shows the Site panel, which has buttons, drop-down lists, and drop-down menus. Most of the buttons are for managing the remote server. The Expand/Collapse button on the far right ▣ is the exception. If you select a Web site in the Site panel and click this button, a larger split window can display both the Site map and a site folder and file list.

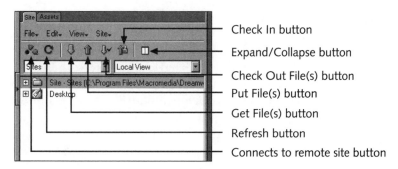

Check In button

Expand/Collapse button

Check Out File(s) button

Put File(s) button

Get File(s) button

Refresh button

Connects to remote site button

4

Figure 4-1   The Site panel

The sites list pop-up menu list on the left of the Site panel provides access to all your defined Web sites. The drop-down list on the right lets you display the site files for the local site (Local view), the remote site (Remote view), or a test site (Testing view), or a hierarchical map (Map view) of the site within the Site panel. When you view the menus on the Site panel, commands that are not available are dimmed out. As in other Windows programs, only commands you can use appear in black type. Available commands are based on your Web site configuration, the document you have open in the document editing window, and other factors. The following discussion of the Site panel focuses on those features you use in developing a local version of your Web site.

The Site panel toolbar contains a range of items that give you full control over site management. Figure 4-2 shows the File menu. The items on this menu let you create and manage files within the Web site, preview them in the Web browsers in which you want to test them, and check hyperlinks to be sure they are correctly configured.

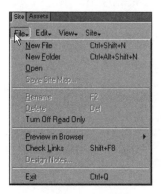

Figure 4-2   Site panel File menu

The Edit menu provides typical file editing commands (such as Cut and Paste), tools for finding and selecting files on both the local and remote sites, a command for duplicating Web sites, and tools for managing the check-in and check-out of files.

Figure 4-3 shows the Site panel View menu. The items on this menu let you configure the view of the Site map and file list that you see in the Site panel. The Refresh command works the same as the Refresh button ⟨image⟩ located at the bottom of the Site panel. This command refreshes the display of the local and remote directory lists. Other commands allow you to hide files and their hyperlinks when you want to focus on a subset of the site, show or hide hidden files and dependent files, display page titles rather than filenames, change the layout of the Site map, display either the Site map or site file structure, and change the number of columns displayed in the Site map.

Figure 4-3   Site panel View menu

The Site panel Site menu in Figure 4-4 provides commands for managing the characteristics of the site, managing the files within the local site (check-in and check-out), and retrieving (Get) and saving (Put) files on the remote site. Other commands allow you to check the hyperlinks on the entire site to be sure that they are properly configured, reconfigure broken links, change the designation of the site home page, and export and import the site settings (for example, to back up the Web site).

Creating the La Bonne Cuisine Web Site

Dreamweaver MX provides a new Site Definition Wizard to set up your Web site, but you can also use its advanced Site Definition dialog box to finish site configuration. In this part of the chapter, you use the wizard to create and initially define the La Bonne Cuisine Web site and the Advanced tab of the Site Definition dialog box to configure the Web site characteristics further. Because this Web site will grow and become more complex as you learn more about Dreamweaver, you need to develop the Web site and design a site layout. This helps you track the different categories of information on the Web site as well as the different types of multimedia assets that you add to make the Web site more attractive and useful.

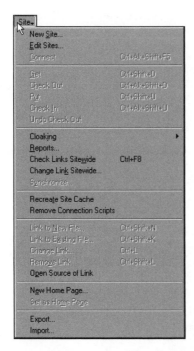

Figure 4-4   Site panel Site menu

 After you define your Web site, be sure that you save new HTML pages and other elements in the correct site directories and identify them as part of a specific Web site. Dreamweaver is set up to manage content within a Web site structure and will prompt you to save the files in one of the directories in the Web site. You will find that developing pages from within the Site panel makes managing the Web site much easier and prevents annoying warning messages that prompt you to save files within the Web site.

The detailed steps that follow guide you through the creation of a Web site to store the files you create for La Bonne Cuisine. You define a Web site for La Bonne Cuisine as a subdirectory nested inside the Sites directory you created in Chapter 1. The Site Definition Wizard helps you create and configure the Web site.

To create the site:

1. Start Dreamweaver and open the Site panel (press function key **F8**), if it is not already open. Create a nested folder named **lbc** within the Sites folder.

2. Click **Site** on the Dreamweaver or Site panel menu bar, and then click **New Site** (review Figure 4-4 for the location of the site functions on this sub-menu). When the Site Definition dialog box opens, click the **Basic** tab to use the Site Definition Wizard. Dreamweaver then prompts you step-by-step for information about your Web site. Type **La Bonne Cuisine** into the input box on the first screen, as shown in Figure 4-5. Then click the **Next** button.

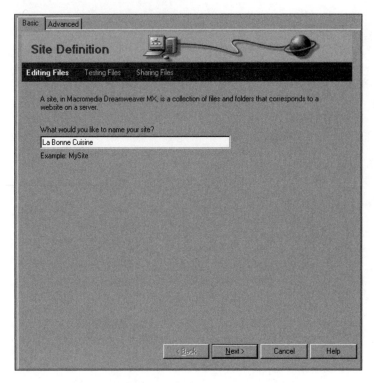

Figure 4-5   Site Definition Wizard

3. On the Editing Files, Part 2 screen, click the **No, I do not want to use a server technology** option button. Then click **Next**.

4. On the Editing Files, Part 3 screen, click the first option button, browse to the lbc folder inside the Sites folder that you set up in Step 1, and then double-click it. Then click the **Select** button. Click the **Next** button to go to the next screen. If Dreamweaver provides the warning message shown in Figure 4-6, click **OK**. If you do not want to see this message again, check the **Don't warn me again.** checkbox before you click **OK**.

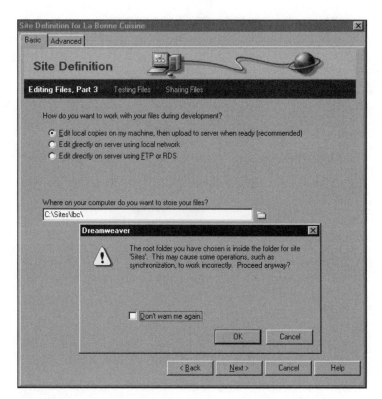

Figure 4-6   Site Definition, Editing Files, Part 3

5. On the Sharing Files screen, select **None** in the drop-down list; you will be working only on the local Web site in this book. Click **Next**.

6. Figure 4-7 shows the feedback screen when you finish the basic site setup. Click the **Done** button. You should now see the La Bonne Cuisine site in the Site panel.

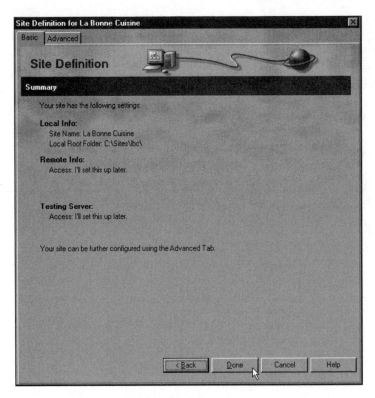

Figure 4-7　Site Definition feedback screen

DESIGNING A WEB SITE STRUCTURE

In earlier chapters of this book, you worked on initial versions of home pages and graphics for the La Bonne Cuisine Web site you just created. Now you can use Dreamweaver to help you design, develop, and manage the entire Web site and its related content.

Note that most Web site developers use a set of naming standards that are influenced by the naming standards in their particular work environment. For example, some Internet Service Providers will not allow files that have uppercase letters in their names, and some operating systems (for example UNIX) treat upper- and lowercase letters as different characters. Thus, many Web site developers do not use uppercase letters in filenames. Also, because browsers may interpret spaces between words differently, your results will be more consistent if you do not use spaces in filenames. Finally, companies frequently set up naming standards for their information systems that developers must follow. Therefore, it is important that you consciously try to use naming standards as you develop the content for your Web site. Meaningful names are as important in HTML development as they are in other types of programming.

Defining a Directory Structure

Before you develop extensive content for your Web site, you will need to define a directory structure for the site by setting up a group of folders. Each folder will hold a different category of elements for the Web site. If a Web site has only a few pages, you *could* place all the files in the **root directory** or top-level directory or folder for the site (Sites\lbc is the root directory for this site), perhaps using a second folder to hold the graphic images. However, your site will not have just a few pages. Because you will be adding many pages and multimedia elements to your La Bonne Cuisine Web site, it is best to design a hierarchical directory structure to manage your site content. To determine what categories of content the Web site will hold, we will review customer requirements for the Web site.

 Note that you should always develop a design for your Web site so that you do not end up with a disorganized mess! Dreamweaver's Web site management tools make it easy to define a directory structure for a Web site before you develop too much content. Before you design the structure of your Web site, you should first think about how to organize the site's content logically.

Hierarchy of Folders

Dreamweaver MX helps you structure a Web site by creating a hierarchy of folders for the different categories of information and files. For example, you might create one folder to hold product information and a separate folder to hold services information. Frequently, Web site developers create at least one separate folder to store the image files for the site. Some developers name this subdirectory images; others call it assets, particularly if it contains more than one type of multimedia file.

If you create numerous multimedia files, you may decide to group each type of multimedia file in a separate folder (for example, images, video, sounds) nested within the assets folder. If assets are shared across the Web site among pages in different folders, the assets folder is often located at the root directory. If assets for each section of the Web site are unique, then each section may have its own assets folder nested within it.

As you can see, you must make choices when designing a Web site, and it is easier to make them before the Web site content becomes very large. One advantage of Dreamweaver MX is that it provides the Site panel, which makes it easier for you to visualize and carry out your Web site design.

The La Bonne Cuisine Main Page

The most complex version of the La Bonne Cuisine main page contains images and hyperlinks to other pages that provide the viewer with information about the organization and its services. One page (aboutlbc.htm) tells about the company, and the others cover several types of services, including food consulting (consulting.htm), excursions (tour.htm), and culinary training (training.htm). Although you created hyperlinks for each of these pages on your La Bonne Cuisine main page, you did not actually create the pages themselves. In reality each of these topics probably requires multiple HTML pages, and may require its own folder in the Web site. It will be much easier to manage and enhance the growing Web site if each category of pages resides in its own folder.

Before deciding how to group the Web pages on your site, you need to examine the customer's ideas and requirements in Table 4-1. These requirements are based on ones that Mary Smith, the owner of La Bonne Cuisine, prepared for her Web site. Mary Smith is a typical small business owner who has lots of experience in her area of expertise and would like to use Internet technology to promote her business. You will use the information in Table 4-1 as you build the La Bonne Cuisine Web site.

Table 4-1   Topics for the La Bonne Cuisine Web Site

Category	Customer Ideas and Requirements
The Owner's Background	Holds Culinary Degrees from Scotland and France, and has used travel and work experiences to: • Own and run a cooking school • Train chefs in a professional chef's school • Work for 2 major manufacturers in product development, and menu and recipe ideas • Consult with restaurants and small business owners • Train sales and marketing people in food—how to eat it, and how to sell it • Teach children and adults about healthy eating and that food is fun
Restaurant Consulting and Product Development	La Bonne Cuisine can offer restaurant owners, managers, and chefs: • New menu ideas • Trendy recipes that fit into menus • Training of kitchen staff on techniques • Manual writing services La Bonne Cuisine can offer assistance to large food companies, small manufacturers, bakeries, and delis to create and launch products such as: • Frozen desserts, cookies, entrees, soups, and sauces • Shelf-stable sauces, salad dressings, and preserves • Deli items • Baked goods
Entertaining and Culinary Training	La Bonne Cuisine can offer knowledgeable assistance with French, Italian, Californian, Mexican, Asian, and Middle Eastern foods and cooking techniques; La Bonne Cuisine can improve your entertaining and culinary skills by: • Helping you plan meals and events in your home or on our premises, if you live in Southern California • Providing shopping and cooking assistance so you can plan and cook for your events at your convenience

Table 4-1   Topics for the La Bonne Cuisine Web Site (continued)

Category	Customer Ideas and Requirements
Culinary Explorations	La Bonne Cuisine can offer specialty tours of the markets, agricultural areas, homes, and restaurants of Southern California, including: • Visits to unique areas like Little Saigon, herb farms, Mexican markets, and fishing areas where the Mediterranean influence still exists • Wine and food tours in California and other parts of the world

Table 4-1 lists the types of services offered by La Bonne Cuisine. Placing the pages for each of these services in its own folder (consulting, training, and tour) would be a logical way to proceed. In addition, the Web site should have a contact folder to hold files containing information about La Bonne Cuisine, the owner, the Web site, and other general information. Also storing the images and other multimedia content for the Web site in an assets folder makes sense. The assets folder will have subfolders for each type of multimedia content (images, movies, and sounds).

Hierarchical Organization of the Site

Web site design requires some basic decisions about the hierarchical organization of the site, or the number of levels of subfolders within subfolders. Because each level of folder nesting adds complexity to the Web site naming structure by adding to the URL length, you should adopt a simple, straightforward, and logical design that allows the grouping of categories of information. The next set of steps helps you set up the design for La Bonne Cuisine using the Dreamweaver MX Site panel. When you finish these steps, the Site panel should look like Figure 4-8.

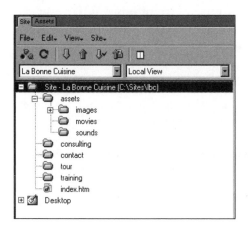

Figure 4-8   Directory structure for La Bonne Cuisine in the Site panel

To work with the Site panel:

1. Start Dreamweaver MX and press the function key **F8** to open the Site panel, if it is not already open. Select **La Bonne Cuisine** from the sites list pop-up menu.

2. The top-level folder for the site is called \Sites\lbc, and the name of the site appears as La Bonne Cuisine on the toolbar. To add the folder for consulting content in this Web site, highlight **\Sites\lbc**, click **File** on the Site panel menu bar, and then click **New Folder**. (You can also do this same task by right-clicking on the folder and selecting **New folder** on the context menu, or by pressing the shortcut key sequence **Ctrl+Alt+Shift+N**.) Type **consulting** over untitled to change the folder name.

3. Highlight the **\Sites\lbc** folder again, before you create each remaining folder, to be sure that they are all nested within the top-level folder or root directory.

4. Repeat Steps 2 and 3 to create the rest of the folders for the Web site: **training**, **tour**, **contact**, and **assets**, as shown in Figure 4-8.

5. The Web site will have three types of multimedia content (images, movies, and sound files), so having separate folders for each type is helpful. To create these subfolders within the assets folder, highlight the **assets** folder, and create the **images**, **movies**, and **sounds** folders within it, as shown in Figure 4-8.

6. Start **Windows Explorer**, copy the following image files from the Chapter4\data\images folder, and paste them into the **\Sites\lbc\assets\images** folder: **aboutusbutton.gif, aboutusover.gif, consultingbutton.gif, consultingover.gif, lamap.gif, lbclogotrans.gif, navbar1c1.gif, navbar1c2.gif, navbar1c3.gif, navbar1c4.gif, navbar2c1.gif, navbar2c2.gif, navbar2c3.gif, navbar2c4.gif, toursbutton.gif, toursover.gif, trainingbutton.gif**, and **trainingover.gif**. If you click the + (plus sign) to the left of the images folder to expand it, you can see the image files listed.

Creating the Home Page

Some Web servers show the directory list for a Web site when the URL for a folder is entered without any specific page name following it. Because most Web site owners prefer to keep their file and directory lists confidential, they name their default home page index.html or index.htm (unless an Internet Server Provider has chosen a different default name). This page appears in a browser if no specific page name is entered. For example, if you type *http://www.myworld.com* (as in Figure 4-9) in your browser, you do not see the Web site directory list, but a page named index.htm. Typing *http://www.myworld.com/index.htm* gives you the same result, as shown in Figure 4-10.

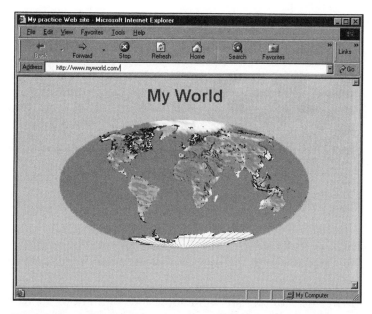

Figure 4-9   The index.htm page for a site displays without a page name in the URL

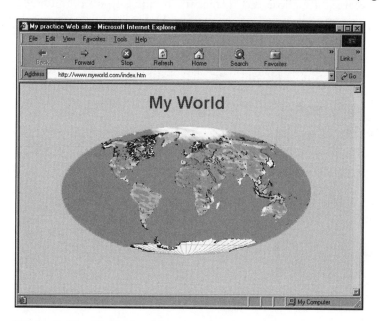

Figure 4-10   The index.htm page for the same site displays with a page name in the URL

When you define your Web site in the Site Definition dialog box, Dreamweaver MX assumes that a page with the name index.html or index.htm is the main page for the Web site. Dreamweaver MX actually looks for pages within the Web site in that order.

To prevent users from seeing the directory structure for your Web site, you have to create a page such as index.html or index.htm.

In the following set of steps you copy and paste index.htm into the top-level directory of the Web site you just created. You then open the Define Sites dialog box to identify index.htm as the home page for your new Web site. In fact, you should observe that Dreamweaver MX assumes index.htm is the home page because it has one of the default home page names that Web servers recognize (as explained above). When you select Site Map Layout in the Define Sites dialog box, Dreamweaver MX automatically inserts index.htm as the home page.

To work with index.htm:

1. Use Windows Explorer to copy **index.htm** from the Chapter4\data folder into the **Sites\lbc** folder.

2. If necessary, start Dreamweaver MX, open the Site panel, and select the **La Bonne Cuisine** site in the sites list pop-up menu, if it is not already selected.

3. Although Dreamweaver usually will choose index.htm from the root directory of the site as the home page for your site, it is prudent to check that Dreamweaver MX chose the correct file by looking on the Site Map Layout category on the Advanced tab of the Site Definition dialog box. Click **Edit Site** in the Site menu in the Site panel.

4. In the Edit Sites dialog box, click **La Bonne Cuisine** to select it if necessary, as shown in Figure 4-11, and then click **Edit**.

Figure 4-11   The Edit Sites dialog box

5. Select the **Advanced** tab of the Site Definition dialog box. The Local Info window in the Category list box is the default selection. All you need to do in the Local Info window is verify that the Refresh Local File List Automatically and Enable Cache checkboxes are selected, to ensure that Dreamweaver MX keeps your file list up-to-date as you develop your Web site.

6. Next, click **Site Map Layout** in the Category list box to open the Site Map Layout window, which is shown in Figure 4-12. Check to be sure that Dreamweaver inserted C:\Sites\lbc\index.htm into the text box. If not, browse to that file, click the filename to select it, and then click **Open** to make it the home page for your Web site.

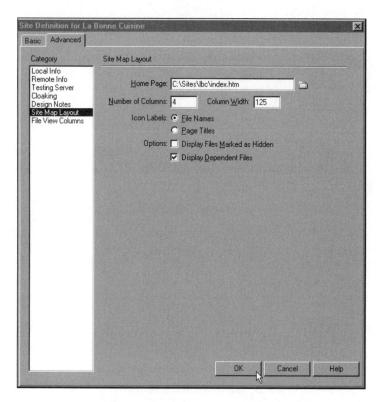

Figure 4-12   Defining the Web site home page

7. Set Number of Columns to **4**, and set column width at **125** pixels. Click the **File Names** option button and then check the **Display Dependent Files** checkbox to display names of the hyperlinked pages and graphics in the Site map. Click **OK** to save.

The default configuration of setting Number of Columns to 200 displays the dependent files in a single row, which is hard to view. You can also display all the dependent files in a single column by setting columns to 1.

8. Finish the process by clicking the **Done** button in the Edit Sites dialog box.

THE SITE MAP

When you set up your Web site, the site configuration included Refresh Local File List Automatically and Enable Cache. As a result, the Site map immediately reflects any changes made to your Web site structure. At this point, the index.htm page for your Web site is at the top of your Web site structure, and the Site map will show the hyperlinks to other pages and to multimedia elements.

Viewing the Expanded Site Map and Files

The following steps show you how to view the current Site map and file lists for La Bonne Cuisine.

To view the Site map:

1. Open Dreamweaver MX if it is not already open. If the Site panel is not visible, press the **F8** function key to open it. Select the **La Bonne Cuisine** site, if necessary.

2. Click the **Expand/Collapse** button 🔲 on the Site panel.

3. The expanded Site panel provides the split view of the local site and the site structure, as shown in Figure 4-13. In order to see this view, you need to click the **Site Map** button 📌 and then choose **Map and Files** on the pop-up menu. The Site map appears with the configuration you set up in the previous section (4 columns, column width of 125).

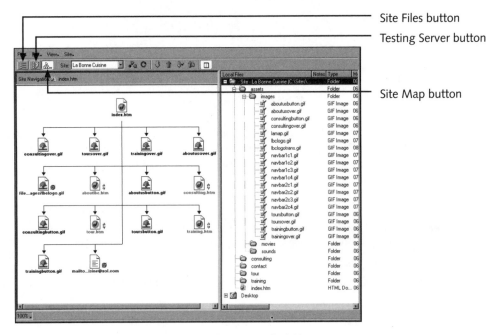

Site Files button

Testing Server button

Site Map button

Figure 4-13   The La Bonne Cuisine Site map and files

Notice that Figure 4-13 shows index.htm at the top level of the Web site structure. As you look at your own Site map, you can see that the color-coding of the filenames indicates the status of the dependent files. The hyperlink that points to the fictional e-mail address is blue, and the hyperlinks that point to nonexistent internal pages are red. Dreamweaver MX does not check to see whether external hyperlinks are valid or not, but it does look for hyperlinked files on the Web site. After you set up the internal hyperlinks correctly, the color coding will change from red to black. In addition, the Site map displays graphics files on the index.htm page because you checked Display Dependent Files when you defined the Site map characteristics in the previous section. If you did not check that feature, the multimedia file links would not appear on the Site map.

Correcting Broken Hyperlinks

In your site, you already know you have **dead links** (incorrect pathnames for hyperlinked files, which Dreamweaver calls **broken links**) because they are red. Dreamweaver also provides a feature to check for broken links and for **orphaned files** (files that are not being linked to by any of the pages in the Web site). You can fix broken links by correcting the pathnames so that they point to the correct files. This is a manual process that can become tedious after a while. Fortunately, after you set up the site structure, Dreamweaver MX provides the Check Links Sitewide command to help you maintain the correct hyperlinks throughout the rest of your project. You can run this command from the expanded Site panel menu bar; from the Site panel, by clicking Site, and then clicking Check Links Sitewide; or by pressing the Ctrl+F8 key sequence:

Be sure that you are working from the Site map or from a saved HTML page within the Web site before you check for broken links. If you check for broken links from the unsaved "untitled.htm" page that initially opens when you open Dreamweaver MX, a dialog box appears with the message "Your document must be saved under the root folder of a defined site. Define a new site containing the folder this file is in, or save the file under the root of an existing site." If you get this message, click Cancel and run the procedure from a page that is part of the Web site.

To correct a broken link for a missing HTML file, you can create a **placeholder** HTML page that has no content but that is in the folder to which the link points. The Site panel opened to Local view makes this process easy. After you have created placeholder pages, you can either open the index.htm page and correct the hyperlinks there or complete the task within the expanded Site panel, open to Map view.

To identify and correct the broken links in Dreamweaver MX:

1. Open the Site panel for La Bonne Cuisine, and display **Local View**. Press the **Ctrl+F8** key combination to check the links.

2. Dreamweaver MX displays the broken links, external links, and orphaned files in the Link Checker panel, as shown in Figure 4-14. Choose **Broken Links** from the Show list box, if necessary. The status bar at the bottom of the Link Checker panel indicates the number of broken links. Taking care of the broken links will remedy some of the orphaned files, but not the image files you copied into the images folder earlier in the chapter. These image files are orphans because you have not yet inserted them into a Web page.

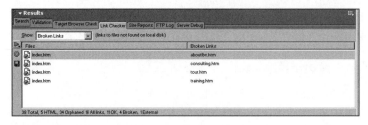

Figure 4-14   The Link Checker panel

3. To create a placeholder HTML file to correct the broken link to the first missing HTML page on the Site map, aboutlbc.htm, right-click the **contact** folder in the Site panel and select **New File**. Change the filename from untitled.htm to **aboutlbc.htm**.

4. Repeat this step to set up placeholder files for **consulting.htm** in the consulting folder, **tour.htm** in the tour folder, and **training.htm** in the training folder.

5. If necessary, click the **Expand/Collapse** button ⬜ in the Site panel to open the expanded Site panel. Click the **Site Map** button 🔠 and select **Map and File**. Right-click the **aboutlbc.htm** broken link in the Site map and click **Change Link**.

6. In the Select HTML File dialog box, open the **contact** folder and select **aboutlbc.htm** so that it appears in the File name text box, as shown in Figure 4-15. Click **OK**. If Dreamweaver MX displays the Update Files dialog box, click the **Update** button to update the hyperlinks. The broken link is mended and the filename on the Site map changes from red to black. Click **OK** to close the Select HTML file dialog box.

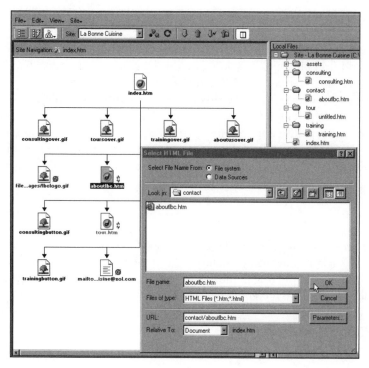

Figure 4-15   Fixing a broken link

7. Run the Check Links Sitewide procedure again (**Ctrl+F8**). There should now be three broken links rather than four.

8. Fix the remaining broken links by locating them on your Site map by their red color. Then create hyperlinks to the appropriate placeholder files you created in Step 4. Run the Check Links Sitewide procedure until there are no more broken links.

9. Save index.htm in the lbc folder. View in the browser to make sure your hyperlinks work.

The URL at the bottom of the dialog box in Figure 4-15 indicates that the address for the file is relative to the document index.htm. Relative addressing is important when you transfer the local Web site structure to a Web server, because Dreamweaver MX maintains the directory structure of your local site on the Web server.

WEB SITE NAVIGATION STRATEGY

The site structure you developed earlier in this chapter makes it easier for you to organize your work and find elements as you maintain the site. On the other hand, Web site navigation is something that you organize for the people who visit and use your Web site. Your objective is to make it easy for them to find the information they need, as well as the information your client wants them to find. That means that you have to design a navigation plan that provides enough information to be useful, but not so much information that the site is cluttered, and the visitor confused. Make your navigation design motto: "Maximize Access, Minimize Clicks!" To meet this motto, you'll need to test your Web site navigation by viewing the Web site as visitors will see it.

 Try to design a navigation scheme that will be easy and intuitive for your Web site visitors to follow. Visitors need to be able to locate related information from a Web page (e.g., information about local food tours), but they also need to be able to jump easily to other parts of the Web site that may have different information (e.g., information about product development). Hyperlinks make it easy to go from anywhere to anywhere on a Web site.

Create a Navigation Plan

The home page sets the standard for navigation on the rest of the Web site. Often it includes a menu page that indicates what is available on the rest of the Web site. However, the home page may or may not be the first page that visitors see. If they simply type in the URL for your Web site without typing any specific HTML page, they begin their visit at index.htm, the page you designated as your home page in Dreamweaver MX. But because visitors may jump into the middle of your Web site from another site, such as a search engine, you need to think about navigation on every page. If they do enter the Web site somewhere in the middle, they should be able to find their way to the Web site home page and other significant pages. Navigation links set expectations about what visitors will find. Navigation links that fulfill visitor expectations increase the usability of your Web site.

Types of Hyperlinks

Navigation links can be text or graphics. The two types of hyperlinks that will be part of your navigation structure are **structural navigation links** (for example, menu bars, navigation bars, image maps, home page buttons) and **associative links** (usually words or phrases in the middle of a body of text that link to other parts of the Web site). Structural navigation links can be text or graphical, and associative links are usually text. Both types of link create visitor expectations. Be sure that your text or graphic link means something in terms of what visitors can expect to find when they jump to the linked information.

Structural navigation links frequently are repeated on all the pages in the Web site, although they can be limited to pages in a particular section of the Web site. Consistency is important for structural navigation links, because visitors find navigating much easier if navigation links such as menu bars are in the same location on every page. Graphics that you use for navigation should also be consistent and meaningful to the visitor. For example, visitors expect that an arrow pointing left will take them back and an arrow pointing up will take them to the top of the page.

You can set up navigation to jump to another Web site, to another page, to a particular place on another page defined by a named anchor tag, or to a particular place on the current page defined by a named anchor tag. **Named anchors** are place markers for a particular area in a document. They make jumping to a particular part of a page possible, as well as jumping to a particular place on another page. This is especially useful on longer pages that present a lot of detailed information, for example, in a glossary of terms on a technical page.

Web site designers often design a navigation strategy that enables visitors to take a tour of the entire site or a subsection of the site as well as jump to any page on the site that interests them. Site navigation has to work for visitors whether they enter a Web site at the home page or somewhere in the middle of the site.

The Use of White Space

Consider the use of white space, which is one or more blank areas that allow visitors to rest their eyes so that they can comprehend the rest of the information on the page. Blank or white areas work especially well to group related categories of information. For example, the site map of the Apple Computer Web site (*www.apple.com/find/sitemap.html*) uses white space to group categories of information on a very large, complex site. Visitors might easily become confused by so many hyperlinks if the links were not divided into categories, with white space separating and framing each category.

Location of Important Information

Consider Web page design when you are laying out your navigation strategy. The top of the page should have meaningful information on it so that visitors do not have to wait for all the graphics to download before they know where they are. If you use a graphical navigation bar or elements, be sure to include <ALT> tags so that visitors who are visually impaired or who have graphics turned off in their browsers may use the tag information to help them navigate. Remember: Visitors may leave your Web site with a click of the mouse if they have to wait too long to view meaningful information!

Text Navigation Links

Wherever you use text for navigation, think about what visitors will expect. The default standard color for an unvisited hyperlink is blue. If you change the color scheme for your Web page, making unvisited hyperlinks some variation of blue is a good idea because visitors can quickly and easily recognize the text as a navigation link. To most people, blue underlined text on a page indicates a hyperlink. Blue underlined text that is not hyperlinked text confuses people because it is not what they expect.

 You can use text hyperlinks to build a menu or act as associative links internally embedded in the text. The first navigation structure for a new Web site is often mocked up with text navigation links that can be replaced later with graphical navigation links.

Text Structural Navigation Links

Some Web sites simply use strings of hyperlink text phrases separated by a delimiter, such as brackets, for their structural navigation links. A text menu bar is easy to create, and easy to change, because it is simply text. Visitors who turn off graphics mode in their browsers can read it; other visitors can read it before graphics download.

In the next set of steps, you create a new text menu bar and fill in some details on one of your placeholder pages. You work from the Site panel, an advantage because Dreamweaver MX manages the file locations! In addition, you use the Point-to-File icon on the Property inspector to link to a file in the Site Files view of the Site panel, a process that lets you set up links quickly with a graphical tool.

To work from the Site panel:

1. Start Dreamweaver MX, if it is not already running. Open the Site panel (function key **F8**), and select **La Bonne Cuisine**, and **Local View**. Double-click the icon for the page **aboutlbc.htm** in the contact folder, to open it for editing in Design view.

2. Modify the Page properties by pressing the **Ctrl+J** key combination. In the title textbox, type **About La Bonne Cuisine**. Leave the color of the hyperlinks alone, but change the text color to a dark red (**#CC0033**). Save the page modifications by clicking **OK**.

3. Type the page heading, **About La Bonne Cuisine**, at the top of the page. Place the insertion point anywhere in the text. Open the Property inspector if it is not already open (**Ctrl+F3**), and click **Heading 1** in the Format drop-down list. Center the heading by clicking the **Align Center** button.
   To save the page, press the **Ctrl+S** key combination.

4. Now you create a prototype text navigation bar, which will work well enough until you decide to replace it with a graphical navigation bar later. On the line below the heading, type the following, which is a shortened version of the hyperlink strings that are used on the menu bar on the home page for the site (**index.htm**):

   [about us][food consulting][culinary excursions][culinary training]

5. Highlight this line and change the properties of the string to **Heading 4** in the Format drop-down list on the Property inspector.

6. In the Site panel, expand the consulting, contact, and tour folders by clicking the **+** buttons to the left of each folder. You then can view the pages inside the folders to which you will create links.

7. Highlight the words **food consulting** on the text navigation bar on the aboutlbc.htm page. Click and hold the **Point-to-File** icon in the Property inspector, and drag the pointer to the file **consulting.htm** in the consulting folder in the Site panel. When you drop it, you set up the link, as shown in Figure 4-16. Close the file.

8. Repeat to create a hyperlink from **culinary excursions** to **tour.htm** in the tour folder, and from **culinary training** to **training.htm** in the training folder. Save the file and view it in a browser. Close the file.

Point-to-File icon

Figure 4-16   Defining a link using the Point-to-File icon

Text Associative Links

One attraction of the Web is that it is possible to hyperlink related information from within the document content. For example, if you mention a specialized term in the middle of a paragraph, a text associative hyperlink can take the visitor to another page that defines the term in more detail. Visitors who already understand the term can keep reading.

Be sure that the text that you underline for the associative hyperlink describes what visitors can expect to find. Be aware that too many associative links in text may distract the visitor and clutter the page.

To create associative links, and to fill in some of the details on one of your place-holder pages:

1. Start Dreamweaver MX, if necessary. Open the Site panel, and then open the document **aboutlbc.htm** for editing. Place the insertion point two lines below the text navigation bar. Then in the Property inspector, if necessary, change the format style to **Paragraph** and change the text alignment to **Align Left** ≣. Type this line: **If you enjoy food, our consulting services are here to meet your needs!**

2. Press **Enter** to go to a new line, and click the **Unordered List** button ≣ in the Property inspector. In the Property inspector, change the text alignment to **Align Left** ≣. Type in the following bullet points, which are based on the information in Table 4-1:

   - **Restaurant Consulting–Provide menu ideas and recipes for restaurants, train kitchen staff, and prepare written manuals**

   - **Culinary Explorations–Offer food tours of ethnic neighborhoods in Southern California, or more extensive food tours in other countries**

   - **Product Development–Develop products for food manufacturers, bakeries, or restaurants**

   - **Entertaining and Culinary Training–Teach people how to plan parties, including shopping, food preparation, and assistance to ensure the party is a success**

3. Highlight the text **Restaurant Consulting** at the beginning of the first bullet point. Click and hold the **Point-to-File** icon 🌐 in the Property inspector. Drag the pointer to the file **consulting.htm** in the consulting folder in the Site panel. This action creates a hyperlink in the same way you did in the previous exercise.

4. Select the text **Culinary Explorations** in the second bullet point. Create a hyperlink to **tour.htm**. Select the text **Product Development** in the third bullet point, and create a hyperlink to **consulting.htm**. Select the text **Entertaining and Culinary Training** in the last bullet point and create a hyperlink to **training.htm**.

5. Save the page and test it in your browser to ensure that the hyperlinks work.

Named Anchors

Named anchors can be very useful in pages that are longer than a single screen. You can use them to jump to the top of the current page or to jump to a definition on a page that has a lot of detailed information. In the following steps you will type the name and address of La Bonne Cuisine at the bottom of the aboutlbc.htm page, and then create a hyperlink to jump to a named anchor at the top of the page.

To work with a named anchor:

1. Start Dreamweaver MX and open **aboutlbc.htm**, if it is not already open. Place your insertion point to the right of the last bullet item (the one that begins "Entertaining and Culinary Training"), and press the **Enter** key to go to a new line. Click the **Unordered List** button in the Property inspector to end the bulleted list. Center the line by clicking **Align Center** in the Property inspector.

2. Insert a horizontal rule on the page by clicking **Horizontal Rule** on the **Common tab** of the **Insert** bar. Next, deselect the horizontal rule by clicking to the right of it, and then press **Enter** to create a new line.

3. Type in the contact information for La Bonne Cuisine on the next four lines: **2395 Lake St., La Verne, CA 91750, 909-123-4567, Contact La Bonne Cuisine**. Highlight these four lines and center-align them.

4. To create a named anchor in Dreamweaver MX, scroll to the top of the page, and put the insertion point before the heading, La Bonne Cuisine. Click **Named Anchor** on the Common tab of the Insert bar.

5. Type **top** in the text box that pops up, and then click **OK**.

6. You should see a Named Anchor icon to the left of the heading, as shown in Figure 4-17. If you do not see it, click **View** on the Dreamweaver workspace menu bar, then click **Invisible Elements**. Save the page.

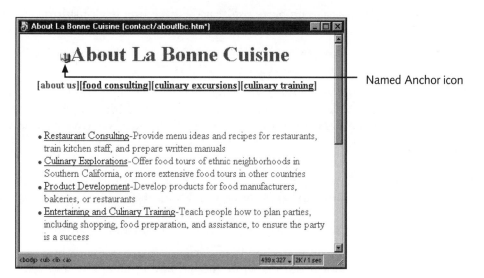

Figure 4-17   Named Anchor icon identifies the page top

7. To link to a named anchor on the same page, scroll down to the bottom of the page. Type **top** on the line below the contact information. Highlight the word **top**, then type **#top** in the Link text box in the Property inspector. Save the file and then test in your browser window. During the test, make sure that the browser window is small so that you see the scroll bar. Click the word **top**; the window should jump to the top of the page.

To create and place named anchors and link to them from a hyperlink on another page, you use the Point-to-File icon ⊕ to create the hyperlink to the second page, and then type the pound sign (#) followed by the named anchor link at the end of the hyperlinked filename.

To work with a named anchor:

1. Open the Site panel, and then double-click **consulting.htm** in the consulting folder to open that placeholder page. Type **Consulting Services** on the first line of the page. Click anywhere inside this text and apply the following formatting in the Property inspector: **Heading 1** format style and **Align Center**.

2. Press the **Enter** key to go to a new line. Change the format style to **Heading 2**, but do not change the center alignment. Type **Restaurant Consulting** on this line, and **Product Development** on the line below it. Make sure that both of these new lines maintain the Heading 2 format style and center alignment.

3. Change the page properties so that the page title is **Consulting Services**, and the text color is dark red (**#CC0033**). Save the page.

4. Place the insertion point to the left of the word **Restaurant** on the second line and create a named anchor called **restaurant**.

5. Add the following three items, in a left-aligned, unordered list, below the heading Restaurant Consulting: **Provide menu ideas and recipes for restaurants**; **Train your kitchen staff**; **Prepare written manuals**. Highlight these lines and select format style **Heading 3** in the Property inspector.

6. Place the insertion point just to the left of the heading Product Development. Click the **Horizontal Rule** button ▦ on the Common tab of the Insert bar, as shown in Figure 4-18. If the Common tab is not visible, you have to click the expander arrow on the Insert bar (shown in Figure 4-18) to open it.

7. Click the **Named Anchor** button ⚓ on the Common tab to insert a named anchor, **product**, before the heading Product Development.

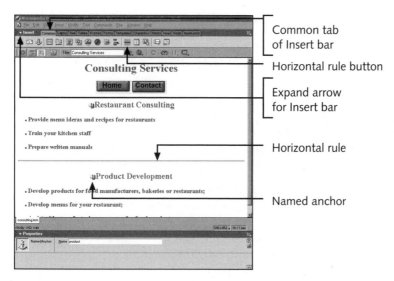

Common tab
of Insert bar

Horizontal rule button

Expand arrow
for Insert bar

Horizontal rule

Named anchor

4

Figure 4-18   Insert horizontal rule

8. Add the following three items, in a left-aligned, unordered (bulleted) list, in format style **Heading 3**, below the heading Product Development:

- **Develop products for food manufacturers, bakeries, or restaurants**
- **Develop menus for your restaurant**
- **Assist with manufacturing processes for food products**

9. Save the file **consulting.htm** to be sure the named anchors are available to other pages. Close the file.

10. Open the **aboutlbc.htm** page and highlight the words **Restaurant Consulting** at the beginning of the first bulleted item. The link to the document you inserted in an earlier exercise (.../consulting/consulting.htm) appears in the Link text box in the Property inspector. To create a link to the named anchor, restaurant, on consulting.htm, type **#restaurant** at the end of the text in the Link text box so that it reads as shown in Figure 4-19. (Note that if the text in the Link text box ends with a forward slash, "#restaurant" must replace that forward slash, not just come after it.)

11. Repeat Step 10 to create a second hyperlink from the phrase Product Development on the page aboutlbc.htm to the named anchor, product, you just created on the page consulting.htm.

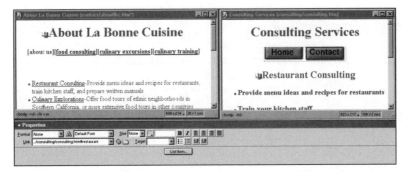

Figure 4-19   Hyperlink to a named anchor in another document

12. Save the file aboutlbc.htm and view that page in your browser window to test the named anchor hyperlinks. Close the file.

Graphic Structural Navigation Links

You can create graphic navigation links as individual icons, buttons, or more extensive graphic navigation bars or image maps. Dreamweaver MX has some powerful tools to help you develop graphic images that will change color or image when you roll over them or click them. Other functions make setting up and hyperlinking an image map easy. Dreamweaver MX also creates hyperlinked Flash buttons and rollover text, two features you learn about in Chapter 8.

Navigation with Icons and Buttons

Navigation is frequently done with icons and buttons. **Icons** are small, usually square graphics (often 32 pixels × 32 pixels in size) that represent meaningful information. People should be able to look at an icon and understand easily what it represents. The hyperlinked images on index.htm are examples of navigation using icons.

Navigation with Navigation Bars

Dreamweaver MX facilitates the creation and programming of navigation bars. Navigation bars are built from a set of buttons. Each button has a set of **button states** that can be a different color or have an altered version of the button image. Dreamweaver MX provides four button states:

- Up image—the normal button state visible when someone opens the page
- Over image—the rollover image visible when the pointer is over the button
- Down image—the image visible when the button is pressed
- Over while down image—the image visible when the displayed page is the same as the one to which the button links

Fireworks MX facilitates the creation of these button states, although you can create a button with four different colors in any graphics program and use it to build the navigation bar in Dreamweaver MX.

The next set of steps shows you how to build a navigation bar in Dreamweaver MX with two buttons (home and contact) already created for you. Dreamweaver MX makes it easy to define the images to be inserted for each of the four button states, and it generates JavaScript to activate the navigation bar.

To build a navigation bar:

1. Open the Site panel for La Bonne Cuisine in Dreamweaver MX, if it is not already open. Double-click the file **consulting.htm**, to open it for editing. This page contains a named anchor in front of the heading Restaurant Consulting. You are going to place the navigation bar immediately under the page heading above the line with the named anchor.

2. Click at the end of the line that says Consulting Services, and press **Enter** to create a new centered line.

3. Insert the navigation bar by selecting the **Navigation Bar** button ▦ on the Common tab on the Insert Bar.

4. In the Insert Navigation Bar dialog box, you can enter information about the button states of each button on the navigation bar. Select **horizontally** in the Insert list box at the bottom to extend the buttons across the page. Then, click the **Browse** button to the right of the Up Image text box to define the image you want to put into that button state for the first **Home** button.

5. To define the Up Image, browse to the **Images** folder, and select **navbar1c1.gif**. Click **OK**. Repeat by selecting the **navbar1c2.gif** in the **Over Image** text box. In the Down Image text box, select **navbar1c3.gif**, and in the Over While Down Image text box, select **navbar1c4.gif**.

6. Type **home** in the Alternate Text text box.

7. In the When Clicked Go to URL text box, define the hyperlinked page by locating the **index.htm** document in the \Sites\lbc folder. Leave Preload Images checked to ensure loading of the navigation bar images when the page is downloaded. Leave Use Tables checked for table layout of the navigation bar. See Figure 4-20.

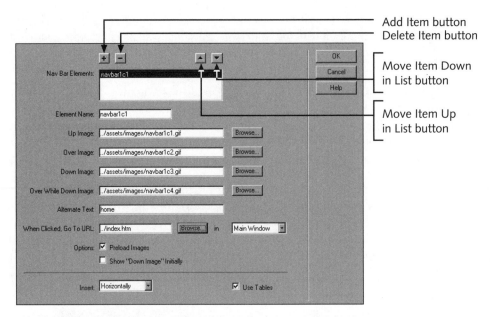

Figure 4-20   Defining images for first button states in the navigation bar

8. To enter information about the second button, **Contacts**, click the **+** button in the upper left side of the Navigation Bar dialog box, shown in Figure 4-20. A new element is defined in the Nav Bar Elements text box. After you type Contacts into the Element Name text box and click elsewhere in the dialog box, Dreamweaver inserts Contacts into the Nav Bar Elements text box.

9. Go to the Up Image textbox and browse to the file **navbar2c1.gif**. Enter the over image (**navbar2c2.gif**), the down image (**navbar2c3.gif**), and the over while down image (**navbar2c4.gif**). Type **home** in the Alternate Text text box. Link the button to the **aboutlbc.htm** page in the contacts folder. Click **OK**.

10. The navigation bar may no longer be centered, because Dreamweaver MX created a table to hold the buttons in the navigation bar. Select this table, if it is not already selected, by clicking one of the buttons and selecting **<table>** in the tag selector. Then click **Center** in the Align list box on the Property inspector, as shown in Figure 4-21.

Figure 4-21   Property inspector for the table that holds the navigation bar

11. Save the page, and preview it in a browser. Note the different button states as you move the cursor over the button, or click it.

Navigation with Image Maps

Image maps have been a popular way of setting up navigation on a Web page, particularly if the image represents a geographic area. The La Bonne Cuisine Web site has a section that is about culinary tours, and it offers several culinary tours of ethnic neighborhoods in Southern California. Thus, an image map that links to pages about ethnic culinary tours would be useful to site visitors. In Dreamweaver MX, you can select any image and define areas and hyperlinks within it to turn the image into an image map.

The expanded Property inspector for an image provides three different drawing tools to create hotspots in different shapes (rectangular, circular, and polygon or freeform). **Hotspots** are areas that contain hyperlinks to other pages, anchors, or elements. Rectangular and circular hotspots are easy to draw. Polygon hotspots provide more unusual shapes. To turn a corner in the polygon, click the mouse to indicate a corner point where the line direction changes. You can adjust the shape of the polygon with the Arrow tool on the left of the Property inspector. If you do not get the shape correct at first, you can move it by dragging it with the cursor, delete it with the Delete key, or press the Ctrl+Z key combination to undo the hotspot shape and then redraw it. It is sometimes easier to delete or undo the hotstop and start over than to adjust the shape of a hotspot.

Do not make your hotspots too small or place them too close together! Visitors have to be able to place their pointer on the hotspot and click it. If the area is too small or if the hotspots overlap, the visitor may be sent to the wrong page or miss the clickable area altogether. The Alt name for the hotspot that you type in its Property inspector also makes each hotspot visible to visitors because it displays as the visitor moves the mouse over the hotspot.

To work with an image map:

1. Open the La Bonne Cuisine Site panel, if it is not already open. Create four placeholder pages, **littletokyo.htm**, **chinatown.htm**, **littleindia.htm**, and **vietnamese.htm** in the tour folder.

2. Double-click the **tour.htm** page in the Local View section of the Site panel. The tour.htm page is empty because it is still a placeholder page.

3. Modify the page properties by typing **Culinary Tours** in the Title: text box above the Design View window.

4. Type **Ethnic Culinary Tours** at the top of the page, change its format style to **Heading 1** and center align the text. Press the **Enter** key to go to a new line.

5. Click the **Image** button 🖼 on the Common tab on the Insert bar. Choose **\Sites\lbc\assets\images\lamap.gif**. Click the image to select it, and then click the **Align Left** button in the Property inspector. The map graphic is now ready to be turned into an image map. If you do not see the map information on the lamap.gif Property inspector, click the down arrow on the right side of the Property inspector to expand it.

6. With the lamap.gif image selected, type **Culinary Tours Image Map** in the Alt text box in the Property inspector. Click the **Rectangular Hotspot Tool** in the Property inspector to create the first hotspot on the image map for Little Saigon, a Vietnamese neighborhood in Orange County.

7. On the lower right portion of the map, draw a rectangle between Garden Grove on the north and Westminster on the south, to cover the word Westminster, as shown in Figure 4-22.

8. The Property inspector now shows a text box containing a # sign for the link from the hotspot. Use Browse for File or point-to-file to link to the page **vietnamese.htm** in the tour folder. Dreamweaver MX creates a hotspot to link to that page from the image map.

9. Type **Vietnamese Culinary Tour** in the Alt textbox, as shown in Figure 4-22. Select **_self** from the Target drop-down list to open the linked page in the same browser window as the tour page.

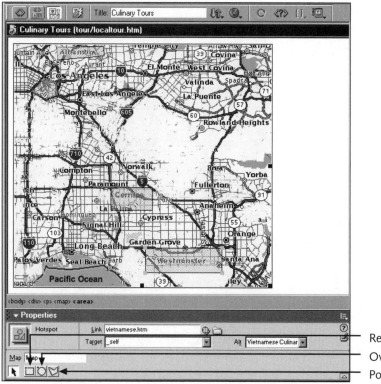

Rectangular Hotspot tool
Oval Hotspot tool
Polygon Hotspot tool

Figure 4-22   Creating a hotspot on an image map

10. Add a hotspot for a Japanese culinary tour in the same way. Click the
Polygon Hotspot Tool and draw a shape in the area shown in Figure
4-23. Each time you need to change the line direction in the polygon you draw,
click the mouse and begin drawing the next side of the polygon. Your polygon should have corners that fit within the shape formed by the intersection
and crossing of the Freeways numbered 5, 10, 60, and 110 in the area just to
the left and below the word Los Angeles. Link the hotspot for this culinary
tour of Little Tokyo to **littletokyo.htm** in the tour folder. Type **Little Tokyo
Culinary Tour** in the Alt text box and select **_self** in the Target drop-down
list in the Property inspector. Save the page and view in your browser.

11. Add a hotspot on the map for a Chinatown tour, by drawing a polygon shape
above freeway10, covering the word Alhambra. Create a hyperlink to the
chinatown.htm page, type **Traditional Chinatown Culinary Tour** in the
Alt text box, and select **_self** in the Target drop-down list.

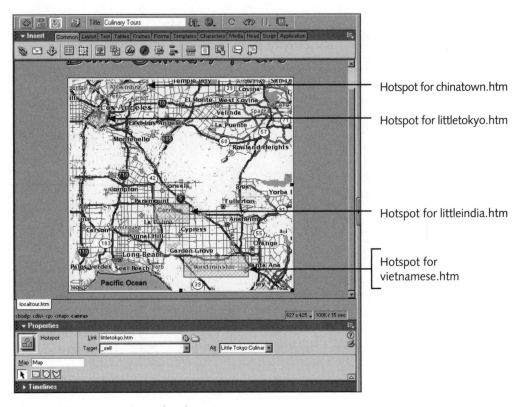

Hotspot for chinatown.htm

Hotspot for littletokyo.htm

Hotspot for littleindia.htm

Hotspot for vietnamese.htm

Figure 4-23   Hotspots on local tour image map

12. Add a hotspot for a Little India tour, by drawing a rectangle covering the word Cerritos. Link the hotspot to **littleindia.htm**, type **Little India Culinary Tour** in the Alt text box, and select **_self** in the Target drop-down list.

13. Save this revised page and review in the browser. Close the page.

CHAPTER SUMMARY

☐ The Dreamweaver MX Site panel makes it easy to create and manage the folders that define your Web site directory structure.

☐ The Local View window on the right side of the expanded Site panel displays the hierarchical directory structure of your Web site.

☐ The Site Map window on the left side of the expanded Site panel makes it easy to visualize and set up hyperlinks between elements (HTML pages and multimedia files) on your Web site.

❐ To help you identify broken links, the Site map shows them in red. You can also check for broken links and orphaned files (ones to which there are no links) using commands on the Site panel Site menu. The expanded Site panel supports the repair of broken links.

❐ Web site directories or folders that have an associated index.htm or index.html file (depending on the server operating system) do not display the file structure of the Web site directory. Web servers assume that a page with one of these names is the home page for the directory and will display that page automatically.

❐ If you choose to refresh the local file list automatically and use caching to speed link updates, Dreamweaver MX automatically updates the Site map when you change any hyperlinks in files in the Web site.

❐ Two types of hyperlinks identify your navigation structure: structural navigation links (e.g., menu bars, navigation bars, image maps, homepage buttons), and associative links (usually hyperlinked works or phrases within page content that link to information on the subject under discussion).

❐ Named anchors are place markers for a particular area in a document. Hyperlinks can jump to named anchors on the same page or on other pages.

❐ The Property inspector provides a Point-to-File icon that makes it easy to set up hyperlinks to another page or a named anchor.

❐ Dreamweaver MX makes it easy to implement graphical structural navigation links of several types: icons and buttons, navigation bars, and image maps.

REVIEW QUESTIONS

1. If you do not want visitors to your Web site to see the file listing of a directory, you need to have a home page defined with the name _____ or _____ .

2. Creating most of your Web site before you design the directory structure for the Web site is a good idea. True or False?

3. You are collaborating with others to build a Web site, and you want to limit the right to work on and update a page on the remote server to one person at a time. The site command you need to set up and use is:

    a. Open Site

    b. Check Out

    c. Check Links Sitewide

    d. Get

4. Associative links are the hyperlinked words or phrases found within the site content that might link to more detailed information about a concept. True or False?

5. Which are the following is a navigation link type? (Choose all that apply.)

   a. associative

   b. structural

   c. external

   d. internal

6. The _____ tag allows you to type a name that will be displayed to identify a graphic for people who have graphics turned off or who are visually impaired.

7. The text box in which you can type in the link to information for an associative link is found in the:

   a. Site map

   b. toolbox

   c. Property inspector

   d. Insert bar

8. On a navigation bar, the button state that normally appears when the page first opens up is:

   a. Up image

   b. Over image

   c. Down image

   d. Over while down image

9. On a navigation bar, the button state that normally appears when you press the button is:

   a. Up image

   b. Over image

   c. Down image

   d. Over while down image

10. The top-level folder or directory of a Web site is called a(n):

    a. Level 1 folder

    b. Web site number one directory

    c. root directory

    d. index directory

11. On a navigation bar, the button state that is visible when the cursor is over the button is called:

    a. Up image

    b. Over image

    c. Down image

    d. Over while down image

12. The three shapes that you can use to define areas on an image map are:

    a. square, oval, and triangle

    b. rectangle, oval, and polygon

    c. polygon, triangle, and circle

    d. oval, polygon, and pyramid

13. The areas on an image map that you draw to contain hyperlinks are called:

    a. cold spots

    b. hotspots

    c. hyperlink spots

    d. map spots

14. The tool available in the Property inspector that makes it easy to drag the pointer to set up hyperlinks is called the _____.

    a. Browse and drop button

    b. Drag and drop button

    c. Point-to-File icon

    d. Folder button

15. Typically, structural navigation links do *not* consist of what types of elements?

    a. buttons and icons

    b. image maps

    c. navigation bars

    d. named anchors

16. Typically, associative links consist of what types of elements?

    a. buttons and icons

    b. image maps

    c. text contained in the page content

    d. navigation bars

17. The command in the Site map that will check for broken links is called _____.

18. The top level of the Web site structure is called the _____.

19. Developers typically name the folder that contains multimedia content
   _____.

20. When you run the Check Links Sitewide command, the broken links are displayed in the:

   a. Property inspector

   b. Site panel

   c. Results panel group

   d. Assets panel

HANDS-ON PROJECTS

Project 4-1

In this project, you set up a practice Web site (myworld) for the rest of the hands-on projects in this chapter.

You must complete Hands-on Project 4-1 before you can complete the remaining projects in this section.

1. Start Dreamweaver MX and open the Site panel (press function key **F8**), if it is not already open. Create a nested folder named **myworld** inside a newly created **ch4practice** folder.

2. Click **Site** on the Dreamweaver or Site panel menu bar, and then click **New Site**. When the Site Definition dialog box opens, select the **Basic tab** to use the Site Definition Wizard. Dreamweaver then prompts you step-by-step for information about your Web site. Type **myworld** into the input box on the first screen. Then click the **Next** button.

3. On the Editing Files, Part 2 screen, click the **No, I do not want to use a server technology** option button. Then click **Next**.

4. On the Editing Files, Part 3 screen, click the first option button, and then browse to the **myworld** folder inside the **ch4practice** folder that you set up in Step 1. Click the **Next** button to go to the next screen.

5. On the Sharing Files screen, select **None** in the drop-down list; you will be working only on the local Web site in this book. Click **Next**, and then click **Done**.

6. The page properties for pages throughout this site are: Background: **#FFFFCC**; Text: **#660099**; Links: **#FF3399**; Visited Links: **#669966**; Active Links, **#CC3333**; and an appropriate title. Create **index.htm** with these page properties, and make index.htm the home page for the site.

7. Create an **images** folder inside the **Chapter4\myworld** folder, as well as placeholder pages for each of the following continents: **namerica.htm, samerica.htm, europe.htm, africa.htm, asia.htm, australia.htm, arctic.htm,** and **antarctica.htm**.

8. Copy the images **worldmap.gif, namericamap.gif, travel1.gif, travel2.gif, travel3.gif, travel4.gif, cities1.gif, cities2.gif, cities3.gif, cities4.gif, food1.gif, food2.gif, food3.gif,** and **food4.gif** from the **Chapter4\data\images** folder into the images folder in the myworld site.

In each of the remaining hands-on projects, you must first open the myworld site in Dreamweaver MX, and then work from the Local view of myworld in the Site panel.

Project 4-2

In this project, you create a text navigation bar for a home page for the Web site myworld that you created in Hands-on Project 4-1.

1. If necessary, create a new page, **index.htm**, adding the page properties defined in Project 4-1.

2. Type a title at the top of the page: **My World** (format style **Heading 1, center alignment**).

3. Type a text navigation bar below the title, format style **Heading 4**:

   [N. America] [S. America] [Europe] [Africa] [Asia] [Australia] [Arctic] [Antarctica]

4. From this text navigation bar, create hyperlinks to the placeholder pages you created in Project 4-1.

5. Save the page and test its hyperlinks in your browser. Close the page.

Project 4-3

In this project, you build an image map using a map of the world.

1. Open **index.htm**. If you did not complete Hands-on Project 4-2, you need to type **My World** at the top of the page (**centered, Heading 1**). Otherwise, continue with Step 2 on the line below the text navigation bar you inserted in Hands-on Project 4-2.

2. Insert and center align the image **worldmap.gif** on the page.

3. Use this image to create an image map with hotspots as links to each continent. Create hyperlinks and alternative names for each of these hotspots, and have the hyperlinked page replace the index.htm page (select Target: **_self**).

4. Save the page and view in your browser. Close the page.

Project 4-4

This project has two parts: you create named anchors on one page and an image map on another page to link to the anchors.

1. Open the page **namerica.htm** and modify its page properties to comply with those defined in Hands-on Project 4-1.

2. At the top of the page, type **North America**.

3. Press the **Enter** key four times, type **Canada**; press the **Enter** key four more times, type **United States of America**; press the **Enter** key four more times, and type **Mexico**. Highlight the lines you created in Steps 2 and 3. Set their format to **Heading 1** and **center aligned**.

4. Create named anchors called **canada**, **usa**, and **mexico** in front of the appropriate lines.

5. Create a new page, **namericamap.htm**, and modify its page properties. Type **North American Map** at the top of the page (**centered**, **Heading 1**). Insert the image file **namericamap.gif** in the center of this page, below the heading.

6. Draw **polygon hotspots** that define Canada, the United States of America, and Mexico. Create hyperlinks to the appropriate named anchors on namerica.htm. Save the pages and view them in your browser.

Project 4-5

In this project, you create a navigation bar for the page europe.htm.

1. Open the page **europe.htm** and edit its page properties.

2. Type **Europe** at the top of the page (**Heading 1**, **center alignment**).

3. Press **Enter** to move down one line, and insert a vertical navigation bar with three buttons that link to pages about travel, cities, and food. Use the button graphics **travel1.gif**, **travel2.gif**, **travel3.gif**, and **travel4.gif** to create the rollover states for the link to travel.htm. Use the button graphics **cities1.gif**, **cities2.gif**, **cities3.gif**, and **cities4.gif** to create the rollover states for the link to cities.htm. Use the button graphics **food1.gif**, **food2.gif**, **food3.gif**, and **food4.gif** to create the rollover states for the link to food.htm.

4. Save the page and view in the browser. Close the page.

Project 4-6

In this project, you check for and fix broken links on the myworld Web site.

1. Open the myworld Web site, if necessary. Click **Check Links Sitewide** on the Site menu in the Site panel. View the list of broken links in the Results panel group.

2. Click the **Save Report** button at the left of the Broken Links File list to save the list as **brokenlinks.txt** in the **ch4practice** folder.

3. Fix the broken links by inserting placeholder pages for **travel.htm**, **cities.htm**, and **food.htm**. Run **Check Links Sitewide** again, until the broken links are all repaired. Save the list showing that there are no broken links as **fixedlinks.txt** in the **ch4practice** folder.

CASE PROJECTS

Locate a map of the place where you live from one of the map programs on the Internet, such as Mapquest (*www.mapquest.com*) or Yahoo Maps (*http://maps.yahoo.com*). Save it as mymap.gif. Create a new page in Dreamweaver MX, and insert the image mymap.gif. Create at least three hotspots on this map that refer to businesses, schools, parks, or other places of interest. Create hyperlinks to the Web sites for those places.

On a separate piece of paper, design an alternative Web site structure for La Bonne Cuisine that is deeper (for example, that has an assets folder for each section of the Web site). Draw out the site map for your alternative Web site structure on a piece of paper. Describe the effects of a deeper Web site structure on Web site management, particularly the creation of hyperlinks.

Find the site map for the Web site of a large company, such as Apple Computer (*www.apple.com/find/sitemap.html*). Figure out the depth and width of the organizational structure of this Web site, based on the directory structure in the site map and the lengths of the URLs. Print out a copy of the site map. Write an analysis that describes what you observe about the navigation strategy for the site.

5

WEB SITE LAYOUT

Tables, Frames, and Layers

In this chapter, you will:

♦ Use Dreamweaver productivity tools and functions to lay out a Web site with tables, frames, and layers

♦ Learn two approaches to table layout that Dreamweaver MX offers to control page layout: Standard and Layout Views

♦ Discover Dreamweaver tools that make it easy to create and manage framesets and the frames they contain

♦ Lay out a Web site using layers and then convert the layers to tables to provide consistent appearance in different browsers

---

In this chapter, you learn how to lay out pages in Dreamweaver using tables, frames, and layers. Understanding how to use these layout tools lets you better control the placement of elements on your Web pages. You can increase the attractiveness and usability of your Web site so that your layout makes sense to the viewer. This chapter not only helps you understand how to use these tools in Web site and page layout, but also helps you understand the advantages and disadvantages of each.

WEB SITE LAYOUT

Using Dreamweaver, you can organize your page layouts using tables, frames, and layers. Tables arrange elements on the page using rows and columns, like spreadsheets or word-processor tables. Web site developers have used tables for HTML layout since 1994.

Frames arrange pages using documents called framesets. **Frameset** documents are not standard HTML documents, because they contain no <body> tags. They are meta-documents that contain layout information for a set of frames, arranged in columns and rows. Each frame can hold and display an individual HTML document; thus, multiple documents can appear simultaneously within a single, unified browser window. User interaction can change the document displayed within one frame without affecting the others in the window. For example, one frame in a frameset frequently contains a menu document. Typically, when the viewer clicks a menu hyperlink, a different document appears in one of the other frames in the frameset, while the menu document remains on the screen.

Layers are a recent addition to HTML. A **layer** is a rectilinear-shaped object that contains some sort of content (for example, an image or text). Layers allow you to position content anywhere on a page, stack content by placing layers on top of one another, hide and show content, and perform simple animation. Because some layer functions are fairly complex and advanced, this chapter introduces you only to the content positioning feature of layers. Chapter 10 covers more complex functions.

Cascading Style Sheets (CSS) (covered in Chapter 10) also provide some additional control over layout. An **internal CSS** allows you to create a style sheet within a document that redefines the format of HTML tags for a single page (for example, changing the font style, size, and color for the content that goes within different header formatting tags). An **external CSS** exists in a separate document on the Web server and provides consistency because it can be used across Web documents. It also decreases download time, because the external CSS downloads to the client browser only once.

The good news about Web site layout HTML tags is that they have improved since tables and frames became part of HTML standards. The bad news is that major browser producers have not agreed on common HTML standards and tags for layers, so this very promising layout option yields output that behaves differently in different browser versions and differently sized browser windows.

Many Web site designers now target their pages for an 800-pixel wide by 600-pixel high monitor, but still try to design the layout to display the most important information in larger or smaller browser windows. You can define the target window sizes for your Web pages, which are displayed in the status bar at the bottom of the Dreamweaver MX Document window in Design and Design and Code views. The browser toolbars and borders occupy a certain amount of the browser window. If you design a page for an 800-pixel wide by 600-pixel high browser window (the size used in this book), the maximum window size that will be displayed is calculated by Dreamweaver to be 760 pixels wide by 420 pixels high. You can change the window size of a page that is not maximized in the Document window by clicking the window size on the status bar and making a selection in the pop-up menu, or by dragging the edges of the HTML document in the Document window. Figure 5-1 shows a window size of 653 × 755 in the status bar. The window size here is reduced to allow you to view the table in both Code and Design Views. You may choose a smaller window size view if your computer monitor is smaller.

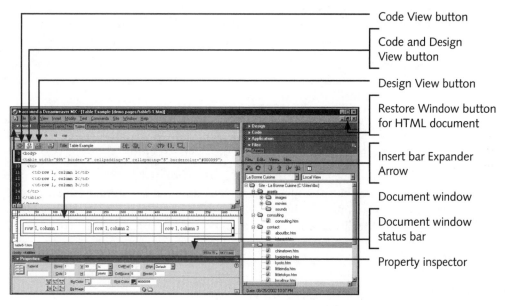

Code View button

Code and Design View button

Design View button

Restore Window button for HTML document

Insert bar Expander Arrow

Document window

Document window status bar

Property inspector

Figure 5-1   Table tags

If you try to click on the window size in the status bar and nothing happens, you need to make sure that the HTML document is not maximized in the Document window. Click the Restore Window button for the Document window in the upper-right corner of the window, shown in Figure 5-1.

LAYOUT WITH TABLES

Widely used in HTML layout, tables were introduced in Netscape Navigator 1.2, providing early Web site designers with much needed layout options. In this section you learn how to define tables for Web page layout.

You define tables in HTML by using the opening and closing tags <table> and </table>. You can also nest tables within tables for further layout options. Table tags structure tables in rows <tr> and individual table data cells <td> within rows. A simple, one-row, three-column table is shown in split Code and Design view in Figure 5-1.

In Dreamweaver MX you can accomplish layout with tables in either Standard view or Layout view. You can switch from one view to the other by clicking the appropriate button on the Layout tab of the Insert bar. If you do not see the tabs available on the Insert bar, you need to click the expander arrow in the left corner of the Insert bar, just below the Dreamweaver menu bar. You must have a page open for editing in Design view to use the buttons on any of the tabs on the Insert bar. However, be aware that switching between views while working on a page with a table may limit the editing capabilities of the view to which you are switching. This chapter helps you understand both methods:

- Standard view allows you to insert tables and then format and adjust them to suit your needs, or to draw page layout with layers and then convert the layers to tables.

- Layout view allows you to draw tables and table cells, adjust their size, and move them around the page layout. Thus, it is more flexible. This mode automatically creates and manages the table structure.

Dreamweaver provides useful tools and features for creating and defining tables. Several tabs on the Insert bar provide tools for creating and modifying tables. The Command menu includes commands that allow you to sort table contents and apply preset table formats. The Modify menu provides a pop-up menu of Table commands, and the Property inspector allows you to edit table attributes. Of course, you can also edit the table tags in the HTML code in Code view.

Table Commands in Dreamweaver

To access the Table commands, click Modify on the Dreamweaver menu bar, and then point to Table. Some commands on this menu are available only when the cursor is inside a table (as in Figure 5-2); others require you to select the entire table; and still others require you to select multiple cells (including rows or columns).

Here is a brief description of each of the Table menu commands:

- Select Table selects the entire table for formatting, for example, to change table width or height. After you select the entire table, you will see a selection bar with drag handles for changing the table size surrounding it as well as a display of table attributes in the Property inspector (as shown in Figure 5-3). The shortcut for selecting a table is the Ctrl+A key combination. You can also select a table by clicking the <table> tag in the tag selector on the status bar at the bottom of the Document window in Design view.

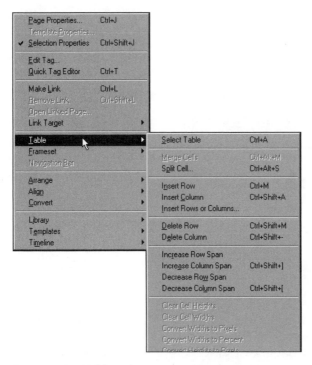

Figure 5-2 Table submenu

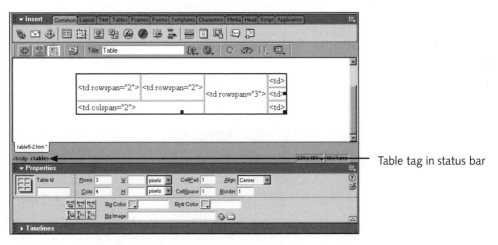

Figure 5-3 Examples of row span and column span in a selected table

> ■ Merge Cells combines two or more table cells into one cell. This command requires you to select at least two adjacent table cells. If you select all three

cells in the table in Figure 5-1 and click Merge Cells (or press the Ctrl+Alt+M key combination), the table row becomes one cell.

- Split Cell divides the selected cell into a specified number of columns or rows. This command is the opposite of the Merge Cells command.

- Insert Row inserts one row above the selected row.

- Insert Column inserts one column to the left of the selected column.

- Insert Rows or Columns inserts one or more rows above or below the selected row, or one or more columns to the left or right of the selected column.

- Delete Row removes the selected row.

- Delete Column removes the selected column.

- Increase Row Span enlarges the height of the selected cell from one row to two rows. The opening table cell tag changes from <td> to <td rowspan="2">. (Selecting two stacked cells in one column and clicking Merge Cells has the same effect.) You can increase row span to include as many rows as the table contains. See Figure 5-3 for examples.

- Increase Column Span enlarges the width of the selected cell from one column to two columns. The opening table cell tag changes from <td> to <td colspan="2">. (Selecting two adjacent row cells and clicking Merge Cells has the same effect.) You can increase column span to include as many columns as the table contains. See Figure 5-3 for examples.

- Decrease Row Span reduces the height of the selected cell by one row. If the rowspan is 2, then the opening table cell tag changes from <td rowspan="2"> to <td>.

- Decrease Column Span reduces the width of the selected cell by one column. If the colspan is 2, then the opening table cell tag changes from <td colspan="2"> to <td>.

- Clear Cell Heights removes all specified pixel or percentage cell row heights. Table row heights then adjust to the height of row contents (if there are cell contents) or to the minimum cell height for the table. Other table attributes (including border size, cell padding, and cell spacing, discussed below) can also affect minimum table height and width.

- Clear Cell Widths removes all specified pixel or percentage cell column widths. Table column widths then adjust to the width of column contents (if there are cell contents) or to the minimum column widths for the table.

- Convert Widths to Pixels changes specified cell and table width from a percentage of the browser window to a fixed number of pixels.

- Convert Widths to Percent changes specified cell and table width from a fixed number of pixels to a percentage of the browser window.

- Convert Heights to Pixels changes specified cell and table height from a percentage of the browser window to a fixed number of pixels.

- Convert Heights to Percent changes specified cell and table height from a fixed number of pixels to a percentage of the browser window.

 Web site developers who want their pages to adjust to browser windows define layout table width in percentages. Setting table width to 95% and centering the layout table should always ensure small margins on both the left and right sides of the page (provided the accumulated width of the table's multimedia content is not wider than the browser window). As you learned in Chapter 4, including space around clusters of content improves Web site usability for the viewer.

Defining Tables and Cells with the Property Inspector

The Property inspector provides an easy way to modify table properties, row or column properties, or single cell properties, depending on what you select. Figure 5-4 shows the Property inspector for an entire table, which defines the attributes of the entire table. The Property inspector for a table cell, row, or column has different attributes.

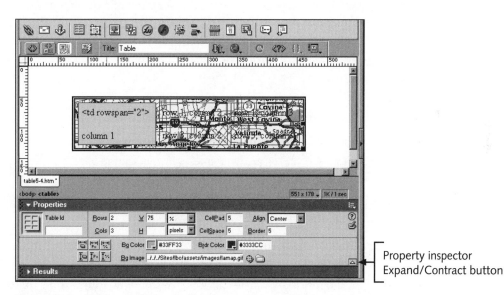

Property inspector
Expand/Contract button

Figure 5-4   Table attributes in the Property inspector

 If you only see one row of options in the Property inspector, click the Expand/Contract arrow △ to see the rest of the options.

Figure 5-4 shows these table attributes in the Property inspector:

- The blank table icon with the words Table Id next to it indicates that the entire table is selected. You can define your own table name, but it only appears within the HTML tag and is not visible in the browser window.

- Rows and Cols (Columns) for the table show two rows and three columns.

- W (table width) is set to 75% of the page width. You can also define table width as a fixed number of pixels.

- H (table height) is unspecified and adjusts to table content.

- CellPad is set to 5 pixels. **Cell padding** provides space between the cell content and the cell boundary or edge.

- CellSpace is also set to 5 pixels. **Cell spacing** specifies the number of pixels between each table cell. Together cell padding and cell spacing ensure that the cell contents are separate, even if the browser width is relatively narrow. Inserting space between content in table cells increases Web page usability for the viewer by separating different Web page elements.

- Align defines the table alignment on the page. This table is aligned in the vertical center of the page. Other options are default (usually interpreted by the browser as left aligned), left, and right.

- Border defines the width of the line around the outside of the table. It is set to 5 pixels to illustrate table properties more fully. For layout purposes, table border is usually set to 0, so that it is invisible when viewing the page in the browser window.

- Help ⃞ opens the context-sensitive help screen for tables.

- Clear Column Widths ⃞ deletes all table column width values from the table.

- Convert Table Widths to Pixels ⃞ converts the table width from a percentage of the browser window to its current width in pixels.

- Convert Table Widths to Percent ⃞ converts the table width from pixels to its current percentage of the browser window.

- Convert Table Heights to Pixels ⃞ converts the table height from a percentage of the browser window to its current height in pixels.

- Clear Row Heights ⃞ deletes all table row height values from the table.

- Convert Table Heights to Percent ⃞ converts the table height from pixels to its percentage of the browser window.

- Bg (Background) Color defines a background color for the table in hexadecimal format. Clicking the color box provides a selection of 216 standard Web safe colors in the Dreamweaver **Color Picker**. You use the Color Picker eyedropper to select one of these colors, and then Dreamweaver inserts the hexadecimal code for your choice. You can also type the hexadecimal code for the color if you know it. The example in Figure 5-4 includes one pink table cell (the cell that contains the text <td rowspan="2">), on the left. The background color for a table cell overrides the table's background color and background image.

■ Brdr (Border) Color defines the outline border color for the entire table.

■ Bg (Background) Image allows you to insert a graphics file as background for the table. As you can see in Figure 5-4, the background image for a table takes precedence over the table's background color.

5

Figure 5-5 shows a table with one cell selected and the Property inspector that defines cell attributes. Changing these attributes alters the layout of the cell and its contents. If you compare the Property inspector for table cells with the Property inspector for text in Figure 1-7, you see many of the same attributes.

■ Format refers to style formats available for text in the table cell.

■ Toggle CSS/HTML mode ▣ lets you switch back and forth between HTML editing features and editing with Cascading Style Sheets (CSS), which you will learn about in Chapter 9.

■ Font Combination defines the fonts for the cell contents from available fonts on the Font list.

■ Link defines the URL of a hyperlinked page for the selected contents in the table cell (text or graphics).

■ Point-to-File and Browse-for-File are tools you can use to define a hyperlink to a document or a named anchor in a linked document.

■ Size refers to font sizes, available in a drop-down list.

■ Text Color defines the font color in hexadecimal format. You can choose the color with the Dreamweaver Color Picker.

■ Text Style and Text Alignment allow you to format content within the table cell.

■ Target defines the window in which the hyperlinked document opens, particularly useful for opening pages inside frames.

■ Unordered (bulleted) and Ordered (numbered) Lists ▤ ▤, and Outdent and Indent Text ▤ ▤ are useful for formatting table cell content.

■ Merges Selected Cells using Spans ▣ provides another way to merge selected adjacent cells.

■ Splits Cell into Rows or Columns ▣ provides another way to split a cell into multiple rows or columns.

- Horz (Horizontal Alignment) lets you define whether the cell contents are left or right aligned, or centered.

- Vert (Vertical Alignment) lets you define the vertical location of the contents within the selected cell (top, middle, bottom, baseline, or default).

- W (Width) lets you define the width of the selected cell or cells in pixels, or as a percentage of the table width, provided you type the **%** sign after the number.

- H (Height) lets you define the height of the selected cell or cells in pixels, or as a percentage of the table height, provided you type the **%** sign after the number.

- No Wrap prevents word wrapping of text within the cell. The cell widens to accommodate the text. If you do not select the No Wrap option, cells expand horizontally at least to fit the longest word and then expand vertically.

- Header, when checked, formats selected cells or rows as a table header. The contents of table header cells are bold and centered by default. Table headers are usually in the top row of the table and are identified by the HTML tag <th>, not <td>.

- Bg (Background) URL of cell lets you define a background image for a cell, column, or row

- Bg (Background Color) defines the background color (in hexadecimal code) for a cell, column, or row via the Color Picker.

- Brdr (Border Color) lets you set a border color for a cell, column, or row.

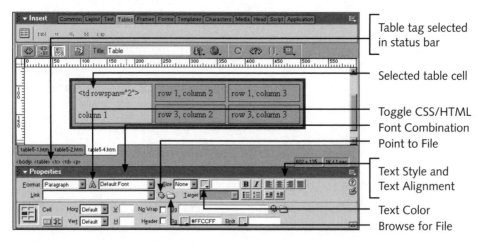

Figure 5-5 Table cell attributes in the Property inspector

Table Layout in Standard View

In this section, you practice what you learned about table layout by developing a new page for the La Bonne Cuisine Web site that links both to the local culinary excursions (on tour.htm) and to an international culinary tour. You create your first table for layout purposes using Dreamweaver Standard view. The next steps help you prepare the pages for table layout.

To prepare the pages for table layout:

1. Copy the following images from the Chapter5\images folder on your Data Disk to the Sites\lbc\assets\images folder on your working drive to use in the exercise in this chapter: **foreigntours.gif, lbclogotrans.gif, tokyonoodles.jpg, tokyotitle.gif, tokyotoyota.jpg, tours.gif, uenotemple.jpg, wasedabg.jpg,** and **worldbg.gif**. If a dialog box asks whether you want to replace files that already exist in the images folder, click **Yes to All**.

Whenever you are asked to insert an image into an HTML page in the La Bonne Cuisine Web site in the chapter exercises, you can find the image in the Sites\lbc\assets\images folder.

2. Start Dreamweaver, and open the Site panel by pressing the **F8** key, if it is not already open. Select the La Bonne Cuisine Web site on the site drop-down list.

    Because tour.htm already has an image map set up to link to various Southern California culinary tours, you can avoid reprogramming the image map by renaming this page localtour.htm in the Local Folder list for the site.

3. To rename the page, open the **tour** folder if it is not already open by clicking the + (plus) sign in front of the folder. Right-click the **tour.htm** file once to select it, then click **Rename** on the pop-up menu and type its new name, **localtour.htm**, over tour.htm. Then press the **Enter** key to complete the renaming step.

4. A dialog box asks whether you want to update the links to **tour.htm** and change them to **localtour.htm**.

5. Click the **Don't Update** button.

6. Next you add two more pages to the tour folder. The first is a replacement page for tour.htm, and the second is the main page for foreigntour.htm. Right-click the **tour** folder and click **New File**. Rename untitled.htm by typing **tour.htm** in its place. Press the **Enter** key to complete the name change. Repeat to create the page **foreigntour.htm**.

7. Double-click **tour.htm** in the Site panel to open it. Press the **Ctrl+J** key combination to open the Page Properties dialog box. Type **Culinary Tours** over Untitled Document in the Title text box. Click the **Browse** button to the right of the Background Image text box and select **wasedabg.jpg** in the

5

Sites\lbc\assets\images folder. Click **OK**. Change the text to dark red by typing **#CC3333** in the Text text box. Type the hexadecimal code **#000099** for dark blue in the Links text box. Click **OK** to save the new page characteristics. Then press the **Ctrl+S** key combination to save the page.

In the next set of steps, you lay out the tour.htm page using two tables. The first table has only one row because it holds header information. It has four columns: two hold graphics and two display information. The second table, which is directly under the first, has three columns and two rows. It contains written information about the tours available from La Bonne Cuisine. Both tables are for layout purposes, have no visible border, are centered, and occupy 95% of the browser width. These table parameters ensure that the page adjusts to different browser widths and provide space on the left and right edges of the page.

Many Web site designers strive to make their pages visible on a single 600-pixel by 800-pixel screen (the screen size for which pages are usually designed today), so that viewers do not have to scroll right or down the screen to view the entire page contents. Formatting tables to be less than 100% of browser width usually makes horizontal scroll bars unnecessary (unless accumulated table content is wider than the browser window). For example, if you insert a 1000-pixel wide image in a table formatted to 100% of the browser width, the resulting table will be at least 1000 pixels wide, in order to hold the image. Web pages that require scrolling down are more difficult to avoid: with this method, as page width decreases, page height generally increases to accommodate page content. In this case, we can reduce page height by using a line break (<br>) tag rather than a paragraph (<p>) tag to separate the two tables. To create a <br> tag, press the Shift+Enter key combination after the first table, rather than the Enter key, which creates a <p> tag to begin the next line. The lower border of the header table will now sit immediately above the top border of the second table. In some cases, it is also possible to insert the second table to the right of the first table without a line break. Because each table in our example is 95 percent of the browser width, the browser cannot place the tables side by side, but will place the second table directly under the first table.

To work within the Document window:

1. Double-click **tour.htm** if it is not already open. If a Dreamweaver message informs you that the file has been changed outside of Dreamweaver and asks if you want to update it, click **Yes**. Make sure the Document window is set to Design view. Expand the Insert bar and open the Layout tab, if necessary.

2. If necessary, click the **Standard View** button on the Layout tab of the Insert bar. Click the **Insert Table** button on the Layout tab to insert a table.

3. Figure 5-6 shows how to configure the table in the Insert Table dialog box. Type **1** in the Rows: text box, **4** in the Columns: text box, **95** in the Width: text box, select **Percent** in the list arrow to the right of the Width: text box, and type **5** in both the Cell Padding and Cell Spacing text boxes to provide space between cells. Type **0** in the Border: text box. Click **OK**.

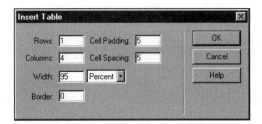

Figure 5-6   Configure a new table

5

4. To center the table, select it, if necessary, by clicking anywhere inside the table, and then click **<table>** in the tag selector at the bottom of the Document window. Select **Center** in the Align drop-down list in the table's Property inspector.

5. Place the insertion point in the left-most table cell, click the **Image** button on the Common tab of the Insert bar, and insert **lbclogotrans.gif** in that table cell. Give the image the Alt name **La Bonne Cuisine logo** in the Property inspector.

6. Click in the second table cell, and type the name of the Web site, **La Bonne Cuisine**. Click anywhere in this text string, and then select **Heading 2** in the Format drop-down list on the Property inspector.

7. Click in the third table cell, press the **Ctrl+Alt+I** key combination, and insert the image **tours.gif**. Give the image the Alt name **tours** in the Property inspector.

8. Click in the fourth table cell and type the words **Special Feature: Culinary Tours**. Click the text to select it, then change the Format style of this text string to **Heading 1** in the Format drop-down list in the Property inspector.

9. Click outside the table to adjust the table cells to the width of their content. The cells with graphics shrink to the width of the graphics, and the cells with text widen to accommodate the text. Save the file **tour.htm** and view it in the browser. Change the browser width and observe what happens. Close the file.

The more detailed information on the page is to be arranged in three columns below the header information. It is possible to format a single table with rows with different numbers of columns (for example, by using the Merge Cells or Split Cells command). However, using two shorter tables makes controlling page layout easier and also reduces download time. In the next steps you insert a new, three-column, two-row table directly below the header table. Be sure that you are in Standard view before you begin. Note that you create hyperlinks to HTML pages that do not yet exist. After you use the Check Links Sitewide Command to reveal broken links, you create placeholder pages for the missing pages.

To insert the table:

1. Open **tour.htm** if it is not already open. Place the insertion point to the right of the first table, and press the **Shift+Enter** key combination to create a <br> tag. Press the **Ctrl+Alt+T** key combination to insert a two-row, three-column table just below the header table. Set table width to **95%**, border to **0**, and cell padding and cell spacing to **5**. Center the table on the page by clicking inside the table, clicking **<table>** in the status bar, and clicking **Center** in the Align drop-down list in the table's Property inspector.

2. Click in the first cell of the first row, change the font size to **5** and the text style to **Bold** and **Italics**, and type **Local Tours: Map!** Select this text and create a hyperlink by typing **localtour.htm** in the Link text box in the Property inspector.

3. Place the insertion point in the second cell of the first row; change the font size to **4**, and the text style to **Bold**. Type **Experience International Cuisine in Southern California**.

4. Place the insertion point in the third cell of the first row, set the font size to **3** and the text style to **Bold**, and click **Unordered List**. Type the bulleted list of local ethnic culinary tours:

   - **Little Saigon**
   - **Little Tokyo**
   - **Chinatown**
   - **Little India**

5. Select the text in each bullet in turn and create a hyperlink to the appropriate page: Little Saigon links to **vietnamese.htm**, Little Tokyo links to **littletokyo.htm**, Chinatown links to **chinatown.htm**, and Little India links to **littleindia.htm**.

6. Click in the first cell in the second row, and modify the text attributes (size **5**, **Bold**, and **Italics**). Type **International Tours**. Select this text and create a hyperlink by typing **foreigntour.htm** in the Link text box.

7. Click in the second cell in the second row and set the font attributes to font size **4**, and **Bold**. Type **Experience the cuisine of Japan**.

8. Click in the last cell of the second row. Set up an unordered (bulleted) list, modify the text attributes to **Bold**, and type two bullet items: **Tokyo** and **Kyoto**. Create a hyperlink to the appropriate pages: Tokyo links to **tokyo.htm** and Kyoto links to **kyoto.htm**. Press the **Ctrl+S** key combination to save the page.

9. Press **F8** to open the La Bonne Cuisine site in the Site panel, if it is not already open. Check for broken links for the site by pressing the **Ctrl+F8** key combination. Look at the list of broken links in the Results panel. Create placeholder pages in the tour folder for the nonexistent pages for which you

created hyperlinks in this exercise using the techniques you learned in Chapter 4. When you finish, check the links for the site again.

10. Save the page, tour.htm, in the Sites\lbc\tour folder, and view it in your browser. Try narrowing the browser window to see what happens to the page layout. Check the hyperlinks to be sure they work. Close the file.

In the browser the page should look like the one shown in Figure 5-7.

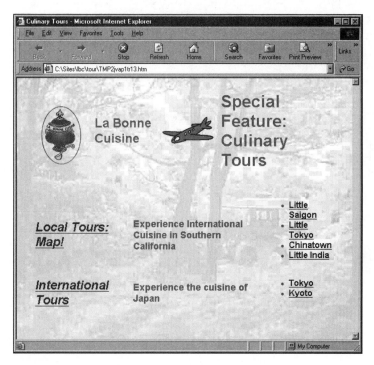

Figure 5-7   Page formatted with Standard view layout tables

A browser window may display your Web page's text in a different font style than the one you use in Dreamweaver Design view. The page displayed in Figure 5-7 has a different font style than the one used to create it in Dreamweaver because the browser has been customized to display a specific font style for all instances of the default font. The font styles you can choose in Dreamweaver or a browser depend on which fonts are installed on your computer.

Table Layout in Layout View

In this section, you learn how to develop table layout using Layout view. When you start Dreamweaver, Standard view is the default. If you need to switch from Standard view to Layout view, click the Layout View button on the Layout tab of the Insert bar (as shown in Figure 5-8), or press the Ctrl+F6 key combination. Unless you turn off the warning, Dreamweaver may display a dialog box informing you that you are switching views. You may have problems working with a table created in Standard view when you switch to Layout view, because Dreamweaver allows you to insert content only into layout cells that you have drawn in Layout view. The table cells from tables you created in Standard view cannot hold content until you draw layout cells into them.

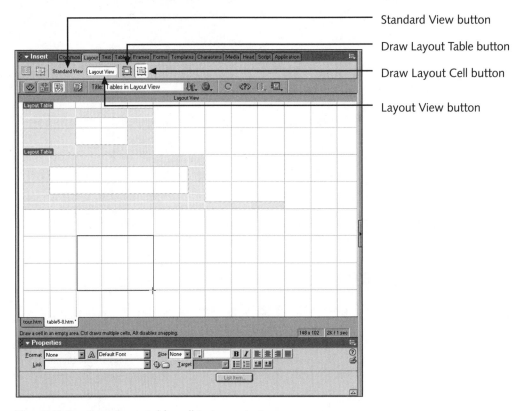

Figure 5-8   Drawing a table cell in Layout view

Layout view allows you to draw layout tables or layout cells on an HTML page. After you draw a layout table, you can draw layout cells within it. If you draw a layout cell outside an existing layout table, Dreamweaver draws a layout table around it, starting at the left margin of the page and the first free line. This means that if you draw your first layout cell in the lower-right quadrant of an HTML page, Dreamweaver inserts a layout table with its upper-left corner in the upper-left corner of the HTML page. If a layout table exists, the top border of the new layout table is immediately below the bottom border of the previous layout table, and the left border of the table is at the left border of the HTML page. Note that Figure 5-8 shows a layout cell being drawn in a space below two existing layout tables. As soon as you release the mouse button and the table cell is drawn, Dreamweaver inserts another table to hold the cell, as shown in Figure 5-9.

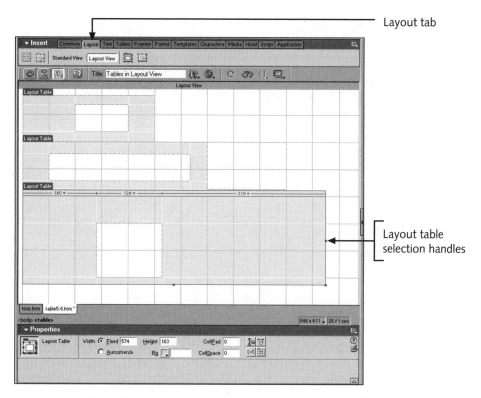

Figure 5-9   The table that Dreamweaver inserts to hold the cell

There are some important differences between creating a table layout in Layout view versus Standard view. In Figures 5-8 and 5-9, you can see a green tab for each table that contains the term Layout Table. Immediately below the tab is a column header area that states the widths of the columns in the table. The table selected in Figure 5-9 has three columns. The width of the left spacer column is 140 pixels, the width of the layout cell is 124 pixels, and the width of the right spacer column is 310 pixels.

When you draw table cells, Dreamweaver inserts columns and rows to create the table layout that you indicated you wanted when you drew the cells. Blue dotted lines outline layout cells you draw in Layout view. These lines turn solid blue when you select the cell. To achieve your table layout, Dreamweaver also inserts spacer cells outlined with faint white lines. You cannot insert content into these spacer cells. To insert content into these spacer cells, you would need to draw layout cells inside them.

Turning on the grid and the ruler in Design view makes it easier to align and draw appropriately sized tables and table cells. Be aware that Dreamweaver automatically snaps new cells to existing cells if you draw them within eight pixels of each other. Dreamweaver also automatically snaps cells to the side of the page if you draw them within eight pixels of the edge. After the layout table or layout cell has been created, you can alter its dimensions by dragging the layout table selection handles (see Figure 5-9) or by selecting the layout cell and dragging the layout cell selection handles, as shown in Figure 5-10. You can move the right and bottom borders of a layout table to resize the table, and you can freely move a layout cell within its layout table.

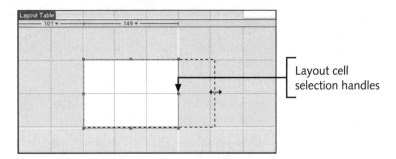

Figure 5-10   Use layout cell selection handles to resize layout cells

The Property inspector for tables in Layout view displays many of the same attributes that it displays for tables in Standard view, although their location on the Property inspector may differ. The Property inspector for tables you drew in Layout view includes one new width attribute, Autostretch. You can use two types of column widths in Layout view: Fixed width and Autostretch. Fixed width, the default setting, specifies a specific numeric width, such as 300 pixels, and appears as a number. Autostretch sets the width to adjust to fit the window size; the layout table will then always fill the browser window, no matter what its size.

You can set only one column in a table to Autostretch by selecting it and clicking the Autostretch option in the Property inspector, or by selecting the column on the column header and selecting Make Column Autostretch from the Column Header menu shown in Figure 5-11. Figure 5-12 shows the column appearance after it has been set to Autostretch. The column header now shows a wavy line rather than a fixed pixel width, and Autostretch is checked in the Property inspector.

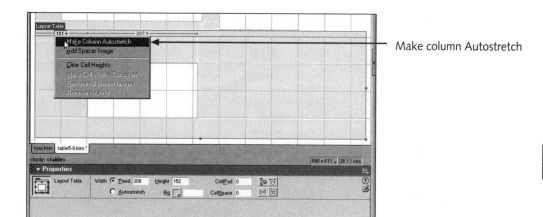

Figure 5-11   Setting a table column to Autostretch

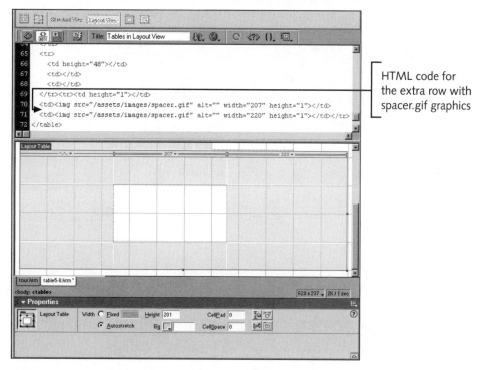

Figure 5-12   Autostretch table column and spacer code

When you designate one column as Autostretch, Dreamweaver asks whether you want to create or insert an existing spacer image, called spacer.gif, to keep the other column widths fixed in size. If you agree, Dreamweaver inserts a one-pixel tall row at the bottom of the table. It then inserts a transparent spacer image that is one pixel high, and one pixel wide, with a display width equal to the column width of the non-Autostretch columns in each of the non-Autostretch table cells in that row. If you choose to insert a pre-existing spacer.gif file, you must specify where this file is saved, usually in the images folder of the Web site. Figure 5-12 shows the HTML code for the extra row, with two table cells that contain spacer.gif. If you later want to change the width of one of these columns, you must remove the spacer.gif file or change its display width to the revised column width. You can also choose not to use a spacer image.

Nested Tables

Nesting tables within tables in Layout view is very easy. All you need to do is draw a table and then draw another table nested within it. Figure 5-13 shows a series of nested tables, as well as table cells within a table. Nesting tables is also possible in Standard view, where they display as shown in Figure 5-14. Comparing these two table layout views gives you a good idea of the differences between them. Layout view provides more flexibility in layout. Replicating the table layout in Figure 5-13 in Standard view would be difficult and time-consuming.

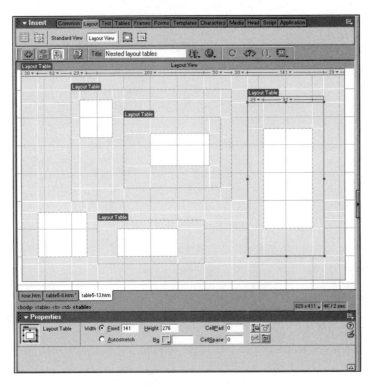

Figure 5-13   Nested tables in Layout view

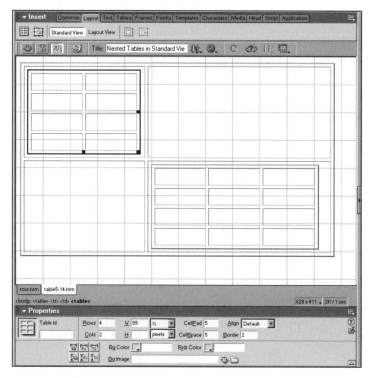

Figure 5-14   Nested tables in Standard view

Practicing Table Layout in Layout View

In this section, you use Layout view to develop the table layout of the page foreigntour.htm. This page links to information about La Bonne Cuisine's international culinary tours, including a proposed tour to Japan. The completed page in Design view should look like Figure 5-15. This page includes one layout table with four layout cells. In the browser window, the completed page should look like Figure 5-16.

 If Dreamweaver is set up for Standard view and you switch to Layout view, Dreamweaver displays a dialog box to warn that you are switching. You can elect not to view this dialog box in the future by clicking the checkbox next to "Don't show me this message again" and clicking OK. There is some value in keeping this reminder (by just clicking OK to close the dialog box), because switching between table layout views may affect existing tables. For example, if you create a table in Standard view, and then switch to Layout view, your table may have empty layout cells that you need to delete before you can create new cells. The choice is yours, but keeping the reminder when switching views may prevent frustration.

Figure 5-15   Design view version of layout in Layout view

To lay out a table:

1. Start Dreamweaver if necessary and open the La Bonne Cuisine Web site. Expand the Insert bar, if necessary. Double-click the file **foreigntour.htm** in the tour folder to open it for editing in Design view. Click the **Layout View** button on the Layout tab of the Insert bar and click **OK** in the warning dialog box, if it appears. Press the **Ctrl+Alt+G** key combination to make the grid visible, and press the **Ctrl+Alt+R** key combination to show the ruler, if they are not visible in Design view.

2. Press the **Ctrl+J** key combination to open the Page Properties dialog box. Type the page title, **Foreign Tours**. Insert a background image, **worldbg.gif**, from the Sites\lbc\assets\images folder. Change the text color to dark green (hexadecimal code **#336600**) and the link color to dark blue-green (hexadecimal code **#336699**). Click **OK**.

Figure 5-16   Browser version of layout in Layout view

3. Click the **Draw Layout Cell** button ⊞ on the Layout tab of the Insert bar, place the insertion point near the top of the page and about 125 pixels from the left margin, then draw a layout cell about 460 pixels wide and 70 pixels high. You can adjust cell width and height by selecting the table cell and changing its dimensions in the Property inspector. To select a table cell, click anywhere inside it and then click the <td> tag on the Document window status bar (displayed in Figure 5-5).

4. Place the insertion point inside the layout cell, click the **Image** button ⊞ on the Common tab of the Insert panel (or press the **Ctrl+Alt+I** key combination), and insert the image **foreigntours.gif** from the Sites\lbc\assets\images folder.

5. Click Draw Layout Cell ⊞ on the Layout tab of the Insert panel, locate the insertion point about 10 pixels from the left margin and 45 pixels from the top of the page, using the ruler to guide you. Draw a layout cell about 100 pixels wide and 100 pixels high. If you draw the second cell within eight pixels of the first, Dreamweaver automatically snaps the new cell to the edge of the existing cell.

6. Place the insertion point inside the layout cell you just drew, press the **Ctrl+Alt+I** key combination, and insert the image **tours.gif** from the Sites\lbc\assets\images folder. Resize the layout table width by dragging its right border as far to the left as possible.

7. Click the **Draw Layout Cell** button ▣ and draw a new layout cell beginning about 120 pixels from the left and 150 pixels from the top of the page. Draw a cell that is about 250 pixels wide and 100 pixels high. Click the cursor inside this table cell. In the Property inspector, change the format to **Heading 2**. Type **Travel with us on our next international culinary tour to Japan!**

8. Click the **Draw Layout Cell** button ▣ and draw a new layout cell about 450 pixels from the left margin and about 125 pixels below the top of the page. Make this cell about 100 pixels wide and 150 pixels high.

9. Place the insertion point in this layout cell, press the **Ctrl+Alt+I** key combination, and insert the image **tokyonoodles.jpg** from the Sites\lbc\assets\images folder. Notice that the table cell expands to hold the image.

10. Save the document, **foreigntour.htm**, and preview it in your browser. Close the file.

LAYOUT WITH FRAMES

After their introduction in Netscape Navigator 2.0, frames became a popular way to lay out Web sites. Using frames, you can organize and display a group of documents on the same page, while still allowing each document to behave independently. You can also nest frames to create more complex layout structures. Some preset frameset structures include nested framesets. Framesets can give a Web site a consistent look, because the contents of some frames, particularly navigation frames, can be the same throughout the Web site. Maintenance may be more efficient, because you need to link to the navigation frame in only one place. Also, download times may be less, because only frame content that changes needs to be downloaded.

Frames have certain disadvantages as well. Frame scroll bars and borders may occupy too much screen real estate in smaller browser windows. If the No Scroll option is set, viewers with smaller browser windows may not be able to scroll to see all the frame contents. It is easy to mix up frame targets so that HTML pages do not load into the intended frame. Printing frame contents can also be harder, because earlier browsers do not print the contents of an entire frameset. Therefore, some Web sites provide print versions of frame content to make printing easier for viewers. Despite all of the drawbacks of frames, they are still widely used, and as a Web developer, you need to know how to create and manage framesets and frames.

You can create framesets in Dreamweaver MX by clicking New on the File menu (or pressing the Ctrl+N key combination) and then selecting the Framesets Category in the New Document dialog box. Figure 5-17 shows the frameset options in the New Document dialog box. This figure also shows the same preset frames available on the Frames tab on the Insert bar when you already have a document open. Remember, a frameset is an HTML document without <body> tags. It contains <frameset> tags instead. The <frameset> tags lay out frame rows and columns within which HTML documents can be displayed. Think of a frameset as a window with a set of panes (or frames) that can each hold an HTML document. The contents of one frame can change and the other frames remain constant. To build more complex configurations, framesets can be nested within framesets.

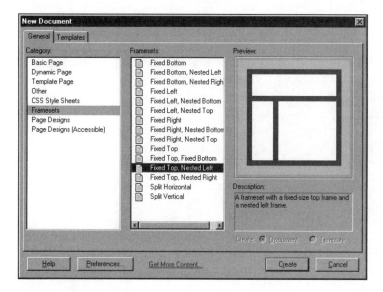

Figure 5-17   Frameset options in New Document dialog box

Figure 5-18 shows the code for a widely used, nested frameset layout. The outer frameset has two rows. The first row frame, named topFrame, holds the HTML document topframe.htm. The second row frame holds a nested frameset with a two-column frame. The left frame, named leftFrame, initially holds the HTML document leftbottom.htm; the right frame, named mainFrame, initially holds the document bottomframe.htm. In Design view, a border of dotted lines surrounds the selected frameset; in the Frames panel shown in Figure 5-19, a dark border surrounds the selection.

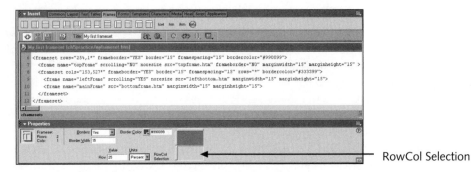

RowCol Selection

Figure 5-18   Frameset HTML tags

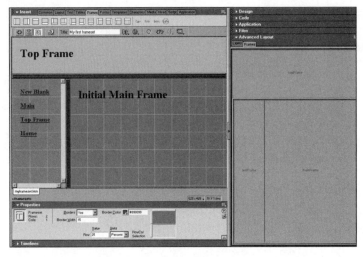

Figure 5-19   Frames category, Frames panel, and Property inspector for a frameset

The Frames panel to the right in Figure 5-19 shows a visual image of the frameset lay-out structure, with the outer frameset selected. You can open the Frames panel by click-ing Other on the Window drop-down menu and then selecting Frames on the pop-up menu, or by pressing the Shift+F2 key combination. Using the Frames panel, you can select the entire frameset by clicking the outer frameset border, or an individual frame by clicking inside the frame.

Frames sound complex, and they can be complex to program in HTML. However, Dreamweaver makes setting up and managing layout with frames easier by helping you visualize that layout. Dreamweaver provides ways to create and modify the frameset doc-ument as well as modify the individual HTML pages inserted into the frames, working from within the frameset display in Design view.

After you define an HTML document as a frameset, you can use the Property inspec-tor, the mouse, and the Frames panel to manage the attributes of the frameset and its contents. When you create a frameset, Dreamweaver creates default frame documents for each frame in the frameset, with names such as UntitledFrame-1.htm. You can either develop these empty documents for your frameset and save them or insert other existing documents by selecting the frame and specifying a document in the Property inspector Src text box. The Dreamweaver Save All command allows you to save the entire frameset and its frame contents.

Although the frameset document is a holder for other documents, giving it a meaningful page title and document name is important. If a visitor bookmarks any page that appears within the frameset, the frameset page title is recorded as the bookmark name, and the frameset document name is recorded as the URL.

Frameset Properties

The Property inspector contains the frameset properties that you can change to define the layout of your frames. If the Property inspector shows no information about the frameset, select the frameset by clicking the frameset border in the Frames panel. The example in Figure 5-19 displays the following parameters in the Property inspector for the outer or parent frameset:

- Frameset indicates the number of frameset rows and columns. The outer frameset has two rows and one column.

- Borders sets frame borders. Setting Borders to Yes results in a narrow gray border with a three-dimensional appearance (whose width and color you can change). Setting Borders to No results in invisible borders. Setting Borders to Default means that the browser determines the display of borders.

- Border Width sets the pixel width of the frameset borders.

- Border Color defines the border color hexadecimal code using the Color Picker.

- RowCol (Row Column) Selection provides a schema of the outer frameset layout so that you can select the row or column for which you would like to change the Value and Units displayed in the bottom row of the Property inspector.

- Value and Units defines the number of pixels or the percentage of the browser window that the row or column selected by RowCol Selection occupies. Setting Units to Relative makes the size of the row or column relative to the space left after allotting space to other rows or columns with specified pixel or percentage sizes.

The following examples may sound complicated, but once you begin using relative units, you will see that they are useful in frameset layout, because they adjust to different browser widths:

- In a two-column frameset, with left frame width set to 80 pixels and the right frame set to Relative Value 1, the width of the left frame is always 80 pixels, but the width of the right frame adjusts to changing browser widths.

- If both frames in a two-column frameset are set to Units Relative, then the values determine the relative size of each. If the first column's value is 2 and the second column's value is 1, then the first column occupies two-thirds of browser width and the second column occupies one-third of browser width.

- Assume there are three columns. The first column's width is in Percent Units with the value 20%; the second column's width is in Relative Units with the value 2; the third column's width is in Relative Units with the value 1. As a result, the second column occupies two-thirds of the width left after allotting 20% of the browser width to the first column.

Frame Properties

Each frame in the frameset also has properties that you can view and adjust in the Property inspector when you select the frame. Frame properties affect layout as well. Reviewing the frame properties in the Property inspector in Figure 5-20 helps you understand these properties. The dotted lines around the selected frame in the Design view window and the dark lines around the same frame in the Frames panel identify the frame whose attributes appear in the Property inspector.

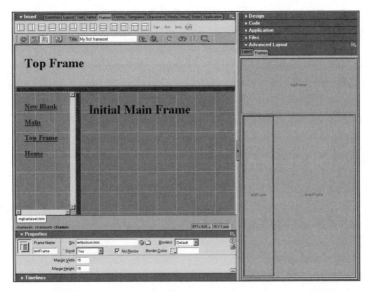

Figure 5-20   Frames category, Frames panel, and Property inspector for a frame

The Property inspector for a frame consists of the following attributes:

- The Frame icon indicates that the displayed information is about one frame.
- Frame Name is the name given to this frame.

- Src (Source Document) provides the name of the source HTML document that appears in the frame. You can create this document from within the frame or load an existing HTML document.

- Borders defines border characteristics (Yes, No, Default). Setting Borders to Yes results in a narrow gray border with a three-dimensional appearance (whose width and color you can change). Setting Borders to No makes borders invisible. Setting Borders to Default means that the browser determines how the borders are displayed. (Remember that these borders are for an individual frame, not the entire frameset.)

- Scroll indicates whether scroll bars are displayed. You can set Scroll to Yes (always display scrollbars), No (never display scrollbars), Auto (display scrollbars if necessary), or Default (allow browser to determine whether scrollbars are displayed). Setting Scroll to No can create problems for viewers with smaller browser windows; they may not be able to scroll to frame content that does not fit in the visible frame space.

- No Resize, if checked, prevents the viewer from resizing the frame. The frame then always remains the preset width and height.

- Border Color provides the hexadecimal code for the border.

- Margin Width and Margin Height define the space in pixels that separates the HTML page that occupies the frame from the edge of the frame (here, 15 pixels).

Inserting Frames in Dreamweaver

You can create a new frameset document from the New Document dialog box, as described earlier, or insert frames into an existing document from the Frames tab on the Insert bar or from the Dreamweaver Insert menu. Each method provides the same preset frameset layout structures. You can also subdivide the frame structure by clicking inside a frame and inserting another frameset within it (called a nested frameset). In fact, several preset frame structures include nested framesets, including the one we have been using as an example.

The New Document dialog box in Dreamweaver MX has slightly different names for each of the frameset layout structures than the Frames tab, which uses the names from earlier versions of Dreamweaver. However, since both offer visual diagrams of the framesets, you can choose the one that matches your layout design. If you want to split one of the frames in your frameset further, you can either select the frame and insert a nested frameset from the Frames tab or the Frames pop-up menu available on the Dreamweaver Insert menu, or you can choose Frameset on the Dreamweaver Modify menu and select one of the split frames options available there (such as the Split Frame Right). You can change the default sizes and parameters of each frameset in its Property inspector.

Saving Framesets

Saving framesets and the frames within them can be confusing, because Dreamweaver gives them all default names starting with "Untitled." You need to adopt a systematic method for saving framesets that includes assigning meaningful names and paying attention to which names you assign to which elements while you are saving them. Options on the Dreamweaver File menu vary depending on whether you select a frame or an entire frameset. To save an individual frame, use the Save Frame or Save Frame As option. Options for saving an entire frameset are as follows:

- Save Frameset opens a dialog box prompting for filename and location. Using the word frameset (or some abbreviation of it) in the name of your frameset makes identifying it easier.

- Save Frameset As saves an existing frameset with a new name or in a new location.

- Save All saves the frameset and the frame documents in each frame. (It also saves any other documents you have open.) If you have not previously saved the frameset documents, Dreamweaver first prompts you to save the frameset document and then prompts you to save each frame within the frameset, beginning with the default main frame (usually the largest one) and then proceeding from the upper-left frame through the remaining frames. You can identify which frame you are being prompted to save by the rope-like dotted line that surrounds the frame in Design view or the solid line around the frame in the Frames panel. If you save the page before you insert the frameset, Dreamweaver assumes that the saved page name belongs in the main frame. The Save All option is also available when a single frame is selected.

Inserting and Managing Framesets and Frames

In the next set of steps, you create a frameset in the New Document dialog box. You will save this practice frameset as myframeset.htm in the Sites\ch5practice folder of your working drive. When Dreamweaver inserts a frameset, it automatically assigns default names to the frames (such as leftFrame and mainFrame) and default document names to the frameset documents (such as UntitledFrameset-1.htm). It uses the name of the document into which you inserted the frameset as the default name for the mainFrame document if you saved it before inserting the frameset, and gives a default name such as UntitledFrame-1.htm to documents in other frames. (Remember that the name of the frame is not the same thing as the name of the document within the frame).

To work with a frameset:

1. Use Windows Explorer to create a **ch5practice** folder inside the Sites folder of your working drive, then create an **images** folder inside the Sites\ch5practice folder. Open Dreamweaver, if it is not already open. If the Frames panel is not open, press the **Shift+F2** key combination to open it.

2. Press the **Ctrl+N** key combination to open the New Document dialog box in Dreamweaver. Select **Framesets** in the Category list, as shown in Figure 5-17. Select **Fixed Top** in the Framesets list to create a frameset with two rows. Click **Create** to create a new frameset.

3. Click **File** on the Dreamweaver menu bar, click **Save All**, and then save the frameset document as **myframeset.htm** in the Sites\ch5practice folder.

4. When prompted for the name of the **mainFrame** document (which has a default name such as untitled.htm), save it as **bottomframe.htm**. The thick, rope-like dotted line around the frame in Design view indicates which frame you are saving. Dreamweaver then prompts for the name of the other frame documents.

5. Save the topFrame document as **topframe.htm**. Verify the names in the **Src input box** in the Property inspector for each frame.

6. Click the outside border of the frameset in the Frames panel to select the entire frameset. In the Property inspector change these attributes of the frameset: Set Borders to **Yes**; set Border Width to **15**; change the Border Color to dark purple (**#990099**).

7. Make sure the entire frameset is still selected by double-checking that a dark border surrounds the entire frameset in the Frames panel. In the Property inspector, select the top row of the frameset in the frameset layout to the right of the RowCol selection. In the Property inspector, change the Units to **Percent** and the Value to **25**. With the entire frameset still selected in the Frames panel, press the **Ctrl+J** key combination to open the Page Properties dialog box. In the Title text box, type **My First Frameset**. Click **OK**.

8. Click **File** on the menu bar, click **Save All**, and save the results in the Sites\ch5practice folder. View the results in your browser window.

In the next set of steps you insert a nested frame inside the bottom frame in the frameset you just created, using the Frames tab on the Insert bar. Notice that Dreamweaver automatically places the document bottomframe.htm into the larger frame and creates an untitled document in the narrower left frame. Also notice that changing the border color of the new frameset overrides the border color of the first frameset, although that may not be the case when you display the frameset in a browser window.

To insert a nested frame:

1. Open the Insert bar by clicking its expander arrow (see Figure 5-20 for its location), if it is not already open. Open the **Frames tab**. Open **myframeset.htm** in Design view if it is not already open. Click in the lower frame in the Frames panel to select it. Insert a two-column nested frameset by clicking **Left Frame** on the Frames tab.

2. With the nested frameset still selected in the Frames panel, click and drag the vertical border separating the left and right frames to the right so that the left frame is about 140 pixels wide. You can also make this change by selecting the nested frameset in the Frames panel and then clicking inside the left frame in

the RowCol Selection schema in the Frameset Property inspector, which is shown in Figure 5-18. You then can change its width by typing **140** in the Col Value input box and selecting **pixels** from the drop-down list. Select the new nested frameset in the Frames panel. In the Property inspector, set Frameset Border to **Yes**, set the border color to **#333399**, and make it **15** pixels wide.

3. In Design view, click and drag the vertical divider of this frameset to make the left frame about **140** pixels wide. You can also make this change by selecting the lower frameset in the RowCol (Row Column) Selection schema in the Property inspector for the frameset, shown in Figure 5-18, and then changing its column width to **140 pixels**.

   Dreamweaver gives the new frame the default name **leftFrame**, as you can see in the Frames panel.

4. Click **File** on the Dreamweaver menu bar, and then click **Save All**. Save the document in leftFrame as **leftbottom.htm** in the Sites\ch5practice folder. Preview the frameset in the browser.

In the next set of steps you change the frame properties and edit the documents within each frame to make them similar to the frameset in Figure 5-20. You select the leftBottom frame, by clicking in the Frames panel. The Property inspector displays the properties of the leftFrame frame.

To modify the frames:

1. Open **myframeset.htm** in Design view if it is not already open. Click inside the top frame in the Frames panel to select it. Change the frame properties in the Property inspector: Set Margin Width and Margin Height to **15**. Click **No Resize** if it is not already checked.

2. Place the insertion point inside the top frame in Design view to modify the document within the frame. Select **Heading 1** in the Format drop-down list on the Property inspector, then type **Top Frame** inside the document. Press the **Ctrl+J** key combination to open the Page Properties dialog box, change the page title to **Top Frame Document**, and change the background color for this frame to green (**#00FF66**). Click **OK**.

3. Click inside leftFrame in the Frames panel to select that frame. Change its properties in the Property inspector: Set Margin Width and Margin Height to **15**. Set Scroll to **Yes**.

4. Click in the left frame in Design view to modify the document within the frame. Select **Heading 3** format, type **New Blank**, then press the **Enter** key to insert a new line. Select **Heading 3** format again if necessary, and type **Main**.

5. Create two more new lines in the left frame in **Heading 3** format. Type **Top Frame** and **Home** on these two lines. Press the **Ctrl+J** key combination to open the Page Properties dialog box, change the page title to **Menu Frame** and the background color to light purple (**#9999FF**). Click **OK**.

6. Click the border around mainFrame in the Frames panel to select that frame. Change the frame properties in the Property inspector: set Margin Width and Margin Height to **15**. Set Scroll to **Auto**.

7. Click inside the main frame in the Document window to modify the document within the frame. Select **Heading 1** format in the Property inspector, and type **Initial Main Frame.** Press the **Ctrl+J** key combination to open the Page Properties dialog box, change the page title to **Home Page** and the background color to dark pink (**#FF0066**). Click **OK**.

8. Click **Save All** on the File menu, and preview in your browser. The results should be similar to the page shown in Figure 5-21 (without the underlines). Note that your browser may display a different default font, depending on its configuration.

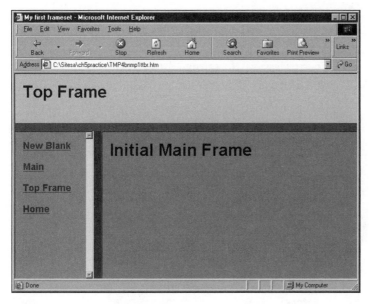

Figure 5-21   myframeset.htm previewed in the browser

In the next set of steps, you add some interactivity to the menu in the left frame to change the contents of the main frame. When you do this, opening your link in the correct target window is critical. Two advantages of Dreamweaver are that it provides default targets (_blank, _parent, _self, _top) and also includes frame targets in the Target list (in this case, mainFrame, leftFrame, topFrame).

- _blank opens the link in a new browser window and keeps the current browser window open.

- _parent opens the link in the parent frameset of the current frame, if it is nested.

- _self opens the link inside the current frame.

- _top opens the link inside the outermost frameset of the current Web page, replacing all the frames.

> If you link to an external Web site, you should choose _top or _blank as the target, because in recent lawsuits involving intellectual property, judges have ruled against opening a Web page belonging to someone else within your own frameset. Thus, in the following steps, whenever you link to an external Web page you open it in a new window by setting the target to _blank. Whenever you open an internal Web page, you can open it in one of the frames within the frameset by setting the target to one of the frames.

To add interactivity:

1. In Design view, open **myframeset.htm** if it is not already open.

2. Select the text **New Blank** in the menu frame. Create a hyperlink by typing a link to the Macromedia Web site (**http://www.macromedia.com**) in the Link text box. Select **_blank** in the Target drop-down list, as shown in Figure 5-22. Use the **Save All** command to save the changes, and then preview in a browser.

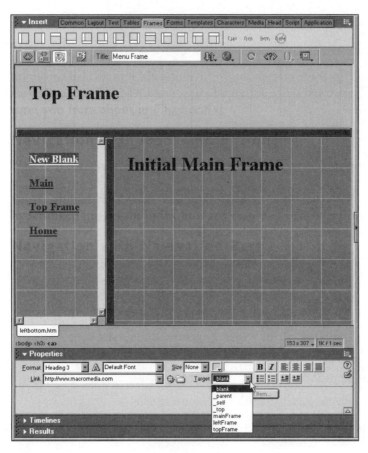

Figure 5-22   Setting target for hyperlinked page

3. Set up a hyperlink for the second navigation link. Select the text **Main** in the menu frame and use the Browse-for-File icon in the Property inspector to select the file **localtour.htm** in the Sites\lbc\tour folder in the La Bonne Cuisine Web site. Select **mainFrame** in the Target list arrow.

4. Repeat Step 3 for the text **Top Frame** in the menu frame, this time selecting the file **aboutlbc.htm** in the Sites\lbc\contact folder and setting the target to **topFrame**.

5. Repeat Step 3 for the text **Home**, with the target **mainFrame**, but this time use the name of the page (**bottomframe.htm**) that originally appears when the frameset opens. This returns the content of mainFrame to its initial state.

6. Click **File** on the Dreamweaver menu bar, then click **Save All**, and view in the browser to see how your menu works.

Figure 5-23 shows the frameset after you click Main in the navigation frame.

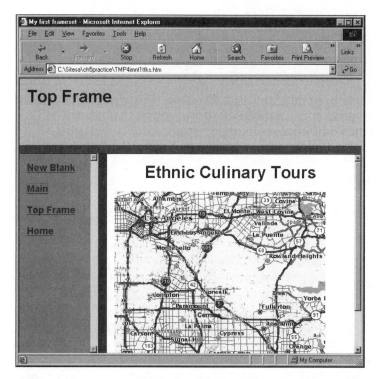

Figure 5-23   Frameset in browser with Main selected

Handling Browsers that Do Not Support Frames

Using the <noframes> tag in a frameset allows you to warn and/or redirect a viewer to Web pages without frames, if the viewer's browser does not support frames. To edit <noframes> content, click Edit NoFrames Content, found under the Frameset command on the Dreamweaver Modify menu. You see a blank NoFrames Content page where you can type your message and insert a hyperlink to an alternative page without frames. The HTML tags for NoFrames go below the frameset tags. To return to the frameset document, click Edit NoFrames Content under the Frameset command on the Dreamweaver Modify menu again. In the following set of steps, you create an alternative path for the viewer whose browser does not support frames.

To create an alternative path:

1. In Design view, open **myframeset.htm** if it is not already open.

2. Click **Modify** on the Dreamweaver menu bar, point to **Frameset**, and then click **Edit NoFrames Content**.

3. Type **Sorry, your browser does not support frames**.

4. Press the **Enter** key and type **Click to continue**. Select the word **Click** and create a hyperlink to **bottomframe.htm**.

5. To return to the Frameset editing window, click the **Edit NoFrames Content** again. Click **File** on the Dreamweaver menu bar, and then click **Save All**.

LAYOUT WITH LAYERS

One great contribution of Dreamweaver MX (as well as Dreamweaver 3 and Dreamweaver 4) to HTML layout is the ability to position content in all sorts of odd-sized rectilinear cells on a page using layers, and then use a Dreamweaver command to convert the layers to tables. Dreamweaver adds extra table cells to preserve the layout structure you created in layers. This table layout displays consistently in different browsers. Layout view in Dreamweaver MX automates much of the layers-to-table layout process for you. Layout view tables may be more difficult to revise later, especially if you become accustomed to the relatively straightforward layers-to-tables method, which can easily be reversed by the tables-to-layers command. Both methods give you much more flexibility than using Standard view tables. You should experiment with both methods (Layout view and layers-to-table) and decide which you prefer. Each layer has an x coordinate that determines its distance in pixels from the left edge of the HTML page, and a y coordinate that determines its distance in pixels from the top of the page. The x and y coordinates are important for page layout, which is two-dimensional. It also has a Z-Index, which defines its stacking order relative to other layers it overlaps, and a visibility property, which indicates whether it is visible or hidden. You can change the stacking order of the layers by dragging and dropping the layers up or down in the Layers panel, as shown in Figure 5-24. You can open the Layers panel by clicking Layers on the Others pop-up on the Dreamweaver Window menu or by pressing the F2 key. The small yellow icons in the left corner of the HTML page in the Document window are invisible elements for the layers. You can see that Layer1 is selected, because it displays layer handles in the Document window, and it is highlighted in the Layers panel.

You cannot convert nested or overlapping layers into tables. You can prevent overlapping or nested layers by clicking the Prevent Overlaps checkbox in the Layers panel, shown in Figure 5-24.

5

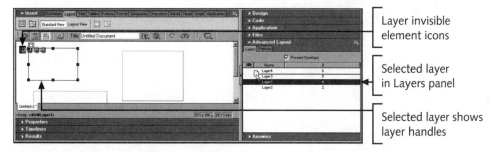

Layer invisible
element icons

Selected layer
in Layers panel

Selected layer shows
layer handles

Figure 5-24   Changing the stacking order of layers in the Layers panel

Layers provide more layout flexibility than frames or Standard view tables because you can use layers to position objects and text anywhere on a page, just as you can with layout cells and layout tables in Layout view. Unfortunately, the results of using layers alone are not predictable, since browsers interpret layer tags differently. Layers also display differently in different-sized browser windows. In addition to their x and y coordinates, layers have width and height attributes that set their physical dimensions. If the browser window is small and the layers' width and height are large enough, then the layers may overlap one another when displayed. Also, you may get variable results depending on the browser resolution and the browser-selected text size.

To draw layers, you must work in Standard view.

Dreamweaver offers two ways to create layers in Standard view:

- Use the Layer command, found on the Dreamweaver Insert menu shown in Figure 5-25, to insert a layer in the upper-left corner of the HTML page in the Dreamweaver editing window. If you insert a second layer this way, you must move the first one elsewhere on the page, or Dreamweaver may nest the second layer inside the first or overlap the two layers.

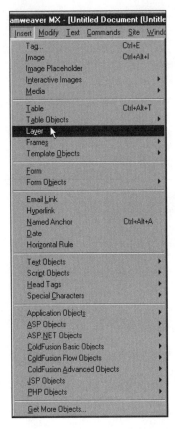

Figure 5-25   Insert a layer from the menu

■ Use the Draw Layer button [img] on the Common tab or Layout tab of the
Insert bar. You can click the button and drag and drop it onto the page to
create a layer that is positioned in the upper-left corner of the HTML page.
This method yields a result very similar to clicking the Layer command on
the Dreamweaver Insert menu, discussed in the previous bullet. To draw a
layer anywhere on the HTML page, click the Draw Layer button [img] on the
Common tab or Layout tab of the Insert bar, and then click anywhere on the
HTML page and draw the layer, as shown on the right side of Figure 5-26.

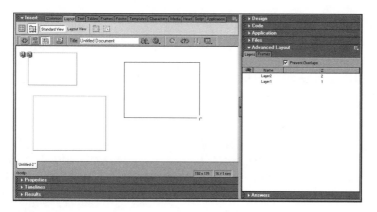

Figure 5-26   Drawing a layer

You can select an existing layer by clicking it in the Layers panel, or by clicking its outer border. If you have inserted a graphic inside the layer, you need to make sure that you select the layer and not the graphic. In Figure 5-27, you can see that the selected layer has a handle in its upper-left corner and that it is highlighted in the Layers panel. If you ever need to move the layer on the page and do not want to change its size, drag it by the layer handle. The black squares on each of the layer edges and corners let you resize the layer. You can also change the dimensions of a layer by changing its width and height parameters in the Property inspector for the layer.

The HTML code for the selected layer in Figure 5-27 shows that a layer is enclosed within <div> tags. A layer has a defined width and height, x and y coordinates that define its position relative to the upper-left corner of the page, and a Z-Index, which indicates its stacking order (and by default, its order of creation). Stacking order can be changed. You learn more about layers in Chapter 10.

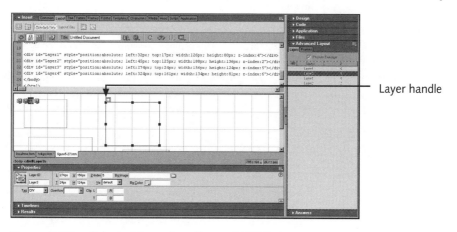

Layer handle

Figure 5-27   Selected layer handles and HTML tags

Layer Properties

When you select a layer, its properties are visible in the Property inspector. You can tell it is selected on the page because its symbol in the upper-left corner of the page is selected, its layer handle and its resizing handles are visible, and it is selected in the Layers panel. Figure 5-27 shows the properties for the selected layer (Layer3 in this example) in the Layer Property inspector:

- Layer ID states that properties are for Layer3. You can change the layer name.

- L (Left) and T (Top) are the x and y coordinates that define the distance in pixels (274 px) from the left edge of the page to the left border of the layer and the distance in pixels (24 px) from the top of the HTML page to the top border of the layer.

- W (Width) and H (Height) define the width of the layer (156 px) and the height of the layer (124 px) in pixels. Width and height can also be percentages.

- Z-Index denotes the stacking order of the layer or order of creation. If you give layers the same x and y coordinates to stack them physically on a page, then higher-numbered layers appear in front of lower-numbered layers. This display method may work differently in Internet Explorer and Netscape Navigator.

- Vis (Visibility) defines the visibility of the layer. Options are default, inherit from parent layer if nested, visible, or hidden. Most browsers interpret default to mean that visibility is inherited from the parent layer, which only applies to a layer nested inside another layer.

- Bg (Background) Image can be used to put a background image in the layer.

- Bg (Background) Color displays the hexadecimal code for a background color.

- Tag is used to create layer refers to the HTML tag choices for layers. SPAN and DIV create CSS layers.

- Overflow lets you define what happens when the content of a CSS layer overflows the size of the layer. Options are Visible, which increases the layer size downward and to the right to make all the layer's content visible; Hidden, which drops any content beyond the layer size; Scroll, which provides scroll bars; and Auto, which provides scroll bars when layer content exceeds layer size.

- Clip (Clip Rectangle) defines the visible area of a layer. You use the L (Left), T (Top), R (Right), and B (Bottom) text boxes to define the area of the layer that is not visible relative to the edges of the layer.

Creating and Managing Layers

In the next set of steps, you use layers to structure a Web page and then convert the layers to tables. You build a page using text and photos for Tokyo, for the proposed culinary tour to Japan.

To create and manage layers:

1. Open Dreamweaver and the La Bonne Cuisine Web site, if necessary. Open **tokyo.htm** in the tour folder in Design view. Press the **Ctrl+F3** key combination and the **F2** key to open the Property inspector and the Layers panel if they are not already open. Click the **Prevent Overlaps** checkbox in the Layers panel to select it. Press the **Ctrl+Alt+G** and the **Ctrl+Alt+R** key combinations to show the grid and the ruler if they are not already open.

2. Press the **Ctrl+J** key combination to open the Page Properties dialog box. Modify the HTML page properties by changing the title to **Tokyo**, the background color to light olive green (hexadecimal code **#CCCC00**), and the text color to dark red (hexadecimal code **#993300**). Click **OK**. Save this page as **tokyo.htm** in the Sites\lbc\tour folder of the La Bonne Cuisine Web site.

3. Click the **Standard View** button on the Layout tab of the Insert bar. Click the **Draw Layer** button [image], and then click **50** pixels from the top and **50** pixels from the left of the page. Drag the insertion point down and to the right to draw a layer on the page that is about **72** pixels high and **164** pixels wide. If the dimensions are not exactly correct, you can select the layer in the Layers panel and type the height and width in the Property inspector.

4. Place the insertion point inside the layer and press the **Ctrl+Alt+I** key combination to open the Insert Image dialog box. Locate and select the image **tokyotitle.gif** from the Sites\lbc\assets\images folder.

5. Use the instructions in Step 3 to draw another layer, this time about **250** pixels from the left and **25** pixels from the top margins of the page. Make it about **240** pixels wide and **84** pixels high.

6. Click in the layer you just drew. In the Property inspector, change the format to **Heading 2** and **italic**. Type **Visit Exciting Tokyo, the Busy Capital of Modern Japan**.

7. Use the instructions in Step 3 to draw another layer, about **150** pixels from the top of the page and **100** pixels from the left margin of the page. Make the layer **174** pixels wide and **216** pixels high. Use the instructions in Step 4 to insert the image **tokyotoyota.jpg** from the Sites\lbc\assets\images folder into this layer.

8. Repeat Step 7 to create a fourth layer, about **200** pixels from the top and **300** pixels from the left margins of the page, **216** pixels wide and **128** pixels high. Insert the image **uenotemple.jpg** from the Sites\lbc\assets\images folder.

9. If you need to move a layer, you can select it by clicking its border or selecting it in the Layer panel. Since the two photographs are close to one another, it is a good idea to move the layer with uenotemple.jpg to the lower right. Click the layer tag in the upper-left corner of its layer and drag it to reposition it, as shown in Figure 5-28. You can also change the layer position by selecting the layer handle and changing the Top position to 225 pixels and the Left position to 340 pixels in the Property inspector.

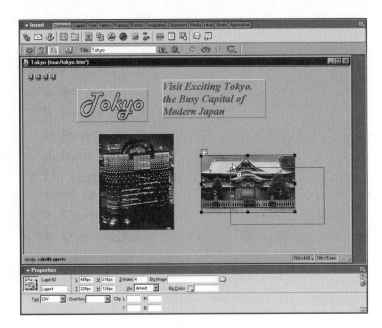

Figure 5-28   Dragging a layer to reposition it

10. Save the page **tokyo.htm** in the Sites\lbc\tour folder.

Now you are ready to complete your layout using the command Convert Layers to Table. The lower group of settings in the Convert Layers to Table dialog box shown in Figure 5-29 converts tables back to layers. The upper group of settings converts layers to tables:

- Most Accurate creates a table cell for every layer and additional table cells to recreate the space between each layer.

- Smallest Collapse Empty Cells means that the layer edges line up if they are within the number of defined pixels (yields fewer empty cells).

- Use Transparent GIFs puts a row of invisible GIF graphics at the bottom of the table. The GIF file, called transparent.gif, is automatically saved in the same folder as the HTML file.

- Center on Page centers the table.

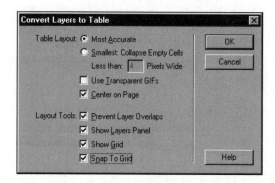

Figure 5-29 Settings for converting layers to tables

To use the Convert Layers to Tables command:

1. Open **tokyo.htm** in Design view, if it is not already open. Make sure you are in Standard view, not Layout view.

2. Click **Modify** on the Dreamweaver menu bar, point to **Convert**, and then click **Layers to Table** to open the Convert Layers to Table dialog box, shown in Figure 5-29. Click the **Most Accurate** option to select it, and the **Center on Page** checkbox to select it. Click to deselect the **Use Transparent GIFs** checkbox if it is selected. Click to select all the check boxes under Layout Tools. Click **OK**.

   Figure 5-30 shows the resulting table. Notice that the table has five rows and seven columns, and that the Layers panel is now empty. The number of rows and columns in your converted table may differ, depending on how precisely you drew the layers and whether you moved the layers to adjust the layout.

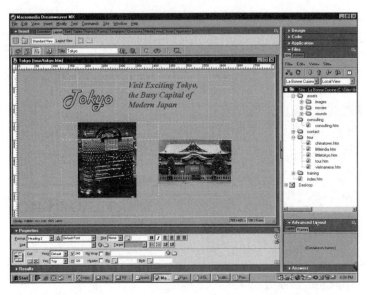

Figure 5-30   Table layout after converting from layers

3. Save the file. View it in the browser.

It should look very similar to the version you viewed before the conversion. If you want to move any of the layers, you can convert the table back to layers, reformat the page, and then convert the layers to a table again.

4. Close **tokyo.htm**.

CHAPTER SUMMARY

❏ Dreamweaver facilitates Web site layout with tools and functions that support development of tables, frames, and layers.

❏ Tables provide a very reliable way to accomplish page layout in Dreamweaver with two options: Standard view and Layout view.

❏ Preparing layout in Standard view means that you create a rectilinear table with rows and columns, which you then adjust by changing the span of table columns and by changing the height and width of table rows and cells. Row and cell height and width can be defined as fixed numbers of pixels or as percentages of the table height and width.

❏ Tables whose width is defined in percentages produce pages that expand and contract to fit different-sized browser windows, as long as the page content is not wider than the browser window.

❑ Layout view facilitates and automates the creation of table layout by letting you draw layout cells anywhere on the HTML page. Dreamweaver automatically creates the layout tables to hold these layout cells.

❑ Layout view allows you to define one column as Autostretch, which means that the column width expands and contracts when the browser window size expands and contracts. Dreamweaver MX places a row at the bottom of the table containing invisible graphics that hold steady the width of the non–Autostretch table cells in the table. The Autostretch cell does not contain one of these graphics, which allows the cell (and its column) to expand and contract.

❑ Frames allow you to develop a consistent site structure in Dreamweaver. Framesets are structures that contain frames, each of which holds a document. Frequently one frame contains a menu, which allows viewers to change the contents of one of the other frames.

❑ Dreamweaver provides tools that make creating, maintaining, and saving framesets and frames easier, provided you develop a methodical way of working with them.

❑ You can use layers to lay out a Web page and then convert the layers to tables to provide better consistency in different browsers. You can convert the table back to layers to adjust layout. This method provides a lot of flexibility in the development of page layout.

5

REVIEW QUESTIONS

1. Web site developers who want their pages to adjust to changing browser widths define layout using table width in _____.

2. Which of these improve Web site usability? (Choose all that apply.)

   a. providing blank space around clusters of information

   b. clear navigation

   c. meaningful navigation links

   d. cluttered page layout

3. The window that lets you set the attributes of whatever object you select (for example, a table, layer, or frame) is called the:

   a. Layer Palette

   b. Property inspector

   c. Launcher

   d. Objects

4. The tool that supplies the hexadecimal code of a Web safe color is the:

a. Color Picker

b. Property inspector

c. Launcher

d. Layers panel

5. The tab on the Insert bar that contains buttons for switching between Layout view and Standard view is called the:

a. Color tab

b. Application tab

c. Common tab

d. Layout tab

6. To draw layout cells on an HTML page you must be in:

a. Drawing view

b. Standard view

c. Layout view

d. Code view

7. The layer tags that define the CSS layers do not include: (Choose all that apply.)

a. SPAN

b. DIV

c. SPACER

d. AUTOSTRETCH

8. Which of the following views in Dreamweaver gives you the most flexibility in layout?

a. Layout View, which allows you to draw layout tables and layout cells

b. Standard View, which lets you increase column span and row span

c. Flexible View, which lets you place items anywhere on the page

d. Frames View, which lets you design frames

9. When a table cell extends across two columns, the cell tag says:

a. <td><td>

b. <td rowspan="2">

c. <td colspan="2">

d. <td div="2">

10. A frameset positioned within a frame is:

 a. layered

 b. embedded

 c. nested

 d. stacked

11. Frameset structure is defined by which of the following:

 a. layers

 b. rows

 c. x and y coordinates

 d. Z-Index

12. One of the properties that defines a table is:

 a. layers

 b. rows

 c. x and y coordinates

 d. Z-Index

13. Which of the following is not used to define layer structure?

 a. Z-Index

 b. rows

 c. x and y coordinates

 d. height and width

14. To convert layers to tables, you have to be sure that:

 a. none of the layers go off the edge of the browser page

 b. no layers are nested

 c. no layers are empty

 d. layer tags are not hidden

15. The frameset tags in a frameset document replace the:

 a. header tags

 b. body tags

 c. table tags

 d. HTML tags

16. The term CSS stands for:

 a. Cascading Style Sheets

 b. Cascading Style Selectors

 c. Class Style Sheets

 d. Cool Style Sheets

17. In a frameset, you cannot set the Units attribute to:

   a. pixels

   b. percent

   c. inches

   d. relative

18. The _____ command prompts you to save the frameset and the frames within in it.

19. The index that denotes the stacking order of a layer is the:

   a. W-Index

   b. X-Index

   c. Y-Index

   d. Z-Index

20. One advantage of using frames for layout is that:

   a. you can easily reuse the same content, such as menu bar frames, throughout your Web site

   b. if the browser window is small, scrollbars can occupy a lot of frame real estate

   c. with frame targets, it is easy to make mistakes that confuse viewers

   d. when viewers bookmark a page within a frame, their bookmark takes them back to the initial set of frameset frames

HANDS-ON PROJECTS

Project 5-1

In this project you lay out a page, kyoto.htm, in Layout view.

1. Copy the following images from the Chapter5\images folder on your Data Disk to the Sites\ch5practice\images folder on your working drive for use in this project: **worldbg.gif**, **kyototitle.gif**, **kyotopalacebridge.jpg**, and **goldentemple.jpg**.

2. Start Dreamweaver in Design view and press the **Ctrl+N** key combination to create a new Web page. Select **Basic Page** in the Category list of the New Document dialog box. Select **HTML** in the Basic Page window and click **Create**. Press the **Ctrl+Alt+G** and **Ctrl+Alt+R** key combinations to show the grid and the ruler, if they are not already visible. Press the **Ctrl+S** key combination and save the page as **kyoto.htm** in the Sites\ch5practice folder.

3. Press the **Ctrl+J** key combination to open the Page Properties dialog box. Change the page title to **Kyoto**, and insert the background image **worldbg.gif** from the Sites\ch5practice\images folder. Click **OK**.

4. On the Layout tab of the Insert bar, click **Layout View**. If the Getting Started in Layout View dialog box appears, click **OK** to close it. Click the **Draw Layout Cell** button and draw a layout cell beginning in the upper-left corner of the page (about 25 pixels from the top and 10 pixels from the left). Make the cell 153 pixels wide and 77 pixels high. Place the insertion point inside the layout cell, press the **Ctrl+Alt+I** key combination, and insert the title graphic, **kyototitle.gif**, from the Sites\ch5practice\images folder.

5. Follow the directions in Step 4 to draw another layout cell to the right and a little lower, beginning at 260 pixels from the left and 50 pixels from the top of the page. Make this layout cell 180 pixels wide and 120 pixels high. Insert the image **kyotopalacebridge.jpg**.

6. Follow the directions in Step 4 to draw another layout cell below the title cell, starting about 125 pixels from the top and 25 pixels from the left. Make the cell 216 pixels wide and 148 pixels high. Insert the image **goldentemple.jpg**.

7. Follow the directions in Step 4 to draw another layout cell, starting about 200 pixels from the top and 275 pixels from the left. Make the cell 183 pixels wide and 66 pixels high. Place the insertion point inside the layout cell, and use the Property inspector to set the format to **Heading 2**. Type **Visit ancient Tokyo**.

8. Save the page **kyoto.htm** in the Sites\ch5practice folder, and view it in your browser.

Project 5-2

In this project you recreate a layout structure similar to the tour.htm page you created earlier in this chapter. You use colspan and rowspan in your table, which has four columns in the first row and three columns in rows 2 and 3. You do not need to include any hyperlinks on this page.

1. Copy the images **wasedabg.gif**, **lbclogotrans.gif**, and **tours.gif** from the Chapter5\images folder on your Data Disk to the Sites\ch5practice\images folder on your working drive for this project. In Dreamweaver open the page **tour.htm** in the Sites\lbc\tour folder so that you can copy and paste text from it into tourcopy.htm, the page you create in this project.

2. Press the **Ctrl+N** key combination to create a new Basic HTML page in Dreamweaver and save it as **tourcopy.htm** in the folder Sites\ch5practice. Modify the page so that it has the same appearance as tour.htm in the La Bonne Cuisine Web site by adding the page title **Culinary Tours**, the background image **wasedabg.gif**, the text color **#CC3333**, and the link color **#000099**.

3. In Standard view, insert a table on this page with **3** rows and **3** columns, **95%** width, and cell padding and cell spacing each equal to **5**. Place the insertion point in the table cell in the first row and first column, and click the **Split cell into rows or columns** button in the Property inspector. Choose **2** columns.

4. Insert the images **lbclogotrans.gif** and **tours.gif** from the Sites\ch5practice\ images folder into the appropriate table cells. Refer to your open copy of tour.htm or to Figure 5-7 to see where the images should be placed. Copy the text and text formatting from tour.htm into the appropriate table cells in tourcopy.htm. Do not include the hyperlinks. If you copy and paste text, you can select the copied text and delete the hyperlinks in the Property inspector.

5. Save the page as **tourcopy.htm** in the folder Sites\ch5practice, view it in your browser, and compare its appearance with tour.htm in the Sites\lbc\tour folder.

Project 5-3

In this project you create a table with percentage widths and change it to fixed pixel widths.

1. Using Windows Explorer, copy the following images from the Chapter5\images folder on your Data Disk to the Sites\ch5practice\images folder on your working drive: **kyototitle.gif, consulting.gif, aboutlbc.gif, cloth.jpg, frenchbakery.jpg**, and **goldentemple.jpg**. If asked whether you want to overwrite existing files, click **Yes to All**.

2. Create a new page and save it as **tablewidths.htm** in the Sites\ch5practice folder.

3. In Standard view, insert a table on this page with **3** rows and **3** columns, **95%** width, and cell padding and cell spacing each equal to **5**. Split the cell in the first row and first column into two columns by placing the insertion point inside the table cell, and clicking the **Split cell into rows or columns** button in the Property inspector. Choose **2** columns.

4. In the first row, insert **kyototitle.gif** in the first cell, **consulting.gif** in the second cell, and **aboutlbc.gif** in the fourth cell. In the second row, insert **frenchbakery.jpg** in the second cell. In the third row, insert **goldentemple.jpg** in the first cell. Save the file **tablewidths.htm**, and view it in your browser to see whether it expands and contracts.

5. Select the **table** in tablewidths.htm, and click the **Convert Table Widths to Pixels** button in the Property inspector. Save the file **tablefixed.htm**, and view it in your browser to see whether it expands and contracts.

Project 5-4

In this project you create a page with layout in Standard view and then edit the page in Layout view.

1. Create a new basic HTML page. Press the **Ctrl+J** key combination and change the page title to **Table Standard**. Click the **Standard View** button on the Layout tab of the Insert bar. Press the **Ctrl+Alt+T** key combination and insert a table with **3** rows and **3** columns, **95%** width, and cell padding and cell spacing each equal to **5**. Type the text **TABLESTANDARD** in each table cell. Save the page as **tablestandard.htm** in the Sites\ch5practice folder on your working drive.

2. Click the **Layout View** button on the Layout tab of the Insert bar. If Dreamweaver displays a dialog box informing you that you are switching layout views, click **OK** to close it. Try to insert a layout cell inside the table you created in Step 1. What happens? Try to insert a layout cell below the table you inserted in Step 1 (the size does not matter). What happens?

Project 5-5

In this project you create a page using Layout view, with an Autostretch column. Dreamweaver provides a spacer.gif file when you indicate that you want to create one and insert it into the non-Autostretch columns of the layout table. You choose where to save this graphics file.

1. Copy the image **tokyonoodles.jpg** from the Chapter5\images folder on your Data Disk to the ch5practice\images folder on your working drive.

2. Create a new HTML page in Dreamweaver. Click the **Layout View** button on the Layout tab of the Insert bar. Press the **Ctrl+J** key combination and change the page title to **Autostretch**. Set window size to **600 × 300** pixels (the display size for a 800 × 600 page size) in the status bar of Design view. To do this, you have to reset the HTML document so that it is not maximized in the Document window. Depending on your screen resolution, you may have to close the panels to the right of the Document window by clicking on the slider on the right edge of the window. Save the page as **autostretch.htm** in the Sites\ch5practice folder on your working drive. Press the **Ctrl+Alt+R** and **Ctrl+Alt+G** key combinations to display the ruler and grid, if they are not visible.

3. Insert a layout table with two layout cells. Draw the first layout cell as close to the upper-left edge of the table as possible and make it at least **100** pixels wide and 150 pixels high. Insert the image **tokyonoodles.jpg** into the cell on the left and resize the cell to fit the graphic (at least **100** pixels wide and **149** pixels high). You can resize a table cell by dragging its edges, or by changing the dimensions in the Table Property inspector. Draw the right layout cell starting **50** pixels from the top and **150** pixels from the left. Make this layout cell **100** pixels high and extend its width to the right edge of the table, which makes it about **600** pixels wide.

4. Place the insertion point inside this layout cell and change the format to **Heading 1** in the Property inspector. Type **This is an example of Autostretch** in the layout cell. Select the layout cell by clicking its edge, and click the **Autostretch** option button in the Property inspector to select it. If Dreamweaver asks whether you want to create a spacer image file, click **OK**, and save the spacer.gif file in the Sites\ch5practice\images folder. Save the file and view in your browser. Expand and contract the browser window to see what happens.

Project 5-6

In this two-part project you first create a frameset with two frames and then add inter-activity between the frames.

1. Copy the images **hiroshimatitle.gif**, **hiroshimacranes.jpg**, **hiroshimaruin.jpg**, and **hiroshimawreaths.jpg** from the Chapter 5\images folder on your Data Disk to the ch5practice\images folder on your working drive.

2. In Dreamweaver, press the **Ctrl+N** key combination to open the New Document dialog box. Choose **Framesets** in the Category list. Then select the **Fixed Top** frameset and click the **Create** button. Set window size to **600 × 300** in the status bar. Press the **Ctrl+Alt+G** and **Ctrl+Alt+R** key combinations to show the grid and ruler in Design view, if they are not already visible. Type **Hiroshima** in the Title textbox. Save the document as **hiroframeset.htm** in the Sites\ch5practice folder. Click **File** on the Dreamweaver menu bar, and then click **Save All**. Name the top frame **hiroshimatop.htm** and the bottom frame **hiroshimahome.htm**.

3. Open the Frames panel and select the top frame. In the Frame Property inspector, set scroll to **Yes**. Select the entire frameset. In the RowCol selection in the Frameset Property inspector, change the top frame's Row Value to **120** and its Units to **Pixels**.

4. Click inside the top frame. Click the **Layout View** button on the Layout tab of the Insert bar. Draw a layout table that is **650** pixels wide and **80** pixels high. Click the **Draw Layout Cell** button, place the insertion point inside the table, and draw a layout cell, beginning in the upper-left corner of the layout table, that is **282** pix-els wide and **75** pixels high. Place the insertion point inside this layout cell, press the **Ctrl+Alt+I** key combination, and insert the image **hiroshimatitle.gif** from the ch5practice\images folder.

5. Draw a second layout cell, immediately to the right of the first, that is **250** pixels wide and **80** pixels high. Type an unordered (bulleted) list inside the cell in bold font with three items: **Hiroshima Ruin**, **Hiroshima Peace Memorial**, and **Home**.

6. Follow the instructions in Step 4 to draw a layout table and layout cell inside the bottom frame. Draw a layout table that is **650** pixels wide and **250** pixels high. Draw a layout cell starting **150** pixels from the left and **50** pixels from the top of the bottom frame. Make the cell **250** pixels wide and **200** pixels high and insert the image **hiroshimacranes.jpg**.

7. Create two more pages with layout similar to the one you created for hiroshimahome.htm. Press the **Ctrl+N** key combination to create a new page and save it as **hiroshimaruin.htm** in the Sites\ch5practice folder. Draw a layout table and a layout cell with the same specifications given in Step 6 and insert the image **hiroshimaruin.jpg** in the layout cell. In the same way, create another new page and save it as **hiroshimamem.htm**. Draw a layout table and a layout cell and insert the image **hiroshimawreaths.jpg**. Save both pages in the Sites\ch5practice folder.

8. Create hyperlinks from the bullets in the top frame that open pages in the bottom frame. Select the text **Hiroshima Ruin** in the top frame and link to **hiroshimaruin.htm**. Select the target **mainFrame** in the Property inspector. Use the same method to create a hyperlink from the text **Hiroshima Peace Memorial** to **hiroshimamem.htm**, and from the text **Home** to **hiroshimahome.htm**. Click **File** on the Dreamweaver menu bar, then click **Save All Frames**, and then test the pages in your browser to make sure that your linked pages open in the bottom of your frameset.

CASE PROJECTS

Browse the Microsoft home page (*www.microsoft.com*). Are tables, frames, or layers used to lay out this page? Also visit the Macromedia home page (*www.macromedia.com*) and the Lotus Notes home page (*www.lotus.com*). Are tables, frames, or layers used to lay out these pages? Try viewing these home pages in different-sized browsers. Compare the types of page layout and the effects of resizing the browser window in a table with a column for each page.

An events company hires you to create the layout for a Web site that offers information about three types of entertainment: music, movies, and TV. Use a frameset and your favorite frameset layout structure to design a prototype for this Web site. Use the buttons musicbutton.gif, moviesbutton.gif, and tvbutton.gif in the Chapter5\images folder to create a menu in one of the frames. Create a home page and pages for music, movies, and TV with information about your favorites. Set up the hyperlinks from the buttons so that they load the pages into the main frame of your frameset.

A travel company hires you to create a Web site for a food tour to Normandy and Britain that they are organizing. Use Layout view to organize three pages for this project: a home page, a page for Normandy, and a page for Britain. The home page should link to the other pages. Use the graphics tours.gif, frenchbakery.jpg, normandysign.jpg, normandyfish.jpg, britishdairy.jpg, britishmarket.jpg, worldbg.gif, and worldmap.gif in the Chapter5\images folder to build your pages.

A travel company hires you to create a Web site for a food tour to Normandy and Britain that they are organizing. Use Layers to organize three pages for this project: a home page, a page for Normandy, and a page for Britain. The home page should link to the other pages. Use the graphics tours.gif, frenchbakery.jpg, normandysign.jpg, normandyfish.jpg, britishdairy.jpg, britishmarket.jpg, worldbg.gif, and worldmap.gif in the Chapter5\images folder to build your pages. After you complete the layout of your pages, convert the layers to tables. If you want to alter the layout of a particular page, convert the table back to layers, change the layout, and then reconvert the layers back to a table. Continue until you are satisfied with the page layout. If you completed the previous Case Project, compare the results. Which method was faster, easier, more flexible for you? Did one method provide more satisfying results for you?

6

UPLOADING A WEB SITE TO THE INTERNET

Domain Names, Web Servers, FTP, and Meta Tags

In this chapter, you will:

♦ Learn about Internet protocols, domain names, and IP addresses

♦ Learn about Web servers and options for posting your Web site

♦ Use Dreamweaver MX to transfer your Web site via FTP

♦ Learn strategies to help people find your site, including implementing meta tags

Coding a Web site is only part of the Web development task. You also need to upload your site to the Web so that people can see it. For a personal Web page, you can often get free Web space to host your site from your ISP or your school. For a commercial site, you need access to a server and you need to register your Internet address so that people can find your page.

In this chapter you learn about various Web hosting options, about the criteria to use when selecting a Web host, and about uploading your site onto the Internet. You also learn how to use search engines and other advertising and promotional schemes to raise the profile of your Web site.

DOMAIN NAMES ON THE WEB

The Internet began as a Department of Defense project when the Defense Advanced Research Projects Agency (DARPA) developed a series of connected data communication nodes to transfer research between geographically separated servers. In 1969, the first three nodes of the ARPANet connected among UCLA, UCSB, and the Stanford Research Institute. Figure 6-1 shows selected events in Internet history. The ARPANet was the predecessor of the NSFNet, once widely used for educational, research, and non-commercial communications. Eventually, the network communication lines were privatized, opening the way for commercial applications and advertising and giving birth to the Internet as we know it today. Along the way, several technical developments emerged that helped organize and control the Internet so that routing of data messages could occur correctly. Figure 6-2 shows the growth of Internet hosts from 1980 to 2000 based upon data from the Internet Software Consortium. The creation of the domain naming system to identify pages uniquely on the Internet was essential to its success. Eventually Web browsers were developed to help users find sites based on content rather than domain name.

The Internet can connect millions of computers successfully, because each computer, Web server, and Web site has a unique address. This address is known as the **Universal Resource Locator (URL)**. The Internet Network Information Center (InterNIC) was the first organization to undertake the task of assigning and managing domain names. Privatized in 1998, the InterNIC has an affiliation with the United States Department of Commerce. Now, private companies, overseen by the Internet Corporation for Assigned Names and Numbers (ICANN), manage domain name registration.

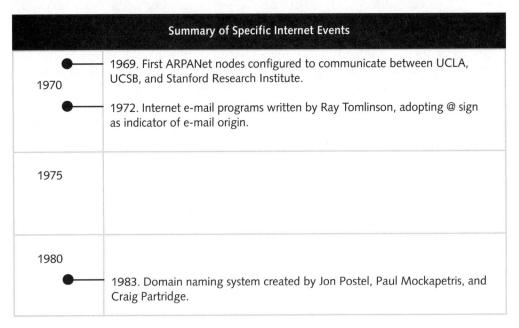

Summary of Specific Internet Events
1970 — 1969. First ARPANet nodes configured to communicate between UCLA, UCSB, and Stanford Research Institute.
1972. Internet e-mail programs written by Ray Tomlinson, adopting @ sign as indicator of e-mail origin.
1975
1980
1983. Domain naming system created by Jon Postel, Paul Mockapetris, and Craig Partridge.

Figure 6-1   Selected events in Internet history

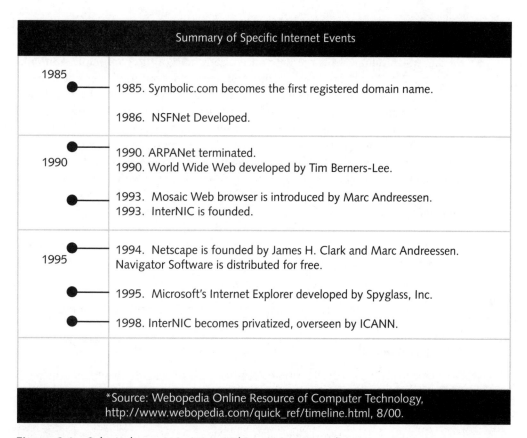

Figure 6-1 Selected events in Internet history (continued)

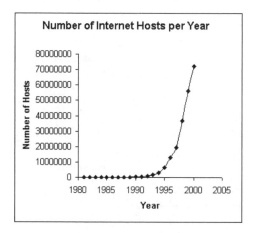

Figure 6-2 Number of Internet hosts by year between 1980 and 2000

Each URL has several components, including a network protocol, a domain name, and, optionally, a file to be accessed. Figure 6–3 shows the format for a typical URL. The first part of the address indicates an access method or network protocol used so that two machines can communicate. A **network protocol** or access method is a specific, predefined format for the bits traveling across the network. If both sides of the communication link know the protocol, then they can translate the messages and communicate. The protocol for the Internet is the Hypertext Transfer Protocol (HTTP), the first part of the address you see on most Web pages. Other examples of access methods include FTP and Telnet. The second piece of the URL designates a machine or server name. On most Web URLs, you see www listed as the beginning of the machine name. The www is not required; frequently, when you navigate through several links into a commercial, government, or academic site, the machine name in the URL changes to something other than www. A server can have any name. However, if your company is the XYZ Corporation, chances are your customers will look for it at *http://www.xyz.com*, not *http://alphabet.xyz.com*. The third part of the URL, a domain name, is listed after the machine name. The **domain name** is the unique identifier for the site. Suffixes that indicate the type of Web site follow domain names. The original six domain name extensions are:

- .com for commercial organizations, such as Sony Corporation or Microsoft

- .edu for educational and academic institutes, such as Claremont McKenna College or the University of Southern California

- .net for network providers, such as Sprint and IBM

- .org for non-profit organizations, such as the Girl Scouts or the National Science Foundation

- .mil for military organizations, such as the Air Force or the Army

- .gov for government agencies, such as the Department of Defense, the White House, or the Department of Commerce

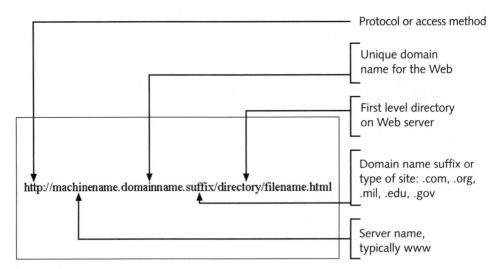

Figure 6-3 URL format

Internet growth has prompted an ongoing discussion about increasing the number of domain name suffixes to create more alternative and descriptive URLs. Currently, seven additional domain name suffixes are available: .aero (travel industry), .biz (business), .coop (cooperatives), info (information services), .museum, .name (for individuals), .pro (professional)). These are listed at the ICANN Web site, http://www.icann.org/tlds/.

After the domain name suffix, you may often see a forward slash (/) followed by text and another forward slash (/), which specifies a directory name on the server that contains the unique domain name. For example, in entering the URL *http://www.csupomona.edu/registrar*, the forward slash (/) instructs the browser to go to the directory called registrar on the csupomona.edu Web site and load the default file, index.html. If the full address is *http://www.csupomona.edu/registrar/studentrecord.htm*, the browser goes to the directory registrar at the csupomona.edu site and finds and loads the HTML file studentrecord.htm. File types found on the Web include:

- .htm or .html for HTML documents

- .txt for plain text documents

- .ppt for PowerPoint presentations (in Internet Explorer, the presentation loads directly into the browser, while in Netscape Navigator, the presentation launches from the local application on your computer; this is true for Excel spreadsheets, .xls, as well)

- .exe for executable programs (your browser gives you the option of executing the file on the server or downloading it to your computer)

Your Web browser can read and access many more types of files.

Domain Name Registration

You should select a simple and memorable domain name to make accessing your Web site easier for users. Your Web address defines your Web identity. When users type your Web site's URL, their machines send messages to another computer called a Domain Name Server. **Domain name servers (DNSs)** are computers located all over the Internet that translate URL requests into Internet Protocol addresses and forward the requests to the appropriate servers. An **Internet Protocol (IP)** address is a representation of a URL that follows a numerical hierarchy and helps route requests all over the world. IP addresses contain four sets of numbers up to three digits in length, separated by periods. For example, 123.123.123.123 and 1.29.234.123 are valid IP addresses. IP addresses are synonymous with domain names. For example, to reach the White House, you type the address *http://www.whitehouse.gov* in your Web browser. If you type *http://198.137.241.43* in the browser instead, your browser also loads the White House home page. The number 198.137.241.43 is the IP address for the White House. All URLs are made up of four numbers between 0 and 255. Today, due to the popularity of the Internet, the availability of unique combinations of four numbers is running out. At some point, it will be necessary to expand the addressing scheme so that more unique numbers are available. Domain name servers translate domain names into IP addresses on the Internet. You can look up IP addresses from several places online simply by typing the domain name; for example, you can retrieve IP addresses and domain names at the Web site *ns.superzone.net/cgi-bin/tools/nslookup*.

Founded in 1993, the InterNIC originally handled all domain name registration for the Internet. For $100, you could register a domain name for two years. As part of the registration, the InterNIC ensured you sole rights to that domain name, and it helped manage ownership and registration changes. Today, several private organizations, called **registrars**, perform this service for the InterNIC, and the price of registration has decreased dramatically. Through these companies, you can check to see if a domain name is taken. If the domain name is not registered, you can register it for a small fee, as little as $15 a year. Some registrars charge more than others and offer more side benefits than others, but all perform the same service of registering your domain name with the InterNIC. You can also now register a domain name for several years if you like.

To find a list of registered domain names and who registered them, you can visit the InterNIC Web site at *www.internic.net*. You can also learn about InterNIC and access a list of approved domain name registrars. The ICANN, at *www.icann.org*, approves the registrars that can register .com, .net, and .org domain names. International ICANN registrars help register foreign domain names. This global network of registrars keeps records and registration information about all domain names on the Internet. The records are available for public use through a Whois directory (*www.netsol.com/cgi-bin/whois/whois*). This directory is useful if you want to purchase a domain name from someone or if you want to clarify a dispute over domain names.

One popular domain name registrar is Dotster, *www.dotster.com*. You can search for available domain names and register them through the Dotster Web site shown in Figure 6-4. The appearance of this Web site may change over time, but the required registration information will remain the same.

Dotster and other companies offer a range of Web-related registration services. They also handle changes to your Web site registration and offer information on many programs and utilities for managing your site traffic and improving your Web business. To see if someone has already registered a domain name, simply enter the name in the text box in the yellow search box on the Dotster Web page, as shown in Figure 6-5. Click the Go button to learn if the domain name is taken.

Figure 6-4   Home page for Dotster

Figure 6-5   Checking domain name status

Figure 6-6 shows the result of a search for LaBonneCuisine.com. Note that while the domain name for our site is already taken, available domain names with different suffixes are listed in the search response. Scrolling down the Web page, variations on the requested domain name are also given, as shown in Figure 6-7. Adding "my", "e", or "about" to the beginning of a domain name or adding "online" or "central" to the end of a domain name often provides a unique name when the exact name is already taken. Using acronyms or abbreviations or placing underscores and dashes in your domain name, you can often create an acceptable, memorable name for your Web site.

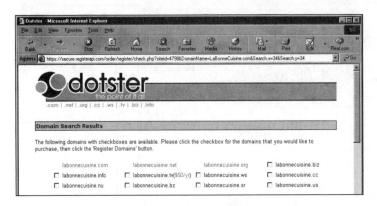

Figure 6-6   Domain name search results

Figure 6-7   Alternative domain name suggestions

After you select a domain name you can register it with you as the owner. To do this, you need information about yourself, what type of service you require, a DNS name and IP address and a credit card number. Service options include information like how long you would like to register the domain name for. You need to provide the name of the individual or organization responsible for the domain name registration, as well as physical and e-mail addresses. The registrar sends registration confirmation to that e-mail address; without it, you cannot register the domain name. You must provide a DNS name and IP address to associate your newly registered domain name with your IP address. You can obtain the DNS name and IP address from your Web host.

Payment is the final step in the registration process. Once you register a domain name, it's yours as long as you renew the registration. For more information about Web hosting, you can visit *www.w3schools.com* and click on Web Hosting.

Domain Name Suffixes for Other Countries

You have probably seen two-letter domain name suffixes such as .ca or .zw. These two-letter suffixes identify countries. The British monarchy's Web site (*www.royal.gov.uk*), for example, has the two-letter suffix .uk, the extension for Web sites originating in the United Kingdom. Similarly, .ca is the extension for Canada, .zw is the extension for Zimbabwe, and .jp is the extension for Japan. You can find a complete list of two-letter country codes at the Web site of the Internet Assigned Numbers Authority (IANA) organization, *www.iana.org/cctld/cctld-whois.htm*. Close to 250 countries have two-letter extensions, including the United States. Sometimes, the domain name suffixes for foreign countries have more than two letters at the end of their addresses. For example, many commercial United Kingdom Web site addresses end with .co.uk.

Although most Web sites in the United States use a .com, .org, or .edu extension, the .us extension is available. You can register a .us Web site for a fee, the same way you would register a .com domain name. The .us domain names follow a geographical hierarchy: US, state, city, and organization. For example, the city of Los Angeles has a personals page located at *http://personals.los-angeles.ca.us/*.

Strategies for Choosing Domain Names

Many small companies register domain names even before they have a Web site, to reserve their company name or something close to it. One quick way to determine if someone has registered the domain name you want is to type it in your Web browser and see if a Web site loads in the browser window. If no one has the domain name, like lbcuisine.com, you are likely to get the standard browser response given when a page does not exist. If a company is using the domain name, the page loads. Sometimes owners put their domain names up for sale. For example, *www.showing.com* gives the sales pitch and contact information shown in Figure 6-8.

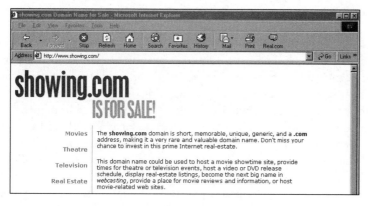

Figure 6-8   Domain name for sale

Considering that the domain name business.com sold for $150,000 in 1997, it is not surprising that people have opportunistically registered domain names hoping to make a huge profit. This type of activity is affectionately known as URL squatting. In one famous case, a writer, Joshua Quittner, discovered that McDonalds.com was an unregistered domain name. He contacted the McDonalds corporation and asked how they could be so negligent. When he got no response, he registered the domain name for himself. Eventually, Quittner gave the McDonalds domain name to the company when it agreed to purchase computer equipment for an elementary school. Some people who register domain names that are trademarks of existing companies are taken to court and stripped of their domain name ownership. It is hard to imagine anyone besides Disney justifying ownership of the domain name Disneyland. On the other hand, a domain name like bird.com could just as easily belong to a pet store as to basketball great Larry Bird.

If the domain name you want is likely to be popular, finding an acceptable alternative domain name may require some thought. As you learned earlier, adding "e", "about", or "my" to the beginning of a phrase can help if someone is already using your exact company name as a domain name. You might also consider words like "online", "to", and "goto". For example, the company About.com owns hundreds of domain names that begin with the word about. You can also use dashes and underscores to change a domain name. You_are_here.com may be an available domain name while youarehere.com is not.

Once you find an available domain name, you might want to register similar domain names as well, so that users who type your domain name wrong might still find your Web site. For example, if you register youarehere.com, urhere.com, u_r_here.com, u-r-here.com, you_are_here.com, and you-are-here.com, and point all these addresses to the same destination, a user with a fuzzy memory is more likely to find your Web site.

WEB SERVERS

The Internet is a network of networks. It is a system of communication lines and computers that spans the globe. Whether you lease a host for your Web site or configure your own host, it is important to understand how your Web site connects to the Internet and how Internet addressing works. Figure 6-9 shows a simplified view of how a person with a home computer can reach a server. As you learned earlier in this chapter, your server has a unique domain name associated with a numerical IP address. Someone looking for your site can find it through the network of special servers called domain name servers (DNSs) located across the Internet. These DNSs have databases of IP addresses that help them route traffic across the Internet. Your Web server consists of hardware, software, and a dedicated communication link providing 24-hour access to the Internet. Software for the server includes an operating system, the documents that comprise your Web site, server software, and programs that help you manage and maintain the server. Your server may also support or connect to a database, or support CGI or Java programs that you run through your Web site. Your physical connection to the Internet can be a simple, albeit slow, phone line, or a high-capacity line leased from the phone company.

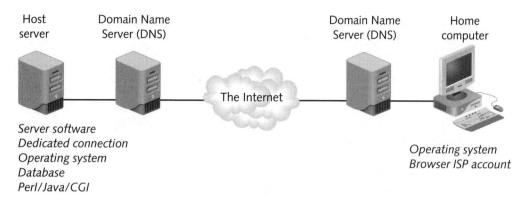

Figure 6-9 Messages across the Internet

Any person on earth with a home computer, a modem, a Web browser, and an Internet Service Provider (ISP) can connect to your Web site. ISPs such as AOL, MSN, and EarthLink provide access to the Internet via local phone numbers. Each time a user connects to the Internet, a dynamic IP address is assigned to that particular session and then released when the sessions ends. When the user starts a Web browser, typically Internet Explorer or Netscape Navigator, and types in an address, the domain name of the address is forwarded to a DNS that translates the domain name into its unique IP address. This IP address is static, not dynamic. This means that a Web site domain name is always associated with the same IP address. The IP address can only change if the owner of the site decides to change it. The request for the site is forwarded across the Internet as a message containing the desired IP address and the return IP address. Once the request reaches the host server, the Web page is transmitted to the requestor and appears in the Web browser.

You can gain access to a Web server in a number of different ways. You can lease space from an ISP on an existing server connected to the Internet, or you can set up and control your own server. Several companies sell server hardware and software offering similar features for Web site control, access, and maintenance. However, there are other things to consider. First, you may expect a lot of traffic on your Web site. In this case, you require high capacity access to your site so that it can handle all of your visitors. If your Web site delivers e-commerce services, your server must have database and security features. You should thoroughly understand the goals of your Web site before you decide how to host it. You should also know how special programs can help you track performance and other statistical information about your site. A variety of products are available to assist you. A Web search for "Web site management tools" will result in numerous alternatives.

Keeping statistics about your Web site can influence decisions you make about technology. For example, very heavy traffic on your Web site can slow performance and irritate users trying to access your site. You may need to ensure that your server has a higher capacity connection to the Internet. This enables more people to reach your site and improves the Web site's performance. You can also learn many useful things about visitors to your site that will help you improve it. You can track the type of Web browser that people use, and the most and least popular pages on your site. You can also determine what geographical region your visitors connect from. Data like this can influence your marketing and design strategy. If most of your visitors are from Japan, you might want to offer a Japanese language version of your Web site. If you want to promote something new on your Web site, you can post the new information on the pages most frequently visited by users of your site. If your site carries advertising, keeping statistics gives you detailed information that you can convey to your clients about the characteristics of visitors to your Web site.

Leasing a Server

Choosing a host for your site saves you the time and money involved in setting up and maintaining your own server. When you lease a server or space on a server from an ISP, you benefit by having access to an Internet host without assuming the cost of setting up and maintaining a server yourself. A Web hosting service typically offers a variety of packages. The company Nvision (*www.nvision.com*) offers a dedicated server starting at $250 per month, or you can lease space on an existing server. Nvision lets you choose between NT and UNIX systems and select basic or premium packages depending upon your needs. For a one-time set-up fee of $35 and a $45 monthly fee, the basic UNIX package has many features, including:

- 70 megabytes of space
- FTP and Telnet accounts
- Perl support
- Database support, including mySQL, mSQL, PostreSQL
- Unlimited e-mail aliases and auto responders
- One POP e-mail account
- Log files and configurable statistics
- cgi-bin directory
- Real Audio/Video basic server
- Instructions for installing scripts, including counters, form mail, guest books, and Web-based e-mail

- Instant crash recovery from online backups
- Unlimited e-mail support
- Virtual hosting support
- Select phone support
- Comprehensive online manual and support

You should look at several hosting services and determine which one suits your needs. Consider the access speeds, technical support, and services they provide. Often additional services mean additional fees. The advantage of using a hosting service is that it is responsible for monitoring and maintaining the server. If it crashes in the middle of the night, a good hosting service has the backup facilities and the technical wherewithal to ensure that your Web site still operates.

Some companies will register your domain name and host your site. If you have already registered your domain name, you can have it transferred to your host so that they can set up your account. Figure 6-10 shows the home page for Feature Price (*www.featureprice.com*).

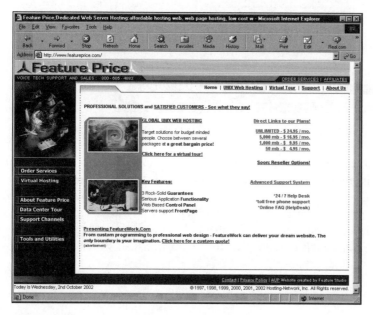

Figure 6-10 Feature Price home page

The ordering process is similar for all Web hosting services. You probably will need to agree to the terms of the hosting service, select a plan, and then pay for the service via credit card. As an example, clicking Order Services on Feature Price opens a page where you can elect to have a secure transaction. Pressing Click Here to Start opens a page where you can view terms and conditions, as shown in Figure 6-11.

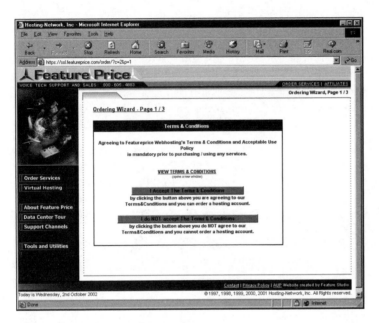

Figure 6-11   Feature Price order page

It is a good idea to read a company's terms and conditions carefully. Many hosts have requirements that you promise not to do anything detrimental to their servers or that you not post materials related to hate crimes and pornography. This is the ethical code of conduct for doing business with Feature Price. Clicking I Accept The Terms & Conditions means that you accept them and you need to uphold your obligation. After accepting the terms, you can select which type of plan suits your needs, as shown in Figure 6-12.

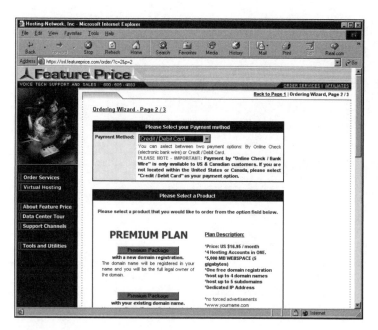

Figure 6-12 Feature Price policy options

As you would expect, more features costs more money. Think about what kind of site you are hosting. How much disk space do you need? Do you need your own e-mail accounts? Reading the options should help you decide. After a plan is selected, you enter ordering information (address, credit card, and domain name) as shown in Figure 6-13. After you've paid, the hosting service will send you DNS information and other information about your account.

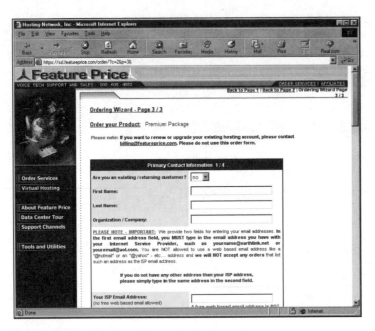

Figure 6-13   Feature Price order information

Setting Up Your Own Server

For a large company, the cost of setting up a server is not an obstacle. The company probably already has high-speed access lines, security, and personnel to maintain and control several Web servers connected to the Internet. For a smaller company with limited resources, the cost of maintaining a Web server may be prohibitive. Table 6-1 lists the approximate costs of various types of Web connections. The fee for a typical phone line is $30 per month, while the fee for a high-speed, T-1 line can be as much as $2000 per month.

Table 6-1   Internet Connection Costs

Access Medium	Capacity	Cost
Phone line (twisted pair)	56 KB/sec	$30/month
ISDN	128 KB/sec	$100–$500/month
DSL	256 KB/sec–1 MB/sec	$30–$120/month
T1	1.544 Mbps	$800–$2000/month
T3	45 Mbps	$2100–$4000/month

If you decide to host your own Web site, you must make several considerations. Are you prepared to accept the costs associated with purchasing server hardware and software and with leasing a dedicated connection to the Internet? Are you prepared to maintain the server? If your goal is to focus on Web design or marketing, hiring an expert to perform these services might be better. If, on the other hand, you plan to manipulate your server a lot and to write executable programs that require special access privileges to the server, setting it up yourself may be wise.

The most popular Web servers include Apache, Microsoft Internet Information Server, and Netscape's Fasttrack and Enterprise Servers. Before selecting a server, you should look at reviews, comparisons, and benchmarking information. To learn what server best meets your needs, you can read trade magazines, access other Web sites that give product evaluations, and visit manufacturers of server equipment or software.

UPLOADING YOUR WEB SITE

6

To upload your site to the Internet, you need a File Transfer Protocol (FTP) program. FTP programs allow you to link to a remote server, enter a password, and then upload and download files using get and put commands. Early FTP programs had a command-line interface and required you to remember filenames and several commands to transfer your files. Today, FTP programs have graphical user interfaces that display files from the server and your local drive, and that allow you to move folders and files with the click of a button or by dragging and dropping them. One very popular FTP program, WS_FTP, comes with the basic software installation on many computers. With this FTP program, you simply select files and use arrows to transfer them to and from the server. Figure 6-14 shows a typical FTP session using WS_FTP. The left side of the screen shows the local hard drive, while the right side of the screen displays the files on the Web server. To move files and directories, you simply click to select them and then click the center arrows to move them to the appropriate location. To configure an FTP program so that it connects to your Web server, you need to know the IP address or name of the server, and you need to have a username and password that enables you to log on to that host.

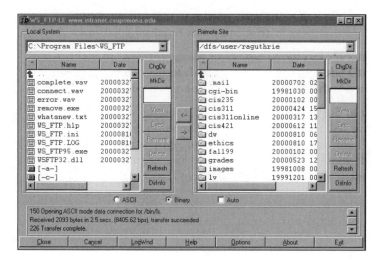

Figure 6-14   FTP session using WS_FTP

Dreamweaver MX has a built-in FTP utility that is similar to independent FTP programs. In Chapter 4, you created a site map and organized your Web site using the Define Sites dialog box. You can also edit the site information, as shown in Figure 6-15, to set up the FTP utility available in Dreamweaver MX.

Figure 6-15   Edit Sites dialog box

Selecting Edit opens the Site Definition dialog box shown in Figure 6-16. It displays seven categories of options: Local Info, Remote Info, Testing Server, Cloaking, Design Notes, Site Map Layout, and File View Columns. To transfer your work to the Internet, you must define the local site information and the remote server information. Figure 6-16 shows the Site Definition dialog box for the local information. Notice that the La Bonne Cuisine site is listed as the site name and the root directory is C:\Sites\lbc.

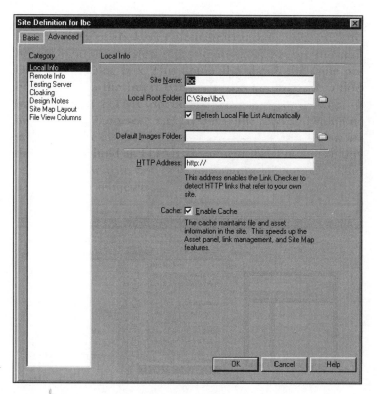

Figure 6-16   Site Definition dialog box

To use FTP to upload your site to the Internet, you must identify the server address and password in the Remote Info category. With the default setting, None, for the Remote Info category screen, no entry boxes are visible. Click the Access: list arrow, as shown in Figure 6-17, and then click FTP. (The FTP option is at the top of the list, and you may need to scroll up to select it.) This makes the Remote Info options available, as shown in Figure 6-18.

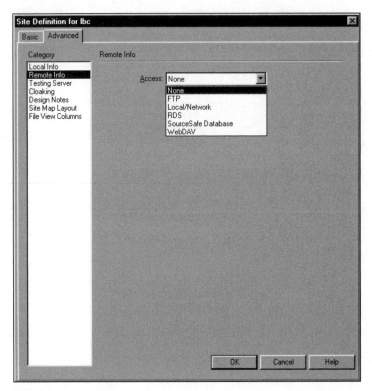

Figure 6-17   Selecting FTP from the Site Definition dialog box

In the text box for the FTP host, you must enter an IP address or name for the Web server. You must also enter a host directory if your site must be put in a specific sub-directory on the server. Finally, you must enter a valid username and password. Click OK to close the window and save the settings. Then click Done on the Site Definition dialog box to save the settings. You can use them every time you want to use FTP to transfer files to and from the La Bonne Cuisine site.

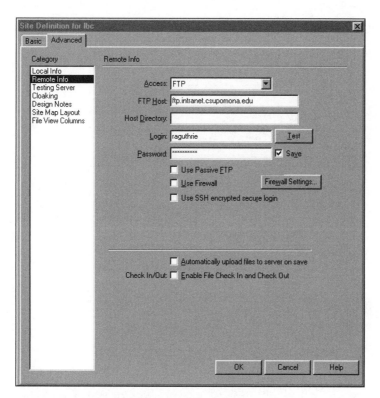

6

Figure 6-18   Remote Site Definition dialog box

When you close the Site Definition dialog box, the Site panel opens. The default view is to show the site menu as part of the Files panel group to the right of the workspace. Dragging the panel group by the gripper and clicking the expander displays the expanded Site panel shown in Figure 6-19. You can change the display of site files using the View pull-down menu on the Sites menu bar and selecting Site Files or Site Map. Note: When the Site panel is expanded, the Site Options menu, at the upper right, is not available. From the View menu, you can select Site Files or Site Map. Alternatively, the buttons at the top of the panel let you click to view Site Files [image], Test Files [image], or the Site Map [image]. If the Site Map option is selected, you can click the Connect button [image] to access the server. If the Test Files button is selected, you can connect to a testing server. Professional developers work on a test server so that they can thoroughly check out their changes before posting them on a live site. When your computer is connected to the server or the test server, the connection icon displays a green dot below the connected cables [image]. When the connection closes, the icon displays disconnected cables above a black dot [image]. Clicking the Refresh button [image] updates the file list on the Web server and on the local site. Click the Get button [image] to transfer files from the server to your local drive. Click the Put button [image] to transfer files from your local drive to the server. You can also simply drag the files with your mouse to transfer them. The next two buttons are for checking out [image] and checking in [image] work. These are typically used if you work in a controlled or shared environment. The last button to the right 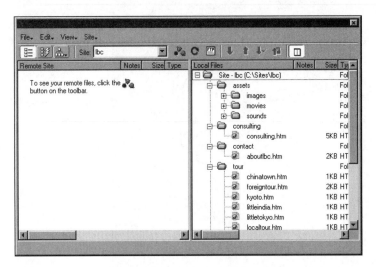 is for expanding and contracting the window so that remote and local sites may be viewed at the same time.

Figure 6-19   La Bonne Cuisine Site panel

The right side of the Site panel shown in Figure 6-19 displays the folders and home page for the lbc site. The left side lists the folders and files on your Web server. To operate the FTP function, you must navigate through the files and select the file or folder you want to transfer by clicking it and then clicking the Get or Put buttons.

Before activating the FTP function, make sure you are connected to the Internet. Click the Connection button to connect to your remote Web server. If you did not save the password to the server, a prompt asks you to enter your password to make the connection. After entering the password, you should observe that the button changes and that the black bullet below the connection icon changes to a green bullet, indicating a successful connection, as shown in Figure 6-20. Under the toolbar are two columns listing files. Files located on your Web server are on the left. On the right, you see all the files you created locally for the La Bonne Cuisine Web site. To transfer the La Bonne Cuisine site to the Web server, you simply click the files to select them and click the Put button. To download a file located on the server, click the file to select it and then click the Get button.

Depending upon your server's configuration and the operating system you use, you may need to set **file protection privileges** for individual files you load on the server. Every file on a Web server has specific access codes that define who can view or manipulate it. File protection privileges include Read, Write, Edit, and Delete. Anyone who has access to the server can erase files set to Delete. Your server may automatically set access privileges to the highest protection, depending upon its configuration. Some FTP programs allow you to change file protection privileges during the FTP session. However, Dreamweaver MX does not have this feature.

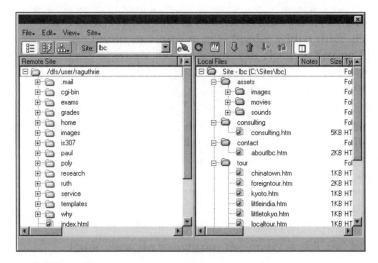

Figure 6-20   Connected to the La Bonne Cuisine Web site

MAKING YOUR WEB SITE VISIBLE

There are various ways of increasing your Web site's visibility. As always, companies use print and television advertising to promote their products and services. Traditional businesses might include their URL in such ads to direct potential customers to a Web site where they can obtain more detailed information about the company. In this case, the URL might be a relatively minor facet of the advertisement. Web-based businesses, however, are likely to make their URLs a central part of any media advertising they produce.

Aside from publicizing a URL in traditional media outlets, there are other useful ways of making your Web site more accessible to users of the Internet. This is important because today the Internet consists of millions of pages. You must maximize the resources available, such as search engines and meta tags, to ensure that interested parties can find your Web site.

Traditional Promotion Channels

Customers have little trouble locating companies on the Internet that are already well known to them, as long as the domain name matches the company name. In fact, existing customers have little trouble locating any company whose domain name matches its company name. But how do people unfamiliar with your company find your Web site? Many organizations already have advertising strategies that use a variety of media to contact existing and potential customers. Newspapers, billboards, television, radio, magazines, business cards, fliers, target marketing mailers, and the Yellow Pages are all examples of traditional advertising methods that you can use to promote your Web site.

Word-of-mouth is also a very effective way to attract more customers to your Web site. Users who have a good experience using your Web site may return there in the future, and they may tell a friend about it. In the early days of the Web, some designers were expert in attracting visitors by sheer novelty. The Web site for the Joe Boxer Company (*www.joeboxer.com*) gained a lot of notoriety by using a hip design and a novel navigation strategy. A promotion on the site allowed people to send e-mail to the server that was eventually routed to the big screen in Times Square. Thousands of people accessed the site just to try it. More recently, a couple who stated that they would "lose their virginity online" gained a lot of free publicity and enjoyed a huge hit rate. As it turned out, the couple were actors and the site was a publicity stunt. Novelty, useful content, and impressive design can all work towards attracting visitors to a Web site through word-of-mouth. Justin Choi, president of Choice Enterprises, designed a popular site for Nitto Tires of Japan. By featuring a sophisticated flash poker game with a sexy animated dealer, something never before done on the Web, the site gained instant popularity, largely created by the buzz about the Web site.

Online Methods for Promoting Your Web Site

You can perform several Web-related activities to help people find your Web site. Once you actually have a Web site hosted on the Internet, registering the site with search engines and including meta tags and well-placed banner advertising may be ways to attract more people to your Web site.

Registering Your Site with a Search Engine

Major search engines usually have a link on their site allowing you to submit your URL for inclusion in their index. The search engines typically provide this service for free. For example, the popular search engine Altavista.com has an Add a URL link at the bottom of the page. To register your site, you simply submit your URL. Altavista reviews the site and determines if it is appropriate for indexing. Altavista also lists extensive information about how it indexes Web pages and about its policies on submitting sites with misleading information. To register a site on Yahoo, the procedure is a little different. Yahoo.com requires you to "suggest a site" for indexing by selecting a lower-level category in their directory, and then entering your site and a short description. Yahoo uses this information to index your site and to give visitors extra information about the site. Listing your Web site with many search engines may seem rather time consuming. For a small fee, you can submit your Web site information once to a registration service that will index your Web site with dozens of search engines.

Even if you do nothing, several search engines will eventually list your site. Search engines use programs called Web crawlers, or spiders, that examine pages on the Internet and index them in a directory. Different search engines use different criteria for indexing pages. So, your page may appear high on one search engine's list and lower on another's. Later in this section, you learn to implement meta tags to improve search engine indexing of your Web site.

Web Rings

A web ring is a group of Web sites devoted to a common theme, linked together in a logical ring. A visitor to one site may follow the ring and find your site because of its alliance with other members of the ring. This can be an effective way to bring traffic to your site from visitors interested in similar topics and information, to the one they originally searched for.

Banner Advertising

A banner ad is a wide rectangular advertisement typically placed at the top of a Web page to advertise a product or service of another site. Figure 6-21 is an example of a banner ad displayed on the Altavista Web site. If you click the banner ad, the advertiser's Web site opens in your browser. You can purchase banner ads from several companies. Usually, the fee depends upon the number of exposures (times the banner is shown) your ad receives. Banner advertising companies sell a set number of exposures for a set fee.

Figure 6-21   Sample banner ad

To target your banner advertisements, you can purchase a keyword from a search engine. This ensures that your banner ad appears when users type a specific word. For example, if your Web site sells saddles, you can have your banner ad appear when a person searches for horses.

If you lack the resources to purchase banner advertising, you might consider enlisting the help of a link exchange. Link exchanges are set up so you can barter banner advertising space with other Web sites. For example, if you agree to post someone else's banner ad on your site 100 times, they will post your ad on their site 100 times. You can find link exchanges for specific topics that help target your advertising. They increase your chances of bringing an interested customer to your site rather than a random, curious Web surfer. For example, if you sell fish or aquatic equipment, the Fish Link Exchange Web site, *www.fishlinkexchange.com*, allows you to trade banner ads with other fish-related companies.

Meta Tags

Meta tags are invisible tags placed in the header of your HTML document that add meta, or higher level, information to your Web site. An example is the description meta tag, which you can use to write a short description of your Web site. There are two categories of meta tags: HTTP-equiv attribute meta tags and Name attribute meta tags. HTTP-equiv attribute tags are used to manipulate the browser into performing some action. The most popular of these is probably the refresh meta tag. Inserting the following code in the header of your HTML document results in the browser opening the Coca-Cola Web site after five seconds.

```
<meta http-equiv="refresh" content="5;URL=http://www.coke.com">
```

The refresh meta tag is often used to redirect an old Web site to a new location or to create an entry page for a Web site. Name attribute meta tags are used for listing information such as keywords, authors, and descriptions. For the La Bonne Cuisine Web site, a keyword meta tag inserted into the header of an HTML document would look like this:

```
<meta name="keywords" content="lbc, la bonne cuisine,
culinary consulting, food product development">
```

This tag ensures that search engines attempting to index the La Bonne Cuisine site utilize the listed keywords to improve the accuracy and ranking of the Web site in their search results.

To insert meta tags in Dreamweaver MX, click the Head tab of the Insert bar, shown in Figure 6-22. The Head tab of the Insert bar helps you add HTML code to the header of your document. These codes do not display text to the viewer of the page; rather, they add value to your Web page by improving Web site indexing, retargeting Web pages, or describing Web site content and development. The six options for header information in Dreamweaver follow:

- Meta 🔳 allows you to designate a name or HTTP-equivalent tag and then designate its attributes.

- Keywords 🔳 allows you to place several descriptive keywords in the header of your site. Search engines use these keywords to help people find relevant information.

- Description 🔳 allows you to describe the Web page in a long string of text.

- Refresh 🔳 allows you to configure a Web page to load a new URL automatically after a defined number of seconds passes. Use this to create new entry pages to Web sites or to redirect users to the new location of a moved Web page.

- Base 🔳 allows you to insert a base tag in the header of your document and makes all hyperlinks on your page relative to the base link you define.

- Link 🔳 allows you to associate one Web page with another by identifying the external page with a link tag.

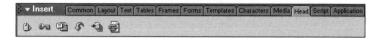

Figure 6-22   The Head tab of the Insert bar

The first button on the left of the Head tab 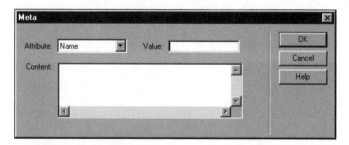 inserts a generic meta tag that requires you to fill in information. Dreamweaver prompts you for some information, but to use this tool, you need to know what type of meta tag you want to insert. Clicking on the Meta button opens the Meta dialog box shown in Figure 6-23. With the Attribute drop-down list, you designate a name or HTTP-equiv type meta tag, and in the Value text box, you specify the type of meta tag you want to insert on your Web page. HTTP-equiv meta tags include the following:

- Expires causes the Web browser to interpret a page as expired after a designated date.

- Pragma prevents Netscape Navigator from caching the page on the local drive when used with a no cache designation.

- Refresh redirects a Web page to another designated URL after a specified number of seconds.

- Set Cookie sets a cookie.

- Window Target controls page display. Usually used to ensure that a Web page does not appear inside a Web page containing frames.

Figure 6-23   Meta dialog box

The format for a meta tag is <Meta attribute="value" content="information">. For example, if you designate an HTTP-equiv attribute, type expires for the value, and type Monday, September 04, 2003 05:30:00 GMT for the content, Dreamweaver formats the tag in the header of the document, as shown in Figure 6-24. This tag makes the page expire at the date and time you specify.

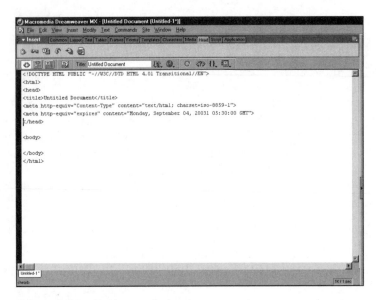

Figure 6-24 Expires meta tag

Name attribute meta tags include the following:

- Description describes the purpose and content of the Web site.

- Generator identifies the Web development tools used to generate the Web site.

- Author names the author of the Web site.

- Keywords lists several keywords that assist search engines in indexing the Web page.

You can insert keywords using the Insert Meta button on the Head tab. However, since keywords are a commonly used meta tag, Dreamweaver provides you with a separate button to insert keywords [icon]. Click this button to open the Keywords dialog box, as shown in Figure 6-25. Then type keywords that describe your Web site. You can list as many as you like; phrases and word combinations are also acceptable, but you should separate each keyword item with commas.

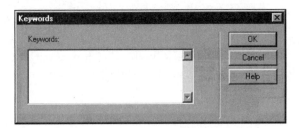

Figure 6-25 Keywords dialog box

Click the Insert Description button ⊞ to insert a Web site description, as shown in Figure 6-26. A search engine that uses your keywords to index your page can also use the description you list in the meta tags to give users information about what your page contains. As with the keyword meta tag, clicking the Description button generates code for a Name attribute meta tag.

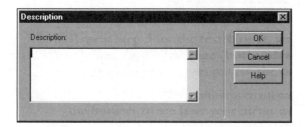

Figure 6-26   Description dialog box

You can use the Insert Refresh button ⟳ to redirect a Web page to another site. Use refresh tags when an old site needs to be redirected to a new URL or when an existing site has an entry page. The entry page is posted for a given number of seconds before the user enters the Web site. Figure 6-27 shows the Refresh dialog box. In the Delay text box, enter a number to specify the number of seconds before the browser loads the new URL. Click the Go To URL radio button, and enter the new URL.

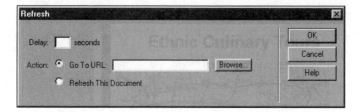

Figure 6-27   Refresh dialog box

The remaining two buttons on the Head tab are slightly different than meta tags. However, they are still invisible tags in the header of the HTML document. You use the Insert Base button ⊞ to specify a URL that all links on the page should be relative to. That is, if you specify the base tag *http://www.lbcuisine.com*, any other links on that page are relative to *that* base tag. When you insert a base tag, you can indicate the relative base reference and target it to a specific window in the Base dialog box, shown in Figure 6-28. The target choices are _blank, _parent, _self, or _top.

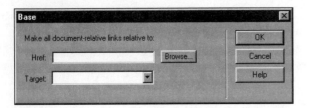

Figure 6-28 Base dialog box

You use the Insert Link button 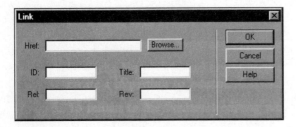 for printing, style sheets, and document navigation. This tag has several attributes, and the Link dialog box shown in Figure 6-29 lists only the common ones. Link tags contained in the header of an HTML document are used in conjunction with style sheets. You learn more about this tag in Chapter 10, which describes how to improve productivity and consistency using style sheets.

Figure 6-29 Link dialog box

Adding Meta Tags to a Web Site

In the next steps, you add meta tags to the La Bonne Cuisine Web site so that search engines can index it appropriately. By carefully selecting your keywords, you improve the search engine ranking of the site. You also create a new index.htm page that becomes the entry page to your La Bonne Cuisine Web site.

To add meta tags:

1. Start Dreamweaver MX if it is not already open. Make sure the Property inspector (Ctrl+F3) and the Head tab of the Insert bar are active.

2. Open the file **index.htm** from the **Sites\lbc** folder by double-clicking the filename.

   You insert meta tags into this page because the La Bonne Cuisine home page is the page that you want search engines to find.

3. Click the **Keywords** button on the Head tab to open the Keywords dialog box. Type the keywords **Food Consulting, Gourmet Food, Food Product Development, Food Tours, Culinary Consulting,** and **Recipe Development** in the text area. Be sure to insert commas between keywords.

Click **OK** in the Keywords dialog box to ensure that the keyword meta tag is inserted into the header of the Web page.

You will not see the meta tag on the page as it is an invisible element contained in the source code inside the header tags of your document.

4. Click the **Show Code view** button in the document toolbar to view the source code. You should see the meta tag containing the keywords you just entered:

```
<meta name="keywords" content="Food Consulting, Gourmet
Food, Food Product Development, Food Tours, Culinary
Consulting, Recipe Development">
```

5. Click the **Show Design view** button to return to Design view.

6. Click the **Description** button 🔳 on the Head tab to open the Description dialog box.

7. In the dialog box, type the text **La Bonne Cuisine provides expert, professional food consulting services, culinary tours, product development and consulting, and culinary training in your home for entertaining.** Click the **OK** button to insert the description meta tag into the header of the HTML document.

8. View the index.htm source code by clicking the **Show Code view** button. You should see the meta tag containing the description you just entered:

```
<meta name="description" content="La Bonne Cuisine
provides expert, professional food consulting services,
culinary tours, product development and consulting, and
culinary training in your home for entertaining.">
```

9. Click the **Show Design view** button to return to Design view.

10. Save this page.

Chapter Summary

- ❏ Before uploading a Web site to the Internet, you need access to a server, a registered domain name, an IP address, and FTP software.

- ❏ Unique addresses called URLs identify pages on the Internet.

- ❏ A domain name is part of the URL. Each domain name is associated with an IP address. To route requests over the Internet, special servers (domain name servers) associate IP addresses with domain names.

- ❏ Domain name suffixes identify what type of Web site you are viewing. The six original domain name suffixes are .com, .edu, .net, .org, .mil, .gov. The new suffixes are .aero, .biz, .coop, .info, .museum, .name, and .pro.

❏ Some URLs have two-letter suffixes that identify Web sites from specific countries. For example, .ca represents Canada and .zw represents Zimbabwe.

❏ FTP software allows you to connect to a remote server to upload (put) and download (get) files. A Dreamweaver MX feature allows you to do this from within the application.

❏ You may wish to lease server space for your Web site instead of maintaining your own server. Considerations in making this decision include costs and resources associated with server maintenance, connection speed, security, and expected traffic. The requirements of the Web site should drive this decision.

❏ You can use several marketing strategies to increase traffic on your Web site. Among them are registering your site with the popular search engines, trading or buying banner ad space, and including meta tags in your HTML documents.

❏ The header of a Web page contains meta tags. Keyword meta tags help search engines index pages. Well-designed meta tags can increase traffic to a Web site because the site is indexed higher in searches for particular topics.

❏ Some uses for meta tags include describing a page, identifying an author, and forwarding (refreshing) one Web page to another.

REVIEW QUESTIONS

1. Which term most closely describes a URL?

   a. Address

   b. FTP

   c. Server

   d. Host

2. What are the essential elements for setting up a Web site?

   a. Server

   b. Hardware/Software

   c. IP Address

   d. All of the above

3. Describe how an IP address is used in accessing Web sites.

4. What is the InterNIC?

5. What organization is responsible for overseeing domain name registration?

   a. Network Solutions

   b. ICANN

   c. Any listed domain name registrar

   d. No one oversees this process.

6. Which of the following is not a valid domain name extension?

    a. .com

    b. .net

    c. .isp

    d. .edu

7. No Web browser can load non-HTML documents. True or False?

8. Registering a domain name on the Web is a free service. True or False?

9. What is the purpose of a DNS?

10. What does it mean to have a dynamic IP address?

11. How can you tell if a domain name you want to use is already taken?

12. What is URL squatting?

    a. Acquiring useful domain names for your own use

    b. Registering a popular domain name and using it to host your Web site

    c. Registering domain names and selling them to the highest bidder

    d. Hijacking domain names from existing sites and posting fictitious Web sites

13. Which of the following are factors in making a Web hosting decision?

    a. Access speed

    b. Security

    c. Server support

    d. all of the above

14. FTP software lets you register your IP address with a DNS. True or False?

15. Which is not necessary for opening an FTP session?

    a. IP address or name

    b. DNS address or name

    c. Username

    d. Password

16. Why is file protection an important consideration when you upload documents to the Internet?

17. Describe three traditional promotion techniques for advertising your Web site.

18. Describe three online promotion techniques for advertising your Web site.

19. The refresh meta tag is used for reloading a Web page that erroneously loads in a Web browser. True or False?

20. A keyword meta tag can improve your Web site's ranking within a Web search engine index. True or False?

6

HANDS-ON PROJECTS

Project 6-1

Joseph Black is looking for a job as a Web developer. His resume is posted on the Web as an HTML page. Add appropriate keywords to help search engines index Joseph's page so a potential employer can find him.

1. Using Windows Explorer, create a new folder named **ch6practice** in the Sites folder on your working drive. Using Windows Explorer, copy the file **joesresume.htm** from your Chapter6 data folder into the Sites\ch6practice folder.

2. Open **joesresume.htm** in Dreamweaver MX.

3. Click the **Head** tab on the Insert bar if it is not already active. Click the **Keywords** button on the Head tab. In the Insert Keywords dialog box, type **resume, IT professional, Web design, employment, Web development skills, technical skills**. Do not forget to type commas between keywords. Click **OK**.

4. Click the **Meta** button on the Head tab. Select the Attribute **Name** and type **author** as the Value. In the Content text area, type **Joseph Black**. Click **OK**.

5. Click the **Show Code view** button to view the HTML code, if necessary. Observe that the meta tags are in the header of your document. Click the **Show Design view** button to return to Design view.

6. Save the file **joesresume.htm** in the Sites\ch6practice folder of your working drive.

Project 6-2

You are the Webmaster for a small company called The Bread Company. The owner asks you to improve its Web site ranking by the major search engines. In this project, you create a page with the company name that contains meta tags for keywords, description, and author. Search engines use the keywords, title, and content of the page to index Web pages. Appropriate content and keywords can make The Bread Company Web site appear in the top 10 selections of major search engines when a viewer enters the word Bread in a search engine. Well-designed meta tags help increase traffic on The Bread Company Web site.

1. Open a new file in Dreamweaver MX. In your new Untitled document, type **The Bread Company Home Page** in the Title text box on the Document toolbar.

2. Type **The Bread Company** in the workspace. Select this text and in the Property inspector set the format to **Heading 1** and the text color to red (**#FF0000**), and click the **Align Center** button. Deselect the text by clicking any blank space in the bottom of the workspace.

3. Click the **Head tab** on the Insert bar if it is not already active. Click the **Description** button 🔲 on the Head tab. In the Description dialog box, type **The home page for The Bread Company with information about products and services. The Bread Company offers fine baked goods to restaurants and hotels all over California**. Click **OK**.

4. Click the **Keywords** button on the Head tab. In the Keywords dialog box, type **The Bread Company, muffins, bagels, bread, croissants, catering, baked goods, weddings, scones**. Do not forget to type commas between keywords. Click **OK**.

5. Click the **Meta** button on the Head tab. Select the Attribute **Name** and type **author** as the Value. In the Content text area, type *your name*. Click **OK**.

6. Click the **Show Code view** button to view the HTML code, if necessary. Observe that four different meta tags are in the header of your document. Click the **Show Design view** button to return to Design view.

7. Save this page as **thebreadcompany.htm** in the Sites\ch6practice folder of your working drive.

Project 6-3

You intend to post some of your academic writing on the Web and want to use meta tags to identify the work as yours. In this project, you type a short poem and then use the Head tab to enter description, author, and copyright meta tags.

1. Open a new file in Dreamweaver MX. In your new untitled document, type **Memorable Quotation by** *Your Name* in the Title text box on the Document toolbar.

2. Type **The integration of television with e-commerce applications will revolutionize the Web in the next five years.** in the workspace. Select the entire quote, and in the Property inspector, format the text to italic and centered, and change the text size to **+4**. Deselect the text by clicking any blank space in the bottom of the workspace.

3. Click the **Head tab** on the Insert bar if it is not already active. Click the **Description** button on the Head tab. Type **This page is a sample of** *your name*'s **quotes**. Click **OK**.

4. Click the **Meta** button on the Head tab. Select the Attribute **Name** and type **author** as the Value. In the Content text area, type *your name*. Click **OK**.

5. Click the **Meta** button on the Head tab. Select the Attribute **Name** and type **copyright** as the Value. In the Content text area, type **Copyright 2003 by** *your name*. Click **OK**.

6. Save this page as **quote.htm** in the Sites\ch6practice folder on your working drive.

6

Project 6-4

Large, complex Web sites with a lot of changing content often use expires meta tags. The expires tag specifies a date on which the page is no longer current. After the specified date, browsers no longer load the page.

1. Open a new file in Dreamweaver MX. In your new Untitled document, type **Digital Web Corporation Home Page** in the Title text box on the Document toolbar.

2. Type the text **Digital Web Corporation** in the blank workspace. Select this text, and in the Property inspector, center and italicize it, and change the text format to **Heading 1**. Deselect the text by clicking any blank space in the bottom of the workspace.

3. In the Head tab, click the **Description** button to open the Description dialog box.

4. In the dialog box, type **This is the home page for the Digital Web Corporation with information about Digital Cameras, Scanners, and Web Development**. Click **OK**.

5. Click the **Meta** button on the Head tab. Select the Attribute **HTTP-equivalent** and type **expires** as the Value. In the Content text area, type **December 20, 2003**. After this date, Web search engines will no longer index this page. Click **OK**.

6. Save this page as **digitalweb.htm** in the Sites\ch6practice folder on your working drive.

Project 6-5

In Project 6-4, you used the expires meta tag to ensure that Web browsers do not load a Web page once it has expired. In this project, you use the pragma meta tag to ensure that a user always sees a fresh, un-cached version of your Web page.

1. In Dreamweaver MX, open the file **digitalweb.htm** from the previous exercise, which is located in the Sites\ch6practice folder, if necessary.

2. On the Head tab, click the **Meta** button to open the Meta dialog box.

3. Select the Attribute **HTTP-equivalent** and type **Cache-Control** as the Value. In the Content text area, type **no-cache**. This means that users' computers will not cache this Web page. Click **OK**.

4. Save this page as **digitalweb2.htm** in the Sites\ch6practice folder on your working drive.

Project 6-6

In this project you create an entry page and a home page for the Human Resources Consulting Corporation (HRCC). The entry page tells visitors what Web site they are about to visit, and that they can expect to enter the site in eight seconds. A refresh meta tag automatically transfers the user to the company's home page. The home page gives the site name and has links to the basic products and services that the human resources firm offers.

1. Open a new file in Dreamweaver MX. Save the file as **entry.htm** in the Sites\ch6practice folder on your working drive.

2. Type **HRCC Entry Page** in the Title text box on the Document toolbar.

3. Type **Welcome to Human Resources Consulting Corporation** in the workspace. Select this text and use the Property inspector to change the text format to **Heading 1** and the text color to red (**#FF0000**). Deselect the text by clicking any blank space in the bottom of the workspace.

4. Press the **Enter** key to move the cursor to the next line. Type **Click here or wait to be connected to the HRCC Home Page**. Select this line of text and use the Property inspector to change the text format to **Heading 4** and the text color to pink (**#FF00FF**). Deselect the text by clicking any blank space in the bottom of the workspace.

5. Select the text **here**, and using the Property inspector, create a link to **home.htm**. Deselect the text by clicking any blank space in the bottom of the workspace.

6. On the Head tab, click the **Refresh** button. In the Refresh dialog box, type **8** for the Delay. Make sure the Go To URL radio button is selected and type **home.htm** in the text box next to it. Click **OK**. Save the file.

7. With entry.htm still open, open a new file and save it as **home.htm** in the Sites\ch6practice folder.

8. Type **HRCC Home Page** in the Title text box on the Document toolbar.

9. In the Dreamweaver MX workspace, type **Human Resources Consulting Corporation**. Press **Enter**. Type **about | consulting | services | placement**.

10. Select the **Human Resources Consulting Corporation** text and use the Property inspector to change the format to **Heading 1**. Deselect the text by clicking any blank space in the bottom of the workspace.

11. Select the text **about** and type **about.htm** in the Link text box in the Property inspector. Do the same for consulting, services, and placement using the links **consulting.htm**, **services.htm**, and **placement.htm**, respectively. (Note: None of these links will actually work because these files do not exist.) Save the file home.htm.

12. Click **Window** on the menu bar and click the file **entry.htm** near the bottom. Preview entry.htm in your Web browser by pressing **F12**. Observe that after 8 seconds, you are transferred to the home page for HRCC. Close the browser window to return to Dreamweaver MX.

6

Project 6-7

The Human Resources Consulting Company that was introduced in Project 6-6 would like to attract traffic to its Web site by swapping advertisements with the Resume Builder Company. In this project, you build a Web page for the company and insert a banner ad on both pages that cross-links these Web sites.

1. Using Windows Explorer, create a folder called **images** in your ch6practice folder on your working drive. Then, copy the files **rcbanner.gif** and **hrccbanner.gif** from the Chapter6\images folder into the Sites\ch6practice\images folder.

2. Open the file **home.htm** in Dreamweaver MX. This file should be located in your Sites\ch6practice folder on your hard drive. The page displays the company name Human Resources Consulting Corporation and a simple text menu. Click at the end of "*placement*" so that your cursor is after all the page's text. Then, press the **Enter** key several times to move the cursor lower on the page.

3. Click the **Image** button on the Common tab, and select the image named **rcbanner.gif** from the ch6practice\images folder.

4. With the image still selected, enter **resumeco.htm** in the Link text box in the Property inspector. This makes the banner a hyperlink to the resume company page.

5. Save this page as **hrcc.htm** in the Sites\ch6practice folder.

6. Open a new file in Dreamweaver MX and save it as **resumeco.htm** in the Sites\ch6practice folder.

7. Type **Resume Builder Company** in the Title text box on the Document tool-bar. Type **Welcome to Resume Builder** in the workspace. Select the text. In the Property inspector, change the format to **Heading 1**, the alignment to **center**, and the text color to red (**#FF0000**). Deselect the text by clicking any blank space in the bottom of the workspace.

8. Open the Page Properties dialog box (**Ctrl+J**), and select a black (**#000000**) background with white (**#FFFFFF**) text. Click **OK**.

9. Press **Enter** twice to position the cursor below the page title. Type the following text: **build a better resume**, **build a career**, and **build your skills**.

10. Select the text **build a better resume** and type **resume.htm** into the Link text box in the Property inspector. Repeat these steps for **build a career** (**career.htm**) and **build your skills** (**skills.htm**). (Note: None of these links will actually work because these files do not exist.) Select all three links. Use the Property inspector to format them as **Heading 2** and center them. Deselect the text by clicking any blank space in the bottom of the workspace.

11. Press **Enter** twice to position the cursor at the bottom of the page.

12. On the Common tab, click the **Image** button and select the image **hrccbanner.gif** from the Sites\ch6practice\images folder.

13. With the image still selected, type **hrcc.htm** in the Link text box in the Property inspector. This makes the banner a hyperlink to the resume company page.

14. Save the page **resumeco.htm**.

15. Preview the resumeco.htm page in your Web browser by clicking the **F12** key. Then, click the banner ad hrcc.htm and notice that it brings you back to the resumeco.htm page. Click the banner on the resumeco.htm page and notice that it opens the hrcc.htm page. Close the browser window to return to Dreamweaver MX.

CASE PROJECTS

A large pet products company, PetStore.com, wants to create a Web site that competes with other major online pet businesses. To increase traffic to its site, the company wants to improve its ranking in the major search engines. Build a Web page for this company that helps search engines index the page by using description and keyword meta tags. Add an expires meta tag so that the page will not be cached after a specific date. Save this page in the Sites\ch6practice folder of your working directory.

PetStore.com decides that the use of meta tags has not increased its traffic as much as it hoped. Part of its new strategy is to use banner advertisements to cross-link its site to other related companies. Create a banner ad in Fireworks for PetStore.com. Create a home page and banner ad for AcmePetSitting.com. Cross-link the banner ads for each site. Save the files in the Sites\ch6practice folder of your working drive. Save the banner advertisements you create in the Sites\ch6practice\images folder.

Search for the keywords Electronics, Saturn, and Microsoft in three major search engines, and see what the top five indexed pages are. Write a brief report addressing the following questions: Are the results similar among the different search engines? Why or why not? How might companies improve their ranking in each search engine?

Go to two major search engines, and determine from their online help how they index Web pages on their site. Then write a brief report that addresses the following questions: Is there a difference in how they find and index pages? How might your strategy differ for gaining a higher search engine ranking for your site with either search engine?

Choose a major search engine, and investigate how you can register your page with it. Write a brief report that addresses the following questions: What are the steps you need to complete? How is this different from hiring a service to register your site with several search engines?

Think of a domain name for a Web site that you would like to register. Go to an Internet registrar. Network Solutions (*www.networksolutions.net*) is one. Complete the steps for registering the domain name. If you are asked for a credit card number, *do not* enter one. You do not need actually to register the domain name, just to figure out how you would do it. Write a brief report that addresses the following questions: Was it difficult to find an unused domain name? Was the registration process difficult? What might you suggest to someone registering a domain name?

7

INTERACTIVE WEB SITE FORMS

Creating and Activating Forms to Gather Client Information

In this chapter, you will:

♦ Learn about the Document Object Model (DOM), forms, and form elements

♦ Lay out and develop forms that accept user input

♦ Insert a jump menu with a Go button, so that users can easily select and open a new Web page

♦ Validate form data fields

♦ Use the Behaviors panel to give users feedback when they submit a form

---

In this chapter, you learn how to increase the interactivity of your Web sites by developing forms that accept information from Web site visitors, provide feedback, and validate the data before it is posted to a Web server. Forms are widely used on the Internet, as well as on intranets and extranets. Examples include survey and guestbook forms that gather information about Web site visitors, and order forms that accept customer orders in e-commerce stores. Interactivity makes the Internet very attractive to many companies, because it enables them to do business anywhere, anytime, using a relatively low-cost communication link with customers and suppliers.

FORMS AND FORM PROCESSING

Forms use two components: HTML source code that describes the form, and either a **server-side** application or a **client-side** script that processes the user-generated form data. The process involves two-way interaction between the client and the server. The client requests an HTML page containing a form, which the Web server downloads to the client. The user fills in and submits the form. If there is a server-side application to process it, the form is posted back to the server, and the server-side application does its work, which frequently involves a database lookup and/or update. The transaction may iterate through several more client/server exchanges before it is finished. Client-side processing of form data is usually simpler. Two examples are scripts that can validate form data before it is posted to the server, and drop-down lists that let users click an item on a drop-down menu to connect to other Web pages.

This Dreamweaver MX book teaches you how to develop forms and generate client-side scripts. It discusses concepts you need to know to design forms that work with server-side applications, but it does not describe how to develop server-side applications.

FORMS AND FORM ELEMENTS

Forms on Web pages resemble the paper forms you see and work with every day. They provide descriptive information (such as directions and labels for the information you are to fill in) and spaces for you to enter information or select choices. HTML provides elements to hold form information, although in comparison with other popular programming languages, such as C++ and Visual Basic, HTML form elements are rather limited in scope and functionality. However, these limitations make HTML forms simpler to understand and program.

Forms, Form Elements, and the Document Object Model (DOM)

The **Document Object Model (DOM)** is a set of standards being defined by the World Wide Web Consortium (W3C, at *www.w3.org*). It defines the attributes of HTML pages that can be programmed and manipulated. Although you don't need to know about HTML form elements and the DOM to create forms in Dreamweaver, knowing a little about them helps you understand what you see behind the scenes in the HTML code. The DOM provides a hierarchical structure. An HTML document can contain one or more forms defined within <form> tags. An individual form can contain one or more form elements (for example, checkboxes, radio buttons). An HTML form is processed in its entirety when the user clicks the form's Submit button. The submit button is programmed to perform a task when clicked. The form's method attribute defines the task, such as posting the data contained within the form to a database.

Inserting Forms and Form Elements

You should find the process of inserting forms and form elements into an HTML page in Dreamweaver MX quite easy, since it is similar to inserting other types of elements. You can do it via the Forms tab on the Insert bar, shown in Figure 7-1, or via the Form and Form Object commands on the Dreamweaver Insert menu, shown in Figure 7-2.

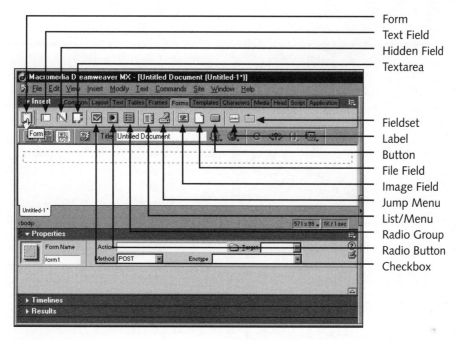

Figure 7-1   Forms tab on the Insert bar

According to the DOM, form elements belong inside forms. The values of the form elements on a form are usually processed when the form is submitted. Usually, you should insert the form first and then insert form elements inside the form tags (represented in Dreamweaver's Design view with a dashed border). Dreamweaver does allow you to insert form elements outside a form, but it asks if you want to insert a form tag around the form element, as shown in the dialog box in Figure 7-3. Clicking the Yes button creates a form around the form element. (If you have already set up a form for this form element and just positioned the cursor in the wrong place, click No, insert the element, and then drag and drop it inside the existing form.)

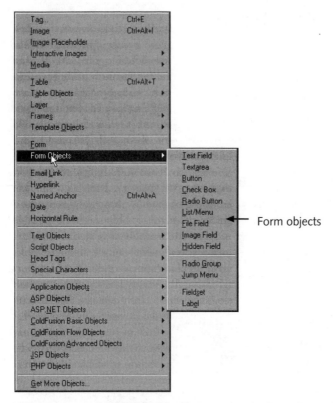

Figure 7-2 Inserting form and form objects from the Insert menu

Figure 7-3 Dialog box prompting to insert a form tag around a form element

Form Properties

Dreamweaver surrounds the form with a dotted red line, an invisible element that viewers cannot see in the browser window. If you cannot see the form borders after you insert a form, click View on the Dreamweaver menu bar, point to Visual Aids, and then click Invisible Elements. The Property inspector shown in Figure 7-1 displays the following attributes of the form enclosed in red dotted lines at the top of the page:

- Form Name assigns a name to the form, which is useful if you write a script to process form data.

- Action refers to a server-side application that will process form data. It has a Browse-for-File icon to help locate the application.

- Method defines how the form data is to be handled. The DOM standard provides methods for DOM objects. There are three choices in the drop-down menu:
  - GET appends form values to the URL defined in the Action field. You cannot use GET for longer forms, because it will append only 8192 characters, which may be too limited to hold all the data on the form that needs to be passed to the server.
  - POST sends the form values in the body of a message together with a request to POST the data to the server URL in the Action field. You can also program POST to perform client-side scripting. If you were using a form for e-commerce to gather orders for goods you sell, you probably would use the POST method to pass the form data to the server.
  - Default uses the browser default, usually GET.

Form Element Properties

The Forms tab on the Insert bar has a button for inserting a form, as well as thirteen other buttons to insert form elements, as shown in Figure 7-1. Form elements also have events and methods, as defined in the DOM. An **event** is some user activity (for example, buttons and checkboxes have onClick events) that initiates an action, for example, a block of JavaScript code that performs a task such as checking whether a text field contains a number. Methods are also available to form elements. The method **focus()** means the form element is active and able to receive input and perform tasks. The method **blur()** means that the form element does not have focus and is not available. The method **select()** keeps track of items that a user selects on a list or menu. Dreamweaver tools manage form element events and methods for you.

Each form element has its own properties, which you can view in the Property inspector when you select the form element. Form element properties differ, depending on the element itself.

Figure 7-4 shows **text field** properties and their HTML tags. Dreamweaver MX treats single line text fields and multi-line **text areas** as variations of the same form element, although they are actually defined as two different form elements in the DOM. Password fields are text fields that display asterisks instead of echoing the text that the user types. The contents of the password field are not encrypted, however, but are masked with asterisks as the user types them into the text box on the form. Encryption requires processing that is beyond the scope of this book.

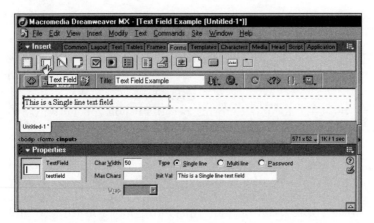

Figure 7-4   Single line text field and its Property inspector

The single line text field properties are as follows:

- TextField assigns a unique name to the field. Text fields must have unique names.

- Char Width defines the maximum number of characters displayed within the text field on the form. It can be less than Max Chars.

- Max Chars defines the maximum number of alphanumeric characters that the user can enter in the field for a single line text field.

- Type defines a text field as Single line, Multi line (a text area field), or Password (displays asterisks).

- Init Val inserts an initial block of text into the field that displays when the form opens. The user can overwrite this text.

Although Dreamweaver MX still lets you create a text area as a multi-line text field, it also lets you create a text area directly. The Property inspector for a multi-line text field or text area, shown in Figure 7-5, differs slightly from the Property inspector for the single line text field in Figure 7-4.

Text areas have two different properties:

- Num Lines sets the height of the field or number of lines for multi-line text fields.

- Wrap determines how the multi-line text wraps when its width exceeds Char Width. Default does not wrap until the user presses the Enter key. Virtual wraps text on the screen but not when the text field data is submitted on the form. Physical wraps the text both on the screen and on the submitted form.

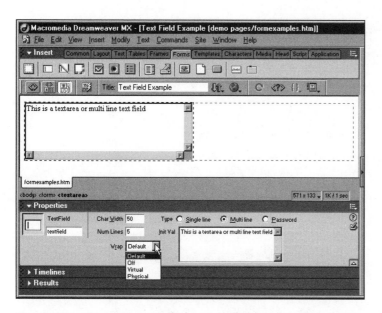

Figure 7-5   Textarea or Multi line text field and its Property inspector

The form element called **hidden fields** allow you to create an element that does not display on the form in the browser but can hold information posted with the form, for example, the user's e-mail address. Hidden fields have names and values that are passed to the server.

A **checkbox** provides a yes/no choice. If a form contains more than one checkbox, as in Figure 7-6, each checkbox has its own name and is independent of the other checkboxes. A user filling out the form could check none, one, or all checkboxes. Figure 7-6 shows a form with multiple checkboxes as well as the Checkbox Property inspector and HTML tags.

The checkbox properties are:

- CheckBox assigns a name to the checkbox. In Figure 7-6, the default name for the first checkbox is "checkbox" and for the second, "checkbox2".

- Checked Value denotes the value of the checkbox when it is checked. This value can be used as the value of a variable when the form is processed.

- Initial State defines whether the checkbox is checked or not when the form first loads.

There are two sets of **radio buttons** in Figure 7-7, the first three share the name "radiobutton," and the second three share the name "RadioGroup1." Each group provides a set of mutually exclusive options from which the user can only select one choice. Each group provides a set of radio buttons with the same name. The radio buttons in a group are mutually exclusive options from which the user can select only one choice.

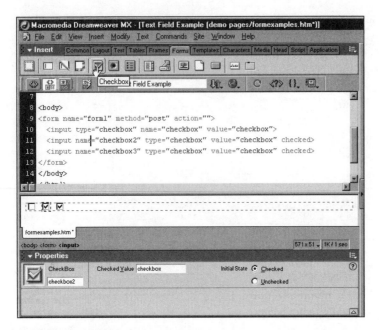

Figure 7-6 Checkbox in Code and Design views, and its Property inspector

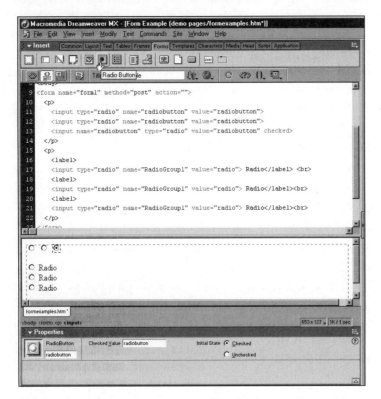

Figure 7-7 Radio buttons and a radio group in Code and Design view

In Dreamweaver MX, you can insert radio buttons one at a time, or you can click Radio Group on the Forms tab to open the Radio Group window shown in Figure 7-8. In this window you can add more radio buttons, change the labels displayed next to each radio button, and format them in a series of single-spaced lines or in a table. The radio button set displayed in the document window shows the resulting radio buttons after you click OK to close the Radio Group dialog box.

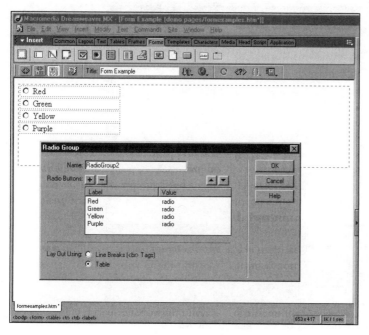

Figure 7-8   Radio Group dialog box options

The radio button properties are as follows:

- RadioButton assigns a name to the button. In Figure 7-7, the first set of radio buttons (created as individual radio buttons) share the same name, "radiobutton," and the second set (created as a Radio Group) share the name "RadioGroup1."

- Checked Value sets the value of the radio button when the user makes a choice. For example, if radio button choices indicate the operating system for a software download, there might be three radio buttons: one for Macintosh, one for Windows 2000, and one for Windows XP. If the user checks the radio button for Macintosh, the value of the radio button is set to Macintosh when the form is submitted for processing.

- Initial State sets the value of the radio button on the form when it is initialized in the browser window. In the first group of radio buttons in Figure 7-7, the third one is checked. In the Property inspector, Dreamweaver lets you set the initial value of more than one radio button in a set to Checked. However, when you view the page in the browser, only the last one in the list will be checked, since only one can be checked at a time.

A **list/menu** makes setting up a scrolling list or a pop-up menu easy. Figure 7-9 shows the HTML code for both types, the Property inspector choices for a scrolling list, and the browser display for both.

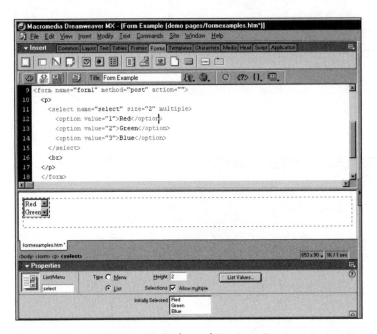

Figure 7-9 List/menu in Code and Design views

The Property inspector for the scrolling list in Figure 7-9 has the following attributes:

- List/Menu assigns a name to the list or menu.

- Type defines whether the element displays a scrolling list or a pop-up menu.

- Height indicates how many list items appear in a scrolling list (but not in a pop-up menu) at one time. If the number of list items is greater than the preset height, a scroll bar provides access to the entire list, as shown in Figure 7-9.

- Selections Allow multiple allows the user to select more than one item from a scrolling list (but not from a pop-up menu). This option is not available on the pop-up menu.

- List Values opens the List Values dialog box (Figure 7-10) for entering or editing list or menu items. Items have labels that appear in the list, as well as values that are sent to the processing application if the item is selected. If no value is specified, the label is sent to the processing application. You can use the + (plus) or − (minus) buttons to add or delete list items, and the up arrow and down arrow buttons to rearrange the items in the list.

- Initially Selected lets you select the default value for the list.

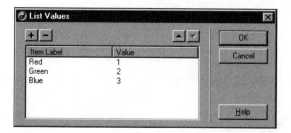

Figure 7-10   Enter List items and values

The **Jump Menu** form element is a Dreamweaver-defined form element that inserts a drop-down menu much like the one described for a list/menu. The difference is that each jump menu item on the list of choices jumps to a predefined URL. The action occurs when a user presses the Enter key after selecting an item on the list or selects an item and clicks an accompanying Go button. The Go button lets the user select the item on the list that is selected by default when the page opens.

Figure 7-11 displays the Property inspector and the HTML code defining a jump menu that links to pages on the La Bonne Cuisine Web site. This jump menu has a Go button. As you can see, the Property inspector for a jump menu is the same as for a list/menu.

When you insert a jump menu on a form, Dreamweaver displays a dialog box that lets you enter text names for the choices on the list and associated URLs (Figure 7-12). You enter the display text and the associated URL for each item, using the + (plus) button to add another item and the − (minus) button to remove an item. The up and down arrow buttons let you move around the list and change the order of items. Two checkboxes provide additional options for your jump menu. The first allows you to insert a Go button. The second allows you to set up the jump menu so that users who use it to jump to another page will see the next item on the jump menu list displayed when they go back to the jump menu. The Open URLs In list contains available windows in which the page can open. If the menu is within a frameset, frame names are listed.

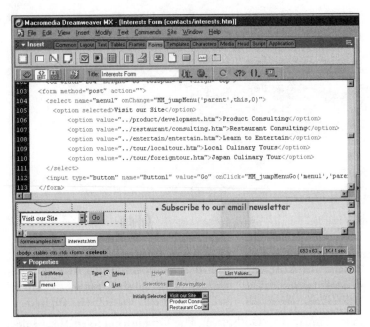

Figure 7-11   Properties of a jump menu and Go button

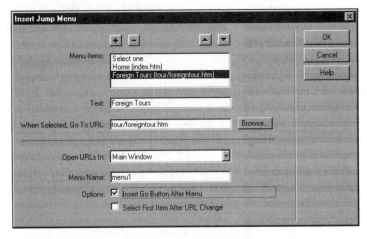

Figure 7-12   Insert Jump Menu dialog box

Image fields work just like submit buttons, except they use images that you insert on the form. Figure 7-13 shows an image field button and a Submit button provided by Dreamweaver.

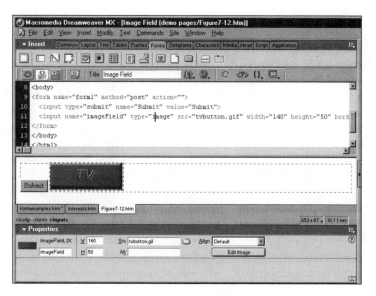

Figure 7-13   Image field used as graphic button

The image field properties follow:

- ImageField assigns a name to the image field. The 2K after the ImageField indicates the size in kilobytes of the image. You can type a name in the input box below the word ImageField.

- W (width) and H (height) define the width and height of the image.

- Src defines the source file for the image field.

- Alt defines alternative text that replaces the image for text-only browsers or for browsers set to download images manually.

- Align lets you align the graphic (similar to other images).

- Edit Image brings up the file in the image editor associated with the file type.

A **file field** allows the user to attach a file stored on the user's computer to the form and transmit it to the server. This rarely used element requires server-side processing, and therefore it is not covered here.

Buttons are form elements essential for processing form data. Dreamweaver provides two form buttons that have specific purposes: Submit processes the action defined for the form; and Reset clears the form data. A programmer can also define buttons that execute scripts. Figure 7-14 shows the Code and Design Views for the three buttons: a Submit form button, a Reset form button, and a programmer-defined button with the label "Play."

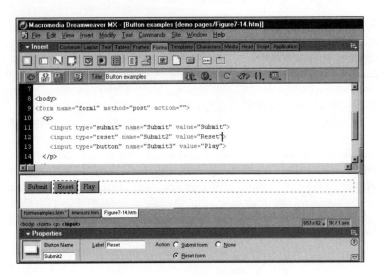

Figure 7-14 Buttons in Code and Design views

The button field properties follow:

- Button Name assigns a name to the button, which by default is "Submit," "Submit2," "Submit3," as in Figure 7-14. You can change this name to make your button(s) easier to identify in form processing.

- Label specifies the text that appears on a Command button.

- Action determines what happens when a user clicks the button. Submit form sets the button to process the completed form and sets the button name to Submit. Reset form sets the button action to clear the form data and sets the button name to Reset. None means the button will be programmed in a scripting language (e.g., JavaScript) to do something when a mouse event occurs.

The **label** element is used to specify labels for controls that do not have implicit labels, for example, text fields, checkboxes, radio buttons, and menus. (Some form controls, such as buttons, automatically have labels associated with them.) An example of a label that associates the text "First name", which would appear on the form, with the text field whose ID is "firstname" looks like this:

```
<LABEL for="firstname">First name: </LABEL>
  <INPUT type="text" id="firstname"><BR>
```

Fieldset is a container tag for a logical group of form elements. It allows you to group related form elements and labels. Grouping makes documents more accessible, because it is easier for users to understand the purpose of the grouped form elements, and to navigate, particularly when the user is relying on speech navigation. For example, if you had a questionnaire about pets, you could use a fieldset to solicit information about dogs and another fieldset to solicit information about cats. Each fieldset has its own label.

LAYOUT AND DEVELOPMENT OF INTERACTIVE FORMS

Form layout is important for the same reasons that page layout is important. Good form layout increases the usability of the form. If you insert a form without considering form layout beforehand, the size of each form object determines how the form looks. Instead of letting form layout just happen, you should try to control it. Tables are especially useful for aligning and balancing form elements, which make them easier for the viewer to scan and comprehend.

In the following exercises you design a form on an HTML page that should be displayed in an 800-pixel by 600-pixel browser window. Dreamweaver lets you define window size in the status bar at the bottom of the window. The maximized size for an 800-by-600-pixel browser window is 760 by 420 pixels, which allows room for the browser toolbars and status bar. In Figure 7-15, which shows interest.htm in the document window, you can see 760 × 420 displayed in the status bar at the bottom of the document window. Clicking the arrow to the right of the numbers in the status bar opens a pop-up menu that lets you select a target browser window size.

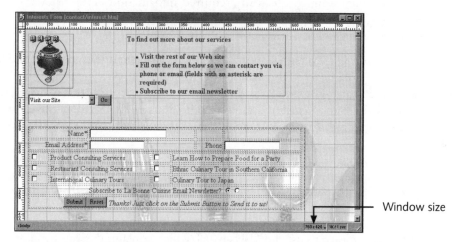

Figure 7-15   Page layout for interest.htm before converting layers to tables

Throughout this book, we have been using the integrated workspace, which is an MDI (Multiple Document Interface) container that holds the current document in the document window, and the Dreamweaver menu bar, docked panels, etc. This workspace is convenient, but depending on your monitor size and screen resolution, you may need to contract the docked panels on the right side to define the correct window size. You also have to be sure that the HTML page in the document window is not maximized within that window before you can define a precise window size.

Creating a Form Layout

The owner of La Bonne Cuisine wants visitors to her Web site to fill out a form indicating which services interest them. Throughout the rest of this chapter, you learn some techniques for client-side handling of the form data, using JavaScript. If you later learn server-side scripting, you will be able to pass the form data to the server for storage and further processing.

The form you develop here is rather short, because people are more likely to complete a form with fewer questions. The customer is only asked for a limited amount of information: name, e-mail address, telephone number (optional), and areas of interest. The owner plans to respond via e-mail, phone calls, or copies of her newsletter. She is also interested in having a jump menu that links to pages on her site containing more detailed information. The page with the form belongs in the Sites\lbc\contact folder of the Web site.

Figure 7-15 shows the layout for this page. You develop a layout using layers and then convert the layers to tables, as shown. Information at the top includes a warning that form fields marked with asterisks are required to submit the form. Warning the viewer about required fields improves Web site usability, because viewers can scan the form and decide whether they want to fill in the required information before they start. Later in this chapter, you learn how to validate the form to check that a user completes the required fields with the correct type of information before the form can be posted.

As mentioned, you use layers to lay out this HTML page and then convert the layers to tables. Two layers hold header information (the logo and the page heading), and two layers hold forms. One form contains a jump menu to help site visitors navigate. The other layer holds a form with an inserted table that helps align the form elements and makes the form easier to read. Figure 7-15 shows the layout for the entire form page.

 When you are drawing layers or table cells of a target size, you can always draw the layer or table cell to the approximate dimensions, and then select it and enter more precise height and width dimensions in the Property inspector.

In this exercise, you learn to use the Assets panel, which contains the assets you have defined for the La Bonne Cuisine Web site, to insert images. The Assets panel is part of the Files panel group and is located on a tab just to the right of the Site panel tab on the docked panels. You also use the Text tab on the Insert bar to modify the text characteristics.

To set up the page and prepare the information at the top of the page, which includes a logo and some informational text:

1. Copy the images **silverbackground.jpg** and **lbclogotrans.gif** from Chapter7\ images folder on your Data Disk to the Sites\lbc\assets\images folder on your working drive. If you see a message asking whether you want to replace the existing files in the Sites\lbc\assets\images folder with the ones you are copying, click the **Yes to all** button.

2. Start Dreamweaver and press the **F8** key to open the Site panel, if it is not already open. Select **LaBonneCuisine** on the drop-down site list. Create a new page inside the contact folder called **interest.htm** by right-clicking the contact folder, and clicking **New File** on the pop-up menu. Rename the file **interest.htm**. Double-click the file to open it in Design view. If the grid and ruler are not visible on the Web page, press the **Ctrl+Alt+G** and **Ctrl+Alt+R** key combinations to make them visible. Click the **Standard View** button on the Layout tab of the Insert bar.

3. Check the window size on the status bar at the bottom of the page in Design view, as shown in Figure 7-15. It should read **760 × 420**, which is the maximized size for an 800-by-600-pixel browser window. If the number is something else, be sure the page is not maximized in the editing window, click the arrow to the right of the number, and select **760 × 420 (800 × 600 maximized)** on the Window Size pop-up menu. Depending on your monitor size and screen resolution, you may have to drag the right edge of the Document window to the right or close the docked panels to the right of the Document window by clicking the sliding arrow between the Document window and the docked panels. If you close the docked panels, you can reopen them once you have resized the Document window.

4. Click **Modify** in the Dreamweaver menu bar, and then click **Page Properties**. Insert **silverbackground.jpg** from Sites\lbc\assets\images for the background image; change the page title to **Interests Form**, the text color to dark red (hexadecimal code **#990000**), and the links color to dark blue (hexadecimal code **#000099**). Save the page.

5. Click the **Common** tab on the Insert bar, and then click the **Draw Layer** button. Place the insertion point about **10** pixels from the left margin and **10** pixels from the top margin, and draw a layer that is about **120** pixels high and **100** pixels wide. Adjust the left and top margins and the layer dimensions in the Property inspector, if necessary.

6. Press the **F11** key to open the Assets panel and select the **Images** icon ▣ to display the site images. Click inside the layer you just created, select the image **lbclogotrans.gif** in the Images list of the Assets panel, and click the **Insert** button at the bottom of the Assets panel to insert the image inside the layer.

7. Click the **Draw Layer** button again and draw another layer starting about **225** pixels from the left margin and **10** pixels from the top margin. Draw a layer about **400** pixels wide and **135** pixels high.

8. Click the **Text** tab of the Insert bar. Click inside the layer and type **To find out more about our services**, and then press **Enter**. Then click **ul** on the Text tab to create an unordered (bulleted) list with the following items: **Visit the rest of our Web site; Fill out the form below so we can contact you via phone or email (fields with an asterisk are required)**; and **Subscribe to our email newsletter**. Select the text and click **B** on the Text tab to make it bold.

9. Save **interest.htm**.

7

In the next set of steps, you develop a jump menu and Go button to help visitors navigate the site. Remember that the layers should not touch or overlap as you develop the page layout.

To develop the jump menu:

1. Open **interest.htm** in the Sites\lbc\contact folder in Dreamweaver, if it is not already open. Be sure you are still in Standard view and have the grid and ruler displayed.

2. Click the **Draw Layer** button [image] on the Common tab of the Insert bar. Place the cursor about **10** pixels from the left and **145** pixels from the top margins of the page. Draw a layer about **190** pixels wide and **25** pixels high.

3. Click in the layer to select it. Click the **Forms** tab on the Insert bar. Click the **Jump Menu** button. Dreamweaver inserts a form to hold these form elements.

4. The first item on your list has no associated URL, because it gives visitors information about what is on the list. Therefore, type **Visit our Site** in the Text text box, and leave the Go To URL text box empty. Then click the **+** button to add another item to the jump menu. Type **Product Consulting** in the Text text box. Click the **Browse** button, and locate and select the file **consulting.htm**, in the Sites\lbc\consulting folder.

5. Enter the remaining information shown in Table 7-1 into the Menu Items and When Selected, Go To URL text boxes, using the **+** (plus) button to add each item.

Table 7-1   Items and Links for Jump Menu

Menu Item	When Selected, Go to URL
Visit Our Site	
Product Consulting	../consulting/consulting.htm
Restaurant Consulting	../consulting/consulting.htm
Learn to Entertain	../training/training.htm
Local Culinary Tours	../tour/localtour.htm
International Culinary Tours	../tour/foreigntour.htm

6. Check the **Insert Go Button After Menu** checkbox, as shown in Figure 7-16, and then click **OK**.

7. Save the page and preview it in your browser.

8. If the layer is not at least **190** pixels wide, the jump menu and Go button may not fit on the same line. Resize the layer width if necessary. Click the choices on the jump menu to ensure that they take you to the associated URL.

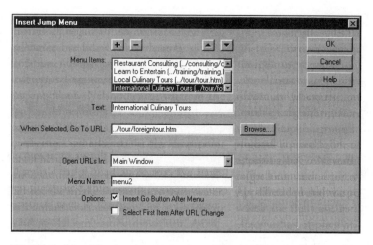

Figure 7-16   The Insert Go Button After Menu checkbox has been checked

If you delete a jump menu from your HTML page because it does not work, and then reinsert a jump menu on the same page, the second jump menu may not work even if you configure it correctly. This occurs because Dreamweaver has not deleted the JavaScript that loads the first jump menu. The browser reads the incorrect JavaScript for the first menu, notes the error, and stops loading the HTML page. If this happens, you need to rebuild the page from the beginning.

The fourth layer you draw holds the form and form elements (laid out with a table) that gather potential customer information for La Bonne Cuisine. The layout for this second form is more complex, because it holds a number of form elements. The steps for building the form are (1) create a layer, (2) insert a form inside it, and (3) insert two tables inside the form. You must create two tables, because the text field elements in the first table are much wider than the checkbox form elements in the second table.

In the following steps, you lay out and insert form elements in the first table, which allow visitors to type their names, e-mail addresses, and phone numbers. You need to switch back and forth between the Forms tab and the Common tab on the Insert bar to perform this exercise.

To work with the table:

1. Open **interest.htm** in Design view, if it is not already open. Be sure Standard view is selected on the Layout tab of the Insert bar.

2. Click the **Draw Layer** button [icon] on the Common tab of the Insert bar. Click the cursor about **10** pixels from the left margin and **215** pixels from the top margin of the page (just below the layer holding the jump menu). Draw a layer about **625** pixels wide and **180** pixels high.

3. Click in the layer. Click the **Form** button  on the Forms tab of the Insert bar. In the Property inspector for the form, type **customer** in the text box right under Form Name.

4. Click in the form you just inserted. Click the **Insert Table** button  on the Common tab of the Insert bar. In the Insert Table dialog box, give the table **2** rows and **4** columns, with width of **99%**. Set border to **0**, cell padding to **1**, and cell spacing to **3**. Click **OK**.

5. Click in the first table cell. Right-align the text in the Property inspector. Type **Name*** inside the cell.

6. Press **Tab** to move to the second cell in the first row of the table. Click the **Text Field** button on the Forms tab of the Insert bar. Select the text field, if necessary, and set the following attributes in the Property inspector: name to **CustName** and Char Width to **35** pixels. Click to select the **Single line** radio button, as in Figure 7-17.

Figure 7-17 Configured text field Property inspector

7. Click in the first cell in the second row. Type **Email Address*** and **Align Right** the text in the Property inspector.

8. Press **Tab** to move to the second cell. Click the **Text Field** button on the Forms tab of the Insert bar. If necessary, select the text field, and in the Property inspector set its name to **email** and Char Width to **25** characters. Click to select the **Single line** radio button.

9. Press **Tab** to move to the next cell, and type **Phone**. Again, right-align this text.

10. Press **Tab** to move to the next cell. Click the **Text Field** button on the Forms tab of the Insert bar. If necessary, select the text field, and set its attributes in the Property inspector: name to **phone** and Char Width to **25** characters. Click to select the **Single line** radio button.

11. Save the page, **interest.htm**, in the Sites\lbc\contact folder, and preview it in the browser.

Now it's time to lay out the rest of the form inside a new table that you insert just to the right of the first table. Because both tables occupy 99% of the browser width, the second table goes directly below the first table with no gap between the borders of the two tables. (If you pressed the Enter key instead to create a new paragraph, you would create a blank line between the two tables, because Dreamweaver inserts a <p> tag.)

In the next steps you create the layout table. You set the columns of the table to the appropriate widths. After you create the table, you merge the four columns in each of the bottom two table rows to make them one column wide.

To work with the table again:

1. Click in the layer you created in the previous set of steps, just to the right of the table you inserted. Press the **Ctrl+Alt+T** key combination to insert another table. Configure this table with **5** rows and **4** columns, border **0**, table width of **99%**, cell padding of **1**, cell spacing of **3**.

2. Drag the cursor down the first column of the first three rows of this table to select the column. In the Property inspector for the selected table cells, type **5%** in the W (width) input box, as shown in Figure 7-18.

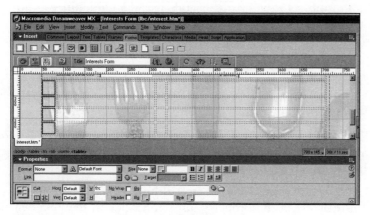

Figure 7-18   Format column width down rows

3. Repeat Step 2 for the second column of the first three rows, but change the column width to **35%** in the Property inspector for the selected table cells.

4. Repeat Step 2 for the third column in the first three rows, and again change the column width to **5%**.

5. Repeat Step 2 for the fourth column of the first three rows, and change the column width to **45%**.

6. Click inside a cell in the fourth row, and then click **<tr>** in the status bar to select the entire fourth row. Click the **Merge Cells** button 🔲 in the Property inspector for the table row to merge these cells. Repeat this process to merge the cells in the fifth row.

7. Save **interest.htm** in the Sites\lbc\contact folder.

The table you just inserted in the form must now be formatted to contain three rows of choices with checkboxes; a fourth row that offers radio button choices to receive the La Bonne Cuisine newsletter; and a fifth row that holds the Submit and Reset buttons. The four columns in the top three rows align the checkboxes and the choices, and the bottom two rows have one column each.

To insert the checkboxes and their labels:

1. Open **interest.htm** in Design view, if it is not already open.

2. Click in the first cell in the second table, and click the **Checkbox** button ☒ on the Forms tab of the Insert bar. Type **product** as the CheckBox Name in the Property inspector. Click in the next cell, and type **Product Consulting Services**.

3. Press **Tab** to move to the next cell, and click the **Checkbox** button on the Forms tab of the Insert bar. Type **entertain** as the CheckBox Name in the Property inspector. Click in the next cell and type **Learn How to Prepare Food for a Party**.

4. Press **Tab** to move to the first cell in the second row, insert a checkbox, and rename it **restaurant** in the Property inspector. Click in the next cell and type **Restaurant Consulting Services**.

5. Press **Tab** to move to the next cell, insert a checkbox, and name it **localtour** in the Property inspector. Click in the next cell and type **Ethnic Culinary Tour in Southern California**.

6. Press **Tab** to move to the first cell in the third row, insert a checkbox, and rename it **intltour** in the Property inspector. Click in the next cell and type **International Culinary Tours**.

7. Press **Tab** to move to the next cell, insert a checkbox, and name it **japan** in the Property inspector. Click in the next cell and type **Culinary Tour to Japan**. Figure 7-19 shows you the layout of this section and the code that creates it. Save the file.

Two radio buttons near the bottom of the form allow the viewer to subscribe to an e-mail newsletter. Both radio buttons have the name "newsletter," because they represent two different answers to the same question. The checked value of the Yes radio button is yes, and the checked value of the No radio button is no. Because we hope that the viewer will subscribe to the newsletter, the Initial State for the Yes radio button is checked, and the Initial State for the No radio button is not checked.

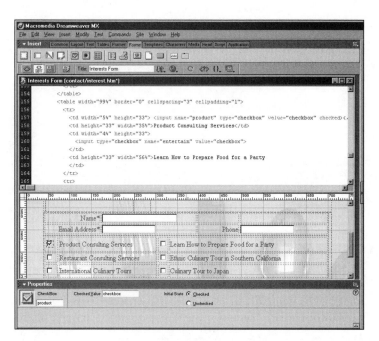

Figure 7-19   Checkboxes and labels and their Property inspector

To work with the radio buttons:

1. Open **interest.htm** in Design view, if it is not already open.

2. Click in the fourth row of the second table. Click the **Align Center** button in the Property inspector for the table cell, type **Subscribe to La Bonne Cuisine Email Newsletter?** Press the **space bar** once.

3. Click the **Radio Button** button on the Forms tab of the Insert bar. Click the **radio button** to select it, if necessary. Type the name **newsletter** in the RadioButton Name text box. Type **Yes** in the Checked Value text box. Click the **Checked** radio button to the right of Initial State.

4. Click in the same table cell just to the right of the radio button you just inserted. Type the text **Yes** and press the **space bar**.

5. Click the **Radio Button** button on the Forms tab of the Insert bar again. In the Property inspector, rename the radio button **newsletter**, set Checked Value to **No**, and click the **Unchecked** radio button to the right of Initial State.

6. Click in the same table cell to the right of the second radio button you inserted. Type **No**.

7. Save **interest.htm** in Sites\lbc\contact folder. Figure 7-20 shows the Property inspector for the first radio button, and the Design and Code Views for both radio buttons.

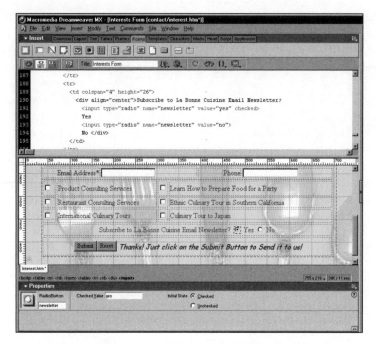

Figure 7-20 Radio button Property inspector and HTML

To insert the buttons and text at the bottom of the form:

1. Click in the bottom row of the table. In the table cell Property inspector, click the **Align Center** button ▤. Click the **Button** button on the Forms tab of the Insert bar. By default, it is the Submit button, which your form needs.

2. Insert a second button just to the right of the first one. Select this button, if necessary. In the button Property inspector, type **reset** in the Button Name text box, and click **Reset form** as its Action, which changes its Label to **Reset**.

3. Click immediately to the right of the second radio button, press the **space bar** and then type **Thanks! Just click on the Submit Button to Send it to us!** Highlight this text and italicize it. Figure 7-21 shows the completed row of the form, with the Property inspector for the Reset button.

4. Save **interest.htm** in the Sites\lbc\contact folder. Preview it in the browser. If you are not satisfied with the layout, adjust it.

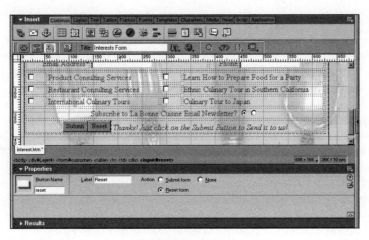

Figure 7-21   Reset button Property inspector

5. If you are happy with the layout, click **Modify** on the Dreamweaver menu bar, point to **Convert**, and then click **Layers to Table**. In the dialog box, click the **Most Accurate** radio button and **Center on Page** checkbox. Deselect any other checkboxes. Click **OK**. Save the page and view in the browser. The browser display should look similar to Figure 7-22.

Figure 7-22   interest.htm form page in browser window

FORM FUNCTIONALITY AND INTERACTIVITY

Your next task is to make the customer form interactive. Dreamweaver provides some interactivity automatically. In this section, you learn how to validate forms and form elements and how to set form actions using Dreamweaver.

Behaviors in Dreamweaver

To add functionality to the form, you should understand something about behaviors and how they work in Dreamweaver. A behavior includes an event and an action. Events are heavily used in event-driven programming languages, such as JavaScript and Visual Basic, to respond to user activity. In Dreamweaver, an event initiates an action, a block of JavaScript code that does some task, such as checking whether a text field contains a number. Typical events for buttons are onMouseOver and onClick.

In the jump menu you just created, you can see an action scripted by Dreamweaver. The Behaviors panel in Figure 7-23 lists the onChange events and the jump menu actions. An onChange event is triggered when the value of a form field or object loses its focus (for example, when the user tabs away from it) and the value within the field has changed. The associated JavaScript code in Code view calls a function, MM_jumpMenu, when the selection in the jump menu changes (the onChange event you see in the Behaviors panel). The JavaScript code for the function MM_jumpMenu in Figure 7-24 is within the <head> tags for the HTML page.

Note You will work more with the Behaviors panel when you attach behaviors to objects in Chapter 10, when you create Dynamic HTML.

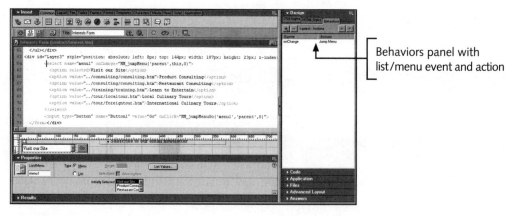

Behaviors panel with list/menu event and action

Figure 7-23   Jump menu Property inspector and HTML code

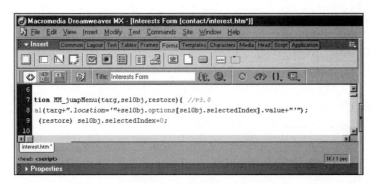

Figure 7-24   JavaScript code for Jump Menu function

You can access the Behaviors panel by clicking Behaviors on the Dreamweaver Window menu or pressing the Shift+F3 key combination. When you click an object in Code or Design view (for example, a form), the Behaviors panel gives you access to the events available to that element, according to the DOM. You can add an event by clicking the + (plus) button and delete an event by clicking the − (minus) button.

Using Behaviors to Validate Forms

Now that you know a little about Dreamweaver behaviors, you need to learn how to set them up to process a form and provide user feedback. The Validate Form action checks the contents of specified text fields to ensure that the user's data entry meets the Validate Form requirements. You can check whether data has been entered and whether that data is of the correct type. For example, you can generate code to check whether the contents of a text field are numeric, or whether they are in e-mail format (that is, they contain an @ symbol with characters before and after it).

You can attach this Validate Form action to individual form fields to validate the field content as the user fills out the form, or you can attach it to the form itself to evaluate multiple fields when the user submits the form. Attaching this action to a form prevents the form from being submitted to the server if fields contain invalid data or if its required fields are not filled out.

If you validate at the individual form element level, validation occurs when the user tabs to the next field (an onBlur() event). If you validate at the form level, validation occurs for the entire form when the user clicks the Submit button, which generates an onSubmit event.

To validate form information at the form level:

1. Open **interest.htm**, if it is not already open. Press the **Shift+F3** key combination to open the **Behaviors panel**, if it is not already open.

2. Click the red form border to select the entire **Customer form**, or click anywhere in the form and then click the **<form#customer>** tag in the tag selector at the bottom of the HTML page in the document window.

3. In the Behaviors panel, click the **+** (plus) button to open a pop-up menu. Click **Validate Form** to open the Validate Form dialog box. Click **text "CustName" in form "customer"** to select it, if necessary, and then click the **Value Required** checkbox. Leave the Anything option selected. An (R) for required appears to the right of the text field name.

4. Select **text "email" in form "customer"**, as shown in Figure 7-25. Check **Value Required** again. Check the **Email Address** radio button at the bottom of the dialog box, so that the content of this field must have the format of an e-mail address. RisEmail appears to the right of the text field name. Click **OK**, and then save the page.

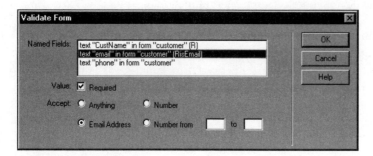

Figure 7-25   Validate Form dialog box

5. Test the validation rules in the browser. Leave required fields blank, type invalid data in the e-mail address field, and click the **Submit** button. Test each field that has validation with both valid and invalid data to be sure it works.

 Setting up numeric validation for the phone number field may be tempting, but remember that phone numbers often contain hyphens and parentheses. Identify only those text fields used in arithmetic operations as numeric.

Client-Side Scripting Feedback

Form validation is an example of client-side feedback for which Dreamweaver generates JavaScript. By writing your own JavaScript code, you can give users other types of feedback when they enter form data and click the Submit button. For example, feedback frequently allows users to review and correct their form data.

Acknowledging that the user is submitting the form in a message box, such as in Figure 7-26, is a very simple kind of feedback. In the next steps, you use the Behaviors panel to create a message box that appears when the user clicks the Submit button on the customer form on interest.htm.

Figure 7-26 Display form feedback in a message box

To produce a feedback message box:

1. Open **interest.htm** in Dreamweaver, if it is not already open. Select the **Submit** button. Press the **Shift+F3** key combination to open the Behaviors panel, if it is not already open, to display the behaviors available for this form element.

2. Click the **+** button in the Behaviors panel and select **Popup Message** on the pop-up menu. Type **Thank you for your interest!**, press the Enter key, and then type **La Bonne Cuisine**. Click **OK**. If you look at the HTML code for the Submit button, it reads:

```
<input name="Submit" type="submit"
onClick="MM_popupMsg('Thank you for your interest!\rLa
Bonne Cuisine')" value="Submit" >
```

3. Save the document **interest.htm** in the Sites\lbc\contact folder. Preview it in the browser, and click the **Submit** button to view the alert box.

CHAPTER SUMMARY

❑ Understanding form elements and their connections to the Document Object Model (DOM) in HTML helps you understand how forms work and how they are processed.

❑ Form elements provide Web site visitors with a lot of options for interactivity. In addition, you can gather information about visitors to your site when they fill out and submit a form.

❑ Form processing usually occurs at the form level, when the user finishes filling out the form and clicks the Submit button. Therefore, individual form elements must be on an actual form if the data they hold is to be posted to a database on a Web server or e-mailed to the site owner.

❑ You can lay out forms using tables, layers, or both. Form layout is as important to Web site usability as page layout.

❑ Dreamweaver automates form validation for individual fields. Validation can happen when the user finishes entering data in each field, or at the form level when the user clicks the Submit button. Dreamweaver automates validation by checking whether a field is filled in, whether it is in e-mail format (with an @ embedded within it), and whether it is numeric. Alert boxes display messages for fields that fail validation.

❑ Dreamweaver supplies standard buttons (Submit and Reset) and also supports the use of images created outside Dreamweaver as buttons. You can program behaviors to respond when the user interacts with form elements or other types of elements on a Web page.

❑ Dreamweaver manages text fields for input. They can be single line or multi-line text fields (also known as text areas). Text fields used for password fields display asterisks, although Dreamweaver does not encrypt the data in the password field before transmitting it.

❑ Dreamweaver lets you generate jump menus, with or without Go buttons. Jump menus are convenient navigation tools that let the user make a selection that takes them to a URL associated with the selected item on a scrolling menu.

❑ The Behaviors panel lets you program events available to each element on an HTML page.

REVIEW QUESTIONS

1. In the hierarchy of the DOM for forms, the following is *not* true:
   a. Documents can hold one or more forms.
   b. Buttons are form elements for processing data.
   c. Forms can hold one or more form elements.
   d. Form elements hold forms.

2. The methods available to forms do *not* include:
   a. E-mail
   b. Get
   c. Default
   d. Post

3. The form element that creates an input field that accepts alphanumeric input is the:
   a. text field
   b. Button
   c. Radio button
   d. Hidden field
   e. File field

4. The form element that provides the choice of one option from among a group of options is the:

a. text field

b. Button

c. Radio button

d. Hidden field

e. File field

5. The form element that lets users browse files on the working drive and upload them as form data is the:

a. text field

b. Button

c. Radio button

d. Hidden field

e. File field

6. The form element that can be used like a button is the:

a. text field

b. Image field

c. Radio button

d. Hidden field

e. File field

7. The form element that does not appear in the browser window is the:

a. text field

b. Button

c. Radio button

d. Hidden field

e. File field

8. The type of text field that displays asterisks rather than letters is the:

a. Hidden field

b. Password field

c. Text area

d. Layer

7

9. Dreamweaver does not automate which type of validation of form elements?

   a. E-mail address

   b. Numeric entry

   c. Required field

   d. Post field

10. You should require numeric entry in a field only if:

    a. You plan to use the information in arithmetic.

    b. It is a telephone number.

    c. It is a zip code.

    d. It is a Social Security number.

11. If you were using a form for e-commerce to gather orders for goods you sell, you probably would use the _____ method to pass the form data to the server.

    a. Post

    b. Get

    c. Default

    d. E-mail

12. The panel that lets you insert images contained within a Web site is called the:

    a. Assets panel

    b. Site panel

    c. Behaviors panel

    d. CSS styles panel

13. The panel in which you can set up methods and actions for a form element is called the:

    a. Assets panel

    b. Site panel

    c. Behaviors panel

    d. CSS styles panel

14. DOM is an acronym for:

    a. Dreamweaver Object Model

    b. Document Object Model

    c. Dynamic Object Model

    d. Dreamweaver Object Map

15. To improve the usability of a form, developers often _____.

    a. warn the users about required fields, so that they can decide whether they want to supply required information before they begin to fill out the form

    b. make the colors of the form very bright

    c. use an attractive image field rather than a submit button to submit the form

    d. extend the form over several pages, so that the users won't know how much information they have to provide

16. In the DOM, the form element that lets the user type a multi-line text field is called the:

    a. Text area

    b. Password field

    c. Scrolling list

    d. Pop-up menu

17. Dreamweaver generates script that encrypts password fields. True or False?

18. The form element that Dreamweaver creates that lets you list a selection of items that sends users to different URLs is called a:

    a. Text area

    b. Password field

    c. Scrolling list

    d. Jump menu

19. The button that Dreamweaver adds to a jump menu is called a _____ button.

    a. Jump

    b. Go

    c. Submit

    d. Reset

20. When Dreamweaver generates code to do e-mail validation for a text field, the validation looks for what character between two strings of text?

    a. %

    b. @

    c. &

    d. #

7

HANDS-ON PROJECTS

Project 7-1

In this project you create a page with a jump menu that uses a Go button.

1. Create a folder named **ch7practice** inside the Sites folder on your working drive, and a folder named **images** inside the ch7practice folder. Copy the images **wasedabg.jpg, cooks.jpg, kyotorr.jpg, kyotopalacebridge.jpg,** and **kyototitle.gif** from the Chapter7\images folder on your Data Disk to the Sites\ch7practice\images folder.

2. Open Dreamweaver, if it is not already open. Create a new basic HTML page in Dreamweaver, and save it as **kyotomenu.htm** in the Sites\ch7practice folder. Press the **Ctrl+Alt+G** key combination to show the grid and the **Ctrl+Alt+R** key combination to show the ruler, if they are not already visible.

3. Press the **Ctrl+J** key combination to open the **Page Properties** dialog box. Change the title of the page to **Kyoto Tour**, and insert the background image **wasedabg.jpg** from Sites\ch7practice\images. Save the file.

4. Create two new pages, **kyotofood.htm** and **kyotostation.htm**. Save them in the Sites\ch7practice folder. Press the **Ctrl+J** key combination to open the **Page Properties** dialog box for each page in turn. Insert the same background graphic, **wasedabg.jpg**, from Sites\ch7practice\images in both pages, and title the first **Kyoto Food** and the second **Kyoto Station.** Save both pages.

5. Press the **Ctrl+Alt+I** key combination to insert the image **cooks.jpg** from Sites\ch7practice\images on the first line of **kyotofood.htm**. Center the image on the page. Save the page.

6. Press the **Ctrl+Alt+I** key combination to insert the image **kyotorr.jpg** from Sites\ch7practice\images onto the first line of **kyotostation.htm**. Center the image on the page. Save the page.

7. Open **kyotomenu.htm** for editing. Press the **Ctrl+F6** key combination to switch to Layout view, if necessary. Draw a layout table that is **600** pixels wide and **300** pixels high.

8. Draw a layout cell in the upper-left corner of the table that is about **200** pixels wide and **100** pixels high. Insert the image **kyototitle.gif** from the Sites\ch7practice\images folder into this layout cell.

9. Draw another layout cell in the same layout table to the right of the first one, starting at the top of the table and **250** pixels from the left margin of the table. Draw this layout cell so that it is **100** pixels high and about **350** pixels wide. Insert a jump menu and Go button from the Forms tab of the Insert bar. Configure the jump menu with two items, **food** and **station**, with the associated URLs for **kyotofood.htm** and **kyotostation.htm** in the Sites\ch7practice folder.

10. Draw another table cell starting about **200** pixels to the right and **150** pixels down from the page margins, using the ruler to guide your starting point. The table cell should be about **200** pixels wide and **120** pixels high. Press the **Ctrl+Alt+I** key combination to insert the image **kyotopalacebridge.jpg** from Sites\ch7practice\images in this table cell.

11. Save the page and test it in the browser to make sure the jump menu works.

Project 7-2

In this project you create a jump menu in a frameset, reusing pages created in Project 7-1.

1. Press the **Ctrl+N** key combination to open the New Document window in Dreamweaver. Select **Framesets** on the General tab of the New Document window. Select the **Fixed Top** frameset and click **Create** to set up the frameset. Press the **Shift+F2** key combination to open the **Frames** panel if it is not already open. Be sure to be in Design view so that the frames will show in the Frames panel. Use the frames in the Frames panel to select frames for editing in the following steps.

2. Click the outer border of the frameset in the Frames panel. In the Property inspector for the frameset, set Row Value to **150** and select **Pixels** on the Units list menu. With the frameset still selected, click **Save All** on the **File** menu. Save the frameset document as **kyotoframeset.htm**, the bottom frame as **kyotobottom.htm**, and the top frame document as **kyototop.htm** in the Sites\ch7practice folder.

3. Edit **kyotobottom.htm**. Press the **Ctrl+J** key combination to open the **Page Properties** dialog box. Type the title **Kyoto Main**, and insert the background image **wasedabg.jpg** from Sites\ch7practice\images. Click in the page and press the **Ctrl+Alt+I** key combination to insert the image **kyotopalacebridge.jpg**. Center the image.

4. Select the top frame in the Frames panel, if necessary. Press the **Ctrl+J** key combination to open the **Page Properties** dialog box. Insert the background image **wasedabg.jpg** from the ch7practice\images folder, and title the page **Kyoto Menu**.

5. Press the **Ctrl+F6** key combination to switch to Layout view, if necessary. Draw a layout table that is about **100** pixels high and **600** pixels wide. Draw a layout cell in the upper-left corner that is about **80** pixels high and **160** pixels wide. Insert the image **kyototitle.gif** from the ch7practice\images folder in this layout cell.

6. Draw another layout cell directly to the right of the first one (but not touching it), starting **200** pixels from the left margin on the rule. Make this layout cell about **80** pixels high and about **270** pixels wide.

7. Place the insertion point in this table cell, and insert a jump menu that includes a Go button using the Forms tab of the Insert bar. Configure the jump menu with two items, **food** and **station**, with the associated URLs for **kyotofood.htm** and **kyotostation.htm**, which are located in the Sites\ch7practice folder. Choose the target **mainFrame** in the **Open URLs In** drop-down list for both items in the list. Click **OK** to save the jump menu.

8. Click the outer border of the frameset in the Frames panel to select it. Click **Save All** on the **File** menu.

9. Test the frameset in the browser to be sure that the jump menu and Go button work correctly, and that the pages open in the lower frame. If the jump menu does not work properly, you should delete it and recreate it.

Project 7-3

In this project you use the Behaviors panel to modify the page kyotobottom.htm that you developed In Project 7-2.

1. Open the frameset **kyotoframeset.htm** in Dreamweaver, if necessary. Place the insertion point to the right of the image kyotopalacebridge.jpg in kyotobottom.htm in the lower frame, and press **Enter** to go to a new line.

2. Insert a button from the Forms tab of the Insert bar. Click **Yes** to any message boxes that appear. Type **More Information** in the label text box, and click the **None** radio button.

3. Press the **Shift+F3** key combination to open the Behaviors panel if it is not already open. Select the button and click the **+** sign on the Behaviors panel. Select **Popup Message** on the pop-up menu. In the Popup Message window, type **Please telephone us for more information**, press **Enter**, and type **Phone: 800-000-0000** on the second line.

4. Save the page and view the changes in the browser.

Project 7-4

In this project you create a form for a company called Party People. The company will use the form to collect information about visitors to its Web site. This project has two parts: creation of the form and validation of its fields.

1. Copy the images **worldbg.gif** and **peopleparty.gif** from the Chapter7\images folder on your Data Disk to the Sites\ch7practice\images folder on your working drive.

2. Start Dreamweaver if necessary. Press the **Ctrl+N** key combination to create a new basic HTML page, and save it as **partyform.htm** in the Sites\ch7practice folder. If the grid and ruler are not showing, press the **Ctrl+Alt+R** and the **Ctrl+Alt+G** key combinations to make them visible. Press the **Ctrl+J** key combination to open the **Page Properties** dialog box. Change the page title to **Party People Form**, and insert **worldbg.gif** from the Sites\ch7practice\images folder as the background image file.

3. In Layout view, click the **Draw Layout Cell** button on the Common tab of the Insert bar starting in the upper-left corner of the HTML page, draw a layout cell that is about **60** pixels high and **300** pixels wide. Notice that Dreamweaver inserts a layout table to hold the layout cell.

4. Click inside this table cell, and press the **Ctrl+Alt+I** key combination to insert the image **peopleparty.gif** from the Sites\ch7practice\images folder.

5. Follow the directions in Step 3 to draw another layout cell starting about **25** pixels from the left margin and **100** pixels from the top of the HTML page. Extend the lower margin of this layout cell to the **450**-pixel line on the ruler, and the right margin to the **450**-pixel line on the ruler. Depending on your monitor size and screen resolution, you may need to contract the Property inspector or the Insert bar to extend the table cell to 450 pixels from the top margin. If either the right or lower margin of the layout table holding this layout cell extends beyond the 450-pixel mark, grab the table margin and drag it back to the table cell margin.

6. Click in the layout cell you just drew and insert a form from the Forms tab of the Insert bar.

7. Click the **Layout** tab on the Insert bar and switch to Standard view. Click inside the form and insert a table in the form with **4** rows and **2** columns, width of **99%**, border of **0**, cell padding of **1**, and cell spacing of **3**.

8. If you closed the Property inspector in Step 5, you need to press the **Ctrl+F3** key combination to reopen it. Type **Name** in the first table cell, press **Tab** to move to the next cell, and insert a text field from the Forms tab of the Insert bar. Click the text field to select it, and type **custname** in the Name text box in the TextField Property inspector. Type **50** in the Char Width text box.

9. Click in the first cell in the second row of the table, and type **Email address**. Press **Tab** to move to the next cell, and insert a text field. In the TextField Property inspector, name the text field **email** and change its Char Width to **50**. Leave the Single line radio button selected.

10. Click in the first cell in the third row, and type **Comments**. Press **Tab** to move to the next cell, and insert a text area. In the Property inspector, change Char Width to **50** and Num Lines to **5**. Type **comments** in the Name text box in the Property inspector.

11. Click in the first cell in the fourth row. Insert a button from the Forms tab of the Insert bar. In the Button Property inspector, change the label name to **Feedback**, but click the **Submit form** radio button. Press **Tab** to move to the last cell, and type **Click here to submit your comments**.

12. Select the **<form>** tag in the status bar, and then press the **Shift+F3** key combination to open the **Behaviors panel** if it is not already open. Click the **+** (plus) button, and then click **Validate Form**. Click to select the **Required** checkbox for the fields **custname** and **email**. Select the field **email** and then click the **Email Address** radio button. Click **OK**.

13. Select the button and click the **+** sign on the Behaviors panel. Select **Popup Message** on the pop-up menu. Type **Thank you for your comments**, press **Enter** to go to a new line, and then type **Have a great day!** in the Popup Message window.

14. Save the page and test the validation in the browser by not entering data in the required fields, and by entering data without the @ sign in the e-mail field.

7

Project 7-5

In this project you create a new page that contains a form with a password field.

1. Create a new page called **password.htm**, and save it in the Sites\ch7practice folder on your working drive. Press the **Ctrl+J** key combination to open the **Page Properties** dialog box, then insert **worldbg.gif** as the background image, and type **Login Page** as the title.

2. Insert a form from the Forms tab of the Insert bar.

3. Insert a text field in the form using the Forms tab of the Insert bar. In the TextField Property inspector, change the name to **password**, click the **Password** radio button to select it, and type **10** in the Char Width and **Max Chars** text boxes.

4. Click to the right of the text field, and type **Enter your secret password of 10 characters or less**.

5. Save the file and test it in the browser. Try to enter a password with more than 10 characters.

Project 7-6

In this project you create two list/menus with the same items. Make one a scrolling list and the other a pop-up menu.

1. Press the **Ctrl+N** key combination to open the New Document window. Create a new basic HTML page and save it as **listmenus.htm** in the Sites\ch7practice folder.

2. Press the **Ctrl+J** key combination to open the **Page Properties** dialog box. Type **Favorite Soft Drinks** in the Title text box, and change the background color to red (**#FF0000**) and the text color to white (**#FFFFFF**). Click **OK**.

3. Type **Choose Your Favorite Soft Drinks** on the first line of the page, and change the format of this line to **Heading 2**. Deselect the text and press **Enter** to go to the next line. Insert a form from the Form tab of the Insert bar. (Note that the dotted outline of the form is not visible because the page's background is red. However, you can always select the form by clicking any of the form elements, and then clicking the <form> tag in the Design view status bar.)

4. In the form, insert two list/menu form elements next to each other.

5. Modify the List/Menu Property inspector of the first list/menu to make it a pop-up menu (click the **Menu** radio button to select it), and name it **popup**. Click the **List Values** button, and type the following Item Labels and corresponding Values: **Coca Cola, Coke; 7-Up, sevenup; Root beer, rootbeer; Tonic water, tonic; Orangina, orangina**.

6. Click the second list/menu to select it. In the Property inspector, make it a scrolling list (click the **List** radio button to select it), and name it **scrolling**. Click the **List Values** button, and type the Item Labels and Values from Step 5. Try set-

ting the height of the List to **1**, to **4**, and to **5**. Each time test the different effect in the browser.

7. Select the scrolling list/menu, and click the **Selections Allow multiple** checkbox in its Property inspector. Test this version of the page in the browser by holding down the Ctrl key to select different nonsequential items on the list or the Shift key to select sequential items on the list.

8. Save the file and view the different list/menus in the browser window.

9. Add a jump menu to the form, to the right of the pop-up menu. Click **Jump Menu** on the Forms tab of the Insert bar. Name the menu **jump** and do not include a Go button. Use the same item labels as the other menus, but insert the URLs for the soft drink Web sites: **Coca Cola: http://www.coke.com**; **7-Up: http://www.7up.com/flash.cfm**; **Root beer: http://www.a-wrootbeer.com/**; **Tonic water: http://www.schweppeseuro.com/**; and **Orangina: http://www.orangina.com/**. Save the page and test in the browser.

7

CASE PROJECTS

1. Access the Macromedia Web site, and download a trial version of Dreamweaver Flash. Analyze the process and write a brief report that addresses the following questions:

   ❑ How does the Macromedia Web site use forms to gather information about customers?

   ❑ What kind of feedback do you receive?

   ❑ Trace the back-and-forth process as you enter data, post it to Macromedia, and receive responses from the server.

   ❑ Look at the HTML source code for each Macromedia page containing a form and for each page that Macromedia returns after you post a form.

   ❑ What form tags do they use?

   ❑ What do the JavaScript functions do?

2. Design a form for a family reunion. Decide what kinds of information you would want family members to submit. Lay it out with colors and text fonts that would appeal to your family. Include a family photo or a clipart graphic to decorate your form page. Perform validation for the fields for which family members would be required to provide information.

3. Design a frameset to display information about courses that your program requires. Create a menu frame and a main frame to display the information. Create at least four pages that display information about the courses in your program that fit in the main frame. Insert a jump menu with a Go button for navigation in your menu frame. Display the informational pages in the main frame when the viewer clicks one of the choices in the jump menu.

4. Your school wants you to design a prototype form for prospective students. You need to request information about the prospective student and the program that interests that person. Use information that you can find on your school's Web site or brochure about the choices prospective students have. Create a form that contains at least text boxes, checkboxes, radio buttons or radio groups, and a submit button. If your school has a Web site, create a jump menu to jump to different pages on the Web site. Use the Behaviors panel to create a pop-up message when the user clicks the Submit button.

8

MULTIMEDIA

Using Dreamweaver to Incorporate Multimedia into Your Web Sites

---

In this chapter, you will:

♦ Understand how Dreamweaver supports multimedia

♦ Learn about tools for inserting multimedia files

♦ Learn about tools for configuring multimedia files

♦ Insert and configure photos, graphics, sound files, and movie files, including Flash and Apple QuickTime movies, into your Web sites

---

By incorporating multimedia files—images, audio, movies, Flash, and other animation—you can make a Web site more interesting for visitors. For example, the Coca Cola (*www.coca-cola.com*) and Universal Studios (*www.universalstudios.com*) Web sites both use Flash extensively to provide interactivity and entertainment and to encourage return visits. Developers of sites like these are very aware of the potential risks of using large multimedia files, because they know that visitors may not wait for files to download, no matter how exciting they are.

You can choose from many software applications that produce multimedia content, including several in the Macromedia family. You already learned about the integration of Fireworks MX and Dreamweaver MX in Chapters 2 and 3. In addition, Dreamweaver MX is integrated with Flash MX, a Macromedia application that helps you produce interactive games and animated movies for the Web. In this chapter, you incorporate various kinds of multimedia content into your Web site using the many tools and features of Dreamweaver.

DREAMWEAVER SUPPORT FOR MULTIMEDIA

Dreamweaver enables you to incorporate a variety of multimedia content into your Web sites. It generates HTML tags to embed different types of multimedia files within Web pages and configures the tags to work in different browser versions. Including multimedia content created in other Macromedia applications is especially easy, because of built-in cross-functionality. But Dreamweaver also works well with multimedia files created with other applications.

Multimedia Quality/File Size Trade-offs

Before you begin incorporating multimedia content into your Web site, you need to understand some important usability issues. When you first learn how to design, insert, and configure multimedia for the Web, it is easy to focus on exciting, high-quality multimedia content. You may be less willing to consider file size and download time. Fast connections to the Web in the classroom laboratory may mask the download times for multimedia content on slower modems. Even though technologies such as Digital Subscriber Lines (DSL) and cable modems are rapidly increasing bandwidth, the core problem of using multimedia on the Web remains the quality/file size trade-off. You should not assume that the viewers of your Web site have ample bandwidth, unless you have a captive audience over a network or an intranet.

Here is a list of things you can do to monitor and control file size:

- Configure Dreamweaver to monitor for file size and display download time for a specific modem speed in the Category section of the Preferences dialog box. (You can easily open this dialog box by pressing the Ctrl+U key combination.) Clicking the Status Bar command in the Preferences dialog box lets you set up information that appears in the status bar in Design view, including the modem speed for which you want to view download times. The status bar shown in Figure 8-1 indicates that the page is 1 kilobyte (KB) in size and takes 1 seconds to download over the default 28.8 kilobits per second modem connection. Figure 8-2 shows how to change the Connection Speed in the list box in the Preferences dialog box.

Figure 8-1   Status bar shows page file size and download time

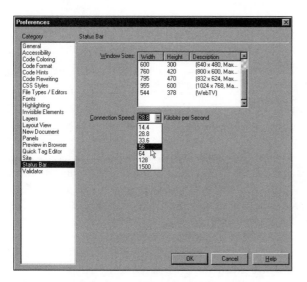

Figure 8-2   Changing Connection Speed preferences

You can also set the window size for which you are optimizing your HTML page. This setting appears just to the left of the file size/modem speed in the document window. You can click the Window Size display in the status bar and select one of the optimized window sizes. If you need additional window sizes, you can define them in the Preferences dialog box shown in Figure 8-2. The example in Figure 8-1 shows 760 × 420, the maximized window size for an 800 × 600 browser window. You cannot have the document editing window maximized when you change the window size. (Review Chapter 7 for an explanation of this requirement.)

- Test download times for pages with multimedia content from an off-site location over a 28.8 modem, to determine how long a typical Web browser takes to download your Web pages.

- Limit the number of colors in an image to reduce file size.

- Compress and optimize multimedia files in application editors, such as Fireworks.

- Use applications that compress multimedia files, such as Goldwave or AudioCatalyst for MP3 audio files and RealProducer for video files.

- Limit the cumulative file size of all objects on a single page. Many Web designers follow a rule of thumb: A Web page should contain no more than 30 KB. Since many users still access the Web via low-speed connections, make minimizing file size one of your primary goals, even if you do not always adhere strictly to the 30 KB limit.

- Reduce the dimensions of images and movies. For example, reducing an image from 300 pixels × 300 pixels to 200 pixels × 200 pixels makes the file significantly smaller.

 Although you can decrease the dimensions of a graphic in Dreamweaver so that it looks smaller, its file size remains the same, since you only changed its appearance on the Web page, not the file itself. You need to open the image in an external editor, change its dimensions, and save it. Doing so reduces the actual image dimensions and file size. Dreamweaver provides a Reset Size button in the image Property inspector that adjusts the display dimensions to the actual width and height of the image.

Setting External Editor Preferences

Dreamweaver lets you define primary and secondary external editors for different types of multimedia files. You then can launch an external editor for a file from within the document window in Design view. Once you save the file, you can switch back to Dreamweaver and see the changes reflected in the file embedded on the Web page. For example, if you need to edit a Flash movie embedded in your Dreamweaver page, you can open it for editing in Flash without leaving Dreamweaver. External editors are attached to specific filename extensions (for example, the .swf extension is attached to Flash). You can add filename extensions and associated external editors by opening the Preferences dialog box (press the Ctrl+U key combination) and clicking File Types Editors in the Category list box.

Figure 8-3 illustrates how to add an application, in this case Adobe ImageReady, as a secondary editor for JPEG (Joint Photographic Experts Group) files. You need to open the Preferences window and choose File Types/Editors in the Category list. Then you select the filename extensions (in this case, .jpg .jpe .jpeg) in the Extensions list box, click the + (plus) button above the Editors list box, and browse to the executable file on your computer. (Note that Fireworks is still defined as the primary external editor for these file types.) If a filename extension is not in the Extensions list, you can click the + (plus) button above the Extensions list box, add the filename extension, and then attach its associated application editor in the same way. Later in this chapter you practice editing an image in an external editor.

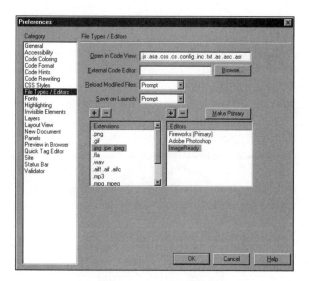

Figure 8-3   Adding an external editor

TYPES OF MULTIMEDIA

Images, audio, and video or movies are three popular types of multimedia content used on the Web.

> In Web development, the terms movie and video are not used very precisely. Both are used to describe digitized movie clips with sound, such as movie trailers offered by entertainment companies on the Web. Flash animations (with sound) are commonly called Flash movies. When you edit a movie with an application like Adobe Premiere, video refers only to the visual part of a movie, separate from the audio or sound portion. In this chapter movie and video are used interchangeably to reflect the terminology you find in the Web development industry.

Image Formats for Photos and Graphics

You already worked with and inserted a number of photos and graphics in earlier chapters in this book, so you are familiar with various file formats used on the Web. Different compression algorithms generate these different file formats.

The JPEG compression algorithm works best with photographs, because it uses a method of analyzing color that better renders continuous tone changes (found in a photo of the sea or the sky, for example). JPEG compression uses RGB (Red Green Blue) color channels and can handle 24-bit color, which translates into millions of colors. JPEG compression is **lossy**, which means that you lose detail when you use JPEG compression.

GIF (CompuServe Graphics Interchange Format) compression uses indexed color, which is limited to a maximum of 8-bit or 256 colors. Compression is accomplished by reducing the number of color bits (and colors) in the image. The compression algorithm analyzes the pixels in an image line by line and changes pixel color to match the available colors. This process works best for graphics with flat color areas. Images with continuous colors, such as photos, tend to become distorted by splotches of color pixels, an effect called **pixelation**. GIF also supports transparent GIFs, which render a background color on the image invisible on the Web page, an effect useful for creating graphical logos and page titles. GIF images are also popular because they are used to create animated GIFs. GIF compression is **lossless**, which means that you do not lose detail when you use GIF compression. However, you do lose color information if you apply GIF compression to a 24-bit image because GIF files are limited to 8-bits of color information or 256 colors.

A new file format for the Web, PNG (Portable Network Graphics), shows great promise because it combines both JPEG and GIF qualities. Not widely used because older browsers cannot display PNG images, PNG is the default file format in Fireworks. Table 8-1 compares the three image file formats.

Table 8-1 Comparison of Image Formats

File Type	Features	Advantages	Disadvantages
JPEG, JPE, JPG	Supports millions of colors (RGB format); compression removes redundant information; client decompresses files after they are downloaded	Preserves photographic images; progressive JPEG downloads file and displays versions of it as it downloads	Lossy compression takes longer to download on client computer because of decompression time; no support for transparency or animation of images
GIF	Displays up to 256 colors (8 bits); requires indexed color; lower numbers of colors require less memory; each pixel is one color	Best for flat, drawn images; can be exported as transparent GIF via GIF89a format; interlaced GIF displays as it downloads; used in GIF animations	Tends to distort photographic images at lower bit rates; converts each pixel to nearest color available in designated color palette; pixelizes images
PNG	Combines best of JPEG and GIF: lossless compression and millions of colors	Displays better on both Mac and PC computers; native file format in Fireworks MX	Not available on older browser versions

Audio Formats

Web browsers recognize and play a variety of audio formats. Audio formats recommended for today's browsers and connections include:

- MPEG Audio Layer 3—The highly popular MP3, a compression that yields relatively high quality and small file size.

- RealAudio—The RealNetworks format (RM), which can be streaming or nonstreaming. A **streaming** audio or video file begins playing as soon as it begins to download. **Nonstreaming** files must completely download before they can begin to play.

- WAV—The default audio format for Microsoft Windows, which comes in compressed and uncompressed formats. Only the larger uncompressed files play in Web browsers.

- MIDI—A file format that uses an algorithm to generate a sound file via the client computer's synthesizer. MIDI files sound different on different computers, since the sound quality depends on the capabilities of a computer's synthesizer.

- WMA—Windows Media Audio, Microsoft's sound format that is becoming more widely used.

- QT—Apple QuickTime, which can be used to create MPEG-4 audio files.

If you need to convert an audio file to a format that plays on the Web, you can use a **ripper**, which converts one audio file format to another through a process called **encoding** or **ripping**. Rippers also optimize and compress the files as they encode them, based on file size parameters that you select. You can easily find shareware or limited-time trial versions of rippers on the Web by searching for the term *CD ripper*. It is also possible to export audio files from video applications in other file formats, such as Macromedia Flash (as SWF or WAV), Apple QuickTime (as MOV), or audio-only files in Adobe Premiere in several formats including QuickTime, RealG2, Windows Media Audio, AVI, and MP3. Flash MX utilizes MP3 to compress audio tracks in movies.

Rippers (as well as applications such as Apple QuickTime and Adobe Premiere) let you set parameters for the audio output that decrease file size. For example, you can decrease file size by choosing mono (one audio channel) rather than stereo (two audio channels) output; by lowering the amount of information or the bit depth of the waveform (for example, from 16-bit to 8-bit), which reduces the amount of information in the waveform; and/or lowering the sampling rate (given in kHz), which eliminates treble frequencies. Each of these methods reduces audio quality as well.

Movie Formats

The main problem with including movies on your Web site is that minimizing their file size minimizes their video and audio quality. It is good practice to warn users of the file size of any movie on your Web site so that they can decide whether to download and watch it before they click its link. You can do several things to lessen the file size problem, such as:

- Decrease movie file size by shortening the movie.

- Break a longer movie into several shorter segments that can be viewed successively if the viewer is interested.

8

- Decrease height and width dimensions of the video display in the video editor.

- Increase the amount of compression.

- Use compression algorithms and file formats that are optimized for viewing on the Web.

- Use external compressors, such as RealProducer or MPEG compression. RealProducer optimizes video and audio and minimizes file size, based on parameters you select concerning the type of audio (for example, music or voice speaking) and video content (for example, talking head, lots of action).

The most common movie formats for the Web are:

- WMV—Windows Media Video from Microsoft.

- AVI—Audio-Video Interleaved, Microsoft Video for Windows.

- MOV—Apple QuickTime format.

- MPEG—Motion Picture Experts Group format.

- RM—RealMedia format, used to compress AVI and MPEG movies. RM movie files can also be streaming or nonstreaming.

- SWF—Flash compression for display on the Web.

Video applications, such as Adobe Premiere and Macromedia Flash, offer multiple file formats for exporting movies. They also allow you to compress audio and video separately. This means that when you create movies for the Web, you can experiment with different file formats, levels of audio and video compression, and video compression algorithms, or **codecs** (encoder/decoder).

Flash movies offer Web developers an exciting alternative for incorporating movies, because Flash files are relatively small. Images are vector-based rather than bitmapped. When you download a vector-based image, you download mathematical information about vectors that describe that image. Changing the vectors that describe the image changes the image. When you download a bitmapped image, you need to download information about every pixel in the image. An image that is 72 dpi (dots or pixels per inch) has 72 pixels in any square inch of the image. If you use 8-bit color, then 8 bits of color information describe each pixel in the image, which accounts for the larger file size of bitmaps. You can use bitmapped images in Flash, but they can increase file size considerably if you do not compress them when you export the Flash movie.

Flash developers employ a number of practices to decrease movie file size, including:

- Reusing the same content throughout the movie, since Flash vector symbols only download once, after which their characteristics (e.g., size, color, visibility) are changed by changing vectors rather than downloading a new version of the symbol.

- Dividing movies into shorter clips, so that subsequent clips download while earlier clips play.

- Looping very short music clips many times, a practice that gives many Flash sites a characteristic rhythmic, thumping sound.

TOOLS FOR INSERTING MULTIMEDIA FILES

In this section you learn about Dreamweaver MX tools for inserting and configuring multimedia content into Web pages, as well as generating Flash rollover buttons and text. Although linking to a multimedia file (which displays in its own browser window) is also possible, your Web site will be more exciting if you use Dreamweaver to integrate multimedia content into the HTML page by inserting or embedding it. You can insert multimedia content from the Insert menu, from the Common and Media tabs on the Insert bar (new in Dreamweaver MX), and from the Assets panel.

The Insert Menu

The Insert menu, shown in Figure 8-4, contains commands for inserting different types of multimedia content, which are also available on the Media tab of the Insert bar. Other types of multimedia content (rollovers, navigation bars, Flash buttons and text, and multimedia files inserted on HTML pages) are also available on the Interactive Images pop-up menu and the Common or Media tabs of the Insert bar. When you click a command on the Insert menu, a dialog box prompts you for the name of the multimedia object you want to insert.

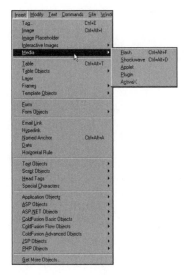

Figure 8-4   Media submenu

The Common and Media Tabs of the Insert bar

Dreamweaver MX provides buttons on the Common and Media tabs of the Insert bar that you can use to insert multimedia files into HMTL pages. You can switch between these tabs by clicking them. The Common tab buttons are shown in Figure 8-5 and the Media tab buttons are shown in Figure 8-6.

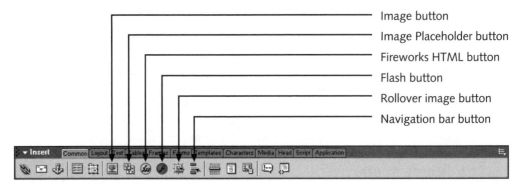

Figure 8-5 Common tab on Insert bar

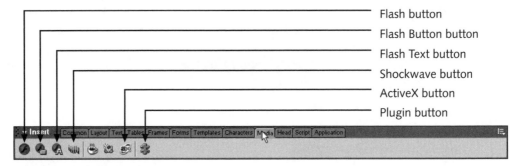

Figure 8-6 Media tab on Insert bar

Functions of the multimedia buttons, starting from the left on the Common tab and continuing on the Media tab, include:

Common Tab

- Image ▣ opens a dialog box to let you select an image to insert at the insertion point.

- Image Placeholder ▧ inserts a placeholder for an image at the insertion point. Clicking this button opens a dialog box in which you can specify a name and dimensions for the placeholder image. You use image placeholders when the artwork for the Web page is not finished.

- Fireworks HTML ⓦ places an HTML document that you prepared in Fireworks at the insertion point. Such a document might include the JavaScript to generate a rollover button.

- Flash ● uses the <object> and <embed> tags to insert a Flash SWF movie onto an HTML page.

- Rollover Image ▤ lets you create a rollover from two image files that you specify. The image you specify as the original image displays until the user moves the mouse across it. At that point the rollover displays.

- Navigation Bar ▤ lets you insert a set of images, such as buttons, to create a vertical or horizontal navigation bar. Each button can have an Up, Down, Over, and Over While Down version of the button.

Media tab multimedia buttons that are not on the Common tab include:

- Flash Button ● lets you customize and create a Flash button with an embedded hyperlink from a preset design, saves it as an SWF movie file, and inserts it onto an HTML page.

- Flash Text ● lets you create and insert an SWF movie with an embedded hyperlink that displays rollover text onto an HTML page.

- Shockwave ▥ lets you insert Shockwave files that are not in Flash SWF format.

- ActiveX ● places an ActiveX control at the insertion point. You can specify a source file and other properties in the Property inspector. When you specify the source file, Dreamweaver inserts both <object> and <embed> tags.

- Plugin ● uses the <embed> tag to insert a multimedia file that requires a Netscape plugin for playback. The name of this button may be misleading, since it inserts a multimedia file rather than a plugin.

The Assets Panel

The Assets panel is one of the windows visible to the right of the Document editing window in Dreamweaver MX. The Assets panel is just to the right of the Site panel when you expand the Files panel group. It lets you quickly insert assets, such as images and movies that are already part of your Web site. If it is not visible, you can open the Assets panel by pressing the F11 key.

 If you want to expand the Assets panel (or any of the other panels), right-click on the panel tab and select Maximize Panel Group. Other panel management commands on the same pop-up menu let you regroup, rename, and close panel groups.

The Assets panel shown in Figure 8-7 displays several categories of assets, including multimedia files located in your Web site:

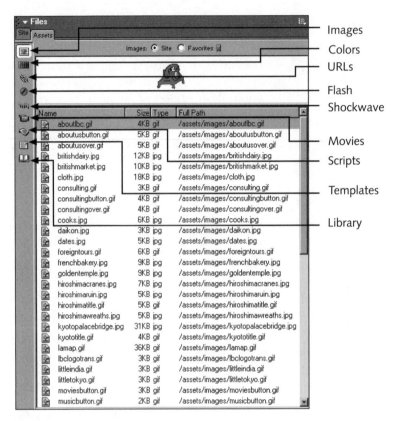

Figure 8-7 The Assets panel

- Images 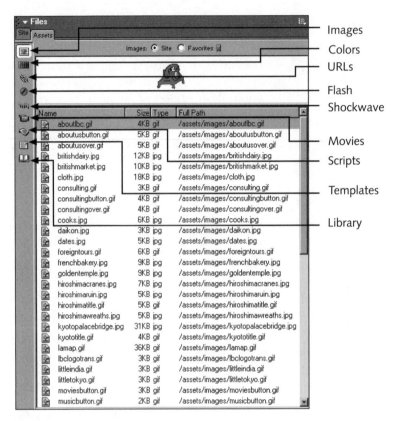 in GIF, JPEG, and PNG formats.
- Colors used in your documents and style sheets (including background colors, and text and link colors).
- URLs external to your Web site to which your documents link.
- Flash movies in SWF format, including Flash buttons and Flash text.
- Shockwave movies not in Flash SWF format.
- Movies in Apple QuickTime or MPEG format
- Scripts stored in independent JavaScript or VBScript files (not embedded in Web pages).
- Templates let you use the same page layout for multiple pages (covered in Chapter 11).

- Library , allows you to store library items, which are elements that you can reuse and automatically update in multiple Web pages (covered in Chapter 11).

The Assets panel only works within a defined Web site for which a site cache exists, such as the La Bonne Cuisine Web site you created in Chapter 4. You can display the files in each asset category by clicking the appropriate icon at the left of the Assets panel shown in Figure 8-7. If you add an asset to one of your Web pages, it is not reflected in the Assets panel unless you rebuild the Web site cache by right-clicking within the Assets panel and then clicking Refresh Site List on the context menu, or by clicking the Refresh Site List button at the bottom of the Assets panel.

If you want to insert an asset into a Web page, you can drag it from the Assets panel onto the Web page in the document editing window, or you can place the insertion point on the location on the Web page, select the asset in the Assets panel, and click the Insert button at the bottom of the Assets panel. You can edit assets from within the Assets panel by selecting the asset and clicking the Edit button at the bottom of the Assets panel, or by double-clicking the asset to open its defined external editor. You can also use the Assets panel to identify a list of favorite assets for quicker access.

TOOLS FOR CONFIGURING MULTIMEDIA FILES

The media file and its controls may look different in different browsers, so previewing your Web site in both browsers from within Dreamweaver is a good idea. Doing so ensures that your target audience can see and hear your multimedia files. Of course, the browser must have the necessary plugin software installed or integrated, or the embedded media file cannot play. When you insert a multimedia file using any of the buttons listed earlier, you can configure properties that govern the appearance of the media file and the media player controls. The following sections discuss the properties available for each of these media objects and the ways to configure them.

> **Tip** MP3 music files are very popular, and you can easily add them to your Web site using the Insert Plugin method described here. However, the viewer may need to download and install a browser plugin that plays MP3 files. You can find these plugins on the Internet by searching for the term *MP3 player*.

Configuring with the Property Inspector

The Property inspector for a multimedia object lets you configure the controls and the Web page appearance. Because many properties are the same for each of these multimedia objects, the properties are only described the first time they appear on one of the object's Property inspectors. You can assume that a property with the same name means the same for subsequent media objects unless otherwise stated.

Chapter 1 of this book describes the attributes of the Property inspector for images. The Property inspectors for image placeholders, rollovers, and navigation bars look almost the same. The Property inspectors for the multimedia files you insert from the Media tab are somewhat different.

Flash

The Flash button on the Common and Media tabs of the Insert bar lets you insert a Flash SWF file on a Web page. The Property inspector in Figure 8-8 shows the properties of a Flash object embedded in a Web page.

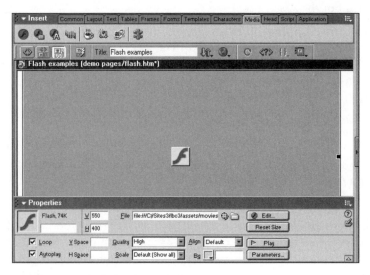

Figure 8-8   Flash SWF properties

If the Flash movie is within the Web site displayed in the Site panel, then the Src text box is visible in the Property inspector. If the movie is not part of the Web site in which you are working, the Src text box is not visible. Src points to the Flash or FLA version of the movie, which you can edit in Flash from within Dreamweaver by clicking the Edit button on the Flash Property inspector. You need to recompress your edited movie for your Web site by exporting it as an SWF file from Flash. Flash shocks or compresses the FLA version of the movie into SWF format, which can be played on the Web in the Flash player. The Flash player is automatically installed in current browsers, and new versions can be readily downloaded and installed from the Macromedia Web site. You should not save the FLA version of the movie within your Web site if you plan to upload the entire site to the Web.

- The text box to the right of the Flash icon lets you specify the name of the plugin for scripting purposes.

- W (width) and H (height) refer to the dimensions of the Flash movie. Dreamweaver uses the actual dimensions of the Flash movie when you insert it onto an HTML page.

- Clicking the Edit button should open up Flash MX (if it is installed on the computer) for editing the Flash (FLA) version of the movie, which you identify in the SRC text box in the Property inspector. The Edit button for Flash works somewhat inconsistently in Dreamweaver MX.

- File identifies the path to the Flash SWF file, with the Point-to-File and Browse-for-File icons. When you drag a Flash object onto the Dreamweaver editing window or click the Flash button on the Common or Media tab of the Insert bar, the Select File dialog box opens.

- Src specifies the path to a Flash source document (FLA) when the Flash movie is part of the Web site you are using. To edit a Flash movie file, you update the movie's source document in Flash format (FLA), and then export it in SWF format.

- Reset Size resets the edited Flash movie to the actual movie size.

- Loop, if checked, configures the movie to play continuously until the user leaves the page.

- Autoplay, if checked, configures the movie to play automatically after the page finishes loading.

- V (vertical) Space and H (horizontal) Space determine the amount of blank space (in pixels) around the Flash movie.

- Quality lets you specify the amount of anti-aliasing used during movie playback, which affects the trade-off between playing speed and visual quality. Low prioritizes speed over quality, Auto Low and Auto High make adjustments once the movie begins to play, High gives priority to the visual quality of the animation (but not to any bitmapped images in the movie), and Best ignores speed and displays the best possible visual quality, including bitmapped images.

- Scale lets you determine how the movie fits into the dimensions set in the width and height fields. The Default (Show all) setting displays the entire movie. No Border fits the movie into the set dimensions so that no borders show. It maintains the original aspect ratio of the Flash movie. Exact Fit scales the movie to the set dimensions, regardless of the aspect ratio.

- Align defines the object's alignment on the page.

- Bg (background color) specifies a background color for the movie area, which appears when the movie loads and after it finishes playing.

- Play/Stop lets you preview the multimedia file in the Document window. Only one is visible at a time. Click the green Play button to see the object in Play mode; click the red Stop button to stop the movie.

- Parameters lets you set parameters for a specific Flash movie in a dialog box. You need to know the name of the parameter and its possible values beforehand, because you need to type them into a list.

Flash Buttons

The Flash Button button on the Media tab of the Insert bar lets you choose, customize, and insert a Flash-animated button from a set of predesigned buttons, some of which allow you to add your own button text. The Property inspector for a Flash Button, which is saved in SWF file format, is very similar to the Property inspector for the Flash movie, shown in Figure 8-8. It lacks the Loop and Autoplay checkboxes and the Src text box, and displays the name Flash Button rather than Flash. When you hyperlink the Flash button to a URL, you embed the URL in the SWF file. Therefore, if you use relative addressing, as we do in the La Bonne Cuisine Web site, the Flash buttons are stored in the same directory or folder as the HTML pages on which they reside.

Flash Text

The Flash Text button on the Media tab of the Insert bar lets you create a small, vector-graphic SWF movie that contains rollover text, which is then inserted onto an HTML page. You select the font from those available on your computer, and type the text. The properties are the same as those for the Flash Button, except the name of the object displays Flash Text rather than Flash Button. The URL of any hyperlinked page is also embedded in the Flash text SWF file, which again must reside in the same directory or folder as the Web page, if you use relative addressing.

 A relative address on an HTML page or embedded in an object such as a Flash button or Flash text is an address that links to a file that is within close proximity within the same Web site. It may be in the same subdirectory as the linking HTML page or object, or it may be in a parent, child, or sibling subdirectory. All of these subdirectories would be within the root directory for the Web site. Fixed addressing means that you include the entire URL address of the link; for example, *www.macromedia.com* is a fixed address. Review the discussion in Chapter 1 about relative addressing for more information.

ActiveX Controls

The ActiveX button on the Media tab of the Insert bar inserts an ActiveX control for a multimedia object. The <object> tags used to insert Microsoft ActiveX controls never became part of standard HTML, and they do not work in Netscape or on Mac computers. When you click the ActiveX button, Dreamweaver places an ActiveX control at the insertion point on the HTML page. To identify the name of the source file that is played by the ActiveX control, you have to check the Embed checkbox on the Property inspector. Then you can click the Browse for File button on the Property inspector to open the Select Netscape Plugin dialog box.

Figure 8-9 shows the Property inspector for an ActiveX control set up to play a sound file. You need to expand the size of the ActiveX control on the Web page to give the user access to all of the media control buttons. Because there are no widely accepted standards for ActiveX controls, you need to consult the documentation for the particular control to learn its possible parameters. Therefore, this discussion is necessarily general.

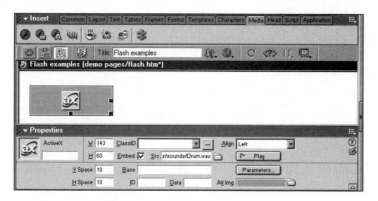

Figure 8-9 ActiveX control properties

The Property inspector for an ActiveX control, shown in Figure 8-9, differs slightly from the Property inspector for the Plugin control, which also works for many multimedia objects. The ActiveX Property inspector lets you configure width and height, vertical and horizontal space around the control, and the object's alignment on the HTML page, in ways similar to the Flash Property inspector.

- W (width) and H (height) refer to the dimensions of the media player controls (start, stop, rewind) for the multimedia object displayed on the HTML page. You usually need to adjust these because the default (32 pixels × 32 pixels) is too small to display all the media player controls. You can adjust the size of the ActiveX control on the Web page, either in the Property inspector or by dragging the black squares on the edges and corners of the object displayed on the Web page.

- ClassID lets you enter the Microsoft ID for the ActiveX control or select an ActiveX control from the list box. If you leave the ClassID blank, the browser identifies the ActiveX control it needs from its list of available ActiveX controls. For example, the Windows Media Player integrated into later versions of Internet Explorer plays many sound and movie files, especially if you click the Embed checkbox.

- Embed adds an <embed> tag within the <object> tag for the ActiveX control. Because Netscape also recognizes the <embed> tag but does not recognize the <object> tag, selecting this option improves the likelihood that your media file actually plays, assuming that the browser can find the necessary plugin or

ActiveX control installed in the browser. Playing ActiveX controls in Netscape requires the purchase of a plugin that most Netscape users do not have. The following example of <object> tags with a set of <embed> tags nested within is set up to play a RealMedia file demo.rm. In this example, Dreamweaver inserted the ClassID identifier, something that Dreamweaver does much more quickly, easily, and correctly than we can.

```
<object classid="clsid:CFCDAA03-8BE4-11cf-B84B-0020AFBBCCFA"
width="443" height="68"> <embed src="images/demo.rm" width="443"
height="68"></embed> </object>
```

- Src (source) refers to the multimedia source document embedded on the HTML page. As usual, clicking the Browse for File button opens a dialog box that lets you locate the media file.

- Base lets you enter a URL that the browser opens if it cannot locate the ActiveX control, so the browser can download the plugin.

- ID lets you enter an optional ActiveX ID parameter that passes information between ActiveX controls.

- Data identifies a data file for the ActiveX control to load, if necessary. RealPlayer and Shockwave Flash do not use this parameter.

- Alt Img (alternative image) lets you enter the URL of an image that appears if the embed option is deselected and the browser cannot display the object.

Plugin for Netscape

The Plugin button on the Media tab of the Insert bar inserts a media file using the HTML <embed> tags that Netscape plugins require. This tag differs from the <object> tag that Internet Explorer uses, although it is possible to nest <embed> tags within <object> tags to improve the chances that both browsers recognize the tags. Figure 8-10 shows the Property inspector for a Netscape plugin.

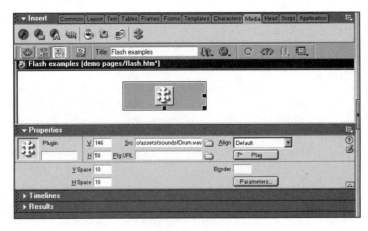

Figure 8-10   Netscape Plugin properties

When you click Plugin on the Media tab, the Select File dialog box opens, so that you can select the media file you want to embed. The Plugin Property inspector lets you access two properties that differ from the Flash and ActiveX properties.

- Plg URL (plugin URL) provides the URL of the Web site where users can download the plugin. Should the user viewing your page not have the required plugin, the browser attempts to download it from this URL.

- Border sets the width of the border around the plugin, although this parameter does not work for all plugins.

Modifying Graphics in the External Editor

In earlier chapters of this book, you inserted graphics files into your Dreamweaver Web site. While you develop your multimedia Web page in Design view, you can open a graphics file in an external editor without leaving Dreamweaver.

You can open an image in an external editor in several ways. If you right-click an image, a pop-up menu lets you choose to edit the image with the default image editor (Fireworks MX), edit the image with other external editors you defined, or optimize the image in Fireworks. You can also select the image, click Edit on the Dreamweaver menu bar, then click Edit with External Editor (or press the Ctrl+E key combination), to open the Preferences window shown in Figure 8-3. A simpler way is to click the image to select it and then click Edit in the Property inspector. After you finish modifying or optimizing the image, you need to save the changes (by clicking Done, for example, in Fireworks MX). The HTML page immediately reflects the changes. If you resize the image in an external editor, you need to click Reset Size in the image Property inspector, because Dreamweaver does not automatically display the image with its new dimensions.

8

INSERTING AND CONFIGURING MULTIMEDIA FILES IN DREAMWEAVER

Now you are familiar with the characteristics of different types of multimedia files and the Dreamweaver tools available to insert and configure them. You are ready to try to include multimedia content on your Web pages. Whenever you insert this content, previewing the page in both Netscape and Internet Explorer is good practice to be sure that both display your file. You should also be able to play embedded media files in Design view by clicking the Play/Stop button in the Property inspector for the multimedia object, although this feature does not always work in Dreamweaver MX. If you want to play all multimedia files on an HTML page, click View on the Dreamweaver menu bar, point to Plugins, and then click Play All (or press the Ctrl+Alt+Shift+P key combination). Use the Stop All command (Ctrl+Alt+Shift+X key combination) to stop playing all multimedia files.

Inserting and Modifying Images

In the following steps, you add images to a Web page using the Assets panel and then open them in Fireworks for editing. You reduce the dimensions of an image and let Fireworks optimize images to reduce file size. Before you begin editing, you need to copy image files into the La Bonne Cuisine images folder, open the Assets panel, turn on the ruler and grid to help with layout in Dreamweaver Design view, and set window sizes to optimize an 800 × 600 browser window.

To insert and modify images:

1. Use Windows Explorer to copy the images **cooks.jpg**, **daikon.jpg**, **littletokyo.jpg**, **littleindia.gif**, **cloth.jpg**, **dates.jpg**, **trainingtitle.gif**, and **training.gif** from the Chapter8\assets\images folder on your Data Disk to the Sites\lbc\assets\images folder on your working drive. If Windows Explorer asks whether you want to overwrite existing files, click **Yes to All**.

2. Start Dreamweaver if it is not already running. Press the **F8** function key to open the Site panel (if it is not already open) and select the **La Bonne Cuisine** Web site. In Design view, open **littleindia.htm**, a placeholder page in the Sites\lbc\tour folder. Press the **F11** key to open the Assets panel, if it is not already open. Press the **Ctrl+Alt+G** and **Ctrl+Alt+R** key combinations to display the grid and the ruler, if they are not already visible. Click **Layout View** on the Layout tab of the Insert bar. If a dialog box opens, click **OK** to close it. Make sure that littleindia.htm is not maximized in the Document editing window, and then click **Window Size** on the status bar (see Figure 8-1). Select **760 × 420** on the pop-up menu to optimize it for an 800 × 600 browser window.

3. Type **Little India Tour** in the Title text box just below the Insert bar. Click **Set Color Scheme** on the Commands drop-down menu. In the Background list, click **Orange**, and in the Text and Links list, click **Grey**, **Yellow**, **Orange**. Click **Apply** to see the change, and click **OK** to close the dialog box.

4. Click the **Draw Layout Table** button ▣ on the Layout tab of the Insert bar. Draw a layout table beginning in the upper-left corner that is about **550** pixels wide and about **400** pixels high. You can adjust the table dimensions in the Property inspector.

5. Click the **Draw Layout Cell** button ▤ on the Layout tab of the Insert bar. Position the cursor in the upper-left corner of the Layout Table, and draw a layout cell about **100** pixels wide and **100** pixels high. Click the **Draw Layout Cell** button again and draw a second layout cell that is **125** pixels from the left margin and **25** pixels from the top page margin, using the ruler. Make this layout cell **400** pixels wide and **100** pixels high. To adjust the dimensions of a layout cell, click the edge of the cell so that the blue outline shows, and change the dimensions in the Property inspector.

6. Place the insertion point in the left layout cell, press **Enter** to leave a blank line, and then type **Tour**. Select the word **Tour** and in the Property inspector, format it as **Heading 1**, click the **Italic** button, and then **Center Align** the text.

7. Place the insertion point in the right layout cell. Click the **Images** icon on the Assets panel. Be sure that the Favorites option button is checked at the top of the Assets panel. If you do not see **littleindia.gif** and the other images you copied into the Web site in Step 1, click the **Refresh Site List** button on the Images Assets panel. Then select the asset **littleindia.gif**, and click the **Insert** button at the bottom of the Assets panel.

8. Select the image **littleindia.gif** on the HTML page, if necessary. In the image Property inspector, click the **Center Align** button, and type **20** in the V Space text box. Click elsewhere on the page to see the change.

9. Click the **Draw Layout Cell** button 🔲 on the Layout tab of the Insert bar. Position the cursor about **75** pixels from the left margin and **200** pixels from the top margin, using the ruler to guide you. Draw a third layout cell that is **101** pixels wide and **146** pixels high. Place the insertion point inside this layout cell, and follow the directions in Step 7 to insert the image **cloth.jpg** from the Assets panel.

10. Click elsewhere on the HTML page to deselect the image. Click the **Draw Layout Cell** button again. Position the cursor about **200** pixels from the left margin and **225** pixels from the top margin using the ruler to guide you. Draw a layout cell that is about **220** pixels wide and **100** pixels high. Place the insertion point inside this layout cell, and type **Visit Little India to view and purchase exotic articles and sample wonderful, tasty foods!** Select the text and change its format to **Heading 3** in the Property inspector.

11. Deselect the text by clicking somewhere else on the page. Click the **Draw Layout Cell** button again. Starting about **450** pixels from the left margin and **225** pixels from the top margin, draw a layout cell about **106** pixels wide and **144** pixels high. Select the image **dates.jpg** in the Assets panel and drag it into the layout cell. In the next steps, you edit the images to optimize them and reduce their file sizes.

12. Be sure you are working in Design view. Click the **cloth.jpg** image to select it. In the Property inspector, click **Edit** to start the primary image editor, Fireworks MX.

8

The first time you use Fireworks, a dialog box may appear asking whether you want to make Fireworks the registered application for .png files. You should click Yes, unless you prefer using a different graphics application whenever you select a .png file for editing. Fireworks stores files in .png format, as you may remember from Chapters 2 and 3. When you open a file in .gif or .jpg format in Fireworks MX, you may be asked if you want to use an existing Fireworks document as the source of the image. Since you did not create these files in Fireworks but copied them into your Web site, you should not have .png versions of the files available. For the purposes of this exercise, you can select Never Use Source PNG on the drop-down list in the Find Source dialog box (if it opens) and click No to close the dialog box.

13. Optimize the image by clicking **2–Up**, which shows the original image and an optimized image with a reduced file size. Select the optimized image on the right, and click **Done** to save the changes. The optimized file is saved and replaced on the HTML page, and you are transferred back to the Dreamweaver document window.

14. Click **dates.jpg** to select it. In the Property inspector, click **Edit** to start the primary image editor. In Fireworks MX, click **Canvas** on the **Modify** menu, and then click **Image Size**. With **Constrain Proportions** and **Resample Image** checked, change the width in the upper text box just under Pixel Dimensions to **72** pixels. The height changes to **104** pixels, because Constrain Proportions is checked. Click **OK**.

15. To optimize the image, click **2–Up**, select the optimized image on the right, and click **Done**.

16. After you are transferred back to Dreamweaver, select the image **dates.jpg** and click **Reset Size** in the Property inspector to view the image displayed on the Web page with its new dimensions.

17. Save the page **littleindia.htm** in the Sites\lbc\tour folder. View the page in the browser. It should look like Figure 8-11. Close **littleindia.htm**.

Inserting Audio Files

You can incorporate sound into your Web pages in two ways: by inserting a hyperlink to an audio file, or by embedding the audio file on the page. In either case, the Web browser opens the audio player identified by that browser as the plugin that plays that file type.

Figure 8-11   littleindia.htm in browser window

Linking to an Audio File

To link to an audio file:

1. Use Windows Explorer to create a **ch8practice** folder inside the Sites folder, and then create an **assets** folder inside the Sites\ch8practice folder. Open this assets folder and create three more folders inside it: **images**, **sounds**, and **movies**. Copy the sound files **CountryRoad.wav** and **CountryRoad1.wav** from the Chapter8\assets\sounds folder to the Sites\ch8practice\assets\sounds folder.

2. Start Dreamweaver if necessary. Press the **Ctrl+N** key combination to create a new page. Click the **General** tab in the New Document window, select **Basic Page**, and click **Create**. Press the **Ctrl+S** key combination to save it as **audio.htm** in the Sites\ch8practice folder. Type **Audio Exercises** in the Title text box just below the Insert bar.

3. Place the insertion point on the page, and type **Listen to Country Road (59 kb)**. Select the words **Country Road**, and in the Property inspector click **Browse for File** to create a hyperlink to the sound file **CountryRoad.wav** in your Sites\ch8practice\assets\sounds folder.

4. Save the page **audio.htm** and preview it in the browser. Click the hyperlink on the page to start the media player that is defined to play a WAV file. Figure 8-12 shows the audio file open in Windows Media Player. Close **audio.htm**.

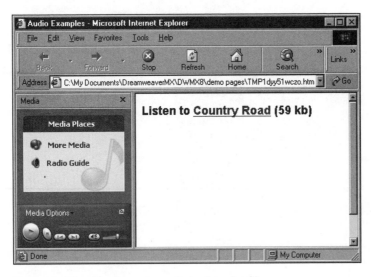

Figure 8-12   Playing a hyperlinked audio file

 Your browser display may look different from Figure 8-12 if a different media player is defined as the plugin to play WAV files in the browser. Configuration for this display in Internet Explorer 6.0 is done by clicking Internet Options on the Tools menu, selecting the Advanced tab, and then checking the Multimedia options "Don't display online media content in the media bar" and "Play sounds in web pages." If you leave the first item unchecked, the display may be slightly different.

Embedding Audio Files

Embedding audio files gives you more control than linking to audio files, since the Property inspector for the embedded object sets parameters for the appearance of the player and the playback of the audio file. When you embed an audio file, Dreamweaver inserts a 32 × 32 pixel icon to represent the object onto the Web page. You must increase the size of this icon if you want the viewer to be able to use the audio player's controls to control (start, stop, rewind, fast forward) the sound. The best size for the icon depends on the plugin identified to play WAV files in the users' browsers. If they use Apple QuickTime, the best setting is 150 pixels wide and 15 pixels high. If they use the Windows Media Player plugin, this setting should be 200 pixels wide and 45 pixels high. Because the latter is preconfigured in the later versions of Internet Explorer, you might want to choose to use this setting if you expect your users to use IE.

To embed an audio file:

1. Open **audio.htm** in Dreamweaver, if it is not already open. Place the insertion point at the end of the line of text you created in the previous exercise, and press **Enter** to go to a new line.

2. Click the **Plugin** button on the Media tab of the Insert bar to open the Select File dialog box. Select **CountryRoad1.wav** in the Sites\ch8practice\assets\sounds folder. Dreamweaver inserts a 32×32 pixel icon that represents the plugin onto the Web page.

3. Save **audio.htm** and preview it in the browser. Figure 8-13 shows how the plugin object looks in Dreamweaver, as well as in two browser windows. Internet Explorer 6 uses the Windows Media Player plugin and Netscape Navigator 6 uses the Apple QuickTime plugin. Because the plugin size is only 32×32 pixels, you see only the play/pause/stopped control.

Figure 8-13   Unresized audio file plugin in Netscape and Internet Explorer

If you want to set Netscape up as a Preview in Browser Option, click Preview in Browser on the Dreamweaver File menu, and then select Edit Browser List. In the Preferences window, click the plus button next to Browsers to open the Add Browser window. Here you can name the browser, and browse to its executable file. Click the secondary browser if you want the default to remain Internet Explorer. If you want to preview your Web pages in earlier versions of browsers that you have installed on your computer, you should define them here.

4. Select the Plugin object and use the Property inspector to resize the plugin (for example, to **150** pixels wide and **15** pixels high for the Apple QuickTime audio plugin and **200** pixels wide and **45** pixels high for the Windows Media

Player audio plugin) to ensure that the plugin controls are visible in both Internet Explorer and Netscape.

5. Save the file **audio.htm** and preview it in a Web browser. In Figure 8-14 you can see the results when the plugin size is configured for Windows Media player in Internet Explorer, which is larger than the Apple QuickTime player displayed in Netscape on the right. Close **audio.htm**.

You may notice in Figure 8-13 and Figure 8-14 that the font in the Internet Explorer browser window differs from the font in Dreamweaver Design view and the Netscape browser window. This occurs because the Internet Explorer browser shown in the figures is configured to display text in Arial font when the font on the HTML page is non-specified or the default font. If you want to display a different font in your Internet Explorer browser, you can start the browser, click Internet Options on the Tools menu, click the General tab, and click the Font button. You can then choose from the fonts available on your computer.

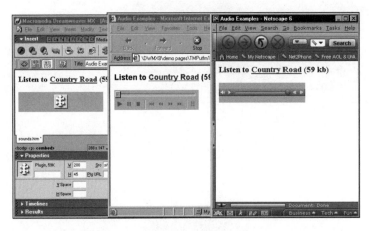

Figure 8-14   Resized audio plugins

Embedding Background Audio

You can embed background audio in a Web page, so that it plays when the page opens without displaying audio controls. Be aware that some visitors may be annoyed if they cannot turn off the audio sound. On the other hand, background audio can be appealing on certain kinds of Web sites, for example, when you are trying to create a mood with music. In the following steps, you reduce the size of the Plugin object to 2 pixels × 2 pixels, creating a barely visible dot, and then configure parameters to hide the Plugin object in the Web browser window, autostart the sound file, and play it in a continuous loop. Older browsers require the width and height attribute; otherwise, you could omit it altogether.

To embed background audio:

1. Use Windows Explorer to copy the file **CountryRoad1.wav** from the Chapter8\assets\sounds folder on your Data Disk to the Sites\lbc\assets\sounds folder on your working drive.

2. Open Dreamweaver if it is not already open, open the Site panel (function key F8) if necessary, select the **La Bonne Cuisine** site, and open the page **localtour.htm** in the tour folder.

3. Place the insertion point immediately to the left of the word *Ethnic* at the top of the page localtour.htm, if necessary. Click the **Plugin** button on the Media tab of the Insert bar to open the Select File dialog box. Select **CountryRoad1.wav** from the Sites\lbc\assets\sounds folder. Click **OK**. The Plugin object should be at the top of the page, so it plays when the page opens.

4. Click the **Plugin object** on the Web page to select it. In the Property inspector, reduce the size of the Plugin object to **2** pixels × **2** pixels by typing **2** in the W and H text boxes.

5. Click the **Parameters** button on the Plugin Property inspector. Type the parameter name **hidden** in the Parameter column. Place the insertion point in the Value column, and type **true**.

6. Click the + (plus) button to add another parameter. Type **autostart** in the Parameter column, and **true** in the Value column.

7. Click the + (plus) button, type **loop** in the Parameter column, and type **true** in the Value column. When you are finished entering parameters, click **OK** as shown in Figure 8-15.

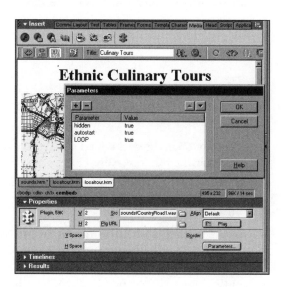

Figure 8-15   Parameters to embed invisible background audio

8. Click **OK**, save the file, and preview the page in a browser. Close the file.

 When you save, close, and reopen this Web page, you may find that Dreamweaver changed the name of the parameter loop from lowercase (loop) to uppercase (LOOP). This does not affect the way the parameter works.

Inserting Video Files

Inserting video files is much like inserting audio files. In this section you insert an Apple QuickTime movie into your Web pages.

 Embedding RealMedia movies in Dreamweaver is difficult. To avoid frustration, you should link to RealMedia movies (RAM and RM file types) so that they display in their own player. You can download RealProducer Basic for free at *www.realnetworks.com/products/producer/info.html*.

Linking to Video Files

Linking to video files in Dreamweaver is very similar to linking to audio files. Because you do not embed the video file in a Web page, you do not need to define its height and width.

 It is easier to link to RealMedia movies and display them in their own player than it is to try to embed them in your Web page in Dreamweaver. The latter requires that you type long strings of information to configure the movie display. If you want to embed RealMedia movies, download RealProducer Basic from *www.realnetworks.com* and follow the directions. You will also need to use RealProducer Basic to upload the RealMedia movie and the HTML page to a Web server.

To link to a video file:

1. Use Windows Explorer to copy the movie file **cookies.mov** from the Chapter8\assets\movies folder to the Sites\ch8practice\assets\movies folder on your working drive.

2. Open Dreamweaver if it is not already open, Press the **Ctrl+N** key combination to create a new page. Click the **General** tab in the New Document window, select **Basic Page**, and click **Create**. Press the **Ctrl+S** key combination to save it as **video.htm** in the Sites\ch8practice folder. Type **Video Exercises** in the Title text box just below the Insert bar.

3. Click on the page. Type the words **Play a QuickTime movie about making cookies in Little Tokyo (2.0 MB)**. Select the words **making cookies**, and in the Property inspector click the **Browse for File** button to create a hyperlink to the file **cookies.mov** in the Sites\ ch8practice\assets\movies folder.

4. Save the file. Preview the page in Internet Explorer and Netscape, if it is installed on your computer. Click the hyperlink to play the Apple QuickTime movie (MOV). Close the file.

Embedding Video Files

Embedding video files is much like embedding audio files. You must make sure that the Plugin object is large enough to play the video and show its controls. You can also set parameters to control how the video plays. In this exercise you use the Assets panel to insert multimedia files and the Property inspector to configure them. Whenever you are going to draw a layout cell, you should first deselect the object (image, plugin, and so on) on which you have just been working. Then click anywhere in a blank part of the HTML page.

To embed video files:

1. Use Windows Explorer to copy the movie file **cookies.mov** from the Chapter8\assets\movies folder on your Data Disk to the Sites\lbc\ assets\movies folder on your working drive.

2. Open Dreamweaver if it is not already open, open the Sites panel (function key F8) if necessary, select the **La Bonne Cuisine** site, and open the page **littletokyo.htm** in the Sites\lbc\tour folder. Press the **Ctrl+Alt+G** and **Ctrl+Alt+R** key combinations to display the grid and the ruler, if they are not already visible. Click **Layout View** on the Layout tab of the Insert bar. Press the **F11** key to open the Assets panel, if it is not already open. Click **Window Size** on the status bar (review Figure 8-1), and choose **760 × 420** to optimize it for an 800 × 600 browser window. Make sure the document window is not maximized when you try to do this.

3. Type **Little Tokyo Culinary Tour** in the Title text box below the Insert bar.

4. Click **Set Color Scheme** on the Commands drop-down menu. In the Background list, click **Orange**, and in the Text and Links list, click **Grey**, **Yellow**, **Orange**. Click **Apply** to see the changes, and click **OK** to close the dialog box.

5. Click the **Draw Layout Table** button ▣ on the Layout tab of the Insert bar. Draw a layout table beginning in the upper-left corner of your workspace that is about **550** pixels wide and about **400** pixels high. Select the table and adjust the dimensions in its Property inspector, if necessary.

6. Deselect the table by clicking elsewhere on the page. Click the **Draw Layout Cell** button ▣ on the Layout tab of the Insert bar. Position the cursor in the upper-left corner of the layout table, and draw a layout cell **100** pixels × **100** pixels. Draw a second layout cell to the right, beginning at the gridline that is **150** pixels from the left and **50** pixels from the top. Make this layout cell about **400** pixels wide and **90** pixels high.

8

7. Place the insertion point in the left cell and press **Enter** to leave a blank line. Type and then select the word **Tour**, and in the Property inspector change it to **Heading 1** Format style, and click the **Italics** and **Align Center** buttons.

8. Place the insertion point in the second cell, and click the **Images** icon on the Assets panel. Select the graphic **littletokyo.jpg** on the list, and click **Insert**. If you do not see the images you copied into the Web site during the earlier activity in this chapter, click the **Refresh Site List** button on the Assets panel. In the Property inspector for the image, click the **Align Center** button and type **20** in the V Space input box. Press **Enter** or click elsewhere on the page to see the results.

9. Deselect the image by clicking elsewhere on the page. Click the **Draw Layout Cell** button ▣ on the Layout tab of the Insert bar. Position the cursor about **25** pixels from the left margin and **150** pixels from the top margin, using the ruler to guide you. Draw a layout cell that is about **200** pixels wide and **210** pixels high. Position the cursor inside this layout cell. Click the **Movies** button on the Assets panel. Select the file **cookies.mov** in the Assets list, and then click **Insert**. If you do not see the movie you copied into the Web site at the beginning of this exercise, click **Refresh Site List** on the Assets panel.

10. Select the **Plugin** object on the HTML page, if it is not already selected. In its Property inspector, type **160** in the W (width) text box and **140** in the H (height) text box to allow space for the movie and the Apple QuickTime Plugin player controls.

11. To center the movie in the table cell, type **20** in the H Space text box in its Property inspector.

12. Select the Plugin object and click the **Play** button on the Property inspector to play the movie. Click the **Stop** button to stop it. Deselect the plugin object on the HTML page.

13. Click the **Draw Layout Cell** button ▣ on the Layout tab of the Insert bar. Begin drawing the layout cell about **250** pixels from the left margin and **150** pixels from the top margin, using the ruler to guide you. Draw a layout cell that is about **300** pixels wide and **75** pixels high. Place the insertion point inside this table cell, and type **Visit Little Tokyo to view and purchase exotic articles and sample wonderful, tasty foods!** Select the text and change its Format style to **Heading 3** in the Property inspector. Again deselect the text by clicking somewhere else on the page.

14. Click the **Draw Layout Cell** button ▣ again. Position the cursor about **275** pixels from the left margin and **250** pixels from the top margin, using the ruler and grid to guide you. Draw a layout cell that is about **235** pixels wide and **145** pixels high. Click the **Images** icon on the Assets panel, and drag

the image **daikon.jpg** into the layout cell. Select the image and type **5** in the Border text box in its Property inspector to place a border around it.

15. Save the file and preview it in both Internet Explorer and Netscape. Close the file.

Inserting Flash Movies

Now that you have experienced inserting audio and video files, inserting Flash movies should be very easy. Flash movies for the Web have the file type SWF (Flash movie). SWF files are compressed versions of Flash movies that are exported from Flash. Flash MX lets you create HTML files with an embedded Flash movie, but you can also use Dreamweaver to embed an existing Flash SWF movie.

When you embed a Flash movie, Dreamweaver sets some default properties in its Property inspector. Dreamweaver inserts an icon for the Flash movie that has exactly the same dimensions as the movie. The Loop parameter is also set by default, so if you do not want the Flash movie to play more than once, you need to click the Loop checkbox to deselect it. The Autoplay parameter is also set by default. In the following exercise, you should leave Autoplay selected, since there is no start button in the movie.

To insert a Flash movie:

1. Use Windows Explorer to copy the file **webwarrior.swf** from the Chapter8\assets\movies folder on your Data Disk to the Sites\ch8practice\ assets\movies folder on your working drive.

2. In Dreamweaver, press the **Ctrl+N** key combination to create a new Basic Page file, as you did in earlier exercises. Save the file as **flash.htm** in the Sites\ch8practice folder. Press the **Ctrl+J** key combination to open the Page Properties dialog box, type **Flash Exercise** in the Title text box, and change the background color to light yellow (**#FFFFCC**), so that it is the same color as the Flash movie. Click **OK**.

3. Click **Flash** on the Common or Media tab of the Insert bar to open the Select Files dialog box. Select the file **webwarrior.swf** from the Sites\ch8practice\assets\movies folder.

4. Save the page. Click **Play** in the Property inspector to view the movie. Click **Stop** (the square red button) to stop it, as shown in Figure 8-16. View the page in both Internet Explorer and Netscape. Close the file.

8

Figure 8-16   Flash movie embedded in HTML page

Inserting Flash Buttons

Dreamweaver MX generates Flash buttons that display rollover animations from a set of predefined designs. You can configure some buttons to hold text. Once you configure a button with the design and text that you want, Dreamweaver inserts it onto the HTML page that is currently open in Design view.

You must take precautions when you generate and insert Flash buttons or Flash text, because Dreamweaver embeds the hyperlinked URL within the Flash SWF movie it creates. Dreamweaver warns that you need to save the HTML page before you insert the Flash button. If you use a relative hyperlink rather than the entire URL of the document to which the button links, you need to save the Flash button in the same folder or directory as the HTML page. A relative hyperlink does not work unless the button and the HTML page are in the same folder or directory as the HTML page housing the Flash object.

To insert and configure a Flash button:

1. Open the Site panel for La Bonne Cuisine, right-click on the **training** folder, select **New File** on the pop-up menu, and create three new HTML files in the training folder: **parties.htm**, **healthy.htm**, and **chefs.htm**.

2. Open the placeholder page **training.htm** in the Sites\lbc\training folder in Dreamweaver. Type **Culinary Training** in the Title text box.

3. Click the **Layout View** button on the Layout tab of the Insert bar, if it is not already selected. Press the **Ctrl+Alt+G** and **Ctrl+Alt+R** key combinations to view the grid and ruler, if they are not already visible. Set Window Size to

760 × 420 (800 × 600 maximized) in the status bar for the page in Design view. Press the **F11** key to open the Assets panel, if it is not already open.

4. Click **Commands** on the Dreamweaver menu bar, then click **Set Color Scheme**. Select **Green** in the Background list, and select **Brown, White, Green** in the Text and Links list. Click **OK**. Save the page.

5. Click the **Draw Layout Table** button 🔲 on the Layout tab of the Insert bar, and draw a table about **550** pixels wide and **400** pixels high.

6. Click the **Draw Layout Cell** button 🔲 on the Layout tab of the Insert bar, place the cursor in the upper-left corner of the table, and draw a layout cell about **300** pixels wide and **130** pixels high. Click the **Images** icon on the Assets panel, and drag the file **trainingtitle.gif** into the layout cell. Select the image, if necessary, and click **Align Center** in the Property inspector.

7. Follow the directions in Step 6 to draw a second layout cell to the right of the first cell that is about **215** pixels wide and **130** pixels high, and insert the image **training.gif**. Center the image and type **15** in the V Space text box.

8. Follow the directions in Step 6 but draw a third layout cell beginning about **180** pixels from the top and about **250** pixels from the left on the ruler. Make this layout cell about **250** pixels wide and **140** pixels high. Insert the image **cooks.jpg** using the Assets panel. Select the image and type **2** in the Border input box to draw a narrow border around it.

9. Click the **Draw Layout Cell** button 🔲 one more time, this time to draw a layout cell for Flash buttons. Begin at the left margin about **180** pixels below the top of the page. Extend the layout cell to the bottom of the table, and make it about **150** pixels wide.

10. Place the insertion point in the last layout cell, then click **Flash Button** button on the Media tab of the Insert bar. In the Insert Flash Button dialog box, shown in Figure 8-17, select **Slider** in the Style text box, and type **Party Planning** in the Button Text text box. Select **Arial Black** in the Font text box, and type **12** in the Size text box. Type **parties.htm** in the Link text box. Type **#CCCC99** in the Bg Color text box. Type **parties.swf** in the Save As text box. Click **Apply** to see the button on the HTML page. Click **OK** to save.

11. Place the insertion point to the right of the parties.swf Flash button and press the **Shift+Enter** key combination to move to the next line without leaving a space between lines. Click the **Flash Button** button again, and insert a button with the same properties as the previous button, but type **Healthy Meals** for the Button Text, **healthy.htm** for the Link, and **healthy.swf** in the Save As text box. Click **OK** to save.

8

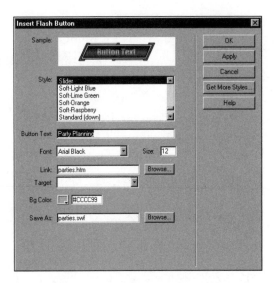

Figure 8-17   Insert Flash Button dialog box

12. Follow the directions in Step 11 to create a third Flash button with the Button Text **Chef Training,** the Link **chefs.htm**, and Save As **chefs.swf**. Click **OK** to save.

13. Save the page **training.htm** in the Sites\lbc\training folder. View the page in the browser, and test the hyperlinks. Close **training.htm**.

14. In Dreamweaver, press the Site tab to the left of the Assets tab to open the Site panel. Notice that Dreamweaver inserted the three Flash buttons into the training folder together with the page training.htm.

Inserting Flash Text

Dreamweaver MX inserts Flash text into your HTML page in Design view. You can configure the characteristics of the font, type your own text, and indicate the URL that opens when the viewer clicks the resulting rollover text. Dreamweaver then produces a Flash SWF movie, which includes the hyperlink information in the same way as the Flash button. Therefore, if you use a hyperlink with a relative address, you must save the Flash text object in the same folder as the Web page.

To insert Flash text into the training.htm page:

1. In Dreamweaver, open the page **training.htm** in the Sites\lbc\training folder. Click the **Layout View** button on the Layout tab of the Insert bar, if it is not already selected. Press the **Ctrl+Alt+G** and **Ctrl+Alt+R** key combinations to view the grid and ruler, if they are not already visible. Set Window Size to **760 × 420** (800 × 600 maximized) in the status bar.

2. Click the **Draw Layout Cell** button 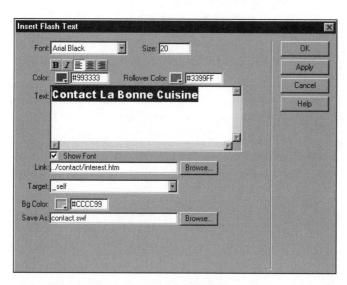 on the Layout tab of the Insert bar. Place the insertion point about **210** pixels from the left and **350** pixels from the top of the page and draw a layout cell about **295** pixels wide and **40** pixels high.

3. Click inside the layout cell you just drew, and then click the **Flash Text** button on the Media tab of the Insert bar.

4. In the Insert Flash Text dialog box, select **Arial Black** in the Font list box. Type **20** in the Size text box, and click the **Align Left** button. Type **#993333** in the Color text box, and type **#3399FF** in the Rollover Color text box. Type **Contact La Bonne Cuisine** in the Text text area.

5. Click the **Browse** button next to the Link text box, and select the file **interest.htm** located in the Sites\lbc\contact folder to create a hyperlink to that page. Type **#CCCC99** in the Bg Color text box. Type **contact.swf** in the Save As text box. Choose **_self** in the Target drop-down list. Figure 8-18 shows the Insert Flash Text dialog box. Click **OK**.

Figure 8-18   Insert Flash Text dialog box

6. Save the file as **training.htm** in the Sites\lbc\training folder. View the file in the browser to see the rollover effects in both the Flash buttons and Flash text. The page should look similar to Figure 8-19, which displays the rollover text color. Close **training.htm**.

Figure 8-19   Flash buttons and Flash text on training.htm

CHAPTER SUMMARY

- ❏ Dreamweaver provides tools that make it easy to insert and configure multimedia content to make Web sites more exciting and attractive.

- ❏ By defining external editors for different types of multimedia content, you can change your multimedia files from within the Dreamweaver editing window and see the results in Dreamweaver after you save the files. This supports optimization of quality and minimization of file size.

- ❏ The Assets panel contains lists of assets available to a Web site and makes it faster and easier to insert objects, including several types of multimedia files, on a Web page.

- ❏ When you embed sound and movie files on an HTML page using an ActiveX control or a Plugin object, you usually need to expand the size of the inserted icon so that viewers can access the controls when they play the image. Dreamweaver also helps you insert background sounds for which no controls appear on the page.

- ❏ The Common and Media tabs of the Insert bar let you insert images and Flash multimedia content, including Flash movies. You can also generate Flash buttons and Flash text that change color as you roll the mouse over them. Some Flash buttons are also animated.

- ❏ Three types of image compression produce image files for display on the Web. JPEG compression works best for photos. GIF compression works best for logos and drawn graphics. You can use GIF for images that display with transparent areas and as frames in animated GIFs. PNG, a new type of file compression, offers some of the best GIF and JPEG features but is not yet widely used, because older browsers do not display PNG images.

❏ Movies for the Web need to be short and compressed. You can embed them within a Web page, or so that they play in various media players set up on visitors' browsers. A good usability practice is to warn visitors of the movie's file size before they start to download it.

❏ In order to make movies and sound files play in the Netscape browser, the Plugin object requires an <embed> tag. Internet Explorer uses ActiveX controls for the same content and requires an <object> tag. Fortunately, Internet Explorer usually recognizes the <embed> tag as well. Since Netscape requires a purchased ActiveX plugin to display ActiveX content, Dreamweaver adds an <embed> tag within the <object> tag to increase the chances that Netscape will display files inserted with an ActiveX control.

REVIEW QUESTIONS

8

1. The big trade-off when incorporating multimedia into your Web sites is between _____ and _____.

2. One higher bandwidth Internet connection that is becoming more popular is the:
   a. cable modem
   b. Ethernet modem
   c. Netware modem
   d. HTTP modem

3. The three image file formats used on the Web are _____, _____, and _____.

4. If you are using relative addressing when you create Flash buttons or Flash text, you need to save:
   a. the Flash button or Flash text in the same directory as the HTML page on which it sits
   b. the Flash button or Flash text in your images directory
   c. your HTML page in a Flash directory
   d. Flash buttons or Flash text in a Flash directory

5. In Dreamweaver, the _____ lets you set the type of connection for which you want to display download time on the status bar at the bottom of the HTML page in Design view.
   a. Common tab of the Insert bar
   b. Preferences dialog box
   c. Property inspector
   d. Behavior panel

6. The download time for a Web page in the Dreamweaver editing window appears on the:

a. Property inspector

b. HTML code

c. Document window status bar

d. Preferences window

7. Many Web designers aim for the maximum memory requirement of _____ per Web page.

a. 10 KB

b. 20 KB

c. 30 KB

d. 100 KB

8. Dreamweaver lets you open external editors for multimedia content that you have inserted onto an HTML page. True or False?

9. The best type of image file format for compressing photographs for the Web so that older Web browsers also recognize them is:

a. JPEG

b. GIF

c. PNG

d. TIFF

10. The best type of image file format for compressing graphics with lots of flat areas (for example, drawings) for the Web so that older Web browsers also recognize them is:

a. JPEG

b. GIF

c. PNG

d. MPEG

11. The newest type of image file format for the Web, which combines characteristics of the other two formats but is NOT recognized by older Web browsers, is:

a. JPEG

b. GIF

c. PNG

d. MP3

12. When you want to insert audio files into your Web site, you can choose to link to them or _____ them.

   a. embed

   b. nest

   c. call

   d. place

13. GIF file format supports a maximum of how many colors?

   a. 216 colors

   b. 256 colors

   c. 255 colors

   d. Millions of colors

14. JPEG file format supports a maximum of how many colors?

   a. 216 colors

   b. 256 colors

   c. 255 colors

   d. Millions of colors

15. You can configure and insert a Flash button from which tab of the Insert bar:

   a. Media tab

   b. Common tab

   c. Layout tab

   d. Frames tab

16. The file format for shocked Flash movies that play on the Web is:

   a. AVI

   b. SWF

   c. MOV

   d. RIP

17. Applications that change the file format of an audio file are commonly called:

   a. shockers

   b. rippers

   c. coders

   d. codecs

8

18. The audio file format that uses an algorithm to reproduce audio files using the synthesizer on the client computer is called:

    a. MIDI

    b. WAV

    c. MP3

    d. RealAudio

19. Choose the reason(s) why Flash movies are much smaller than bitmapped movies (such as those produced by video editors like Premiere):

    a. They use vector-based symbols that only need to be downloaded once.

    b. They often use a series of smaller movie clips, so that one can play while the next downloads.

    c. They use short sound clips that only download once but loop repeatedly.

    d. They export MP3 sound, which gives quality sound with low memory requirements.

20. The HTML tags that embed multimedia files into Netscape and Internet Explorer differ, but both browsers usually recognize which HTML tag?

    a. <object>

    b. <embed>

    c. <plugin>

    d. <activex>

HANDS-ON PROJECTS

Project 8-1

In this project you embed a video file and provide a link to the download site for the Apple QuickTime player.

1. If you did not copy the file **cookies.mov** from the Chapter8\assets\movies folder on your Data Disk to the Sites\ch8practice\assets\movies folder on your working drive for an exercise earlier in the chapter, use Windows Explorer to do that before you start Step 2.

2. Download the current version of the Apple QuickTime Download button to display it on your Web page. The button is currently labeled **QuickTime Free Download** and is named **getquicktime.gif**. You should visit the Apple QuickTime Web site (*http://www.apple.com/quicktime*) and locate the current version of the button image that is used to download Apple QuickTime. To save it, right-click the graphic, and click **Save Picture As**. Save the button image in your Sites\ch8practice\assets\images folder. If you cannot locate a copy of this graphic

on the Apple Web site, you can copy one from the Chapter8\assets\images folder on your working drive.

3. Create a new HTML page in the Sites\ch8practice folder called **myvideo.htm**. Click the **Standard View** button on the Layout tab of the Insert bar, if it is not already selected.

4. Press the **Ctrl+J** key combination to open the Page Properties dialog box, and enter the title **My Video Page**, make the background black (**#000000**), and make the text color white (**#FFFFFF**). Click **OK**.

5. Type **My Video Page** at the top of this page, and then select this text. In the Property inspector change the Format style to **Heading 1** and center the text. Place the insertion point after the text **My Video Page**, and press the **Enter** key to go to the next line.

6. Click the **Insert Table** button on the Common tab of the Insert bar to insert a table to hold your movie. The table should have **2** rows, **2** columns, **0** borders, cell padding and cell spacing both equal to **5**, and be **85%** of the page width and centered on the HTML page.

7. Place the insertion point in the first table cell, and type **Video shows a baker preparing cookies in a shop in Little Tokyo**. Press the **Enter** key and then type **The movie is 2 MB in size**. Press the **Enter** key again, and then type **The movie should start playing when it finishes downloading**.

8. Press the **Tab** key to move to the next cell in the row. Select the table cell by clicking the **<td>** tag on the Design view status bar. Click inside the table cell, and then click the **Align Center** button in the table cell Property inspector. Click the **Plugin** button on the Media tab of the Insert bar and select the movie **cookies.mov** from the Sites\ch8practice\assets\movies folder. Click the **Plugin object** in the table cell to select it. In its Property inspector, increase the Plugin object's width to **152** pixels and height to **138** pixels to display the movie controls. Save the page and preview it in both Netscape and Internet Explorer.

9. Place the insertion point in row 2, column 1, and type **If you do not have Apple QuickTime loaded on your computer, you can get it by clicking the QuickTime button to the right**.

10. Place the insertion point in row 2, column 2 of the table, and press the **Ctrl+Alt+I** key combination to insert the image you downloaded from the Apple Web site in Step 2, which is saved in the Sites\ch8practice\assets\images folder. Create a hyperlink to the URL on the Apple Web site where you can download the free version of the Apple QuickTime Player, currently *http://www.apple.com/quicktime/download*. If the URL on the Apple Web site changed, search the Apple Web site for it, and copy and paste the link into the Link text box.

11. Save the page and preview it in both browsers.

Project 8-2

In this project you alter the page you developed in Project 8-1 by changing the parameters for playing the movie and alerting viewers about how to start and stop the movie with the movie controls.

1. Open the **myvideo.htm** page you created in Hands-on Project 8-1 and saved in the Sites\ch8practice folder. Save the page again as **myvideo1.htm** in the same folder.

2. Select the Plugin object for the video **cookies.mov**. Click the **Parameters** button in the Plugin Property inspector to open the Parameters window.

3. Type **autostart** in the Parameter column and **false** in the Value column. This parameter means that the movie does not automatically begin playing once it is downloaded; the viewer must start the movie by clicking the control. Click the + (plus) button to add a new parameter, and type **loop** in the Parameter column, and **false** in the Value column. Click **OK**.

4. Place the insertion point in the first table cell. Highlight the text **The movie should start playing when it finishes downloading**, and type **Press the VCR start control to start the movie** to replace it. Press the **Enter** key to go to a new line. Below this instruction, type another message telling the viewer how to stop the movie: **Press the VCR stop control to stop it**.

5. Save the Web page and view it in the browser. Note that the Play button changes to Pause once you click it to start the movie.

Project 8-3

In this project you embed an audio file in a layout table and set up links to the Web sites where viewers can download plugin applications. You display a download button on your Web page with a link to the URL at *www.real.com* from which viewers can download Real Player basic free of charge, as well as a button to download Apple QuickTime.

1. Use Windows Explorer to copy **getquicktime.gif** and **realplayer.gif** from the Chapter8\assets\images folder on your Data Disk to the Sites\ch8practice\assets\images folder on your working drive.

2. If you did not copy the audio file **CountryRoad.wav** from the Chapter8\assets\sounds folder to the Sites\ch8practice\assets\sounds folder for an exercise earlier in the chapter, use Windows Explorer to do that before you proceed to Step 3.

3. Press the **Ctrl+N** key combination to create a new basic HTML page, and press the **Ctrl+S** key combination to save it as **myaudio.htm** in the Sites\ch8practice folder. Click the **Standard View** button on the Layout tab of the Insert bar, if it is not already selected.

4. Type **My Audio Files** in the Title text box below the Insert bar. Click **Set Color Scheme** on the Commands drop-down menu, and change the background to **Blue** and the text to **White**, **Green**, **Yellow** for this page.

5. At the top of the Web page, type **My Audio Resource Page**. Select the text, use the Property inspector to change its Format style to **Heading 1**, and center the text. Deselect the text. Press the **Enter** key to go to a new line.

6. Click the **Insert Table** button on the Common tab of the Insert bar to create a table to hold your audio content. The table should have **2** rows, **2** columns, **0** borders, cell padding and cell spacing both equal to **5**, and be **85%** of the page width. Use the table Property inspector to center align the table on the HTML page.

7. Place the insertion point in the first table cell and type **Press the stop control to stop the music playing**. Left align this text.

8. Press the **Enter** key to go to a new line, and insert a Plugin object to embed the audio file **CountryRoad.wav** from the Sites\ch8practice\assets\sounds folder. Modify the size of the Plugin object to show the start and stop buttons in the browser window. If you use the Apple QuickTime plugin to play WAV audio files, set the plugin dimensions to **150** pixels wide and **15** pixels high. If you use the Windows Media Player plugin, set the plugin dimensions to **200** pixels wide and **45** pixels high.

9. Place the insertion point inside the first table cell in the second row, and create a hyperlink to download the Apple QuickTime player. Type **Download the free Apple QuickTime player if you do not have it already installed on your computer**. Highlight the word **Download** and create a hyperlink to the download site at: *http://www.apple.com/quicktime/download*.

10. Click at the end of the text you just typed and press the **Enter** key to move to a new line. Press the **Ctrl+Alt+I** key combination to insert the **getquicktime.gif** image. Right align the image, select it, and create another hyperlink to the same Apple QuickTime player download site to which you linked in Step 9.

11. Place the insertion point in the second table cell in the second row, and type **Download the free, basic RealAudio player if you do not have it already installed on your computer**. Highlight the word **Download** and create a hyperlink to the current download site for Real Player basic: *http://www.real.com*. Deselect the text. Press the **Enter** key to move to a new line.

12. Press **Ctrl+Alt+I** to insert the image **realplayer.gif**. Right align the image, select it, and create another hyperlink to the same RealAudio player download site to which you linked in Step 11.

13. Save the file and view it in Internet Explorer. Check the hyperlinks to be sure they all work.

Project 8-4

In this project you change the parameters for playing the WAV file audio.htm, created in Project 8-3, and tell viewers how to start and stop the movie with the movie controls.

1. Open **myaudio.htm** in the Sites\ch8practice folder. Save it as **myaudio1.htm** in the same folder.

2. Select the audio **CountryRoad.wav** and click the **Parameters** button in the Property inspector to open the Parameters window.

3. Type **autostart** in the Parameter column, and type **false** in the Value column.

4. Click the + (plus) button, and type **loop** in the Parameter column and **true** in the Value column. Click **OK** to close the Parameter window.

5. The music no longer begins to play when the page loads in the browser, so change the text in the first table cell. Type **Press the start control to start playing the song and the stop control to stop it**.

6. Save the page and view it in Internet Explorer.

Project 8-5

In this project you embed a Flash movie in a Web page.

1. Use Windows Explorer to copy the file **tours.swf** from the Chapter8\assets\movies folder on your Data Disk to the Sites\ch8practice\assets\movies folder on your working drive.

2. Press the **Ctrl+N** key combination to create a new page, and press the **Ctrl+S** key combination to save it as **flashtour.htm** in the Sites\ch8practice folder.

3. Press the **Ctrl+J** key combination, and change the page title to **Tours Flash Page**. Click **Set Color Scheme** on the Commands drop-down menu, and select a **Yellow** background, and **Purple**, **Pink**, **Green** text and links.

4. Type **Flash Tour** at the top of the page with **Heading 1** format, **center** aligned.

5. Press the **Enter** key to go down one line, click **Flash** on the Common tab of the Insert bar, and select the Flash movie **tours.swf** from the Sites\ch8practice\assets\movies folder.

6. Use the Property inspector to change the Flash movie attributes and display. Type **5** in the V Space and H Space input boxes. Play the Flash movie on the page by clicking the **Play** button in the Property inspector. Adjust Quality to **Low**, and play the movie again.

7. Change Quality back to **High**, and save the page **flashtour.htm** in the Sites\ch8practice folder. View the page in both browsers.

Project 8-6

In this project you create a page with Flash buttons.

1. Use Windows Explorer to copy the images **peopleparty.gif** and **medshrimp.jpg** from the Chapter8\assets\images folder on your Data Disk to the Sites\ch8practice\assets\images folder on your working drive.

2. Press the **Ctrl+N** key combination to create a new page. Press the **Ctrl+S** key combination to save the new page as **flashbuttons.htm** in the Sites\ch8practice folder. Press the **Ctrl+Alt+G** and **Ctrl+Alt+R** key combinations to view the

grid and the ruler, if they are not visible. Click **Layout View** on the Layout tab of the Insert bar, if it is not already selected.

3. Type **Parties** in the Title text box. Click **Set Color Scheme** on the Commands drop-down menu to change the color scheme to **Green** background with **Brown**, **Green**, **Blue** text and links.

4. Click the **Draw Layout Table** button on the Layout tab of the Insert bar to draw a table about **550** pixels wide and **450** pixels high. Draw a layout cell **550** pixels wide and **115** pixels high, beginning in the upper-left corner of the table. Type **Flash! Flash! Flash!** with **Heading 1** Format style, *italicized*, and **center** alignment. Press the **Enter** key to go to the line below the heading, and press the **Ctrl+Alt+I** key combination to insert the image **peopleparty.gif** from the Sites\ch8practice\assets\images folder. The image should also be **center** aligned.

5. Click the **Draw Layout Cell** button on the Layout tab of the Insert bar. Place the cursor about **275** pixels from the left and **170** pixels from the top of the page, using the ruler. Draw a table cell about **226** pixels wide and **200** pixels high. Press the **Ctrl+Alt+I** key combination to insert in this table cell the image **medshrimp.jpg** from the Sites\ch8practice\assets\images folder. Type **5** in the Border input box in the Property inspector for the image.

6. Click the **Draw Layout Cell** button again. Place the cursor about **25** pixels from the left margin and **190** pixels from the top page margin, using the ruler. Draw a layout cell that is about **200** pixels wide and **120** pixels high. Select the layout cell and click **Center** in the Horz list box.

7. Click inside the layout cell you just drew. Click the **Flash Button** button on the Media tab of the Insert bar to insert the Flash buttons listed below into this layout cell. When you finish configuring a Flash button, click **OK** to close the Insert Flash Button dialog box, and then press **Shift+Enter** before you insert the next Flash button. The Flash buttons should be located immediately under one another. For all buttons, choose the Flash button style **Chrome Bar**, and the default font style and size. Set the background color to **#CCFFCC** to match the page color.

Button Text	Link to Page	Save As
Beach Party	**beachparty.htm**	**beachparty.swf**
Kids' Party	**kidsparty.htm**	**kidsparty.swf**
Dog Party	**dogparty.htm**	**dogparty.swf**
Pool Party	**poolparty.htm**	**poolparty.swf**
Home	**home.htm**	**home.swf**

8. Click the **Draw Layout Cell** button and place the cursor about **75** pixels from the left margin and **325** pixels from the top page margin. Draw a layout cell that is about **155** pixels wide and **50** pixels high.

9. Place the insertion point in this layout cell, and click the **Flash Text** button on the Media tab of the Insert bar. In the Text input box, type **E-mail us at** on the first line and type **partypeople@xol.com** on the second line. Select an informal

8

font (such as **Comic Sans MS**), Size **15**, **Bold**, **left** aligned, a subdued blue-green Color (**#336699**), a tan Rollover Color (**#CC9966**), and light green Bg (background) Color (**#CCFFCC**) to match the page color. Type **mailto:partypeople@xol.com** as the link. Save as **emailtext.swf**. Click **OK**.

10. Save the page and create placeholder pages in the Sites\ch8practice folder for all the linked pages (**beachparty.htm**, **kidsparty.htm**, **dogparty.htm**, **poolparty.htm**, and **home.htm**) that do not exist. View in the browser.

Project 8-7

In this project you create a page for the Children's Party with Flash text.

1. Use Windows Explorer to copy **childtitle.gif** and **kids.jpg** from the Chapter8\assets\images folder on your Data Disk to the Sites\ch8practice\assets\images folder on your working drive.

2. Open the **kidsparty.htm** page you created in Hands-on Project 8-6. If you did not complete that project, you can simply press the **Ctrl+N** key combination to create a new page, and press the **Ctrl+S** key combination to save it as **kidsparty.htm**, and save it in the Sites\ch8practice folder.

3. Type **Kids Party** in the Title text box. Click **Set Color Scheme** on the **Commands** drop-down menu, and choose the color scheme with a **Yellow** background and **Purple**, **Pink**, **Green** text and links. Press the **Ctrl+Alt+R** and **Ctrl+Alt+G** key combinations to view the ruler and grid, if they are not visible on the HTML page.

4. Click the **Layout View** button on the Layout tab of the Insert bar, if it is not already selected. Click the **Draw Layout Table** button to draw a layout table about **550** pixels wide and **400** pixels high.

5. Click the **Draw Layout Cell** button. Place the cursor in the upper-left corner of the layout table, and draw a table cell about **550** pixels wide and **70** pixels high. Insert the image **childtitle.gif** from the Sites\ch8practice\assets\images folder. Center it in the layout cell.

6. Follow the directions in Step 5 to draw another layout cell starting about **150** pixels from the page top and **50** pixels from the left margin on the ruler. Make it about **240** pixels wide and **210** pixels high.

7. Click inside the table cell you drew in Step 6. Click **Flash text** on the Media tab of the Insert bar. Select an informal text style available on your computer (such as **Lucida Handwriting**, **Jokerman**, or **Comic Sans MS**, with size **40**). Define the font Color as **#6666CC**, the Rollover Color as **#FF00FF**, and the Bg (background) Color as **#FFFFCC** for each Flash text SWF file. The first Flash text should read **Balloons**, link to **balloons.htm**, and be saved as **balloons.swf**. (Note that you must click **OK** when you finish creating each Flash text SWF file, and then press **Enter** to go to a new line before inserting the next Flash text.) The next Flash text should read **Clowns**, link to **clowns.htm**, and be saved as **clowns.swf**. The third Flash text should read **Cake**, link to **kidsfood.htm**, and be named **kidsfood.swf**. Click **OK** when you finish creating the Flash text.

Note that you must click **OK** when you finish creating each Flash text SWF file, and then press **Enter** to go to a new line before inserting the next Flash text. Click **OK** when you finish creating the Flash text.

8. Click the **Draw Layout Cell** button. Place the cursor about **325** pixels from the left and **200** pixels from the top, using the ruler. Draw a layout cell about **210** pixels wide and **145** pixels high. Insert the image **kids.jpg** from the Sites\ch8practice\ assets\images folder. Select the image, if necessary, and type **5** in the Border input box in the image's Property inspector.

9. Save the page **kidsparty.htm** in the Sites\ch8practice folder. Create placeholder pages for the missing files (**balloons.htm**, **clowns.htm**, and **kidsfood.htm**). View **kidsparty.htm** in the browser to see the rollover effects.

CASE PROJECTS

Visit the Apple movie trailers Web site (www.apple.com/trailers) to view movie trailers in Apple QuickTime (MOV) or RealVideo format. Go to at least three movie company trailer sites within the Apple Web site, and analyze how they display the movie trailers. Do they warn the viewer about (1) the need for a certain viewer; (2) the file size of the movie trailers; and (3) the player plugins they need to view the movie trailers? Do they provide links to the required plugin? Do they offer movies for different plugins with different compression levels suitable for different bandwidth levels? Do they increase the usability of their movie Web sites in any other ways? Is the time you spend waiting for the movies to download worthwhile?

You have been hired to build a multimedia Web site for a food company that sells your favorite kind of food. Find multimedia content that is appropriate for your Web site. Use photos, Flash text, and Flash buttons to make it exciting. Create titles and edit and optimize your photos in Fireworks MX. Create a menu page and at least 5 other pages for your food site.

Create a small multimedia Web site about your class, your school, your family, or any other topic for which you have multimedia content. Use digital or scanned photos, create titles with Fireworks or Flash Text, and use audio or video files that may be available to you. Use Fireworks to crop and optimize photos for the Web. Create a menu using Flash buttons to link to the pages on your Web site.

9

STYLE SHEETS

Using Inline, Internal, and External Style Sheets

In this chapter, you will:

◆ Learn about the basic elements of style sheets

◆ Learn how to use inline, internal, and external style sheets

◆ Apply Cascading Style Sheets

◆ Use CSS selectors

◆ Link Web pages to external style sheets

Style sheets give Web developers control over many aspects of page design. Styles in HTML are very similar to templates and styles in word-processing applications. Dreamweaver MX builds code to control text, spacing, background, and placement attributes on a Web page into a set of rules that you can apply to lines of text, entire pages, or entire Web sites. Applied to an entire Web site, these rules guarantee a consistent format and style for the site's content. Consistency is very important in Web design, because it gives users a sense of familiarity across pages and simplifies navigation. Style sheets also simplify Web site maintenance. If you design each page individually, then changing one particular feature of the site requires you to edit each page individually. Style sheets let you set the rules in one file, so that changing an aspect of the style requires only one modification.

In this chapter you learn to apply HTML and Cascading Style Sheet (CSS) styles. Using CSS, you redefine HTML tags, create your own custom styles, and learn to use CSS selectors to change the attributes of hyperlinks. You also learn how to export the styles that you create in a style sheet, so that you can use them on other Web pages.

INTRODUCTION TO STYLE SHEETS

Style sheets, or Cascading Style Sheets (CSS), are a system used with HTML that allows a developer to tightly control the style of page properties and text. For example, without CSS, changing all Heading 1 tags to red, italic, underscore, requires you to select the text in each Heading 1, clicking the Property inspector three times for every change. Changing every Heading 1 tag on a large Web site takes hundreds of clicks on many pages. This work is tedious and prone to error. Style sheets were developed to solve these problems. Using a style sheet, you can define your own styles and apply them to a line of text, an HTML document, or an entire Web site. Furthermore, style sheets can control more than just text attributes such as bold, italic, and underscore. You can use them to control spacing, font face, type size, line spacing, background, alignment, margins, and almost any attribute you can think of.

In an HTML document, the tag <style> indicates the beginning of a style definition, and the tag </style> indicates that the style definition is complete. Figure 9-1 shows an internal style for changing all Heading 1 tags to red. A **selector**, followed by a **declaration** controlling the properties of the selector, defines the syntax of the style as follows:

selector {declaration}

For example:

```
H1 {color: #FF0000}
```

H1 is the selector and {color: #FF0000} is the declaration statement. This code makes Heading 1 text red. You can also group multiple properties within one style using semicolons to separate the properties. For example:

```
H1 {color: #FF0000; font-style: italic; font-weight: bold}
```

This code, when contained in the header of a document, formats all H1 tags in red, italic, and bold. You can also apply a set of properties to multiple tags by separating the tags with commas at the beginning of the statement. For example:

```
H1, H2, H3 {color: #FF0000; font-style: italic;
font-weight: bold}
```

This code, when contained in the header of a document, makes all h1, h2, and h3 tags red, italic, and bold.

After you define the attributes for a specific tag, you can apply the tag throughout a document or Web site. You accomplish this by means of inheritance. **Inheritance** means that some values are inherited by the children of the respective element. Predefining the properties of the h1 header ensures that all h1 headers share the same properties.

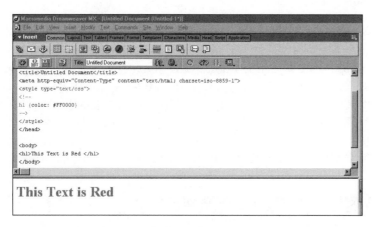

Figure 9-1   Style example from the Dreamweaver MX HTML source window

Because of inheritance, you can change properties throughout a document by placing a style in the body tag. For example, changing font-family to Helvetica in the HTML body tag (`<body font-family: Helvetica>`) formats all text in Helvetica. This is much easier than changing the font by hand throughout the document. If you later decide to change the font to sans-serif, you merely change the body tag of the document.

In addition to redefining the attributes of existing HTML tags, style sheets let you define custom classes that you can apply throughout your document or Web site. In effect, a **custom class** is a custom HTML tag. Instead of using a predefined tag as the selector, you define your own selector, preceded by a period. For example:

```
.place {font-family: Arial; font-size: 9pt; font-style:
italic; color: #0000FF}
```

This code defines a class named place that you can apply to the body of the HTML document inside a paragraph tag. For example:

```
<p class="place">place_text</p>
```

Adding the custom class to the <p> tag in the style definition ensures that the style is applied to an entire paragraph. You can also define a style to apply to a segment of text by using a <span> tag. You define the custom tag in the header and call it using a class name in the body of the document. More examples of this are provided in the following sections. Later in this chapter you define and use your own classes.

Style sheets are also called Cascading Style Sheets because you can apply multiple style sheets to one Web page. The sheets cascade so that a new style sheet overrides the styles set by the older style sheet. This feature is attractive because you can apply a general style sheet to your entire Web site and then apply more specific style sheets to different sections of your Web site, depending upon your requirements.

The code examples you've seen so far are contained in the header of a document. However, in creating a consistent style to your entire site, you want to have the same styles for each of your Web pages. To do this, you can create an external style sheet and link every page to it. Figure 9-2 shows styles saved to an external style sheet and a Web page that links to the style sheet. The style sheet extension is .css for Cascading Style Sheet. The styles defined in the file resemble a long list of formatting rules, listed one after the other. As you can imagine, if you had to type all these rules yourself it would be quite tedious. Dreamweaver MX has detailed assistance for building internal style sheets as well as for building and linking to external style sheets, which saves time and prevents syntax and stylistic errors.

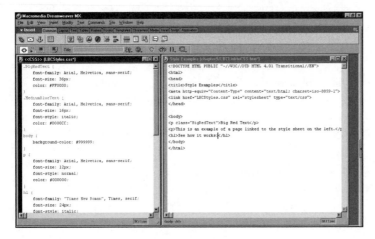

Figure 9-2   CSS format and link to CSS

It is important to keep in mind that not all browsers support all styles. A style sheet that appears one way in Explorer may look different in Netscape. Testing your work in Explorer and Netscape and on different platforms is essential to ensuring the integrity of your design.

HTML AND CSS STYLES PANELS

You can apply three types of styles to HTML documents. **Inline styles** are the least powerful, applied by writing the style definition into the tag in the body of your HTML document. To apply styles more widely, you can use an **internal style**, declaring the custom class in the head of the HTML document. Referencing that class then affects all content of the HTML document with that tag. To apply styles throughout an entire Web site, you can define an **external style sheet**, which is a separate file that contains all your style rules. In this section, you will learn about HTML and CSS styles. HTML styles are used if you want to format text that is used frequently throughout a small site. The styles are applied to selected text or paragraphs. CSS styles are used when you have a larger site and want to control the format of many aspects of the site through custom styles defined in a style sheet.

To access the HTML Styles panel in Dreamweaver, click Window on the menu bar, then click HTML Styles, or press the Ctrl+F11 key combination. If your Design panel group is open, you can also access HTML Styles or CSS Styles by clicking the tab in the panel group. The HTML Styles panel is shown in Figure 9-3. Notice that this panel contains two predefined HTML styles. Clicking the first item in the list 🖉 lets you clear HTML styles from selected text, while clicking the second item 🖋 lets you clear an HTML style from an entire paragraph. As you add HTML styles, a few more icons help you identify the styles defined in the panel. The style items that begin with the letter a are styles that you can apply to text selections |a. These style items clear any previously existing styles. A plus sign **a+** follows additive styles, which are applied in addition to a pre-existing style. A paragraph tag ¶ precedes styles that you can apply to an entire paragraph. A paragraph style can also appear with a plus sign, indicating an additive style. If you select the checkbox in the lower-left corner of the HTML Styles panel, you apply your styles as soon as you select them. To create a style, click the New Style button 🔳, and to delete a style, simply select it and click the Delete Style button 🔳. Clicking twice on a style lets you change its properties. You can access all these functions from the Options menu in the upper-right corner of the panel group. This menu also includes the Duplicate command, which can be useful when you want to create a style similar to one that already exists. You can duplicate the existing style and then edit it to suit to your needs.

9

Figure 9-3   HTML Styles panel

To access the CSS Styles panel to define and edit internal and external styles, click Window on the menu bar and then click CSS Styles, or press the Shift+F11 key combination. (See Figure 9-4.) The CSS Styles panel is similar to the HTML Styles panel. In the panel, the custom styles you create are listed. With the Apply Styles option checked, you apply a style by selecting the element on the page and clicking the style name in the panel. Clicking the other radio button, Edit Styles, displays a list of your defined styles or style sheets within the panel. Double-clicking a style allows you to change its attributes. Once a style is changed, your document automatically shows the changes. With the CSS Styles panel, you can link to an external style sheet (Attach Style Sheet 🔳) or edit a style sheet (Edit Style Sheet 🔳). An external style sheet typically contains several style definitions. When you attach it to your HTML document, you apply the styles defined in the external style sheet to your document and make them available in your Styles panel so that you can select them. Clicking the Attach Style Sheet button 🔳 lets you browse for and select the external style sheet. If you want to open and edit an existing style in your current document, click the Edit Style Sheet button 🔳.

Figure 9-4   CSS Styles panel

Using HTML Styles

The simplest way to change styles is to embed defined style formats within existing tags in an HTML document. Using the HTML Styles panel, you can define styles that you wish to apply frequently. Instead of selecting each property from the Property inspector, you select the text you wish to change and then apply a style from the HTML Styles panel. If the styles used on your Web page are even moderately complex, this is much faster than entering fonts, colors, and sizes separately for each instance in the document. It also prevents you from making an error, because the styles are defined in one place. When you want to create a new style, click the New Style button ⊞. This opens the Define HTML Style dialog box shown in Figure 9-5. In this dialog box, you can set the following options:

- The Name text box is used to name the style and place its name in the HTML Styles panel.

- The Apply To choices are used to determine how the styles are applied. Choose Selection to ensure that the style is applied only to selected text. Choose Paragraph to ensure that the style is always applied to an entire paragraph.

- When Applying is used to either apply the style by adding it to an existing style (Add to Existing Style), or you can clear the existing style (Clear Existing Style) and apply the new style to plain text. For example, if you have bold text and you apply a style that was red, Arial font, adding the style to an existing style results in bold, red, Arial text. Clearing the old style before applying the new style results in red Arial text.

- Font Attributes set font characteristics using various drop-down lists and text boxes.

- Paragraph Attributes set attributes for paragraphs, HTML headers, and preformatted text. You can also select alignment properties for these attributes. These are available only if the Paragraph option is selected under Apply To.

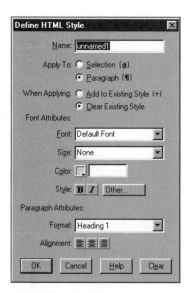

Figure 9-5   Define HTML Style dialog box

Creating and Applying Inline Styles

To practice working with styles in this chapter, you develop the consulting portion of the La Bonne Cuisine Web site. La Bonne Cuisine assists its clients in developing recipes, testing food products, and improving manufacturing processes. Most content for the consulting portion of the site has been developed for you, so you can practice using styles without creating pages from scratch. However, you do need to specify colors and styles. Images and text also are provided for the files linked to the consulting portion of the La Bonne Cuisine site. Later in this chapter, you alter these design elements using other style sheet techniques.

To specify colors and styles:

1. Using Windows Explorer, copy the files **consulting.htm**, **cfp.htm**, **manufacturing.htm**, **recipecards.htm**, and **tastetesting.htm** from your Chapter9\consulting data folder into the Sites\lbc\consulting folder on your working drive. The file consulting.htm replaces an existing file. The other files are new to the site. Use Windows Explorer to copy the images **consulting.gif**, **fajitapizza.jpg**, **fajitasRecipeCard.jpg**, and **manufacturing.jpg** from the Chapter9\assets\images data folder to your Sites\lbc\assets\images folder.

2. Launch Dreamweaver MX. Press **F8** to open the Site panel (if it is not already open) and select the **La Bonne Cuisine** Web site. In Design view, open the file **consulting.htm** in the Sites\lbc\consulting folder. The file consulting.htm is an HTML page describing La Bonne Cuisine's consulting services.

3. Press **Ctrl+F11** to open the HTML Styles panel, if it is not already open. Click the **New Style** button ⊞ on the HTML Styles panel to open the Define HTML Style dialog box. You are creating a question style to format the two questions on the page.

4. In the Name text box, type **question style**. Select the following attributes:
   - Apply To: **Selection** (this applies the style to selected text, instead of an entire paragraph)
   - When Applying: **Clear Existing Style** (this option clears any pre-existing styles, although this page has none)
   - Color: **#CC3399** (pinkish-purple)
   - Style: **Bold, Italic**

   Click **OK**.

   Notice that the new style, question style, now appears at the bottom of the list on the HTML Styles panel.

5. On the consulting.htm page, select the third line of text, "**Are you looking for new menu ideas?**". In the HTML Styles panel, click **question style**. Deselect the text and observe that the text's appearance changes so it has the attributes you defined in Step 4.

6. Scroll down the Dreamweaver workspace, and select the text "**Are you attempting to launch a food product or looking for a creative idea to enhance existing products?**". Click **question style** again in the HTML Styles panel to change the style of the second question.

 When you use the HTML Styles panel, you must select text and then apply the style every time you want to use it. If you edit an HTML style, it must be re-applied to show the change in the style attributes.

7. Save the file **consulting.htm**.

Using Cascading Style Sheets

Another kind of style you can apply within Dreamweaver MX is called CSS style. When you click the New CSS Style button 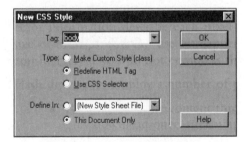 on the CSS Styles panel, the New CSS Style dialog box opens, as shown in Figure 9-6. This dialog box gives you three options for the type of CSS style: Make Custom Style (class), Redefine HTML Tag, and Use CSS Selector.

Figure 9-6   New CSS Style dialog box

The Type and Define In radio buttons on the New CSS Style dialog box are by default set to Make Custom Style and (New Style Sheet File), respectively. When you click the

Redefine HTML Tag radio button, the list at the top of the dialog box becomes a Tag list, from which you select the HTML tag you want to redefine. If you click the Make Custom Style radio button, the list becomes a Name text box, in which you enter your own class name. If you click the Use CSS Selector radio button, you select one of four selectors from the list.

The simplest way to create a CSS is by redefining an HTML tag. This option allows you to modify an existing HTML tag, for instance h1, and assign it different properties that apply whenever you use an h1 tag. When you use this option, the h1 tags in the body of your code remain the same. That is, all h1 headings appear as h1 with no additional attributes. However, in the header of your code, the tag has been redefined with a new style attribute, as described in the previous section.

A second way to create a CSS style is by creating your own custom class. This option is like redefining an HTML tag, except that you define a unique class that you can select from the CSS Styles panel and use whenever you see fit. In essence, you create your own HTML tag and access it by referencing the class name. The last option for creating a CSS Style is to select Use CSS Selector. You can use the CSS Selector option to group tags that share attributes or to change the appearance of hyperlink attributes. You practice using each of these methods in the sections below.

Redefining HTML Tags

To redefine an HTML tag, select the Redefine HTML Tag radio button on the New CSS Style dialog box. This activates the Tag drop-down list at the top of the dialog box. From this list, you can select the tag you wish to redefine, as shown in Figure 9-7. At the bottom of the New CSS Style dialog box, you can select the scope of your tag definition by clicking either the radio button for New Style Sheet File or for This Document Only. If you select New Style Sheet File, you are prompted to save the style sheet on your working drive with the name you select. Choosing This Document Only creates a list of styles that you can use in the current document and then export later to an external style sheet if you want to use it elsewhere. After you select a tag to redefine and choose This Document Only, your screen should resemble Figure 9-8. The title bar at the top of this dialog box indicates which HTML style you are redefining. Figure 9-8 shows that you are redefining the style for the h1 tag.

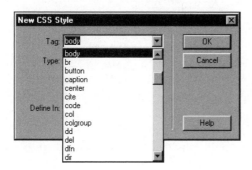

Figure 9-7   Tag selection in the New CSS Style dialog box

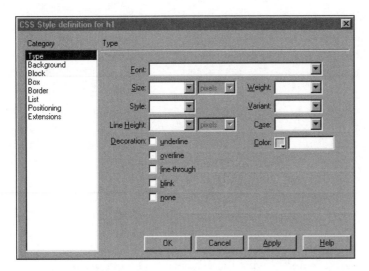

Figure 9-8   Defining a style

The CSS Style definition dialog box changes depending upon which category you select. Each category controls different settings. Figure 9-9 shows the CSS Style definition dialog box for the category Background, which is quite different from the Type Style definition dialog box. The CSS Style Definition dialog box lists eight categories:

- Type changes text characteristics such as font, size, and color.

- Background controls background characteristics such as using a color background or an image, or creating a fixed or scrolling background.

- Block controls spacing and alignment of text and lines on the HTML page.

- Box changes box attributes such as height, width, padding, and margins.

- Border changes the attributes of borders around text such as thickness and color.

- List controls list attributes such as text type and bullet appearance.

- Positioning defines positioning of text on the screen.

- Extensions controls page breaks and the visual appearance of the cursor.

Suppose that you want to make all h1 tags red, all h2 tags white, all h1 and h2 tags Arial font, and your document's background blue, as shown in Figure 9-10. To accomplish this, you redefine these HTML tags using the CSS Styles panel and then the changes are automatically applied to your document. In Figure 9-10, you see that the code between the body tags looks like a typical HTML page. The pair of style tags, <style> and </style>, in the header of the document, indicates that a style is being defined. The three redefined tags (h1, h2, and body) are shown between the style tags in the source code. Notice that the selected text on the page, "Fantastic", is defined as an h2 header in the source code and that the style above defines h2 as white and Arial.

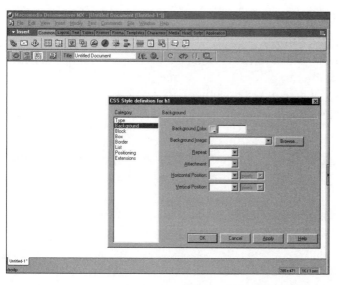

Figure 9-9   Setting the style for the Background Category

9

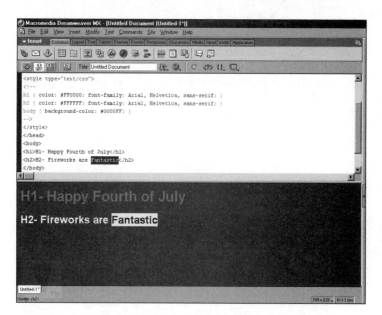

Figure 9-10   Redefined HTML styles and source code

Defining a Custom Class

The process of defining a custom class is virtually the same as redefining an HTML tag. However, instead of using the HTML tag, you give your newly defined tag a unique name that you can use throughout your code. You define the tag in the header of your document and can call it anywhere in the document. To define a custom class, select the Make Custom Style radio button. The default name *.unnamed1* appears in the Name text box, as shown in Figure 9-11. (Note that the name cannot include spaces or unusual characters.) Just type over this text to give the custom style an appropriate name. Select This Document Only in the Define In option. After you click the OK button, the same CSS Style definition dialog box that you used in the previous section (see Figure 9-8) appears.

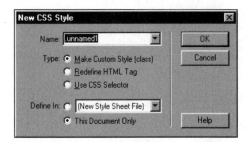

Figure 9-11   Make Custom Style (class) selection from the New CSS Style dialog box

Suppose you want to recreate the page shown in Figure 9-10 using custom styles instead of redefining HTML tags. You need to create a new style named .BigRedText by selecting Make Custom Style so that your screen looks like Figure 9-12. From the CSS Style definition dialog box, choose characteristics for red text and a larger text size for the Type category. (See Figure 9-13.)

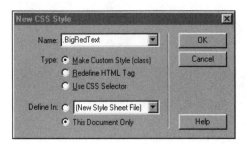

Figure 9-12   Naming a custom style for .BigRedText

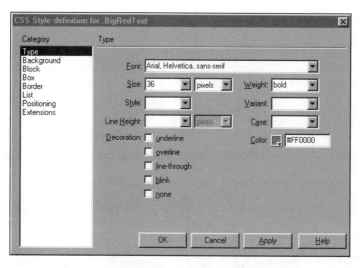

Figure 9-13   Setting the Type style for .BigRedText

Figure 9-14 shows the CSS Styles panel with the text "Happy Fourth of July." By selecting the text and clicking .BigRedText from the Styles dialog box, you can apply the style to the document (assuming that the Apply Styles option is chosen). The icon to the left of the CSS Styles *ʃ* indicates that the style applies to this document only. (The icon indicating an external style sheet is used is *⊞ʃ* .) You can also clear a style by selecting text with a defined style and then clicking the icon *ʃ* at the top of the styles panel. Custom styles are useful if special elements of text throughout a page need to be consistent. For example, if you want every phone number on a contact page to be of sans-serif font face, purple, and bold, you could define a custom class called .PhoneNumbers. You could then apply this style to every phone number on your page.

Figure 9-14   Applying a custom style from the CSS Styles panel

You apply custom styles to your HTML code when you call the style name in the body of the HTML document. Figure 9-15 shows the CSS Styles panel on a page similar to the one shown in Figure 9-10. Figure 9-16 displays the source code used to create these custom styles. In the document header, you still see the style tags, <style> and </style>. Between those tags the custom styles .BigRedText and .MedWhiteText are defined. Brackets following the style name enclose the attributes for these styles. In the body of the HTML document, the styles are called using a <p> tag and a class designator that calls the class by name. For example, `<p class="BigRedText">Happy Fourth of July</p>` formats the text "Happy Fourth of July" using the class .BigRedText.

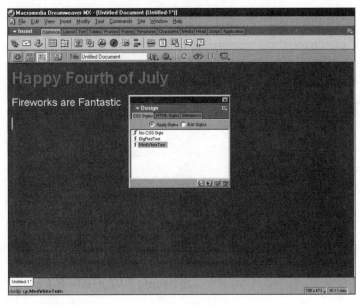

Figure 9-15   Applying custom styles

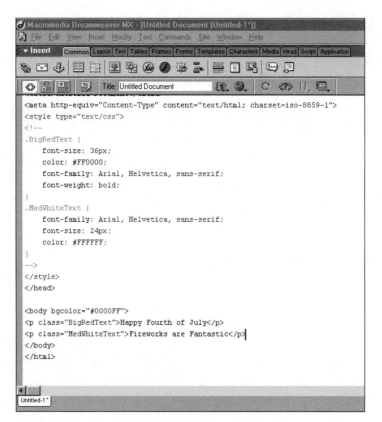

```
<meta http-equiv="Content-Type" content="text/html; charset=iso-8859-1">
<style type="text/css">
<!--
.BigRedText {
    font-size: 36px;
    color: #FF0000;
    font-family: Arial, Helvetica, sans-serif;
    font-weight: bold;
}
.MedWhiteText {
    font-family: Arial, Helvetica, sans-serif;
    font-size: 24px;
    color: #FFFFFF;
}
-->
</style>
</head>

<body bgcolor="#0000FF">
<p class="BigRedText">Happy Fourth of July</p>
<p class="MedWhiteText">Fireworks are Fantastic</p>
</body>
</html>
```

Figure 9-16   Source code for custom styles

Editing an Existing Style

An advantage of using HTML or custom styles is that you can change the look of an entire page simply by redefining the styles that make up that page. Without styles, you need to change all text on the page using the Property inspector. Using styles, you can change the style and apply it to the entire page. This saves time and ensures that your document remains consistent.

To edit an HTML or a custom style, you can double-click the style on the list on the CSS Styles panel, or you can select the style and click the Edit Style Sheet button ![icon]. Either of these actions opens the CSS Style definition dialog box shown in Figure 9-9. If the Apply Styles option is checked, be sure you double-click to edit a style. If you click only once, you may end up applying the style to an element selected on the page.

At the top of the CSS Styles panel, you can also click the Edit Styles radio button. The Styles panel then reformats to list your styles and attributes, as shown in Figure 9-17. From this view, you can edit and manage your styles. Again, you can change the attributes of each style by double-clicking the style or clicking the Edit Style Sheet button ![icon].

Figure 9-17   CSS Styles panel, Edit Styles view

Creating and Applying Custom Styles

In the next steps, you edit the consulting.htm page of the La Bonne Cuisine Web site. First, you redefine HTML tags for the h1 and h2 headings on the page. Then, you define custom styles for specific page elements.

To define HTML tags and custom styles:

1. Open Dreamweaver MX if it is not already open, and press **F8** to open the Site panel, if necessary. Select the **La Bonne Cuisine** site, and open the page **consulting.htm** in the consulting folder.

2. Press **Shift+F11** to open the CSS Styles panel, if it is not already open. Click the **Edit Styles** radio button so you can see what styles are defined for this document.

3. Click the **New CSS Style** button ⊞ to open the New CSS Style dialog box. Click the **Redefine HTML Tag** radio button. Click the **This Document Only** radio button to limit the style's scope to the current document. Click the **Tag** list arrow, and then click **h1**. Click **OK**. The CSS Style definition for h1 dialog box opens.

4. In the Type category, select the following attributes:
   - Weight: **bold**
   - Case: **uppercase**
   - Color: **#660066** (deep purple)

5. Under Category, click **Background** to access a new set of attributes. Type **#00CCCC** in the Background Color text box to change the background color for h1 to an aquagreen. Click **OK**. Observe that the Heading 1 text already contained in your document now appears with the new style.

6. Click the **New CSS Style** button ⊞. Ensure that the **Redefine HTML Tag** radio button and the **This Document Only** radio button are still selected. Click the **Tag** list arrow, and then click **h2** on the list. Click **OK**. The CSS Style definition for h2 dialog box opens.

7. In the Color text box of the Type category, type **#0066FF** (blue). Click **OK**. Observe that the Heading 2 text in your document is now blue.

8. Click the **New CSS Style** button ⊞. Ensure that the radio buttons for **Redefine HTML Tag** and **This Document Only** are selected. Click the **Tag** list arrow, and then click **p** on the list. Click **OK**. The CSS Style definition for p dialog box opens.

9. In the Type category, select:

   ■ Font: **Arial, Helvetica, sans-serif**

   ■ Size: **14 pixels**

10. Under Category, click **Block** to access a new set of attributes. Type **20** in the Text Indent text box. The value should be set automatically to **points**. Click **OK**.

11. Press **F12** to preview this page in your Web browser. Close your browser when you finish previewing the page. Save the page **consulting.htm**.

The next set of styles you define are known as custom styles. You define these for introductory text in paragraphs, for keywords, and for lists.

To define and apply custom styles:

1. Open Dreamweaver MX if it is not already open, press **F8** open the Site panel, if necessary, select the **La Bonne Cuisine** site, and open the page **consulting.htm** in the consulting folder.

2. Press **Shift+F11** to open the CSS Styles panel, if it is not already open. Click the **Edit Styles** radio button so you can see what styles are defined for this document.

3. In the CSS Styles panel, click the **New CSS Style** button ⊞. If it is not already selected, click the **Make Custom Style (class)** radio button. Under the option Define In, select **This Document Only**. Type **paraintro** in the Name text box. Click **OK**. The CSS Style definition for paraintro dialog box opens.

4. In the Type category, select:

   ■ Weight: **bold**

   ■ Color: **#009999** (aquagreen)

   Click **OK**. In the CSS Styles panel, you see the style paraintro.

9

5. Click the **Apply Styles** radio button in the CSS Styles panel. You should see your paraintro style in the panel. Select the text "**Trendy recipes that will fit into your menus**," and then click **paraintro** in the CSS Styles panel to change the text style to bold, green. You must deselect the text to see the style change.

6. Apply this style to the remainder of the paragraph introductions (Training kitchen staff on techniques, Manual Writing, Product Development, and Product Testing) on this Web page by selecting the text and clicking the **paraintro** style in the CSS Styles panel.

7. Click the **New CSS Style** button ⊞. Ensure that the radio buttons for **Make Custom Style (class)** and **This Document Only** are selected. Type **focuswords** in the Name text box. Click **OK**. The CSS Style definition for .focuswords dialog box opens.

8. Under the Type category, select the following attributes:

   - Weight: **bold**
   - Style: **italic**
   - Color: **#333333** (gray)

   Click **OK**. The style focuswords appears in the CSS Styles panel.

9. Click **focuswords** in the CSS Styles panel to apply this style to the following phrases by selecting the text:

   - Specializing in international cuisine for over 15 years
   - development of vegetarian and heart-healthy cuisine
   - storage and presentation techniques
   - 15 years of product development experience

   The gray emphasized text style shows in your workspace.

10. Press **F12** to preview this page in your Web browser. Save this file.

Using CSS Selectors

CSS selectors is the third option for creating CSS styles. Using CSS selectors, you can either group styles into one similar style, or you can define a style for links, active links, visited links, and hovers. Perhaps you have seen a Web site with responsive hyperlinks made of text rollovers. You can use CSS selectors to create a rollover effect that does not require the use of images.

If you want to apply a specific, consistent attribute to many tags, you can use grouping with CSS selectors. For example, suppose you want all your heading text to be blue. You could group all the heading tags using the CSS selector option in the Styles panel. Then, whenever you add a heading to your document, its color is always the same blue you defined using the CSS selector. To group HTML tags into a single style, you can type the tag names into the New Style dialog box using commas to separate them, as shown in Figure 9-18. Clicking OK opens the CSS Style definition dialog box, so that you can select a common style for the set of tags.

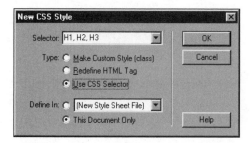

Figure 9-18 Defining a style for multiple tags using the CSS Selector

Grouping these HTML tags and using a similar style is another efficient way to achieve consistency on a Web page. Furthermore, if you decide to change the three headings to green, you need only edit the style and change one color tag from blue to green. The style will be applied to the entire page.

You can also use CSS selectors to alter the link, active link, visited link, and hover options for hyperlinks. To do this from the New CSS Style dialog box, select Use CSS Selector option, and select the element you want to change from the Selector drop-down list shown in Figure 9-19. When you use this option, you actually define a style for your link options within the header of your document. When you create links, they have the attributes you define in the header of the document.

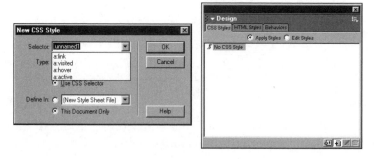

Figure 9-19 Redefining hyperlink attributes

Suppose you want to create a page on which hyperlink text is pink, bold, Arial font. When a viewer moves the pointer over the hyperlink, you want the text to enlarge and turn a deeper color of pink. To do this, you use a CSS selector, creating a new style in the CSS Style definition dialog box for a:link and a:hover. Figure 9-20 shows how your source code looks. The selectors are defined in the header of the document, and look like custom classes. When you preview this page in your Web browser, you see the hyperlink styles implemented. Note that Netscape 4.x does not support this style.

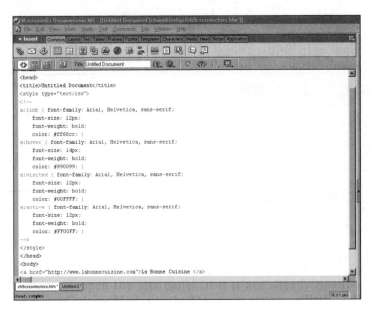

Figure 9-20 Source code for CSS selectors

Note

Using the CSS Selector, you can create hyperlinks with no underlined text. To do this from the CSS Styles panel, create a new style designated CSS selector. The text list menu gives you options for a:active, a:hover, a:link, and a:visited. Select a:link. Then, in the Type category of the CSS Styles definition dialog box for a:link, make sure to select the none checkbox under Decoration. You can apply this attribute to a:active, a:hover, and a:visited as well.

Creating and Implementing CSS Selectors

In the steps below you edit the consulting.htm page of the La Bonne Cuisine Web site to change the link attributes using CSS selectors. You change the hyperlinks so they appear with the default blue text and no underline. When a viewer moves the pointer over the text (a:hover), it appears underlined, bold, and a bit lighter than the default blue text. A visited (a:visited) or active (a:active) link appears as gray underlined text. The page contains links for contacting La Bonne Cuisine and to other portions of the Web site. You also add links for three samples of La Bonne Cuisine's services.

To specify link attributes and add links:

1. Open Dreamweaver MX if it is not already open, press **F8** to open the Site panel, if necessary, select the **La Bonne Cuisine** site, and open the page **consulting.htm** in the consulting folder.

2. Press **Shift+F11** to open the CSS Styles panel, if it is not already open. Click the **Edit Styles** radio button on the CSS Styles panel so you can see the styles associated with this document.

3. Click the **New CSS Style** button [+]. Click the **Use CSS Selector** radio button to select it, and click the **This Document Only** radio button to select it. The CSS selectors let you change the appearance of hyperlinks on the Web page by using a style. Click the **Selector** list arrow, and click **a:link**. Click **OK**. The CSS Style Definition for a:link dialog box opens.

4. In the Type category, click the **none** checkbox under Decoration to select it. Select **#3366FF** in the Color text box. Click **OK**. This removes underlining from hyperlink text.

5. Click the **New CSS Style** button [+]. Ensure that the radio buttons **Use CSS Selector** and **This Document Only** are selected. Click the **Selector** list arrow, and click **a:hover**. Click **OK**. The CSS Style definition for a:hover dialog box opens. In the Type category, select:

   ■ Weight: **bold**

   ■ Color: **#FFCC00** (blue)

   ■ Decoration: **none**

   Click **OK**.

6. In the CSS Styles panel, make sure **a:hover** is selected by clicking it with your mouse. Choose **Duplicate** from the Design panel group Options menu. The Duplicate CSS Style dialog box opens. Click the **Selector** drop-down list, and click **a:visited**. Click **OK**.

7. Repeat Step 6, but this time, click **a:active** in the Selector drop-down list. Click **OK**.

8. Preview the page in your Web browser (**F12**), and observe that the hyperlinks at the bottom of the page are not underlined. (Note that the hover effect may not work in some browser versions.) Close your Web browser when you finish previewing the page.

9. Save this page.

Linking to an External Style Sheet

In the previous sections, you defined styles that applied to one document only. Most Web sites are considerably larger than one page and more complex. By linking to an external style sheet you can apply styles uniformly to an entire Web site instead of individual pages. For example, consider a Web site with 50 pages linked to a style sheet that defines styles for h1, h2, and the custom class .specialitems. If you decide to change the color and size of the h1 and h2 headings and set the .specialitems custom class to Arial, bold, 14 point, you need only edit the external style sheet, rather than change each of the 50 pages. Every h1, h2, and .specialitem class adopts the new style.

An external style sheet has the file extension .css. That is, julystyle.css is a valid name for a style sheet, while julystyle.htm is not. To use an external style sheet, the HTML document must contain a link to the style sheet in the header of the document. You format the link as follows:

```
<link rel="stylesheet" href="julystyle.css">
```

You must place this link between the head tags at the top of the HTML document. Every document that uses the styles defined in the style sheet must contain a link to the file.

If you have already defined styles for one page and wish to use them throughout a Web site, the Options menu on the CSS Styles panel (see Figure 9-21) lets you export styles. Alternatively, you can click File on the Dreamweaver menu bar, point to Export, and then click Export CSS Styles.

 When you export the style sheet, this doesn't automatically link the style sheet to the page from which you exported. Those styles are still defined internally to that document.

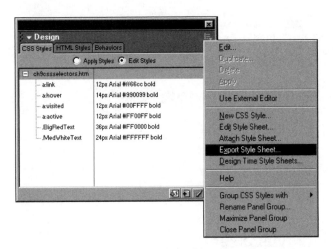

Figure 9-21   Exporting CSS styles

When prompted for a filename, you should name the file descriptively, so that you can readily access it. Figure 9-22 shows the Export Styles dialog box, naming a style sheet for summer styles. You need to ensure that the filename extension is .css, not .htm.

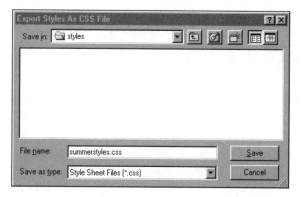

Figure 9-22   Saving an external style sheet

After you save the external style sheet, you can open a new or existing Web page, open the CSS Styles panel and link to the external style sheet by clicking the Attach Style Sheet button ![button]. A dialog box opens, shown in Figure 9-23, which enables you to import the styles or simply link to the existing style sheet. You can browse your directory structure for the style sheet file. Remember to select a .css file. When you select the file, Dreamweaver inserts a link in the HTML code, as shown in Figure 9-24.

9

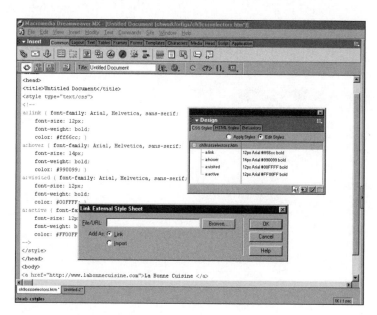

Figure 9-23   Linking to a style sheet

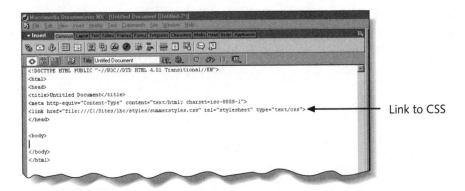

Figure 9-24 Source code displaying link to external style sheet

If you know you will use an external style sheet when you begin editing a page, you can click the Define In radio button, and then select New Style Sheet File, as shown in Figure 9-25. Selecting this option lets you create the style sheet file externally before you begin editing your page. As you define new styles while you work, you can save them in the external style sheet rather than saving them in the header of the Web page you are editing. After the styles are saved in an external style sheet, you can apply the external style sheet to as many HTML documents as you like by attaching them using the CSS Styles panel. You can define both internal and external styles for an HTML document. Styles called from an external style sheet show a linked style icon ☰ᶠ next to the custom style name, as shown in Figure 9-26.

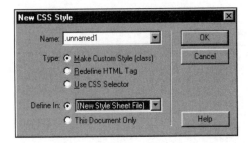

Figure 9-25 Selecting New Style Sheet File

Figure 9-26   CSS Styles panel showing attached styles

Creating and Implementing External Style Sheets

In the following steps, you export the styles you created on the consulting.htm page of the La Bonne Cuisine Web site so that you can apply them to more Web pages.

To export and apply styles:

1. Open Dreamweaver MX if it is not already open, press **F8** to open the Site panel, if necessary, select the **La Bonne Cuisine** site, and open the page **consulting.htm** in the consulting folder.

2. Choose **Export Style Sheet** from the Design panel group Options menu. The Export Styles As CSS File dialog box opens.

3. In the Export Styles As CSS File dialog box, type **consultingstyles.css** as the name of the file and make sure to save it in the Sites\lbc\consulting folder on your working drive. The Save as type text box should indicate Style Sheet Files. Click **Save**. After you export this file, you can link other pages to it to apply these styles.

4. In Dreamweaver MX, open the file **manufacturing.htm** located in the Sites\lbc\consulting folder. You can find it in the consulting folder in the La Bonne Cuisine Site panel.

5. Press **Shift+F11** to open the CSS Styles panel, if it is not already open.

6. Click the **Attach Style Sheet** button 🔗 to open the Link External Style Sheet dialog box. Make sure the **Link** radio button is selected after Add As.

7. Click **Browse**, and navigate to and select the file **consultingstyles.css** that you just created in the Sites\lbc\consulting folder. Click **OK**. Observe that it appears in the text box. Click **OK**.

8. Observe that some changes occurred on the page.

9. Open the files **tastetesting.htm** and **recipecards.htm**, and repeat Steps 5 through 7 to create links to the consultingstyle.css style sheet.

10. Save your work for all files.

11. Preview all the modified pages in your Web browser to see that the effects have been applied. You can preview the consulting.htm Web page and then click the hyperlinks at the bottom to preview the other pages. Close your browser when you finish.

CHAPTER SUMMARY

❏ You can use style sheets to give your Web sites a coherent, consistent appearance and to edit your Web pages more efficiently, because you can make format changes to style sheets and apply them to an entire page or an entire site.

❏ Dreamweaver MX helps you create HTML styles and CSS styles (internal or external styles) by providing a series of style definition menus and dialog boxes in which you specify style attributes.

❏ CSS styles can be applied to an entire Web page.

❏ Using the CSS Selector option in the CSS Styles panel, you can redefine the attributes of a hyperlink. The four hyperlink states are active, hover, link, and visited. By redefining the styles for each of these states, you can create unique hyperlink attributes.

❏ You can create an external style sheet by exporting an existing document's styles to a .css file. You can link several HTML documents to the .css file to achieve the same style formatting as the original document.

REVIEW QUESTIONS

1. What are some advantages of using style sheets? Choose all that apply.

   a. Style sheets ensure consistency throughout a Web site.

   b. Style sheets can override existing styles.

   c. Style sheets make Web site changes and maintenance more efficient.

   d. Style sheets can be used to create rollover text.

2. In the following source code, what does "h1" represent?

   ```
   h1 {color: #FF0000}
   ```

   a. Selector

   b. Declaration

   c. Assignment statement

   d. Hexadecimal color code

3. In the following source code, what does "color: #FF0000" represent?

    ```
    H1 {color: #FF0000}
    ```

    a. Selector

    b. Declaration

    c. Assignment statement

    d. Hexadecimal color code

4. Regarding style sheets, what does the concept of inheritance mean?

5. Which tag indicates that a style is defined in the source code?

    a. <style>

    b. <css>

    c. <link>

    d. <style sheet>

6. What are the three types of styles used in HTML documents?

7. Why is a style sheet called cascading?

8. HTML styles can change the color and font of text. True or False?

9. You can apply CSS styles to multiple documents. True or False?

10. Choose the three style formats you can create with the CSS Styles panel:

    a. Redefine HTML tags

    b. Make Custom Style

    c. Use CSS Selector

    d. Export Global Styles

11. Redefining HTML tags requires you to create another name for the tag. True or False?

12. Using the CSS Selector option in Dreamweaver MX, you can: (choose all that apply)

    a. redefine HTML tags.

    b. group HTML tags into one style.

    c. change hyperlink attributes.

    d. define a custom class.

13. How is a custom class implemented in the HTML source code?

14. In the code sample below, "BigRedText" is:

    ```
    <span class="BigRedText">Happy Fourth of July</span>
    ```

    a. a canned definition for that style.

    b. an assigned name for a custom class.

    c. a redefined HTML tag.

    d. all of the above.

9

15. To change an existing style, you must delete it from the CSS Styles panel. True or False?

16. Which of the following are options for redefining hyperlink attributes using the CSS Selector? (Choose all that apply.)

    a. a:hover

    b. a:link

    c. a:over

    d. a:href

17. How do you create a hyperlink without underlined text?

18. Using Dreamweaver MX to group HTML tags into a style requires you to edit the source code. True or False?

19. You can create an external style sheet by exporting CSS styles from an open document. True or False?

20. An external style sheet must be called prior to the beginning of an HTML document. True or False?

HANDS-ON PROJECTS

Project 9-1

In this project you use HTML styles to format a Web page with the instructions for frying an egg.

1. Using Windows Explorer, create the folder **ch9practice** in the Sites directory on your working drive. Create a folder called **images** within the ch9practice folder. Copy the file **eggs.htm** from the Chapter9 data folder to your Sites\ch9practice folder.

2. Open the **eggs.htm** file in Dreamweaver MX. The eggs.htm file contains plain text with no formatting. Open the HTML Styles panel (**Ctrl+F11**), if it is not already open. In this exercise, you use the HTML Styles panel and the Properties inspector (**Ctrl+F3**).

3. Click the **New Style** button [image] at the bottom of the HTML Styles panel. The Define HTML Style dialog box opens. In the **Name** text box, type **Egg Title**. Click the radio buttons to select **Selection** and **Clear Existing Style**. Change the Font Attributes to Font: **Arial**, **Helvetica**, **sans-serif**, Size: **+5**, Color: **#CC6600** (orange), Style: **bold**, **italicized**. Click **OK**. An HTML style named Egg Title appears in the panel.

4. Select the text **Tutorial on How to Fry an Egg**, and click **Egg Title** in the styles list on the HTML Styles panel. Deselect the text and observe that you applied the style.

5. Select the text listing the five items needed to fry the egg (**Frying Pan**, **Butter**, **Eggs**, **Stove**, and **Spatula**), and click the **Unordered List** button in the Properties panel to create a bulleted list.

6. Click the **New CSS Style** button at the bottom of the HTML Styles panel to open the Define HTML Style dialog box. In the Name text box, type **Egg Subtitle**. Click to select the radio buttons for **Paragraph** and **Clear Existing Style**. Change the Font Attributes to Font: **Arial**, **Helvetica**, **sans-serif**, Size: **+1**, Color: **#FFCC00** (gold), Style: **bold**. Click **OK**. The new style name appears in the HTML Styles panel.

7. Select the text **Necessary Items:** and click **Egg Subtitle** in the styles list on the HTML Styles panel. Deselect the text and observe that you applied the style. Repeat this step to apply the Egg Subtitle style to the text **Directions** and **Yum! Yum!**.

8. Click the **New Style** button on the HTML Styles panel again. In the **Name** text box, type **Red Text**. Click to select the radio buttons for **Selection** and **Add to Existing Style**. Set the Font attribute to **Default Font**, the Size attribute to **None**, and make sure that the Bold and Italic styles are not selected. Change the text color to **#FF0000** (red). Click **OK**. The new style name appears in the HTML Styles panel.

9. Select the bulleted list and click the style **Red Text** in the HTML Styles panel. Deselect the text and observe the red text in the bulleted list. Select the paragraph of text that gives directions for frying the egg, and click the **Red Text** style again. The paragraph appears with red text.

10. Select the text **Yum! Yum!**, and click the style **Red Text** in the HTML Styles panel. Deselect the text and observe that the text is red and still has the previously existing style (Arial font with size +1). The Red Text style overlays the Egg Subtitle style.

11. Double-click the **Red Text** style in the HTML Styles panel to open the Define HTML Style dialog box for Red Text. Click the radio button for **Clear Existing Style** to select it. Click **OK**. Observe that the plus sign on the icon next to the Red Text style disappeared. Select the **Yum! Yum!** text again, and click the **Red Text** style. Deselect the text to see the previously existing style cleared and the text with only a red color. Select the **Yum! Yum!** text again, and click the **Egg Subtitle** style in the HTML Styles panel to reapply the style.

12. Save the page **eggs.htm** in your Sites\ch9practice folder.

Project 9-2

In this project you use CSS styles to give a Web resume a more interesting appearance.

1. Using Windows Explorer copy the file **joesresume.htm** from the Chapter9 data folder into your Sites\ch9practice folder. Open the **joesresume.htm** file in Dreamweaver MX. You are going to edit a plain text file listing Joe Black's accomplishments. Open the CSS Styles panel (**Shift+F11**), if it is not already

open. Make sure the radio button for **Apply Styles** is selected in the Styles panel so you can apply the styles you create. You use the CSS Styles panel throughout this exercise. No other panels are necessary.

2. Click the **New CSS Style** button ⊞ at the bottom of the CSS Styles panel to open the New CSS Style dialog box. Click to select the radio buttons for **Make Custom Style (class)** under Type, and **This Document Only** under Define In. In the **Name** text box, type **name**. Click **OK**. The CSS Style definition for .name dialog box opens.

3. In the CSS Style definition dialog box, under the Type category, select the following settings:

   ❑ Font: **Arial, Helvetica, sans-serif**

   ❑ Color: **#0000FF** (blue)

   ❑ Size: **16**

   ❑ Style: **italic**

   Click **OK**. The CSS style name appears in the list of styles in the CSS Styles panel.

4. Click the **New CSS Style** button ⊞ on the CSS Styles panel again. Ensure that the radio buttons are selected for **Make Custom Style (class)** under Type, and **This Document Only** under Define In. In the **Name** text box, type **topics**. Click **OK**. The CSS Style definition for .topics dialog box opens.

5. In the CSS Style definition dialog box, under the Type category, select the following settings:

   ❑ Font: **Arial, Helvetica, sans-serif**

   ❑ Color: **#333333** (gray)

   ❑ Size: **14**

   Click **OK**.

6. Click the **New CSS Style** button ⊞ on the CSS Styles panel again. Ensure that the radio buttons are selected for **Make Custom Style (class)** under Type, and **This Document Only** under Define In. In the **Name** text box, type **objective**. Click **OK**. The CSS Style definition for .objective dialog box opens.

7. In the CSS Style definition for .objective dialog box, under the Type category, select the following settings:

   ❑ Color: **#0066FF** (blue)

   ❑ Size: **14**

   ❑ Style: **italic**

   Click **OK**.

8. Observe that the CSS Styles panel displays the three styles you just created.

9. Select Joe Black's name and address in the workspace, and click the style **name**. Deselect the text and observe that the name and address text is now blue and italic.

10. Select all text describing the objective, and click the **objective** style in the CSS Styles panel. Deselect the text and observe that it is now blue and italicized.

11. Select the text **Previous Work Experience**, and click the **topics** style in the CSS Styles panel. Deselect the text and observe that it is now smaller and gray. Apply the topic style to the text **Skills and Education** by selecting the text and clicking the **topics** style in the CSS Styles panel.

12. Save **joesresume.htm**. Preview the page in your Web browser (**F12**). Close the browser window when you finish previewing your page.

Project 9-3

In this project you use the same CSS styles that you created in Project 9-2. To do this, you export the styles from joesresume.htm and import them into janesresume.htm. You also use some more advanced features of CSS styles to give Jane's resume a more interesting appearance.

1. In Dreamweaver MX, open the file **joesresume.htm** that you edited in Project 9-2, if it is not already open. Click **File** on the Dreamweaver menu bar, point to **Export**, and then click **CSS Styles**. In the Export Styles As CSS File dialog box, type **resume.css** as the filename for the external style sheet. Make sure you save the file **resume.css** in your ch9practice folder. Click **Save**.

2. Using Windows Explorer, copy the file **janesresume.htm** from the Chapter9 data folder to your Sites\ch9practice folder. Copy the file **monogram.gif** from the Chapter9\images data folder to your Sites\ch9practice\images folder. Open the file **janesresume.htm** in Dreamweaver MX.

3. Open the CSS Styles panel (**Shift+F11**), if it is not already open. Click the **Attach Style Sheet** button to open the Link External Style Sheet dialog box. With the **Link** radio button selected, click **Browse** and select the file **resume.css** located in the ch9practice folder. Click **OK**. Click **OK** again to link to the file. In the CSS Styles panel, you see the styles you created in the previous project (name, topics, and objective). You can also see that they are linked to janesresume.htm via a style sheet.

4. Make sure the radio button for **Apply Styles** is selected at the top of the CSS Styles panel. Select Jane's name and address, and apply the **name** style by clicking it in the CSS Styles panel.

5. Select the text **Education** and apply the **topics** style by clicking it in the CSS Styles panel. Repeat for the text **Work Experience**, **Skills**, and **Other**.

6. Click the **New CSS Style** button at the bottom of the CSS Styles panel to open the New CSS Style dialog box. Click to select the radio buttons for **Redefine HTML Tag** under Type and **This Document Only** under Define In. In the **Tag** text box, use the list arrow to select the **body** tag. Click **OK**. The CSS Style definition for body dialog box opens.

7. In the CSS Style definition dialog box, click the **Background** category. Click the **Browse** button for the Background Image text box. Click to select the file **monogram.gif** from the Sites\ch9practice\images folder. Click **OK**. In the Repeat text box, use the list arrow to select **no–repeat**. For the Attachment option, select **fixed**. For Horizontal Position, select **center**. For Vertical Position, select **center**. Click **OK**.

8. Save **janesresume.htm**.

9. Preview the page in your Web browser (**F12**). If you use Internet Explorer, you see that the monogram remains centered on the page while the text scrolls. (This effect does not work in Netscape Navigator 4.x.) Close the browser when you finish previewing the page.

Project 9-4

In this project you use CSS styles to create a simple, controlled format for a campus newspaper.

1. Using Windows Explorer, copy the file **campusnews.htm** from the Chapter9 data folder into your Sites\ch9practice folder. In Dreamweaver MX, open the file **campusnews.htm**.

2. Open the CSS Styles panel (**Shift+F11**), if it is not already open.

3. Click the **New CSS Style** button ⊞ at the bottom of the CSS Styles panel to open the New CSS Style dialog box. Ensure that the radio buttons are selected for **Make Custom Style (class)** under Type, and **New Style Sheet File** under Define In. In the **Name** text box, type **papertitle**. Click **OK**. A dialog box prompts you for a style sheet name. Name the style sheet **news.css**, and make sure to save this file in the ch9practice folder. Click **Save**. The CSS Style definition for .papertitle in news.css dialog box opens.

4. Under the Type category, select the following attributes:

   ❑ Font: **Arial**, **Helvetica**, **sans-serif**

   ❑ Size: **36**

   ❑ Color: **#FFFFFF** (white)

   Click **OK**.

5. Select the text **Inter Campus News** in the Dreamweaver workspace, and apply the **papertitle** style by clicking it in the CSS Styles panel. Deselect the text to see its changed appearance.

6. Click the **New CSS Style** button ⊞ at the bottom of the CSS Styles panel to open the New CSS Style dialog box. Ensure that the radio buttons for **Make Custom Style (class)** under Type, and **news.css** under Define In are selected. In the **Name** text box, type **issue**. Click **OK**. The CSS Style Definition for .issue in news.css dialog box opens.

7. Under the Type category, select the following attributes:
   - Size: **36**
   - Style: **italic**
   - Weight: **bold**
   - Color: **#000000** (black)

   Select the **Block** category, then select **right** in the Text Align text box. Click **OK**.

8. Select the text **This Issue:** in the Dreamweaver workspace, and apply the **issue** style by clicking it in the CSS Styles panel. Select the text **15 April 2003**, and apply the **issue** style again.

9. Click the **New CSS Style** button ⊞ to open the New CSS Style dialog box. Ensure that the radio buttons are selected for **Make Custom Style (class)** under Type, and **news.css** under Define In. In the **Name** text box, type **subtitle**. Click **OK**. The CSS Style definition for .subtitle in news.css dialog box opens.

10. Under the Type category, select the following attributes:
    - Font: **Arial, Helvetica, sans-serif**
    - Size: **14**
    - Color: **#FF6600** (orange)

    Click **OK**.

11. Select the text **An Online Publication of CU**, and apply the **subtitle** style by clicking it in the CSS Styles panel. Repeat this step for the text in the upper-right corner of the table that lists the topics that the paper contains (Summer Jobs through Deans Report, inclusive). Deselect the text to see the style applied.

12. Click the **New CSS Style** button ⊞ to open the New CSS Style dialog box. Ensure that the radio buttons are selected for **Make Custom Style (class)** under Type, and **news.css** under Define In. In the **Name** text box, type **copytitle**. Click **OK**. The CSS Style definition for .copytitle in news.css dialog box opens.

13. Under the Type category, select the following attributes:
    - Font: **Arial, Helvetica, sans-serif**
    - Size: **14**
    - Color: **#000000** (black)

    Click **OK**.

14. Select the text **Finding a Summer Job that is Right for You**, and apply the **copytitle** style by clicking it in the CSS Styles panel. Repeat for the text **Campus Drug Use** and **Dean's Report**.

9

15. Click the **New CSS Style** button 🖃 to open the New CSS Style dialog box. Ensure that the radio buttons are selected for **Make Custom Style (class)** under Type, and **news.css** under Define In. In the **Name** text box, type **copytext**. Click **OK**. The CSS Style definition for .copytext in news.css dialog box opens.

16. Under the Type category, select the following attributes:

    ⊐ Font: **Times New Roman**, **Times**, **serif**

    ⊐ Size: **12**

    ⊐ Color: **#000099** (dark blue)

    Click **OK**.

17. Select the text of each paragraph in the news, and apply the **copytext** style by clicking it in the CSS Styles panel. You should apply this style to four paragraphs.

18. Preview your page (**F12**). Close the browser window when you finish previewing. Save the file **campusnews.htm**.

Project 9-5

In this project you open the campusnews.htm file that you created in Project 9-4 and change the appearance of the Web page by editing the external style sheet.

1. Using Windows Explorer, duplicate the files **news.css** and **campusnews.htm** in the Sites\ch9practice folder, and rename the copies **news2.css** and **campusnews2.htm**, respectively. Open the file **campusnews2.htm** in Dreamweaver MX.

2. The file campusnews2.htm is still linked to the external style sheet news.css. You need to relink this file to news2.css. Open the CSS Styles panel (**Shift + F11**) if it is not already open. Make sure the **Edit Styles** radio button at the top of the panel is selected. Click the file **news.css** to select it and click **Delete Style** 🗑 to eliminate the link to the old style sheet. Click the **Attach Style Sheet** button ⊶ at the bottom of the CSS Styles panel. With the **Link** radio button selected, click **Browse**, and locate the file news2.css in the ch9practice folder. Select **news2.css** by clicking it. Click **OK** to close the Select Style Sheet File dialog box. Click **OK** again to close the Link External Style Sheet dialog box. Because the two files are the same, your document should look like it did when you first opened it. Now you can edit news2.css without affecting your original file from the previous exercise.

3. Click the **Edit Style Sheet** button 🖼 to open the Edit Style Sheet dialog box. Select **news2.css** and click the **Edit** button. A dialog box opens listing the five styles you created in Project 9-4.

4. Click the **papertitle** style and press the **Edit** button. The CSS Style definition for .papertitle in news.css dialog box opens. In the Type category, change the color of the text from white to **#FFFF00** (yellow). Click **OK**.

5. Double-click the **copytext** style to open the CSS Style definition for .copytext in news2.css dialog box. In the Type category, change the text color to **#FFFFFF** (white). Click **OK**.

6. Double-click the **copytitle** style to open the CSS Style definition for .copytitle in news2.css dialog box. In the Type category, change the text color to **#FF0000** (red). Click **OK**.

7. In the news2.css dialog box, click **New** to open the New CSS Style dialog box. Click the **Redefine HTML Tag** radio button to select it. In the Tag list box, select **body**. Make sure **news2.css** is selected under Define In. Click **OK**. The CSS Style definition dialog box opens. Click **Background** under Category and change the Background Color to **#000000** (black). Click **OK**.

8. Click **Save** in the news2.css window. Click **Done** in the Edit Style Sheet dialog box. Observe that the page has changed.

9. Preview the page (**F12**). Close your browser when you finish previewing the page. Save the file **campusnews2.htm**.

Project 9-6

In this project you add hyperlinks to campusnews.htm and format them using CSS selectors to create a rollover effect.

1. In Dreamweaver MX, open the file **campusnews.htm** in your ch9practice folder on your working drive.

2. Open the CSS Styles panel (**Shift+F11**), if it is not already open. Click the **Attach Style Sheet** button [image] to open the Link External Style Sheet dialog box. With the radio button for **Link** selected, click **Browse**. Type **links.css** in the File name text box, and make sure the Sites\ch9practice folder is selected. Click **OK**. Click **OK** again. You will be prompted that the file does not exist. Click **Yes** to create it and return to your document.

3. Click the radio button for **Edit Styles** at the top of the CSS Styles panel. Click **links.css** to select it. Click the **New CSS Style** button [image] at the bottom of the CSS Styles panel to open the New CSS Style dialog box. Click the **Use CSS Selector** radio button to select it. In the Selector text box, use the list arrow to select **a:link**. In the Define In text box, make sure **links.css** is selected. Click **OK**. The CSS Style definition for a:link in links.css dialog box opens.

4. In the CSS Style definition dialog box, under the Type category, select the following attributes:

   ❑ Decoration: **none**

   ❑ Weight: **bold**

   ❑ Color: **#0000FF** (blue)

   Click **OK**.

5. Click the **New CSS Style** button [image] to open the New CSS Style dialog box. The radio buttons should still be selected for **Use CSS Selector**, and for **links.css** in the Define In text box. In the Selector text box, use the list arrow to select **a:hover**. Click **OK**. The CSS Style definition for a:hover in links.css dialog box opens.

9

6. In the CSS Style definition dialog box, under the Type category, select the following attributes:

   ❑ Decoration: **none**

   ❑ Weight: **bold**

   ❑ Color: **#FF6600** (orange)

   Click **OK**.

7. Repeat Steps 5 and 6 for the remaining CSS selectors, a:visited and a:active, setting the attributes to Decoration: **none**, Weight: **bold**, and Color: **#FF0000** (red).

8. Save this page as **campusnews3.htm** in your Sites\ch9practice folder.

9. Preview your page (**F12**). In Internet Explorer the text looks like a rollover (blue text turns red) when the pointer passes over it. Underlines for hyperlinks are absent. Close your Web browser.

CASE PROJECTS

Create external style sheets for Halloween, Fourth of July, and New Year's Eve, selecting appropriate colors and fonts for the three holidays. Create a personal Web page that contains information about you: your birthdate, your activities and hobbies, your favorite TV show, etc. Apply the different style sheets to your personal Web page. Did you capture the style for each holiday? What happens when you link to more than one style sheet?

Create a resume in Dreamweaver MX that uses HTML styles. Use specific styles to make your resume more readable and to highlight specific expertise.

Build a simple navigation bar for a site that promotes tourism in Mexico. Using CSS selectors, create three different rollover effects. Which one is most aesthetically appealing and why? Choose your best effect and use it to create a navigation bar with six links that comprise the Baja Tours navigation bar. Create a home page for the Baja Tours company that includes your navigation bar.

Build a Web site for a small business that designs custom perfumes for individual clients. Kate's Perfume interviews clients, gets to know their personalities and scent preferences, and then assists them in designing their personalized perfumes. Customers can also purchase aromatherapy soaps, candles, and bath accessories. The style of the site should be controlled by an external style sheet. The navigation menu shown on each page should use CSS Selectors to eliminate the underline decoration and show rollover text. There should be five subpages to this site.

Pick a topic for a small business page for which you would like to build a Web site. Think about the target audience, the objective of the Web site, and the type of content that your customers would expect on your site. Build a Web site that takes advantage of internal and external styles to make page development and maintenance more efficient.

DYNAMIC HTML

Working with Layers, Behaviors, and Timelines

In this chapter, you will:

♦ Discover how Dynamic HTML (DHTML) can enliven Web sites

♦ Create and manipulate layers "on top" of your Web document

♦ Create Dreamweaver MX behaviors and event handlers to control layers

♦ Create simple animation using layers on a timeline

Adding interactive, dynamic content to a Web site lets you engage the user in a more tactile, visual way. User interaction with your Web site is an electronic handshake with your customer. The more time users spend on a Web site, the stronger their relationship with the company.

In Chapter 5, you learned to lay out a Web page using layers. After you completed the layout, you used a Dreamweaver MX utility to convert the layers into an HTML table. This is a fast, visual way to create a controlled layout without the restrictions of working initially with a table. In this chapter, you create and then manipulate layers using the Timelines and Behaviors panels, so that the layers appear to move on the page. You create this movement using Dreamweaver MX-generated JavaScript. Positioning and manipulating layers with JavaScript is called Dynamic HTML.

DYNAMIC HTML

Dynamic HTML (DHTML) refers to the combined use of HTML and JavaScript to make a page that users can control or respond to. For example, a Web page can contain an animated graphic with play, stop, and pause buttons that users can click to control the animation. The page is interactive because the user controls what happens. Dreamweaver MX helps you develop DHTML Web pages by generating and providing panels on which you can create and configure layers, animation, and pre-scripted behaviors. The code that executes DHTML combines JavaScript and HTML. **JavaScript** is the default script language in most Web browsers. Programming in JavaScript lets you create a more responsive and dynamic page. JavaScript functions appear within <script> tags in your document and are called in the code when a specific event handler is executed. An **event handler** is a method that activates a function or action. Examples of JavaScript event handlers include onLoad, onClick, onMouseDown, onMouseOver, onMouseUp, and onDrop. When activated, the event handler or action causes a specified behavior or event to take place on your Web page. Event handlers are usually easy to understand. For example, the onClick event is the user clicking the mouse button. Some event handlers have less obvious meanings, such as OnFocus. The OnFocus event occurs when the user clicks an object or presses the Tab key to get to an object. A text field in a form could be the OnFocus object.

Netscape Navigator and Internet Explorer support some different event handlers. Dreamweaver MX provides a quick lookup feature, so that you can easily see which event handlers are available and test them in either browser. A pseudocode example of an event handler in action is "onLoad, play the animation." This tells the browser to execute a JavaScript function controlling the animation when the Web page loads.

The following code shows the simplest rollover you could create.

```
<A HREF="http://www.lbcuisine.com"
onMouseOver="document.logo.src='images/glow_lbclogo.gif'"
onMouseOut="document.logo.src='images/lbclogo.gif'">

<IMG SRC="images/lbclogo.gif" WIDTH=100 HEIGHT=118 BORDER=0
NAME="logo"></A>
```

The first line sets up a hyperlink to the La Bonne Cuisine Web site. The second line lists an event handler, onMouseover, that indicates to load the file glow_lbclogo.gif from the images subfolder when the mouse is placed over the image. The third line tells the browser to load the image lbclogo.gif when the mouse moves off the image, onMouseout. The next line of code sets the initial image that is displayed on the page, which is the onMouseout image, lbclogo.gif. This is a very simple script that would be placed in the body of your Web page. However, it is too simple for today's Web sites. Using JavaScript, you can preload your images in the header of your document, making your rollovers much more responsive. Dreamweaver MX does this for you by writing JavaScript functions in the header of the document when you create a rollover. Similarly, with DHTML, the JavaScript is generated for you as functions created in the header of the file.

Flash is another animation tool, which creates vector-based animation that typically loads and runs quickly, with smoother and more movie-like visual effects. To run Flash animation, users must download a Flash plugin. DHTML, on the other hand, requires no plugin.

When incorporating animated graphics into your Web sites, be careful to provide easy exits, so that users are not forced to view something. A user might find the animation frivolous, may have already seen it, or may not have the system resources or connection speed to view the graphics successfully. Adding a skip button to your Web page lets users bypass the animation and go directly to page content. Consider what type of client visits the site to determine how much animation and dynamic content to include.

LAYERS

10

Layers let you place (stack) objects on top of other objects or text on a Web page. In Chapter 5 you created layers and then converted them into tables to control the layout of a Web site. In this chapter, you stack and overlap the layers and program them to move on your Web page. You can control layer attributes, such as starting and stopping position on the page, and the stack position with respect to the other layers on the page.

To insert a layer on a Web page, click the Draw Layer button 📰 on the Insert bar Common tab shown in Figure 10-1, and then click and drag the crosshairs on the workspace to draw the layer. (Note that you must be in Standard view to draw layers.) A layer on the workspace looks like a blank box, as shown in the top rectangle in Figure 10-2. These outlines are invisible when you preview your page or when you upload it to the Internet. When you select a layer, small black squares, called handles, appear around the layer; you can click and drag these handles to resize a layer. To select a layer, you can click inside the layer, click the tab at the top of the layer, or click the edge of the layer. Clicking inside the layer lets you add content to it. Clicking the Layer tab selects the layer so that you can modify its attributes. When you want to reposition a layer, drag it by the Layer tab in the upper-left corner of the layer.

Draw Layer button

Figure 10-1   Common tab of the Insert bar

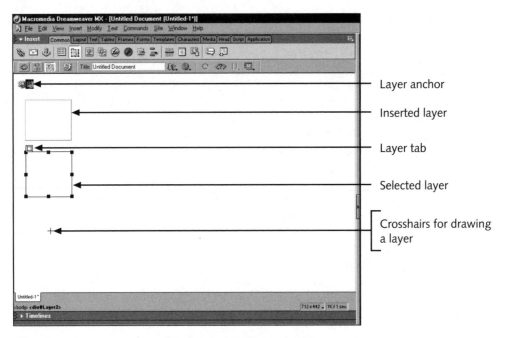

Figure 10-2   Layers in Dreamweaver MX workspace

 Note When you want to drag a layer or change its properties in the Property inspector, you must select it. Be careful to select the layer and not its contents. When you select a layer, black handles appear around it. However, if you select a graphic inside a layer, the selected graphic displays similar black handles. To be sure that you select the layer, click inside it and then click the Layer tab in the upper-left corner of the layer.

Notice the small icons at the top of the workspace ▦ in Figure 10-2. Every time you create a layer, one of these icons appears. The icon remains in the same place, regardless of the layer's position on the workspace, because the layer is encoded here. If you delete an icon, you also delete its associated layer. If you select an icon, you select its associated layer.

You can access the code for embedding the layer by selecting the layer and clicking the Show Code view button ◈. In the source code, layers are implemented within the body of the HTML document as follows:

```
<div id="Layer1" style="position:absolute; left:22px; top:69px; width:105px; height:88px;
z-index:1"></div>
```

A division (div) tag is used to insert the layer, and "id" is an arbitrary identifier you use to name your layer. For example, if a layer contains your company logo, "mylogo" might be a more appropriate name than "Layer1." Following the style tag, the layer coordinates are listed in pixels. This determines the layer's position on the page. The last layer element is the Z-index. The **Z-index** indicates layer order when your page has multiple layers. A Z-index of 1 indicates the lowest level—that is, one level above the main HTML page. A Z-index of 2 indicates that a layer is two layers above the main page. The layer with the highest Z-index is the top layer.

If you have more than one layer in your workspace, the Layers panel can help you to manage them. To open the Layers panel, you can click Window on the Dreamweaver menu bar, point to Others, then click Layers, or you can press the F2 key. The Layers panel is part of the Advanced Layout panel group with Frames.

The sample Layers panel shown in Figure 10-3 displays three layers, with Layer1 selected. In the workspace that corresponds to this Layers panel, the handles would show for Layer1, because it is selected. You can resize a selected layer, add text to it, or drag it to a new position in the workspace. In Figure 10-3 the closed eye image indicates that Layer2 is hidden. No eye indicates that a layer is in the default state (showing but not defined as showing explicitly in the code), and the open eye indicates that a layer is visible. When working with multiple layers, you may sometimes find it easier to turn off some layers so that you can focus only on certain layers. If layers overlap, Layers 2 and 3 may obscure part of Layer1. The Prevent Overlaps checkbox, shown at the top of the Layers panel in Figure 10-3, can prevent layers from overlapping. This is very useful if you plan to create layers and then convert them to tables, or if you do not want any of your layers to be obscured. You can also prevent overlapping layers by clicking Modify on the Dreamweaver menu bar, pointing to Arrange, and then clicking Prevent Layer Overlaps.

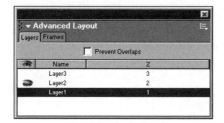

Figure 10-3   Layers panel

Adding content to layers is exactly like adding content to a Web page. You simply position the pointer inside the layer and type text, or insert images, tables, or hyperlinks. Figure 10-4 shows how you could use layers to position text and a graphic so that they appear to build on one another in a cascading fashion. You can see that four different layers exist, because they appear in the workspace as overlapping rectangles and are listed in the Layers panel. In the Layers panel, layer names have been changed to indicate the layers' contents. The layer lbclogo contains the La Bonne Cuisine logo and has the Z-index 1, indicating that it is on the lowest level. The latext layer is above this layer, so the text appears on top of the graphic. A similar effect is shown for Layers 3 and 4, where text appears to be on top of the text of the layer beneath. If you want to change the Z-index positioning of a layer, simply select the layer in the Layers panel and drag it to the desired position. Prior to the development of DHTML, placing page elements on top of one another was impossible. Regular HTML just places one item after the other in a vertical, one-dimensional manner. DHTML lets you position objects in an *xyz*, three-dimensional coordinate system: *x* pixels from the left, *y* pixels from the top, and *z* layers above the primary page.

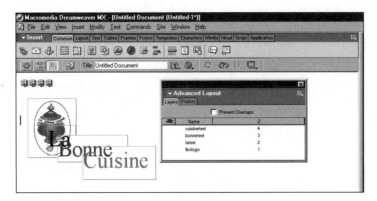

Figure 10-4   Multiple overlapping layers

You can nest one layer within another by inserting a layer within an existing layer. Simply hold down the Ctrl key when inserting the new layer. When you reposition the parent layer in the workspace, the child layer moves with it automatically. The child layer inherits the parent layer's properties.

You may have suspected that the Property inspector changes when you select a layer. If you select the lbclogo layer, the Layer Property inspector appears, as shown in Figure 10-5. The Layer ID text box displays the layer name. The Property inspector displays the layer attributes:

- L (Left) controls the layer's horizontal position. The layer is positioned the specified number of pixels from the left of the browser window.

- T (Top) controls the layer's vertical position. The layer is positioned the specified number of pixels below the top of the browser window.

- W (Width) controls the layer's width in pixels.

- H (Height) controls the layer's height in pixels.

- Z-index controls the layer level with respect to the HTML document and other layers on the page. Lower Z-index numbers indicate lower levels.

- Vis (Visibility) controls how a layer appears, using the attributes default, inherit, visible, and hidden. The attribute inherit causes the layer to inherit a parent layer's attributes when the layers are nested. Visible causes the layer and all its contents to appear on the screen. A hidden attribute makes the layer invisible.

- Bg (Background) Image indicates what graphic is used for the layer background.

- Bg (Background) Color indicates a hexadecimal color value for the layer's background.

- Tag alters the type of HTML tag that contains the layer. The SPAN and DIV tags both can be used to create layers.

- Overflow controls how the layer displays information that exceeds the layer boundaries. A visible designation ensures that text or images outside the layer boundary display. A hidden designation hides the overflow of text or images. Adding a scroll attribute embeds a scroll bar, so the user can scroll to see the image. The auto attribute adds scroll bars as well, if the image or text is outside the layer boundaries. Note that the overflow setting does not work in Netscape 4.*x*.

- Clip clips the rectangle a given number of pixels from the left (L), top (T), right (R), or bottom (B). Similar to cropping an image in Fireworks, this ensures that only the part of the layer containing the image appears.

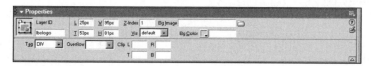

Figure 10-5 Property inspector for a layer

10

Layers and Style Sheets

In addition to freeform drawing of a layer in the workspace, you can create layers in two other ways. You can click Insert on the Dreamweaver menu bar and then click Layer. A layer you insert using this method is automatically sized according to the layer defaults set in Dreamweaver MX. (You learn about layer defaults later in this chapter.) You can also insert layers using style sheets. In Chapter 9 you learned how to control text attributes using the CSS Style definition dialog box. The panel has several categories that let you change text characteristics. Among these categories is one for positioning, which lets you insert a layer by defining it in a style sheet. The advantage to defining layers in a style sheet is that you can use the style definition over and over again. If you want to insert a layer with the same attributes on many pages of your Web site, you can define it in an external style sheet and then insert it whenever you need it. Figure 10-6 shows the Positioning category of the CSS Style definition dialog box. The position attributes match the ones displayed on the Layer Property inspector shown in Figure 10-5. The only difference is in your source code; instead of defining the positioning attributes as part of the DIV tag, you define them using styles—that is, as a class in the header of the HTML document or in an external style sheet.

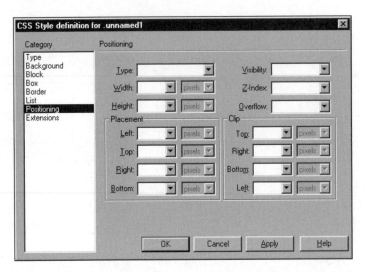

Figure 10-6   Positioning category of the CSS Style definition dialog box

Absolute and Relative Positioning

Absolute positioning of layers is like absolute sizing of text. If the position is absolute, the layer's position on the Web page is fixed. The location is a specific number of pixels from the left of the browser window and the top of the browser window. In **relative positioning** the layer's position is relative to another object on the page. This is useful because when a user resizes a window, sequential HTML text may change to fit the resized browser. For example, if a Web page contains a simple table with text that covers 75% of the browser window, resizing the window also resizes and therefore reformats the text. Using a relative position for the layer can maintain the layer display with respect to the table instead of the browser window. Another way to use relative positioning is to create a layer with an absolute position and then create another layer with a position relative to that first layer. Similarly, you can place a layer in a table, and the positioning will be relative to the table rather than to the browser window. You use absolute positioning much more often than relative positioning. Absolute positioning offers more control, and the browser displays more predictable results. You need to apply and test relative layers carefully, because their appearance is unpredictable in different browsers and in resized browser windows.

When using relative positioning of layers, previewing your Web page in both Internet Explorer and Netscape Navigator is smart. Working with relative layers can be difficult; they don't always appear where you expect. Absolute layering is much more common.

Layer Defaults

Modifying layer defaults is useful when you want to insert several layers with the same attributes. You can set the layer characteristics in the Layer Preferences dialog box and then use the Insert menu to insert multiple layers with the same characteristics. To access the Layer Preferences dialog box, click Edit on the Dreamweaver menu bar, then click Preferences. The Preferences dialog box has many categories. If you click the Layers category, you see the dialog box shown in Figure 10-7. Most layer preferences shown match those defined earlier for the Property inspector for layers. There are two other options, Nesting and Netscape 4 Compatibility. Nesting means that you can nest one layer inside another. The Netscape 4 Compatibility option compensates for a problem in Netscape Navigator 4.*x* browsers. In Netscape Navigator versions 4.*x*, an error causes layers to lose their display coordinates when the Netscape browser is resized. By selecting the checkbox for Netscape 4 Compatibility, you can ensure that the resizing problem with the Netscape 4.*x* browsers does not interfere with your layers' positions when a user resizes the browser window. This option is checked by default in Dreamweaver MX.

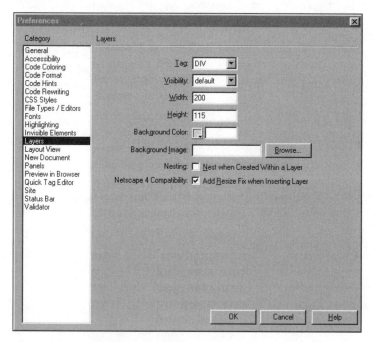

Figure 10-7 Preferences dialog box

10

BEHAVIORS

Once you create and position a layer, you can manipulate it using events and behaviors. Dreamweaver MX helps you manipulate layers by coding JavaScript functions that move, hide, and display layers at specific locations. The layer's position is important in the code, because Dreamweaver MX builds a function to move the layer based upon the layer's coordinates.

As you learned earlier in this chapter, event handlers activate JavaScript functions. An event handler causes some action to occur when a user activates it by doing something on the Web page. For example, if a user clicks a button to play animation, the event handler is OnClick. Dreamweaver MX helps you to write scripts that perform actions when events occur. An **action** is a function, defined in the header of the HTML document, that executes once an event handler is activated. By attaching an event to an action, you can create a behavior on a Web page.

Dreamweaver MX generates the JavaScript code that executes the action called by the event handler via the Behaviors panel. To open the Behaviors panel, click Window on the Dreamweaver menu bar, then click Behaviors, or press the Shift+F3 key combination. Figure 10-8 shows the Behaviors panel. After inserting a layer, you can use the Behaviors panel to build a behavior by selecting and attaching an event to an action. On the Behaviors panel, the + (plus) and - (minus) buttons let you add and delete actions. Figure 10-9 shows the extensive list of actions available in Dreamweaver MX on the Action (+) pop-up menu when the body tag, a hyperlink, or an image is selected. You can select the last option, Get More Behaviors, to access the Macromedia Web site, where you can download other behaviors. The first list option, Call JavaScript, lets you enter your own JavaScript code.

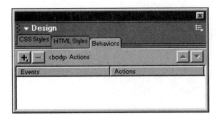

Figure 10-8   Behaviors panel

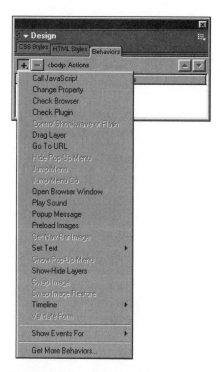

Figure 10-9   Actions (+) pop-up menu

Different event handlers are available, depending upon which version of which browser you select. Figure 10-10 shows the list from which you can select the browser's event handlers you want to use. You can select 3.0 and Later Browsers, 4.0 and Later Browsers, or a specific version of Internet Explorer or Netscape Navigator. To test your behaviors, you can access a Dreamweaver MX built-in utility by clicking File on the Dreamweaver menu bar, then clicking Check Page and Check Target Browsers. Using this utility, you can select a specific browser and receive a brief error report indicating any browser incompatibilities.

10

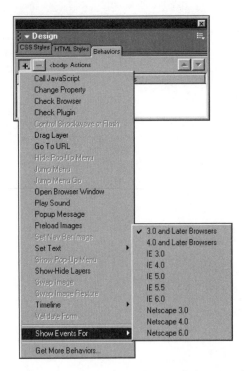

Figure 10-10   Behaviors panel showing browser selection

After selecting an action, you need to enter parameters that help the action to operate. A dialog box associated with the action you select lets you enter parameters for that action. An event handler is automatically added for you. To change the event handler to suit your behavior, click the triangle to the right of the event and select from the list of events that appears, as shown in Figure 10-11.

Setting Status Bar Text

A simple example that demonstrates the use of the Behaviors panel is setting the text of the status bar in the Browser window. In the following steps, you write text that is to appear in the status bar when the Web page is loaded. To do this, you open the Behaviors panel, add the behavior and then activate the behavior when the page loads.

To change the status bar text:

1. Click the **F8** function key to open the Site panel (if it is not already open) and select the **La Bonne Cuisine** Web site. In Design view, open the file **consulting.htm** in the Sites\lbc\consulting folder. The file consulting.htm is an HTML page describing La Bonne Cuisine's consulting services.

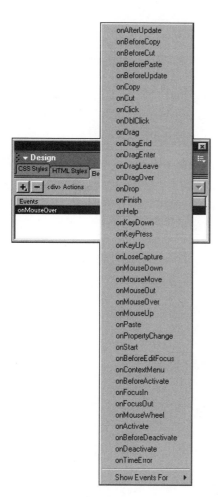

Figure 10-11   Adding an event handler using the Behaviors panel

2. Open the Behaviors panel if it is not already open (**Shift + F3**). With your cursor in the document to the right of the table, click the **Actions (+)** pop-up menu, point to **Show Events For**, and click **4.0 and Later Browsers**. Then, click the **Actions (+)** pop-up menu, point to **Set Text**, and then click **Set Text of Status Bar**. The Set Text of Status Bar dialog box opens, as shown in Figure 10-12.

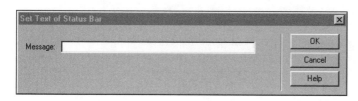

Figure 10-12   Set Text of Status Bar dialog box

3. Click the body tag on the tag selector, which is at the bottom of the Document window. Type **Welcome to La Bonne Cuisine. Have a nice day!!!** in the message text box in the Set Text of Status Bar dialog box. Click **OK**.

4. Click the Events list arrow in the Behaviors panel, and select the event handler **OnLoad**. Your final Behaviors panel displays the event and action shown in Figure 10-13. If you need to edit the text of the status bar, simply double-click the action in the Behaviors panel.

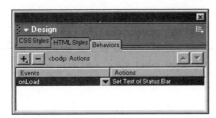

Figure 10-13   Behaviors panel with status bar event added

5. Save the file. Press **F12** to preview the status bar text. Figure 10-14 shows the resulting status bar previewed in a Web browser.

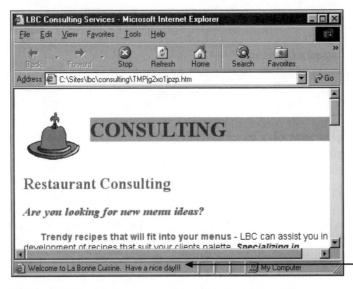

Status bar text

Figure 10-14   Status bar as it appears in a Web browser

Dreamweaver MX lets you select a script that checks the browser version and redirects the user to the appropriate URL. This may be useful if you need to design a Web site that has two different versions, one for Internet Explorer and one for Netscape Navigator users. You can access this option via the Behaviors panel by selecting the behavior Check Browser and entering the appropriate URLs.

Creating a Drag Layer Action

One way to make a Web page more dynamic is to design it so that users can drag and rearrange layers on the page, for example to dress a figure, arrange furniture, or put toys in a box. The goal is to give users more dynamic experiences with the page, because they control it—the page responds to users' actions. To create the dragging effect, you need to attach behaviors to layers. In the steps below, you create a paper doll Web page that lets users dress a doll by dragging layers across the screen. To accomplish this, you need to place the layers where you would like them to be dropped, set a drop target (a left/top coordinate where you want the drag action to stop), and then reposition the layers where you want them to appear when the page first loads into the browser.

To create a drag layer action:

1. Using Windows Explorer, create a folder called **ch10practice** in the Sites directory on your working drive. Create a subfolder called **images** within the ch10practice folder. Copy the files **hat.gif**, **pants.gif**, **doll.gif**, and **shirt.gif** from the Chapter10\images data folder into your Sites\ch10practice\images folder. Copy the file **paperdoll.htm** from the Chapter10 folder into your Sites\ch10practice folder.

2. Make sure that the Property inspector (Ctrl+F3) and the Layers (F2) and Behaviors (Shift+F3) panels are open. Open the file **paperdoll.htm** in Dreamweaver. Notice that hat, shirt, and pants images are available for the stick figure in the right of the workspace.

3. In the Behaviors panel, click the **Actions (+)** pop-up menu, point to **Show Events For**, then click **4.0 and Later Browsers**.

   In the Layers panel, you should see four layers. The Z-index for the doll layer is 1, because the doll is positioned below the clothing layers. Notice that the clothing layers are named hat, shirt, and pants. Assigning appropriate names to the layers helps you when you define their behaviors.

4. In the Layers panel, make sure that the **Prevent Overlaps** checkbox is unchecked. Select the layer containing the hat by clicking the layer in the workspace. Make sure the layer, and not the image, is selected. Black handles appear around the layer, and the Property inspector indicates the hat layer's location and size. Drag the hat layer to position it on the head of the doll. The coordinates in the Property inspector should show **400**px in the L text box and **40**px in the T text box. If you have trouble dragging the hat layer to this position, you can type the coordinates into the Property inspector to move the layer.

5. Click the body tag on the tag selector, which is at the bottom of the Document window. Click the **Actions (+)** pop-up menu on the Behaviors panel, and click **Drag Layer** in the Actions list. The Drag Layer dialog box opens, as shown in Figure 10-15. In the Basic tab, click the **Layer** list arrow and click layer **hat** because you want the user to drag the hat layer. In the

10

Movement list box leave the value **Unconstrained**, so that the user can drag the layer anywhere on the page. (Constraining the drag option lets you constrain the dragging motion for the layer.) Click **Get Current Position** to use the layer's current location as the Drop Target location. Type **50** in the Snap if Within text box. This causes the layer to snap to the designated position if the user drags it within 50 pixels. The default is 50 pixels. Click **OK** to close the Drag Layer dialog box.

Dreamweaver generates JavaScript language instructions for dragging the layer onto the specified area, in effect placing the hat on the doll.

In the Behaviors panel, you can see an event, onLoad, listed to the left of the action Drag Layer.

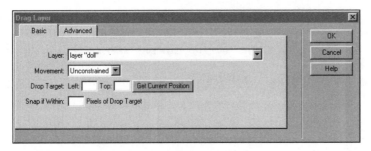

Figure 10-15   Drag Layer dialog box

6. Select the layer containing the shirt by clicking the layer in the workspace. Drag the shirt layer to position it on the body of the doll. Set the coordinates in the Property inspector to **460**px in the L text box and **225**px in the T text box. Click the body tag on the tag selector, which is at the bottom of the Document window. Click the **Actions (+)** pop-up menu on the Behaviors panel, and click **Drag Layer** in the Actions list. The Drag Layer dialog box opens. In the Basic tab, click the **Layer** list arrow and click the layer **shirt** because you want the user to drag the shirt layer. In the Movement list box, leave the value **Unconstrained**. Click **Get Current Position**. In the Snap if Within text box, type **50**. Click **OK** to close the Drag Layer dialog box. If necessary, click the **Actions** list arrow and click **onLoad**.

7. Select the layer containing the pants by clicking the layer in the workspace and then clicking the tab at the top of the layer. Drag the pants layer to position it on the body of the doll. Set the coordinates in the Property inspector to **450**px in the L text box and **280**px in the T text box. Click the body tag on the tag selector, which is at the bottom of the Document window. Click the **Actions (+)** pop-up menu on the Behaviors panel, and click **Drag Layer** in the Actions list. The Drag Layer dialog box opens. In the Basic tab, click the **Layer** list arrow and click the **pants** layer because you want the user to drag the pants layer. In the Movement list box, leave the value **Unconstrained**. Click **Get Current Position**. In the Snap if Within text

box, type **50**. Click **OK** to close the Drag Layer dialog box. If necessary, click the **Actions** list arrow and select **onLoad**.

8. In the Dreamweaver workspace, click the **hat** layer to select it, and then click its **Layer** tab. In the Property inspector, type the coordinates L **50**px and T **50**px. The hat layer should move to that position in the workspace. (You can also relocate the layers by dragging them by the Layer tab, but using the Property inspector is more precise.) Click the **shirt** layer to select it, and then click its **Layer** tab. In the Property inspector, type the coordinates L **50**px and T **200**px. Click the **pants** layer to select it, and then click its **Layer** tab. In the Property inspector, type the coordinates L **50**px and T **350**px. The doll should now be on the right side of your workspace and the three clothing items on the left.

9. Save the page **paperdoll.htm**, and preview it in your Web browser (**F12**). Test the page by holding down the mouse button on one clothing item and dragging the item to dress the paper doll. Observe that each item snaps to the correct position when you drag it to within 50 pixels of the desired location.

More Behaviors

Figure 10-9 shows many of the behaviors that you can add to your Web pages. You can add behaviors for specific browsers and versions, or for multiple browsers and versions. The Behaviors panel helps you by displaying the behaviors available for the browser version or versions you select. You can investigate many of these behaviors independently as you become more experienced. You can also connect to the Macromedia Web site and download more pre-scripted behaviors.

10

TIMELINES

Using DHTML, you can animate layers in a timeline. A **timeline** contains layers in specific positions at different frames, ordered sequentially. A **frame** is one cell or one point of time in an animation. In a movie, frames recorded sequentially give the illusion of motion, because enough frames are captured so that the viewer's mind fills in any gaps in motion.

Using a timeline, you can place specifically positioned layers into frames to create smooth animation. To do this in DHTML, you first create the layer that you want to animate and then create a JavaScript function that controls how the layer moves. If you want a graphic of a dove to start in the upper-left corner of the workspace and move diagonally to the lower-right corner, you would insert the dove graphic in a layer and then write a function to animate it by moving it an increasing number of x pixels from the left and y pixels from the top, until it reaches the desired destination. To create the animation in Dreamweaver MX, you define the first and final frames of the animation; Dreamweaver MX writes the code to script the diagonal frames in between.

To script animations with Dreamweaver MX, you use a timeline that lets you build your animation and control its timing and other attributes. Figure 10-16 shows the Timelines panel. You can open it by clicking Others on the Dreamweaver Window menu and selecting Timelines, or pressing the Alt+F9 key combination.

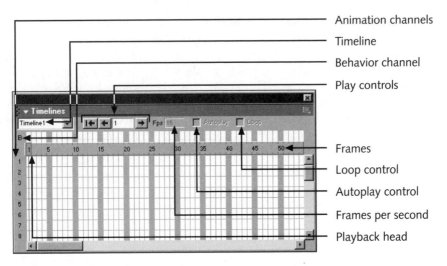

Animation channels
Timeline
Behavior channel
Play controls
Frames
Loop control
Autoplay control
Frames per second
Playback head

Figure 10-16   Timelines panel

The Timelines panel contains several horizontal animation channels. To animate layers, you drag them into the animation channels and then move the layers to the desired coordinates for specific frames. The horizontal bar marked with a B is a behavior channel, where you can insert actions using the Behaviors panel. The number bar separating the behavior channel from the animation channels represents frame numbers. The number bar helps you to control how many frames your animation contains or to identify in which frame you want an action to occur. A text box above the behavior channel displays the number of frames per second (FPS). A larger number of frames per second yields higher quality animation, while too few frames per second might create choppy animation. By placing layers in a timeline, you can orchestrate the timing and movement of several layers on a Web page. Placing individual layers in different animation channels, you can start and end them on different frames, so layers appear and disappear, creating a complex animation.

You can preview and control your animation using the Timeline panel's command buttons. These buttons let you advance or reverse animation frame-by-frame. You can also control the animation with the Playback head, shown on the Frames number bar as a red rectangle with a red tracer line below it. By dragging this Playback head, you can move the timeline to a specific frame and see how the animation operates in the workspace.

To make your animation play continuously when the Web page loads, you need to select the checkboxes for Loop and for Autoplay. Selecting the Autoplay checkbox ensures that your timeline plays when the Web page loads. The Loop checkbox, when selected, ensures that your timeline plays continually, looping from the end frame to frame 1, over and over again. Clicking the Options menu in the upper-right corner of the Timelines panel displays the editing menu shown in Figure 10-17. For example, you can use this menu to add additional timelines, creating more complex animation. You can move between different timelines by clicking the list arrow next to the timeline text box.

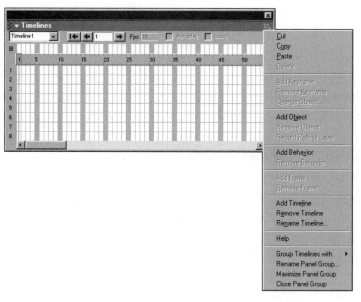

Figure 10-17   Timelines panel Options menu

The steps involved in creating animation using Dreamweaver MX are not difficult, but you must do them with precision for the animation to work. The general steps for creating a simple, linear animation using the Timelines panel follow:

- *Insert the layer.* Insert a layer onto your Web page. Add graphics or text to the layer, so that it has visible content.

- *Drag the layer into the timeline.* Drag and drop the layer into a timeline animation channel in the Timelines panel. The animation timeline automatically appears in the Timelines panel, as shown in Figure 10-18. When you first use this procedure, the message shown in Figure 10-19 appears. You can close this dialog box by clicking OK. You can prevent this dialog box from appearing again by clicking the "Don't show me this message again" checkbox. The animation shown in Figure 10-18 is 15 frames long, begins on Frame 1, and ends on Frame 15. It plays at 15 frames per second when the Web page loads. A small circle inside a frame indicates that a keyframe exists. Keyframes exist in this example to define the beginning and end of the animation. You can also insert them along the animation to control changes in the path of the layer.

10

- *Move the layer to the desired position for specific timeline frames.* Click the last frame of the animation channel containing that layer, Frame 15. The frame turns a darker purple color than the rest of the timeline. Drag the layer by the layer handle to position it in the workspace where you want the animation to end. A straight line displays the path of the animation, as shown in Figure 10-20. When you preview the animation in your Web browser, this line does not show.

- *Select play options.* Click the Autoplay checkbox if you want the animation to play when the page loads. Click the Loop checkbox if you want the animation to play continually.

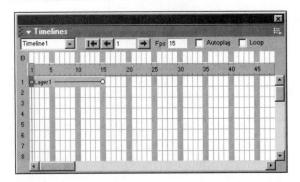

Figure 10-18   Layer in animation channel 1

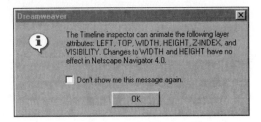

Figure 10-19   Pop-up message displayed when using the Timelines panel

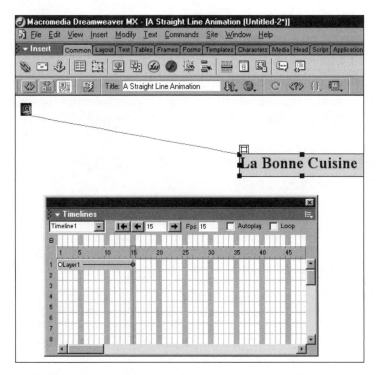

Figure 10-20   Straight-line animation

You can change the animation's length by clicking the last frame of a layer in an animation channel and dragging it out or in to lengthen or shorten the animation. You can also move the entire layer, so that the animation starts at a frame other than Frame 1. This very simple animation can be easily created visually. While one sliding layer is not an astounding feat, animating several layers in unison can create an impressive visual effect. To do this, you use multiple layers controlled by separate animation channels. You can also insert keyframes anywhere along a layer's animation channel and create behaviors associated with that keyframe. Working on the timing and placement of multiple layers can be quite time consuming. However, when done correctly, your work can result in a very pleasing application of animation on a Web page.

Creating a Linear Animation

In the steps below, you use the Timelines panel to animate three layers that contain the text La, Bonne, and Cuisine, respectively.

To animate three layers:

1. Using Windows Explorer, copy the file **textanimation.htm** from the Chapter10 data folder into your Sites\ch10practice folder and then open the file in Dreamweaver.

Make sure the Property inspector (**Ctrl+F3**), the Layers panel (**F2**) and the Timelines panel (**Alt+F9**) are open.

2. Click the **La** layer to select it, and then click the **Layer** tab. Drag the layer into the first animation channel in the Timelines panel.

   A dialog box, shown in Figure 10-19, may open, explaining that the Timeline inspector can control layer attributes and that Netscape 4.0 does not process changes to width and height attributes. If this window does not appear, that is fine. It is just an explanation and is unnecessary for animating your layers. If it does open, click the **Don't show me this message again** checkbox, if you wish, and click **OK** to close the dialog box.

3. Observe that a lavender bar appears in animation channel 1, with keyframes at Frames 1 and 15. Observe also that the timeline in the animation channel is labeled La. Select **keyframe 15** by clicking the small circle in Frame 15. Drag the lavender bar to position the end keyframe under Frame 30 of the animation. Now, the animation will play for 30 frames at a rate of 15 frames per second.

4. Select **keyframe 1** by clicking the small circle in Frame 1. With the La layer still selected, in the Property inspector type **500** in the L text box and **500** in the T text box. Press **Enter**. The layer is repositioned in the workspace for the first keyframe and an animation guide, indicated by a black line, appears on the screen. You can play the animation by dragging the red Playback head across the frames in the Timelines panel. As the red Playback head passes over the frames, you should see the layer move. (*Note:* You can also reposition layers in the timeline by dragging them over a path in the workspace.)

5. Click the **Bonne** layer to select it, and then click the **Layer** tab. Drag and drop the layer into animation channel 2. Click the last keyframe of the timeline in animation channel 2, and drag the timeline to **Frame 20**. Click the first frame of animation channel 2, and in the Property inspector type **30** in the L text box and **500** in the T text box. Press **Enter**.

6. Click the **Cuisine** layer to select it, and then click its **Layer tab**. Drag and drop the layer into animation channel 3. Click the last keyframe of the timeline in animation channel 3, and drag the timeline to **Frame 20**. Click the first frame of animation channel 3, and in the Property inspector type **500** in the L text box and **5** in the T text box. Press **Enter**.

7. Click the **Autoplay** checkbox in the Timelines panel to ensure that the animation plays when the page loads. Click **OK** in the message dialog box that appears.

8. Save this file and preview the animation in your Web browser (**F12**). The animation should begin with the text layers in three different areas of the screen and then show them moving to the center of the screen where they all meet to show the name of the company.

Creating a Non-linear Animation

Sometimes you may want to create animation that travels along a non-linear path to create a movement that seems more natural, or even to create a movement that seems random. Web pages use this effect to show a bird flying across the page and then landing in some specific area. It has also been applied as a marketing strategy, in which a monkey scrambles across the page until the user "catches" it (that is, clicks it). Catching the monkey earns the user a 20% discount on an online purchase. Of course, the user always catches the monkey but feels success and has an incentive to purchase a product online. In the steps below, you create a layer that travels in a non-linear path by dragging the layer over the workspace. This animation is not precisely positioned, because you drag the mouse freehand over the workspace.

To create a non-linear animation:

1. Using Windows Explorer, copy the file **boxanimation.htm** from the Chapter10 data folder into the Sites\ch10practice folder on your working drive and open the file in Dreamweaver. The file boxanimation.htm appears as a blank page with a small layer that has a blue background.

2. Make sure the Timelines panel (**Alt+F9**) is open. Click the **Layer** to select it. Right-click the **Layer tab**, then click **Record Path** on the context menu, as shown in Figure 10-21.

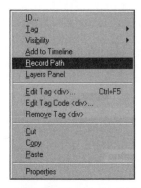

Figure 10-21   Recording a non-linear path for a layer

3. Click and hold the **Layer tab**, and drag the layer around the screen to delineate the animation path. You can create loops, arcs, and zig-zags on the non-linear path of this layer. As you drag, gray dots appear in the workspace, marking your path. When you release the mouse button, a complex timeline with keyframes appears in animation channel 1 in the Timelines panel. The path you created for the layer becomes a thin black line, as shown in Figure 10-22.

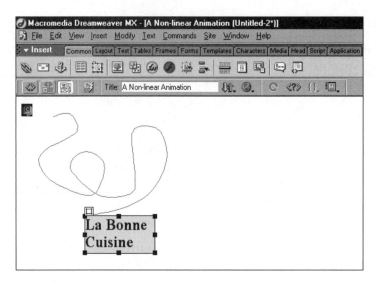

Figure 10-22 Non-linear path for a layer

4. Click the **Autoplay** checkbox in the Timelines panel. If a message dialog box appears, click the **Don't show me this message again** checkbox, if you wish, then click **OK**.

5. Click the **Loop** checkbox in the Timelines panel. If a message dialog box appears, click the **Don't show me this message again** checkbox, if you wish, then click **OK**.

6. Save the file **boxanimation.htm**. Preview it in your Web browser (**F12**). This animation works in both Netscape Navigator and Internet Explorer. Observe that the path is followed by the layer and repeated. Close the browser window when you finish.

You can attach a behavior to your timeline so a dynamic event occurs as your timeline plays. For example, the timeline could transfer the user to a new URL once it stops playing. To attach a behavior to a timeline, you insert a keyframe in the behavior channel near the top of the Timelines panel and then use the Behaviors panel to script the action.

Adding Controls to Animation

Another way to make your Web sites more engaging is to let visitors control the animation. For example, if a lengthy animation introduces your Web site, you might include a "skip" button. Users who have already seen the animation or don't want to see it, can use the button to access the pages containing the information they seek. Sometimes, complex animation serves as an entry page to a Web site. In this case, you can loop the animation and then offer the user a link that says "Enter." When the user clicks Enter, the linked site opens in the browser window. In this section, you add two clickable links: PLAY, to play the animation, and STOP, to pause the animation.

To add user controls to your animation:

1. Open the file **boxanimation.htm** in the ch10practice folder in Dreamweaver. In the Timelines panel (**Alt+F9**), uncheck the **Autoplay** option. Make sure that the Property inspector (**Ctrl+F3**) and the Behaviors panel (**Shift+F3**) are open. Click in the workspace.

2. Press **Enter** twice to move down a few lines in the workspace.

3. Type the text **PLAY** in the workspace. Press **Enter**. Type the text **STOP**.

4. Select the text **PLAY** and in the Property inspector, type **#** in the Link text box. (The # acts as a placeholder so that the text appears as a link but only activates a behavior on the current page.) Press **Enter**. In the Behaviors panel, click the **Actions (+)** pop-up menu, point to **Show Events For**, and click **4.0 and Later Browsers**.

5. In the Behaviors panel, click the **Actions (+)** pop-up menu again, point to **Timeline**, and click **Play Timeline**. The Play Timeline dialog appears, with Timeline 1 selected in the Play Timeline list box. Click **OK**. In the Behaviors panel, OnClick should be listed under Events and Play Timeline under Actions.

6. In the Dreamweaver workspace, select the text **STOP**, and in the Property inspector type **#** in the Link text box. Press **Enter**.

7. In the Behaviors panel, click the **Actions (+)** pop-up menu, point to **Timeline**, and click **Stop Timeline**. The Stop Timeline dialog box appears, indicating that all timelines will stop. Click **OK**. In the Behaviors panel, OnClick should be listed under Events and Stop Timeline under Actions.

8. Save this file as **box_control.htm** in the Sites\ch10practice folder on your working drive.

9. Preview this page (**F12**). Click the **STOP** and **PLAY** buttons to see that the animation now has controls. Close the browser window when you finish previewing.

 You can create graphic buttons in Fireworks and design your page so that the user actually presses a button with a behavior attached to it, rather than clicking a hyperlink.

ERROR CHECKING

When you create a page with complex layers and behaviors, it is important to test your page thoroughly. Many browsers and browser versions do not support the same event handlers, and your Web page may not work as you designed it. Dreamweaver MX allows you to test your page in different browsers and generates an error report indicating what incompatibilities exist. To check for browser compatibility, click File on the Dreamweaver menu bar, point to Check Page, and then click Check Target Browsers, as shown in Figure 10-23. To use this feature in Dreamweaver MX, you must first save your page.

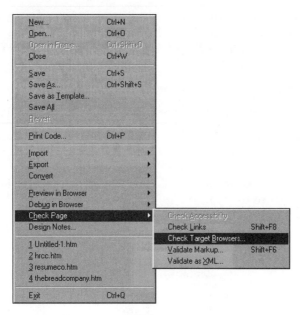

Figure 10-23   Checking target browser compatibility

A dialog box, shown in Figure 10-24, lets you click the browser type and version against which you want to check your page. Holding the Ctrl or Shift key down, you can select multiple browsers. The error report is generated automatically and displayed in the Target Browser Check panel, as shown in Figure 10-25, for a page created to animate one layer and allow a user to drag another. The report was generated for all versions of the Netscape browser. In it, you can see what elements are not supported by which browser version. To access the Results panel, you can select Results from the Dreamweaver Window menu and then Target Browser Check, as well as other test and validation tools.

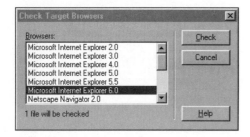

Figure 10-24   Check Target Browsers dialog box

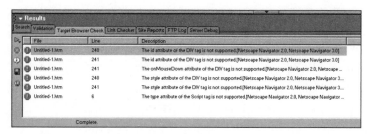

Figure 10-25   Target Browser Check panel

CHAPTER SUMMARY

❑ DHTML combines HTML and JavaScript to create a more interesting and sometimes interactive Web page. Dreamweaver MX generates JavaScript code for you when you use the Timelines, Behaviors, and Layers panels.

❑ Using layers, you can position objects on top of a Web page by specifying the number of pixels from the left and top of the browser window, and the layer order out from the page. A Z-index indicates the layer order of the Web page. The lower the Z-index, the lower the layer's level location on the page. You can position layers relatively or absolutely, and overlap them.

❑ The Layers panel helps you to identify and organize layers. You can rearrange layers, name layers, and set layers' values to hidden and visible using this panel.

❑ Using the Timelines panel, you can animate individual layers in animation channels by dragging each layer into the Timelines panel. The Timelines panel lets you control the speed and length of animation, and attributes such as Autoplay (so that the animation automatically plays when the page loads) or Loop (so that animation plays continuously).

❑ You can animate layers on both a linear and non-linear path. You can add keyframes to change the direction of an animation. You can drag keyframes to change the start and end time for different animated layers on the same timeline.

❑ The Behaviors panel helps you connect events with actions. For example, selecting the Drag Layer option from the Behaviors panel produces DHTML code that lets a user drag a layer freely around the Web browser. The page is dynamic in that the user can move or change its content.

❑ You can attach a behavior to any frame in an animation timeline, so that an event occurs when that frame of animation plays. You might use this to send a message to the user when animation ends, or to send the user to another URL.

❑ You can insert controls so that the user can control animation. Using behaviors, you can enable the user to stop or start the animation timeline so that the user controls the animation.

REVIEW QUESTIONS

1. What are some advantages of using DHTML? (Choose all that apply.)

   a. It can enhance a Web page by animating objects.

   b. You can make a Web page more interactive.

   c. No special plugins are required for DHTML code to operate.

   d. It does not require programming languages like JavaScript.

2. What is an interactive Web page?

3. Using DHTML, you can position layers in a left, top, Z-index coordinate system. True or False?

4. Which Z-index indicates the layer on the top level (all other layers are underneath) of the Web page?

   a. 0

   b. 1

   c. 2

   d. 3

5. What page elements can you insert in a layer? (Choose all that apply.)

   a. Text

   b. Images

   c. Tables

   d. Rollovers

6. Layers in Dreamweaver MX must not overlap. True or False?

7. What parameters do you use to position a layer on a Web page?

   a. Left and Top

   b. Right and Top

   c. Height and Width

   d. Left and Right

8. Explain the difference between relative and absolute positioning.

9. Which of the following are JavaScript event handlers? (Choose all that apply.)

   a. OnClick

   b. OnMouseOver

   c. OnMouseUp

   d. OnRelease

10. What is the difference between an event and an action?

11. The Drag Layer option in the Behaviors panel lets you create:

   a. animation through timelines.

   b. objects on the Web that the user can manipulate.

   c. multiple layers working in conjunction for some task.

   d. none of the above.

12. You can hide layers by deleting them using the command Delete Behavior. True or False?

13. Which of the following is not a feature of the Timelines panel?

   a. Animation channels

   b. Behavior channel

   c. Keyframes

   d. Seconds indicated by a number line

14. Describe the process of creating an animation that takes one image and breaks it apart into three areas of the screen.

15. What is the behavior channel in the Timelines panel used for?

16. What is FPS? What effect does a greater or lower FPS have on the speed of the animation?

17. Selecting the Autoplay checkbox in the Timelines panel ensures that your animation plays automatically when the Web page loads in the Web browser. True or False?

18. Selecting the Loop checkbox in the Timelines panel ensures that your animation loops when the Web page loads in the Web browser. True or False?

19. Inserting a behavior midway through the animation timeline for a layer creates an error in the animation. True or False?

20. Describe the process for adding user controls to an animation that runs in a continual loop.

HANDS-ON PROJECTS

Project 10-1

Currently, the Adventure Travel Company has a home page that has a Heading 1 title at the top with the company name. The company's owner thinks this is a boring way to display the company name and wants you to create something more graphically appealing. You decide to create a new title for the company using overlapping text layers and absolute positioning.

   1. Open a new file in Dreamweaver. In this file, you insert four layers. Three will contain text and one will contain a colored background. The layers will overlap to create an appealing title for the Adventure Travel Company home page.

2. Make sure that the Layers panel (**F2**) and the Property inspector (**Ctrl+F3**) are open. Make sure Dreamweaver is in Standard view by clicking the **Layout** tab and then **Standard View**.

3. In the Title text box at the top of the workspace, type **Adventure Travel**. Click in the workspace.

4. Click **Insert** on the Dreamweaver menu bar, and then click **Layer**. The text Layer1 appears in the Layers panel, and the layer appears in the workspace. Click **Layer1** to select it in the Layers panel. It is highlighted by a blue bar once you select it, and handles appear around the layer. Double-click the text **Layer1** in the Layers panel, and type the text **block** to rename the layer. Press **Enter**. With the layer still selected, enter the following properties in the Property inspector:

   ◘ L (left): **24**

   ◘ T (top): **40**

   ◘ W (width): **100**

   ◘ H (height): **100**

   ◘ Bg Color: **#CC6600** (orange)

   The layer is repositioned on the screen, displaying new attributes. Click elsewhere in the workspace to deselect the layer.

5. Repeat Step 4 to create a second layer, and name it **block2**. Enter the following properties in the Property inspector:

   ◘ L (left): **57**

   ◘ T (top): **17**

   ◘ W (width): **100**

   ◘ H (height): **100**

   ◘ Bg Color: **#006633** (green)

   The layer is repositioned on the screen, displaying new attributes. Click elsewhere in the workspace to deselect the layer.

6. Repeat Step 4 to create a third layer, and name it **text**. Enter the following properties in the Property inspector:

   ◘ L (left): **73**

   ◘ T (top): **52**

   ◘ W (width): **350**

   ◘ H (height): **61**

   The layer is repositioned on the screen, displaying new size and position attributes.

7. Click in the text layer so that you can add text. Type the text **Adventure Travel** in the text layer. Select the text and enter the following settings in the Property inspector:

◻ Size: **+4**

◻ Font: **bold**, **italic**

◻ Text color: **#FF9900** (light orange)

The text shows in the layer, and the layer is positioned on top of the color layers.

8. Save this file as **adventure.htm** in the Sites\ch10practice folder on your working drive.

9. Preview the page (**F12**). Close the browser window when you finish previewing.

Project 10-2

The president of Adventure Travel reviewed the logo you developed in Project 10-1. While he is much more pleased with this logo on the top of the company home page, he still feels that the Web site is too static. Create a DHTML animation that moves the layers of the logo from separate positions on the page to the joined position at the top.

1. Open the file **adventure.htm** located in the Sites\ch10practice folder.

2. Make sure that the Property inspector (**Ctrl+F3**), the Layers panel (**F2**), and the Timelines panel (**Alt+F9**) are open.

3. Click the block layer in the Layers panel to select the orange layer. Drag and drop the layer into animation channel 1 on the Timelines panel. A lavender timeline appears in animation channel 1.

4. A message box, shown in Figure 10-19, may appear, if you did not turn it off permanently. Click the **Don't show me this message again** checkbox, if you wish, then click **OK** to close it.

5. Click the first keyframe of the block timeline in the animation channel. When selected, the first keyframe becomes a darker color than the rest of the timeline. Place your mouse over the block Layer tab, and drag it straight down your workspace. A black line should indicate the path.

6. With the layer still selected, in the Property inspector type **20** in the L text box and **520** in the T text box.

7. Repeat Steps 3 through 6 for the **block2** layer, but drag it into animation channel 2 and in the Property inspector type coordinates **800** L and **17** T.

8. Repeat Steps 3 through 6 for the **text** layer, but drag it into animation channel 3 and in the Property inspector type coordinates **600** L and **600** T.

9. Click the **Autoplay** checkbox at the top of the Timelines panel. This causes your animation to play when the Web page loads into the Web browser.

10. Save this file as **adventure_animation.htm** in the Sites\ch10practice folder on your working drive.

10

11. Preview this page (**F12**). If you wish to view the animation more than once, you need to press the Refresh button on your browser. Close the browser window when you finish previewing.

Project 10-3

The president of Adventure Travel is very happy. He has one more request. He wants a pop-up window to display a message welcoming the user once the animation plays. To do this, you add a behavior to the timeline that opens the message window.

1. Open the file **adventure_animation.htm** in the Sites\ch10practice folder, if it is not already open.

2. Make sure that the Timelines panel (**Alt+F9**) and the Behaviors panel (**Shift+F3**) are open.

3. In the Timelines panel, you see three animation channels with block, block2, and text timelines. The behavior channel located above these animation channels is marked with a B. Click the last frame of the animation to select it. Then click **Frame 15** in the Behavior channel. The frame turns black once you select it, and the Playback head moves to the last frame of the animation.

4. Click the **Actions (+)** pop-up menu in the Behaviors panel. Point to **Show Events For**, then click **4.0 and Later Browsers**.

5. Click the **Actions (+)** pop-up menu in the Behaviors panel again, and then click **Popup Message**. The Popup Message dialog box opens. Type the text **Welcome to Adventure Travel** in the text area in the message box. Click **OK**. In the Behaviors panel, you can see that your action has been scripted. In the Timelines panel, you see a dash in Frame 15 in the behavior channel.

6. Make sure that the **Autoplay** checkbox is checked in the Timelines panel.

7. Save this file as **adventure_popup.htm** in the Sites\ch10practice folder on your working drive. If a message dialog box opens, click the **Don't show me this message again** checkbox, if you wish, then click **OK**.

8. Preview this page (**F12**). When you finish previewing, you need to close the pop-up message before you can refresh or close the browser window.

Project 10-4

You have been asked to program a DHTML animation that takes a layer of text and moves it on a non-linear path around the Web page. You use the Timelines panel and the Property inspector to accomplish this by dragging the layer on a non-linear path.

1. Open a new file in Dreamweaver. Make sure that the Property inspector (**Ctrl+F3**), the Layers panel (**F2**), and the Timelines panel (**Alt+F9**) are open.

2. In the Title text box at the top of the workspace, type **Hello**. Press **Enter**.

3. Click **Insert** on the Dreamweaver menu bar, then click **Layer**. A layer appears at the top of the workspace.

4. Click **Layer1** in the Layers panel to select it. Make sure you see the black handles around the layer; if not, you did not select it properly. In the Property inspector, set the following layer attributes:

◘ L (left): **50**

◘ T (top): **50**

◘ W (width): **50**

◘ H (height): **50**

The layer is repositioned on the screen, according to the new size and position attributes.

5. Click in the layer so that you can add text. Type the text **Hello** in the text layer. Select the text and in the Property inspector, set the style to **bold**.

6. Click the layer to select it. Right-click the **Layer** tab and then click **Record Path**. Drag the layer around the workspace. The path is recorded for you in animation channel 1. Release the mouse button when your path is complete. (This is not a precise step. Your results vary depending upon where you drag the layer.)

7. In the Timelines panel, click the **Autoplay** and **Loop** checkboxes to select them, if they are not already selected. This ensures that your animation plays when the page loads and that the animation plays continuously.

8. Save this file as **hello.htm** in your Sites\ch10practice folder.

9. Preview this page (**F12**). Close the browser window when you finish previewing.

Project 10-5

In this project you alter the Web page you developed in Project 10-4 to include PLAY and STOP controls that the user can operate.

1. Open the file **hello.htm**, if it is not already open. The file is located in the Sites\ch10practice folder. You should see one layer with the text Hello in it.

2. In the Timelines panel (**Alt+F9**), uncheck the **Autoplay** option. Make sure that the Property inspector (**Ctrl+F3**) and the Behaviors panel (**Shift+F3**) are open.

3. To let the user control the animation, you need to add clickable links that have behaviors attached to them. Instead of linking to another page, these links play and pause the animation.

4. In the Title text box at the top of the workspace, change the title from Hello to **Hello Control** and click in the workspace. Press **Enter** twice to move down a few lines in the workspace.

5. Type the text **PLAY** in the workspace. Press **Enter**. Type the text **STOP**.

6. Select the text **PLAY** and in the Property inspector, type # in the Link text box. Press **Enter**. In the Behaviors panel, click the **Actions (+)** pop-up menu, point to **Show Events For**, and click **4.0 and Later Browsers**.

10

7. In the Behaviors panel, click the **Actions (+)** pop-up menu again, point to **Timeline**, and then click **Play Timeline**. A dialog box appears, indicating that Timeline 1 will play. Click **OK**.

8. Select the text **STOP** and in the Property inspector, type **#** in the Link text box. Press **Enter**.

9. In the Behaviors panel, click the **Actions (+)** pop-up menu, point to **Timeline**, and then click **Stop Timeline**. A dialog box appears, indicating that all timelines will be stopped. Click **OK**.

10. Save this file as **hello_control.htm** in the Sites\ch10practice folder on your working drive.

11. Preview this page (**F12**). Click the **STOP** and **PLAY** buttons to test the animation controls. Close the browser window when you finish previewing.

CASE PROJECTS

You are Webmaster for a site that gives small children opportunities to use computers. Create a DHTML page that permits children to clean their rooms by dragging their clothes into a basket. You will need to use the drag action to move the clothing layers. You will need to use the hide layer action to make the layers disappear when a child drops the clothes in the basket.

Create a personal Web site. You may use the one you created in the Chapter 9 Case Projects. Use the Behaviors panel to insert an action to stop and play sound on your Web page.

Create a simple movie to serve as an entry page to a business site for a cellular service company. The movie should play for 20 seconds and include multiple layers of text on a black background. Three different animations of text should fly across the screen: "Are you listening?" "Can you hear it?" and "Call us!" A link should be available to the user to skip the animation and go to the business page immediately. Try playing a background sound with your animation.

11

DREAMWEAVER PRODUCTIVITY TOOLS

Libraries, Templates, Browser Targeting, and Accessibility

In this chapter, you will:

♦ Learn about Dreamweaver MX productivity tools that make Web site creation and maintenance easier and more efficient

♦ Create, store, and utilize reusable objects in Dreamweaver libraries to enhance Web development productivity

♦ Create and use Dreamweaver templates to give your Web pages a consistent look and feel

♦ Use productivity tools to create, maintain, clean up, validate, and debug code

♦ Use Dreamweaver to test your Web site and HTML documents for accessibility and browser compatibility

---

In this chapter, you learn how to use more advanced Dreamweaver MX productivity tools. Thus far, you have learned how to use Dreamweaver to design and build a Web site, page-by-page. The Dreamweaver features in this chapter enhance productivity and take some drudgework out of developing, maintaining, and testing a complete Web site. Learning to use libraries and templates, taking advantage of code productivity tools, and preparing sites that are accessible to disabled users—and that target specific browsers—can help you develop and maintain Web sites that are attractive, consistent, and easy for your viewers to navigate and use.

Dreamweaver MX Productivity Tools

In Chapter 8, you used the Dreamweaver MX Assets panel to insert multimedia content. The Assets panel also provides access to library items and templates, two categories of assets that provide convenient storage for objects, HTML code, and page designs that you can reuse throughout your Web site. When you change items stored in a library or alter a template, Dreamweaver MX propagates the changes throughout your Web site or to selected pages.

Library items and templates provide similar opportunities to reuse objects and page design, but library items provide more flexibility and templates provide more control. If one person is responsible for designing a Web site, and if layout is likely to change, then library items provide more flexibility in making changes. If a group of developers are collaborating to build a Web site and only one developer has the right to change the design and layout, then templates are a better choice. Until you become comfortable using libraries and templates separately, do not use both together on the same page because managing them becomes confusing.

Dreamweaver MX also provides productivity tools that help you create, modify, validate, clean up, and test code on your Web site, and prepare HTML pages that are accessible and compatible with different browser versions.

Dreamweaver MX Libraries

Dreamweaver libraries are similar to the other, more familiar type of library. They are repositories of information that you can borrow and use again and again. Dreamweaver libraries contain library items, such as images and text, which are available for reuse throughout a Web site. Libraries actually store the HTML source code that either links to an existing object, such as an image, or defines the characteristics and content of information, such as text. Library items are great productivity tools, because once you set up and insert a library item, you can edit the library item, save the changes, and propagate them to individual pages or to every Web site page that uses them. You cannot edit instances of library items on Web pages unless you detach the instance from the library item. Detached library items are not updated when you modify the library item.

Setting up Library Items

Dreamweaver MX stores library items in a library subdirectory that resides within the local root folder of the Web site. The Library Assets panel displays library items associated with a Web site. Click Assets on the Dreamweaver Window menu, or press the F11 key to open the Assets panel. Then click the Library icon to open the Library Assets panel, shown in Figure 11-1.

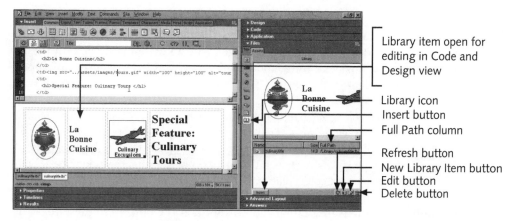

Library item open for editing in Code and Design view

Library icon
Insert button
Full Path column

Refresh button
New Library Item button
Edit button
Delete button

Figure 11-1   Library Assets panel and library item in Code and Design view

Dreamweaver library items can contain any element stored within the <body> tags of an HTML page: images, navigation bars, text, tables, forms, Java applets, ActiveX objects, and plugin objects. If the library item links to an object, such as an image, and you move the object into a different folder, Dreamweaver prompts you to update the links to the object. The filename extension for a library item is .lbi. The left side of Figure 11-1 shows the Code and Design view for this table library item selected in the Assets panel, culinarytitle.lbi. The HTML code for this library item contains table formatting, formatted text, and the pathnames and locations of images, their Alt tags, and their dimensions.

Library items cannot contain style sheets or timelines, because both belong within <head> tags, not <body> tags. However, you can create a library item with an element that includes a Dreamweaver behavior; Dreamweaver copies to the library item file the element, the element's event handler (e.g., onClick, onLoad, or onMouseOver), and the action that is called when the event occurs. Dreamweaver does not copy the associated JavaScript functions into the library item. When you insert the library item into a document, Dreamweaver automatically inserts the appropriate JavaScript functions into the <head> section of that document (if they aren't already there). However, if you (and not Dreamweaver) write the JavaScript code associated with the library item, then you have to use the Call JavaScript behavior to execute the code.

Setting up a library item is as easy as drag and drop. You need only select an object on a Web page and drag it into the Library Assets panel to initialize it as a library item. For example, to create the library item in Figure 11-1, you need to select the table that contains the images and text and drag it into the Library Assets panel. You then type the name of the library item, and Dreamweaver MX adds the .lbi filename extension and stores the item in the Web site library, as shown in the Full Path column of the Library Assets panel list. Giving the library item a meaningful name is important, as it helps you easily locate the item. You can change the name of a library item later, and Dreamweaver

11

will prompt you to update the library item filename on the pages that use it. A library item on an HTML page is usually highlighted in yellow. However, the yellow highlighting usually does not appear on images. Instead, when you click on the library item image on the Web page, it dims, and the library item Property inspector appears, instead of the image Property inspector.

It is possible to change the highlight colors for library items and locked and editable regions of a template by opening the Preferences dialog box (Ctrl+U), selecting Highlighting, and choosing other colors. You might want to change highlight colors if the pages on which you are working have similar background colors that make the highlight color hard to see.

The buttons for managing Library items appear at the bottom of the Library Assets panel in Figure 11-1, and are reused on some of the other categories of the Assets panel, sometimes with different names:

- Insert inserts the library item selected in the Library Assets panel into an HTML page.

- Refresh Site List refreshes the list of site assets to reflect changes when you add assets to or delete them from the Web site.

- New Library Item creates a new library item from any item highlighted on an HTML page.

- Edit opens the library item within Dreamweaver, as shown in Figure 11-1.

- Delete deletes the selected library item from the library but not from the Web pages on which it is inserted. You cannot undo the deletion of library items, but you can always restore a library item by selecting an instance of it on a Web page and recreating it in the Library Assets panel.

A number of useful Library Assets panel options, including the ones available as buttons on the Library Assets panel, are also available on the Options menu accessible from the expander arrow button at the top of the panel. Figure 11-2 shows this pop-up menu for the same image library item. Figure 11-1 shows the library item in its own editing window, while Figure 11-2 shows it inserted and highlighted in yellow on a Web page.

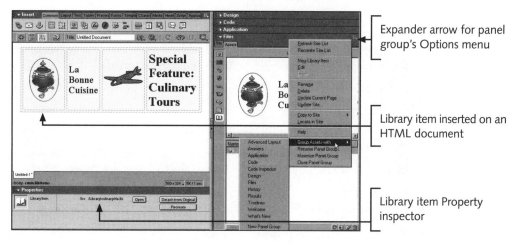

Expander arrow for panel group's Options menu

Library item inserted on an HTML document

Library item Property inspector

Figure 11-2   Library Assets panel Options menu and library item on an HTML document

This pop-up menu contains several of the commands represented by buttons at the bottom of the Library Assets panel and also offers additional productivity commands. Some of these commands involve the arrangement of panel groups, which you can display, remove, and regroup as part of the dockable panels on the right side of the new Dreamweaver MX integrated workspace layout. All of the commands are listed, but explanations only cover the ones that were not explained earlier in the discussion of the Library Assets panel:

- **Refresh Site List**

- **Recreate Site List** rebuilds the list of site assets from scratch. You need to do this, for example, after you copy assets into the Web site using Windows Explorer.

- **New Library Item**

- **Edit**

- **Insert** is dimmed on the menu because the document window contains the library item rather than a page into which the library item could be inserted.

- **Rename** lets you type a new name for the library item.

- **Delete**

- **Update Current Page** updates the current document with the current versions of all library items.

- **Update Site** opens the dialog box shown in Figure 11-3, which provides two search options: search all the pages on the Web site for library items and/or templates, or search for files that use the item selected in the Assets panel. You can select either option in the Look in: drop-down list. If you select Entire Site, you select a Web site in the second drop-down list at the

11

top of the dialog box. You can choose to update library items and/or templates in the Update checkboxes. Clicking the Done button performs the updates and, with the Show Log checkbox selected, displays an update log at the bottom of the dialog box, as shown in Figure 11-3.

- **Copy to Site** lists other Web sites to which you can copy the selected library item.

- **Locate in Site** shows the selected library item in the Library folder for the Site files list.

- **Help** opens the Dreamweaver MX Help files for the Assets panel.

- **Group Assets with** provides a pop-up menu that lets you group the Assets panel with a different panel group.

- **Rename Panel Group** lets you give the panel group a different name.

- **Maximize Panel Group** lets you maximize the size of the panel group in the vertical space available in the Dreamweaver MX integrated workspace layout. The Library Assets panel in Figure 11-2 is maximized.

- **Close Panel Group** closes the panel group that is open and removes it from the dockable panels.

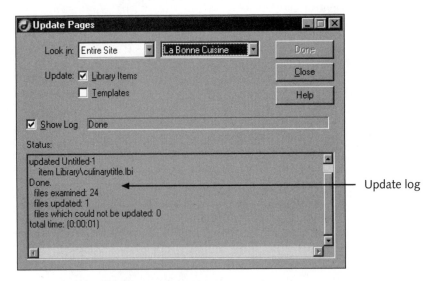

Update log

Figure 11-3   Update Pages dialog box

The library item Property inspector shown in Figure 11-4 provides information about the library item and offers options for managing library items:

- **Src** (source) provides the pathname to the location of the library item in the Library folder. You cannot edit this information from the Property inspector.

- **Open** opens the library item for editing in the same way as the Edit button in the Library Assets panel.

- **Detach from Original** breaks the link between the source file and the selected library item. You can then edit the library item on the HTML page, but it no longer is updated when you modify the library item itself.

- **Recreate** overwrites the original library item with its current version. This is useful if the original library item is missing or was deleted.

Figure 11-4   Library item Property inspector

Using Library Items

The real productivity enhancer of library items is the ability to create a library item, insert it on multiple HTML pages in a Web site, and then easily propagate changes to the library item throughout the Web site. The next steps show you how to create library items that you can use on multiple pages in the tour section of the La Bonne Cuisine Web site. The first library item is a text string announcing the next culinary tour, which you can insert on pages in the tour folder. Each time you change the tour information, you only need to update the text in the library item. Then Dreamweaver replaces the contents of the library item on all pages that contain it. The second library item is a table containing graphics and text found at the top of the page tour.htm. You can include this table on pages for local culinary tours to give them a consistent look.

When you insert a library item onto an HTML page, Dreamweaver displays the tag selector `<mm:libitem>` in the status bar in the Document window. The library item also appears with a yellow highlight.

When you create a text library item, Dreamweaver MX does not always include text formatting as part of the library item. For example, it may not center the text in the culinarytour library item you create in the next set of steps, even though it was centered on the Web page shown in Figure 11-5. If this happens, you can edit the library item by selecting it from the Library Assets panel and clicking Edit. You can then configure text formatting for the library item in its Property inspector and press the Ctrl+S key combination to save it. When Dreamweaver asks whether you want to update the pages that contain the library item, you click Update.

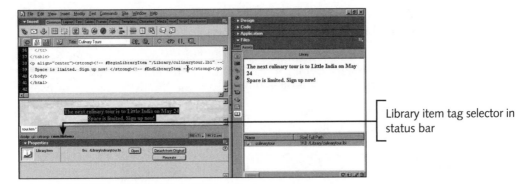

Figure 11-5 Creating a library item

To create a library item:

1. Start Dreamweaver MX, if it is not already running. Press the **F8** key to open the Site panel, if it is not already open. Select **La Bonne Cuisine** in the drop-down list to view the Site files.

2. Double-click the page **tour.htm** in the tour folder of the La Bonne Cuisine Web site to open it for editing in Design view. Click the **Assets** tab to the right of the Site tab on the Files Group. Click the **Library** icon to open the Library Assets panel.

3. Click to the right of the lower table in the HTML document, and press the **Enter** key to move to a new line. Type **The next culinary tour is to Little India on May 24**. Create a line break (**Shift+Enter**). Type **Space is limited. Sign up now!** Highlight both lines of text, and in the Property inspector, make them **bold** and **center aligned**.

4. Click the **<p>** tag in the tag selector to select the text, and then click the **New Library Item** button in the Library Assets panel. Type **culinarytour** as the name of the library item in the Library Assets panel. Press the **Enter** key or click elsewhere in a blank area of the Library Assets panel list or the workspace to complete the entry.

5. If the library item is not centered, click the **Edit** button on the Library Assets panel, highlight the text in the Design View editing window, center align it in the Property inspector, and save it (**Ctrl+S**).

6. If Dreamweaver displays the Update Library Items dialog box shown in Figure 11-6, which asks whether you want to update the library item in the file /tour/tour.htm, click the **Update** button. Dreamweaver then displays a dialog box, similar to the one in Figure 11-3, with a log file showing that it updated the page. Click **OK**. Click **Close** to close the dialog box. Close any open windows.

Sometimes there is a brief delay before the Update Library Items dialog box opens. If you do not see it immediately after you add a new library item, it should open when you try to move on to some other activity in Dreamweaver.

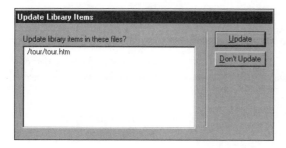

Figure 11-6   Prompt to update a library item

7. To create the second library item, click anywhere inside the table at the top of the tour.htm page and then click the **<table>** selector tag in the status bar to select the table. Click the new **New Library Item** button in the Library Assets panel. Enter **culinarytitle** as the name of the library item on the Library Assets panel. If Dreamweaver displays a dialog box similar to the one shown in Figure 11-6, click **Update**. You should then see the Update Pages log file shown in Figures 11-3 and 11-7.

8. Save the page **tour.htm** (**Ctrl+S**). Close the page.

11

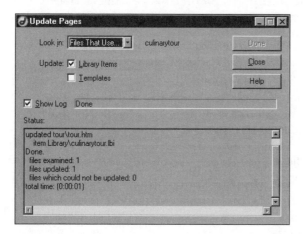

Figure 11-7   Update Pages log file

In the next steps, you use library items to update the local tour pages in the tour folder to give them a consistent appearance. Two pages, chinatown.htm and vietnamese.htm, are currently placeholder pages without content. Therefore you need to modify their page characteristics and insert content as well as library items. The other two pages, littleindia.htm and littletokyo.htm, already contain page content.

In this exercise you use Standard view to modify page layout. Because Layout view was used to develop these pages, they display blank rows and columns and have fixed pixel widths when you open them in Standard view. You need to delete blank table rows to reduce page length, center-align the tables, and change table widths to 95% to be consistent with the library item table you just created. After you delete any rows that cross all columns in the table, you can simply insert the two library items you just created at the top and bottom of the page, and the layout is finished. If you insert the culinarytitle library item immediately to the left of the table, Dreamweaver places the culinarytitle table immediately above the existing table without inserting a `<p>` tag and a blank line, which also reduces page length.

In the next steps, you use the library items culinarytour and culinarytitle to develop new pages and update existing ones. You then modify the culinarytour contents and have Dreamweaver make changes everywhere culinarytour appears on the Web site.

To develop and update pages:

1. Use Windows Explorer to copy the images you use in the chapter exercises from the Chapter11\images data folder to your Sites\lbc\assets\images folder: **beach.jpg, britishdairy.jpg, bubbles.jpg, chefstraining.gif, childtitle.gif, chinatown.gif, chinatownmarket.jpg, contactover.gif, contactup.gif, entertain.gif, entertain.jpg, ethnictours.gif, healthymeals.gif, kidspartyover.gif, kidspartyup.gif, littlesaigon.gif, medparty.gif, medpartyover.gif, medpartyup.gif, medsalad.jpg, medtable.jpg, partyhelp.gif, partyhelpover.gif, partyhelpup.gif, partyplanning.gif, picnicsover.gif, picnicsup.gif, picnictitle.gif**, and **vietnamese.jpg**. If you are asked whether you want to overwrite existing files, click **Yes to All**.

2. Start Dreamweaver if necessary, and press the **F8** key to open the Site panel if it is not already open. Open the **La Bonne Cuisine** Web site if it is not open.

3. In the Site panel, double-click **chinatown.htm** in the tour section to open it in Design view. Be sure **Standard View** is selected on the Layout tab of the Insert bar. Type the title **Chinatown Tour** in the Title text box on the title bar. Click **Set Color Scheme** on the Dreamweaver Commands menu. In the Background list, click **Orange**, and in the Text and Links list, click **Grey, Yellow, Orange**. Click **Apply** to see the changes, and click **OK** to close the dialog box. Save the page.

4. Open the Assets panel by clicking on the **Assets tab** in the Files Group. Then click the **Library** icon, if necessary. If the Update Library Items dialog box opens, click **Update**.

5. Place the insertion point on the Web page, if necessary, select the library item **culinarytitle** from the Library Assets panel, and click **Insert** on the Library Assets panel to insert culinarytitle at the top of the page. Click the Web page below the library item.

6. Click the **Insert Table** button on the Common tab of the Insert bar, and insert a table with **1** row, **2** columns, width **95%**, and cell spacing and cell padding set to **5**. Click anywhere inside the table, and select the **<table>** selector tag in the status bar. In the table Property inspector, click **Center** in the Align drop-down list. Place the insertion point in the first table cell, click the **Images** icon on the Library Assets panel to open the Images Assets panel, select the image **chinatown.gif**, and click **Insert** to insert it. If you do not see the images you copied into the Web site at the beginning of this exercise, click **Refresh Site List** on the Images Assets panel. Click inside the second cell, and use the same method to insert the image **chinatownmarket.jpg** from the Images Assets panel. In the image Property inspector, type **3** in the Border text box to put a border around **chinatownmarket.jpg**.

7. Place the insertion point to the right of the table, and press the **Enter** key to go to a new line. Click the **Library** icon on the Assets panel to switch to the Library Assets panel. Select **culinarytour** on the list, and click **Insert** to insert it at the bottom of the page. Save the page and view it in the browser. Close the page.

8. Follow the directions in Steps 3 through 7 to update **vietnamese.htm** in the tour folder. Type **Little Saigon Tour** in the Title text box, and set the color scheme as you did for chinatown.htm. Again insert the **culinarytitle** and **culinarytour** library items. Insert a table as you did in Step 6, and insert the images **littlesaigon.gif** and **vietnamese.jpg** (with a 3-pixel border) in the appropriate table cells. Save the page and view it in the browser. Close the page.

9. Open **littleindia.htm**. When you developed this page in Layout view, Dreamweaver inserted blank rows to complete the layout you requested. To delete these extra blank rows that add to page length, click and drag over any blank row that extends across the table to select it. Delete the row (**Ctrl+Shift+M**). After you finish deleting any blank rows, click anywhere in the table and select the **<table>** selector tag in the status bar. Click the **Convert Table Widths to Percent** button on the table Property inspector. Type **95** in the W text box, and be sure **%** is selected on the drop-down list to its right. Click **Center** in the Align drop-down list.

10. Click to the left of the table containing the images, but do not create a new line. Instead select the library item **culinarytitle** in the Library Assets panel, and click **Insert** on the Library Assets panel to insert it at the top of the page immediately above the table. Click to the right of the table containing the images, and press the **Enter** key to go to a new line at the bottom of the page. Select **culinarytour** from the list in the Library Assets panel, and click **Insert** to insert it at the bottom of the page. Save the page and view it in the browser. Close the page.

11. Open **littletokyo.htm**. Follow the directions in Steps 9 and 10 to update this page. Save the page and view it in the browser.

11

12. Change the contents of the **culinarytour** library item to reflect a new date. Select **culinarytour** in the Library Assets panel, and click **Edit**. When Dreamweaver opens the text string for editing, select the text **India** and type **Tokyo** over it. Select **May 24** and change it to **June 2**. Save the library item (**Ctrl+S**). When Dreamweaver displays an Update Library Items dialog box similar to Figure 11-6, click **Update**. Dreamweaver then updates the library item on each page and displays an update log similar to Figure 11-7. Click **Close** to close the dialog box. To see the update, view **littletokyo.htm** in the browser.

13. Close the browser.

It is possible to delete library items and still leave them on the HTML pages on which they were inserted. However, you cannot edit the library item on the HTML page unless you select it on the HTML page and click Detach from Original in the library item Property inspector shown in Figure 11-4. If you do not detach deleted library items, they remain on the HTML page, and you cannot edit them. They also show as broken links when you run the Check Links Sitewide command. In the next steps, you format the localtour.htm page to make it similar to the other local tour pages you just formatted. You also create a library item from a text string, delete it from the Library Assets panel, and detach it from its original page so it becomes editable again.

To create, delete, and detach a library item:

1. Open the page **localtour.htm** in the tour folder in Dreamweaver. Click **Set Color Scheme** on the Dreamweaver Commands menu. In the Background list, click **Orange**, and in the Text and Links list, click **Grey, Yellow, Orange**. Click **OK**.

2. Highlight the words **Ethnic Culinary Tours** at the top of localtour.htm. Open the **Library Assets** panel. Click the **New Library Item** button to create a library item, and name it **ethnictours**. Press the **Enter** key or click in a blank area of the Library Assets panel list or on the HTML document in the Document window to complete the entry.

3. Be sure that **ethnictours** is still selected in the Library Assets panel. Delete it by clicking the **Delete** button on the Library Assets panel. When Dreamweaver prompts "Are you sure you want to delete ethnictours?", click **Yes**.

4. When you click the **ethnictours.lbi** library item on the page localtour.htm, you see the library item Property inspector. The text is highlighted, because Dreamweaver still considers it a library item that you cannot edit on the localtour.htm page. Click **Detach from Original** in the library item Property inspector. Dreamweaver displays a warning message: "If you make this item editable, it will no longer be possible to automatically update it when the original changes." If you do not want to see this message in the future you can click the **Don't warn me again** checkbox, but letting Dreamweaver warn you is probably safer. Click **OK**. The highlighting disappears and you again can edit the text.

5. Highlight the text **Ethnic Culinary Tours** on localtour.htm, and press the **Delete** key. Be careful not to delete the plugin object to its immediate left, which is only 2 pixels by 2 pixels in size. Click the **Images** icon on the Assets panel to switch to the Images Assets panel. Highlight **ethnictours.gif** in the Images Assets panel, and click **Insert**.

6. Select the image map **lamap.gif** on the page localtour.htm. In its Property inspector, select **Align Center** and type **4** in the Border text box.

7. Place the insertion point to the right of the image map. Press the **Enter** key to go to a new line. Highlight the **culinarytour** library item in the Library Assets panel, and click **Insert**. Save the page and view it in the browser. Close the page.

DREAMWEAVER MX TEMPLATES

Like libraries, templates provide reusable objects. They provide similar productivity advantages, because you can change the look and feel of an entire Web site by changing a template and then propagating the changes throughout the site. With a template you can lock certain parts of each Web page as uneditable regions and define other parts as editable. From a usability standpoint, a Web site designed with a template provides consistent layout, color, and navigation, all of which help visitors to understand and navigate the Web site. In addition to the Templates category of the Assets panel, Dreamweaver MX provides new support for creating and using templates in the Templates tab of the Insert bar, and in the New Document dialog box, which lists the templates for your Web site on a Templates tab. Dreamweaver MX also comes with a number of page designs that can be used in the New Document dialog box to create HTML documents with designs, such as forms, articles, and product catalogs. These page designs can be created as documents or templates. Macromedia currently offers a tutorial as well as free Dreamweaver templates at *www.macromedia.com/software/dreamweaver/download/templates/*.

Setting up Templates

When you create a template, all of the regions on the page are locked or uneditable, with the exception of the page title. You must define which regions are editable. In addition, the page properties stored within the `<body>` tags of the template are locked. Dreamweaver defines the page title on each template as the editable region doctitle, which allows you to change the document title for each template-based page.

The filename extension for Dreamweaver templates is .dwt. Dreamweaver creates a Templates folder at your site root directory to hold any templates you define for the Web site. It also adds the templates to the Templates tab in the New Document dialog box so that you can easily create new pages based on your template.

11

You can define and manage templates from the Templates Assets panel by opening the Assets panel and clicking the Templates icon. The Templates Assets panel shown in Figure 11-8 is very similar to the Library Assets panel in Figure 11-1, except that it has an Apply button in place of an Insert button, because you apply templates to Web pages. The new Templates tab on the Insert bar provides immediate access to template commands, some of which apply only to HTML documents that retrieve data from a database. The commands on the Templates tab are described in the following list:

- **Make Template** opens a dialog box to save the HTML document open in the Document window as a template.

- **Make Nested Template** creates a template whose design and editable regions are based on another template. To create a nested template, you first create and save a document based on an existing template. When you click Make Nested Template, you can further define editable regions in areas originally defined as editable from the base template. Nested templates let you create variations on a parent template and give you more flexibility in developing different sections of your Web site. When you change the parent template, the changes are propagated to the nested templates.

- **Editable Region** lets you designate which areas of the template are available for updating in documents based on the template.

- **Optional Region** designates a region of the template-based document that may or may not be shown. The Web programmer who develops a page based on the template uses a conditional *if* statement to control the display of the optional region on the template-based page.

- **Repeating Region** adds multiple copies of the selected region in a template-based document. Repeating regions help you control the layout of regions that are repeated in a page. They are used on catalog pages, for example, to repeat data from a list of items. You may use them when you develop an application that accesses and updates a database.

- **Editable Optional Region** creates an optional region that allows the Web programmer to decide whether the content is displayed, as well as make edits to the content if desired. Editable regions are controlled by conditional statements.

- **Repeating Table** lets you define a table and then define the location of editable regions in each cell in the table. You define options to control which rows of data that come from a database are included in the repeating region.

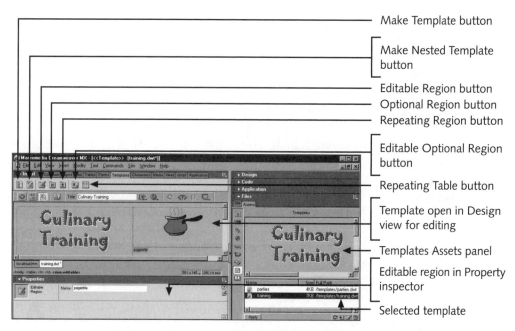

Make Template button

Make Nested Template button

Editable Region button

Optional Region button

Repeating Region button

Editable Optional Region button

Repeating Table button

Template open in Design view for editing

Templates Assets panel

Editable region in Property inspector

Selected template

Figure 11-8   Template in Design view, Templates Assets panel, and Templates tab on the Insert bar

11

Usually HTML tags enclose regions that you can edit. For example, you can designate as editable an entire table by making the `<table>` tag editable, an individual table cell by making the `<td>` tag editable, or text within a table cell by making the `<p>` tag editable. What is editable depends on the tags you select as editable. If you select the table cell tag `<td>`, you can add different kinds of content, such as images or text, to the table cell. If you select a text string within the table cell, then the editable region can only hold text; you cannot insert other types of media into the table cell. Once you define a region as editable, the tag selector `<mm:editable>` appears in the status bar in Design view.

Layers and layer content are also separate elements. If you make a layer editable, you can change its position. If you make layer content editable you can change the contents of the layer. If you have problems with editable areas when using templates, check the HTML code to see which tags are defined as editable.

Creating a Template from an HTML Page

Designing a template for a Web site is fairly simple once you know how you want the Web site to look. You can derive templates from existing HTML pages or create new pages initially as templates. When you save the first template for a Web site, Dreamweaver creates a Templates folder at the local root folder for the Web site.

When you save the first template for a Web site, Dreamweaver creates a Templates folder at the local root folder for the Web site to hold all the templates for the site. If you are creating a template from an existing Web page, you need to decide what regions of the page are locked and what regions you can change. Try to keep as much of the template locked as possible to minimize the number of items you need to insert individually in each page. Even if you can change a region, you can save yourself a lot of work by including plugin objects and placeholder text or images to indicate what type of content should be in that region. Then you can just change the names of the actual files to be inserted with the plugins or image tags.

The next steps show you how to create and save templates from an existing Web page. Your starting page is training.htm. This page has a title image, a table cell with contact information in Flash text, and a navigation menu with Flash buttons that link to other pages in the training folder: parties.htm, healthy.htm, and chefs.htm. In the following exercise, you add two Flash buttons to the navigation menu before saving the page as a template. You must create the Flash buttons on the training.htm page before you turn it into a template, so that relative URL links in the Flash buttons are saved in the training folder. Doing this assures that the Flash button hyperlinks will work on pages you create from the template, which are also saved in the training folder.

In this exercise, you work in Standard view, because it is easier to change and delete table cells before you turn them into editable regions in the template. You split the table cell containing the training.gif image into two rows, so that you can insert an appropriate title image for each of the three Web pages that use this template. One additional editable cell holds an appropriate photo.

After you save an existing Web page as a template, Dreamweaver does several things. It updates the Templates Assets panel, creates a Templates folder in the Web site if this is the first template for the Web site, places the template inside the Templates folder, and changes the title bar at the top of the Document window to read: `<<Template>>` [`templatename.dwt`]. You then select elements on the template that can be changed, and modify them to make them editable. In the following steps, you make an empty table cell and an image editable. You should be able to insert any new content you want inside the editable table cell and replace the editable image with another image. If you save the template without defining editable regions, Dreamweaver warns you, but you can still click OK, save the template, and open or work on it later to create your editable regions.

To create a template from an existing Web page:

1. Open the file **training.htm**, located in the training folder of the La Bonne Cuisine Web site, in Design view. Be sure **Standard View** is selected on the Layout tab of the Insert bar. Open the **Assets** panel, if it is not already open, by pressing the F11 function key. Select **Templates** on the Assets panel. The list on the Templates Assets panel should be empty.

2. Click the image **training.gif**, which looks like a cooking pot, on training.htm to select it. In the image Property inspector, delete **15** from the V space text box. Click in the table cell that holds this image, and open the Split Cell dialog box (**Ctrl+Alt+S**). Click the **Rows** radio button, and type **2**

in the Number of Rows list, as shown in Figure 11-9. Click **OK** to create an additional table cell below the training.gif image.

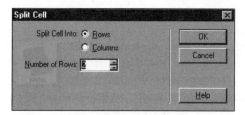

Figure 11-9   Split Cell dialog box

3. Click to the right of the Flash button that says Chef Training, and press **Shift+Enter** to go to the next line without leaving a space. Click the **Flash Button** button on the Media tab of the Insert bar. In the Insert Flash Button dialog box, select **Slider** in the Style text box, and type **Home** in the Button Text text box. Select **Arial Black** in the Font text box, and type **12** in the Size text box. Click **Browse** to the right of the Link text box, and create a hyperlink to the file **index.htm** in the Sites\lbc folder. Type **#CCCC99** in the Bg Color text box. Type **home.swf** in the Save As text box. Click **Apply** to see the button on the HTML page. Click **OK** to save the Flash button. Save the page (**Ctrl+S**). Test the new link in the browser to make sure it works correctly.

4. Click to the right of the Flash button that says Chef Training again, and press **Shift+Enter** to go to the next line without leaving a space. Follow the directions in Step 3 to create another Flash button with the text **Training** that links to the **training.htm** page, and save it as **training.swf** (as shown in Figure 11-10). Your Training Flash button should be between the Chef Training and Home Flash buttons.

Figure 11-10   Save As Template dialog box

5. Click the **Make Template** button on the Templates tab of the Insert bar to save training.htm as a template. In the Save As Template dialog box, choose the **La Bonne Cuisine** Web site. The word **training** (the name of the HTML page) should appear automatically in the Save As text box, as shown

in Figure 11-10. Click **Save**. Look in the Templates Assets panel to see the training template with \Templates\training.dwt listed in the Full Path column. Since this is the first template in this Web site, Dreamweaver creates a Templates folder to hold the template. Click on the Site tab of the Files panel group to see this new Templates folder that holds your training.dwt template. Because you are now working with a template, you should see the template name (training.dwt) in the title bar at the top of the workspace.

6. Select the new table cell you inserted in Step 2 by clicking inside it and selecting the **<td>** selector tag in the status bar. Click the **Editable Region** button on the Templates tab of the Insert bar to open the **New Editable Region** dialog box. Type **pagetitle** in the Name text box, as shown in Figure 11-11, and click **OK**.

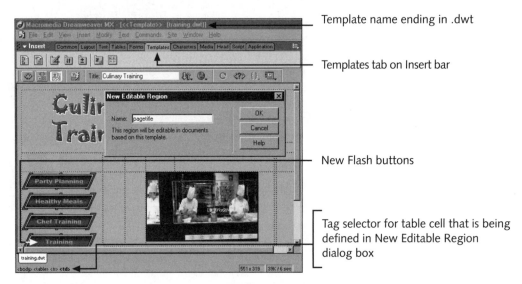

Figure 11-11   New Editable Region dialog box

7. Select the image **cooks.jpg**. Click the **Editable Region** button again. Type **photo** in the Name text box, and click **OK**. Select the photo and delete it from the page, so that you can replace it with other images on the pages you create from the template. Figure 11-12 shows the editable regions, and the HTML code for the photo editable region. If your photo region is not centered in the table cell, select the **<td>** tag in the tag selector, and click the **Align Center** button in the Property inspector.

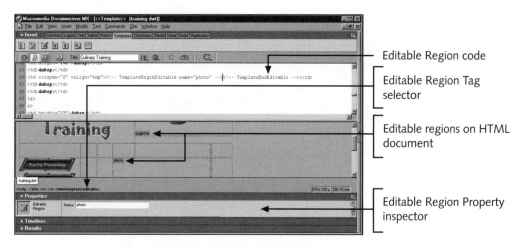

Figure 11-12   Design and Code view for editable region

8. Save the changes you made to the template (**Ctrl+S**). In a later exercise in this chapter, you use this template to update several pages. Close the template.

Creating a Template from Scratch

Creating a new template from scratch in Dreamweaver MX is very much like preparing one from an existing HTML page. First you create a new blank page and save it as a template. You define the page's title, background color or graphic, font colors, etc. As you lay out the template, you define locked and editable regions, and then you fill in the content of the locked regions.

To complete this simple procedure:

1. Open the **La Bonne Cuisine** Web site in Dreamweaver, if it is not already open. Create a new page (**Ctrl+N**). On the General tab of the New Document dialog box, select the **Template Page** category. Then select **HTML Template** in the Template Page list as shown in Figure 11-13, and click **Create** to create a new template in the Document window. Save it as a template by clicking **Save** on the Dreamweaver File menu. Dreamweaver may warn you that you do not have any editable regions on your template. Click **OK** to close this dialog box. In the Save As Template dialog box, select **La Bonne Cuisine** from the Site list, and type **parties** in the Save As text box. Then click **Save**.

2. Be sure you are in Standard view. Press the **F11** key to open the Assets panel, if it is not already open. Click the **Templates** icon to view your new template in the Templates Assets panel. Then click the **Images** icon to display the Images Assets panel.

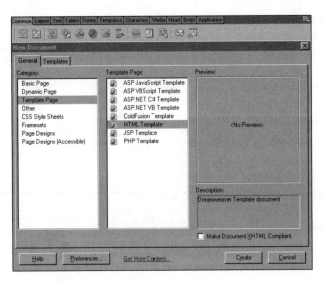

Figure 11-13 New Document dialog box settings for creating a new template

3. Open the **Page Properties** dialog box (**Ctrl+J**). Type **Parties** in the Title text box, and change the Background color to **#99CCCC**, the Text color to **#9933CC**, the Links color to **#003399**, the **Visited Links** color to **#CC99FF**, and the Active Links color to **#9933FF**. Click **OK** to save the settings.

4. Click the **Insert Table** button on the Common tab of the Insert bar to insert a table with **4** rows and **1** column, **95%** of page width, cell padding and cell spacing both **5**, and border **0**. Click **OK**. Click and drag down the first two rows to select them, and click **Align Center** button in the Property inspector. Click in the fourth row, then click the **Align Center** in the Property inspector.

5. Click in the top row of the table and select the image **partyhelp.gif** in the Images Assets panel. Click **Insert** to insert the image into the table cell. Leave this area locked so that this image is present on every page that uses this template.

6. Click in the second row and select the **<td>** tag selector in the status window to select the table cell. Click the **Editable Region** button on the Templates tab of the Insert bar to open the New Editable Region dialog box. Name the editable region **titlebar** and click **OK**.

7. Click in the third row, and in the Property inspector, click the **Split cells into rows or columns** button. Select the **Columns** radio button, and select **2** in Number of Columns list. Click **OK**. Click in the left column, unless it is already selected, and in the Property inspector, type **40%** in the W (width) text box.

8. Create the first of four rollovers to serve as a menu. Click in the first column in the third row. Click the **Rollover Image** button in the Common tab of the Insert bar. The settings for the first rollover image are shown in Figure 11-14. Accept the default image name that Dreamweaver inserts. For the original image, browse to **partyhelpup.gif** in the images folder. Browse to **partyhelpover.gif** for the rollover image. Leave **Preload Rollover Image** checked. Type **Party Help** in the Alternate Text: text box. Type **entertain.htm** in the URL text box. (This page does not exist yet, so you cannot browse to it.) Click **OK** to place the rollover image in the HTML document.

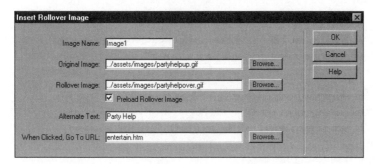

Figure 11-14   Insert Rollover Image dialog box

9. Click to the right of the Party Help rollover image. Press the **Enter** key to move to the next line.

10. Follow the directions in Steps 8 and 9 to insert three more rollover images. The second rollover should use **picnicsup.gif** and **picnicsover.gif**, display **Picnics** as its alternate text, and link to **picnics.htm**. The third rollover should use **medpartyup.gif** and **medpartyover.gif**, display **Mediterranean Party** as its alternate text, and link to **medparty.htm**. The fourth button should use **kidspartyup.gif** and **kidspartyover.gif**, display **Kids' Party** as its alternate text, and link to **kidsparty.htm**.

11. Click in the second column in the third row. Center align the contents of the cell in the Property inspector. Click the **<td>** selector tag in the status bar to select the table cell. Click Editable Region on the Templates tab of the Insert bar to open the New Editable Region dialog box. Name the editable region **photoarea** and click **OK**.

12. Place the insertion point in the bottom row of the table, and follow the directions in Step 8 to insert the rollover images **contactup.gif**, and **contactover.gif**. Type **Contact La Bonne Cuisine** as the alternate text. Browse to **interest.htm** in the **contact** folder to identify When Clicked, Go To URL.

13. Save the changes to the template (**Ctrl+S**). Close the template.

Using Templates in Web Design

In the next exercise, you use templates to format existing pages in the training section quickly. Then you use the parties template to create new pages. Using templates in this exercise makes developing the training section of your Web site easy and quick.

To format existing pages with a template:

1. Open the **La Bonne Cuisine** Web site in Dreamweaver, if it is not already open. Open the page **healthy.htm** in the training folder to edit in Design view. Press the **F11** key to open the Assets panel, if it is not already open. Click **Templates** on the Assets panel to display the list of available templates.

2. Select **training** in the template list, and click **Apply** to apply the template to healthy.htm. In the Title text box at the top of the workspace, type additional text to change the page title from Culinary Training to **Culinary Training: Healthy Meals**.

3. Click the **Images** icon on the Assets panel to display the images for the Web site. Select the image **healthymeals.gif** in the Images Assets panel and drag it into the light blue editable region marker that says pagetitle on healthy.htm, as shown in Figure 11-15.

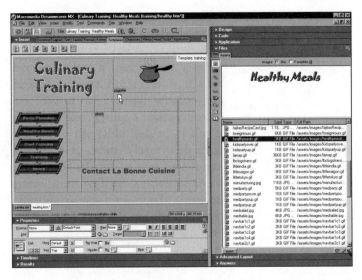

Figure 11-15   Dragging image into editable region on template-based HTML page

4. Follow the directions in Step 3 to insert the image **medsalad.jpg** into the photo editable region. Select the image, if it is not already selected, and type **4** in the Border text box in the image Property inspector. Save the page and view it in the browser. Close the page.

5. Open the page **chefs.htm** in the training folder, and follow the directions in Steps 2 through 4 to apply the training template and complete this page. Change the page title to **Culinary Training: Chef's Training**. Insert the image **chefstraining.gif** in the pagetitle editable region, and **britishdairy.jpg** in the photo editable region (again with a 4-pixel border). Save the page and view it in the browser. Close the page.

6. Open the page **parties.htm** in the training folder, and again follow the directions in Steps 2 through 4 to apply the training template and complete this page. Change the page title to **Culinary Training: Party Planning**. Insert **partyplanning.gif** into the pagetitle editable region and **medtable.jpg** into the photo editable region (again with a 4-pixel border). Both images should be center aligned. Place the insertion point to the right of the image **partyplanning.gif**, and press the **Enter** key to go to a new line. Type **Help with Entertainment?** and select it. In the Property inspector, change the text to the **Arial** font family, make it **bold** and **center aligned**. Type **entertain.htm** in the Link text box to create a hyperlink. Save the page and test it in the browser. Close the page.

7. Click **New** on the Dreamweaver File menu to open the New Document window. Click the **Templates** tab, then select **La Bonne Cuisine** in the list of sites, and **parties** in the Templates list for that Web site. Leave the Update Page when Template Changes checkbox checked, and then click **Create** to close the New Document dialog box and create the page. Dreamweaver creates a page with the two editable regions you defined. Save the page as **entertain.htm** in the Sites\lbc\training folder. Change the page title to **Parties: Help to Entertain**. Drag the image **entertain.gif** into the titlebar editable region (center align in the table cell, if necessary). Drag the image **entertain.jpg** into the photoarea editable region. In the Property inspector, type **4** in the Border text box for the **entertain.jpg** image. Save the page and view it in the browser. Close the page.

8. Repeat Step 7 using the **parties** template to create these pages in the training folder: (1) **picnics.htm**, (2) **medparty.htm**, and (3) **kidsparty.htm**. Title these pages: (1) **Parties: Picnics**, (2) **Parties: Mediterranean Party**, and (3) **Parties: Kids' Party**. Then insert images into the titlebar editable region on each page: (1) **picnictitle.gif**, (2) **medparty.gif**, and (3) **childtitle.gif**. Insert images in the photoarea editable region on each page: (1) **beach.jpg**, (2) **medtable.jpg**, and (3) **bubbles.jpg**. Again, place a 4-pixel border around the photos in the photoarea editable region on each page. Save each page and view it in the browser. Close each page after viewing it.

11

Changing the Web Design via the Template

Using a template as the basis of many Web pages eliminates a lot of tedious work. When you want to change these pages, you only need to change the template and then propagate the changes throughout the Web site, just as you did with the Library items. In the next steps, you add text to the template and update the pages to include that text.

To change Web design with a template:

1. Open the **La Bonne Cuisine** Web site in Dreamweaver, if it is not already open. Press the **F11** key to open the Assets panel, if it is not already open. Click the **Templates** icon to view the Templates Assets panel.

2. Open the **parties** template for editing by selecting it in the Templates Assets panel and clicking the **Edit** button.

3. Click to the left of the Flash Text object that says Contact La Bonne Cuisine, and press the **Enter** key to insert a blank line above it. Position the cursor on this new blank line and type the text **Contact us about upcoming training sessions!** Select this text, and in the Property inspector, choose the **Arial** font family, and make it **bold italic**. Center the text if it is not already centered.

4. Save the template (**Ctrl+S**), which opens the Update Template Files dialog box (see Figure 11-16). Click the **Update** button to see the Update Pages dialog box (see Figure 11-17).

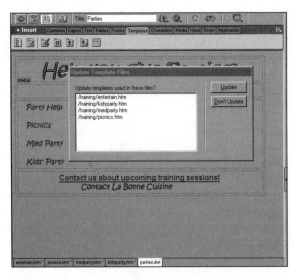

Figure 11-16 Update Template Files dialog box

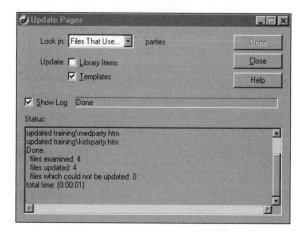

Figure 11-17   Update Pages dialog box

5. View the pages based on the training template in the browser to see the changes. Close the pages.

PRODUCTIVITY TOOLS FOR MANAGING CODE

Throughout most of this book you have been working in Design view or in Design and Code view to develop the HTML documents and framesets for your Web site. As you become more experienced, you may also want to fine tune or modify HTML code. Dreamweaver MX tools help you add comments, write, modify, clean up, and validate HTML code, and test and debug JavaScript. You can also find and replace page content and HTML code (including tag attributes) with Dreamweaver MX.

HTML Code Editing

Commenting code is good programming practice, because it allows you to document program modules and variables and explain changes and bug fixes. The Comment button on the Common tab of the Insert bar helps you comment HTML code by placing it within comment tags (`<!-- -->`). If you click the Comment button in Code view, Dreamweaver inserts the comment tags and you can type your comment in the blank space between the two sets of dashes, as shown in Figure 11-18. If you are in Design view, you click an object or text on the HTML page, click the Comment button, and Dreamweaver opens up the Comments dialog box. After you type in your comment and click OK, the comment is inserted in the HTML code, and a hidden tag is inserted on the HTML page in Design view. If you click on this hidden tag, the Property inspector for the comment opens.

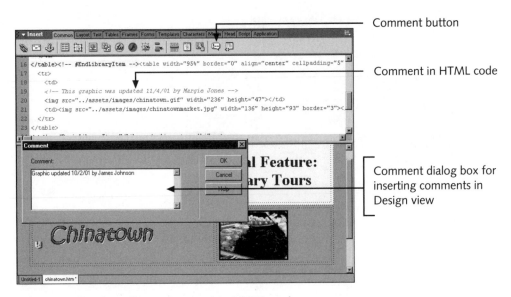

Figure 11-18 Inserting a comment in HTML code

You have already changed the tag attributes of text or objects on your HTML document by selecting the text or object and modifying its attributes in the Property inspector. The tag attributes then change to reflect the Property inspector attributes. The tag editor and the Quick Tag Editor also help you change tag attributes. Right-clicking an object, such as the image in Figure 11-19, displays a context menu with both tag editors. Right-clicking the tag selector for the object provides access to the Quick Tag Editor.

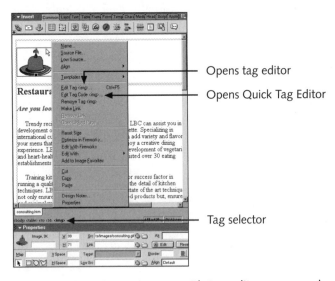

Figure 11-19 Context menu with tag editor commands

The Edit Tag <img> command opens the tag editor, a window that lets you set attributes (also available in the Property inspector) for the selected object. If you click the Tag Info expander arrow, the window shows reference information about the tag, as shown in Figure 11-20. This information is also available in the Reference panel, which is part of the Code panel group. This panel provides information and code examples from O'Reilly reference books.

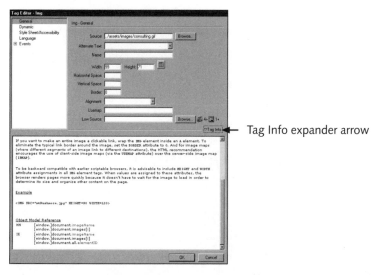

Tag Info expander arrow

Figure 11-20   Tag Editor dialog box with expanded tag information

The Edit Tag Code <img> command opens the Quick Tag Editor, shown in Figure 11-21. The Quick Tag Editor lets you type in the HTML code for tag attributes. It has three modes, which are available depending on the object that is selected by pressing Ctrl+T:

- Insert HTML mode lets you insert new HTML code.

- Edit Tag mode, which is visible in Figure 11-21, lets you edit an existing tag.

- Wrap Tag mode lets you wrap a new tag around the current selection.

Another tool that helps you manage HTML tags is the Tag Chooser, which lets you select a tag to insert into your HTML code. You right-click anywhere in a document that is displayed in Code view and select Insert Tag on the context window to open the window in Figure 11-22. You can choose from many types of tags. The Tag Chooser also expands to give you reference information about the tag and an example of its use. After you select a tag in this window, the tag editor opens.

11

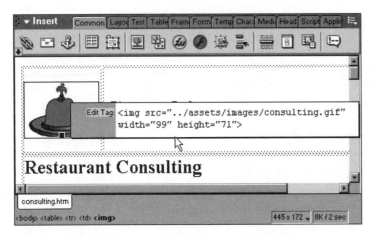

Figure 11-21   Quick Tag Editor

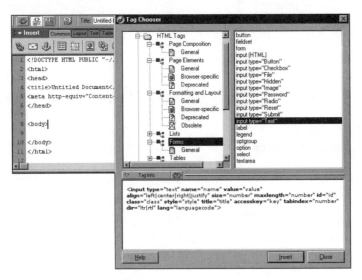

Figure 11-22   Tag Chooser

The Tag Inspector panel is part of the Code panel group. Figure 11-23 shows the HTML tags for an HTML document and the attributes for an image, which is selected in the Tag Inspector.

Selected tag

Tag attributes

Figure 11-23   Tag Inspector panel

You can find and replace text or code within a single HTML document, selected files, a directory, or an entire Web site. You can search for text, text surrounded by specific tags, or HTML tags and attributes. You use different commands to search for files, and to search for text and/or HTML. Figure 11-24 shows the Find and Replace window that searches the La Bonne Cuisine Web site for `<img>` tags with the border attribute set to 4 pixels. The results panel below shows a list of tags that meet the criterion, when the Find All button is clicked. If the Find Next button is clicked, then the next instance is displayed in the Document window. If the Replace All button were clicked, the border attribute would change for all of the images.

11

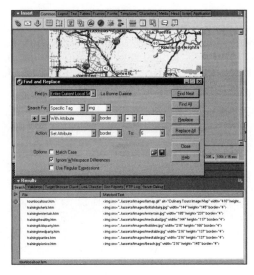

Figure 11-24   Find and Replace window and results for image attribute

HTML Code Cleanup

Dreamweaver MX provides other utilities to help you manage HTML code. Newer Internet browser versions overlook missing tags and other HTML errors and guess what you meant. However, it is best to create clean HTML code for your Web site, because a browser may misinterpret what you meant or older versions of browsers may refuse to load your page. Dreamweaver MX has a utility that cleans up HTML code, for example, by adding missing closing tags. You can import HTML documents that are saved as HTML in Microsoft Word without losing the formatting and functions from the HTML document saved in Word. When you import such a document, a Dreamweaver MX utility, Clean Up Word HTML, deletes some of the unnecessary HTML code that Microsoft Word inserts in the HTML document. Saving Microsoft Word documents as HTML documents can be quite convenient if the Word document is one that already exists. You can quickly see the value of these utilities by loading in a Word HTML document and running the utility to clean it up.

In order to have access to the Import command on the File menu in the Dreamweaver workspace, you need to have a document open in Dreamweaver, such as the blank document untitled.htm that Dreamweaver creates when it first opens. If you have closed all the documents in the Document window in Dreamweaver, you will have to open one up or create a new blank one to do the exercise.

To work with HTML code cleanup:

1. Using Windows Explorer, create a new folder named **ch11practice** within your Sites folder. Copy the Microsoft Word HTML document, **chapter11.htm**, from the Chapter11 data folder to the ch11practice folder.

2. Open Dreamweaver, if it is not open. Click **Import** on the File menu in the Dreamweaver workspace. If you already had Dreamweaver open, but did not have a page open in the Document window, you will need to create or open an existing HTML page in order to have access to the import command on the File menu. Then click **Word HTML** on the pop-up menu. Select **chapter11.htm**, and click **Open**.

3. **Word 2000/2002** should be selected in the Clean Up HTML from drop-down list. Leave all of the checkboxes checked in the Clean Up Word HTML dialog box, as shown in Figure 11-25. Click **OK**. A warning box then shows you all of the extra code that Dreamweaver is removing from the Word HTML document. Click **OK** to continue.

4. Click **Clean Up HTML** on the Commands menu in Dreamweaver workspace to check that the HTML code cleanup worked. Check all the checkboxes except Specific Tag(s). Dreamweaver will ask you to reconsider special markup tags, since that may remove template or library tags. Because this document does not contain any special Dreamweaver markup tags, you can click **OK**. The dialog box should say that there is nothing to clean up.

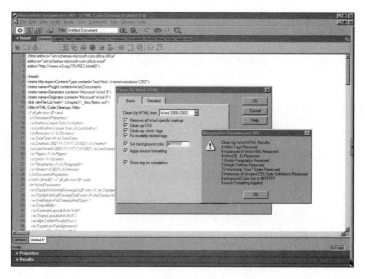

Figure 11-25   Importing and cleaning up a Word HTML document

5. Save the document as **converted.htm** in the ch11practice folder. Open and compare the two documents, chapter11.htm and converted.htm, in the browser window. Right-click each HTML document in the browser window and click **View Source**. Compare the source code for these documents to see what code Dreamweaver MX removed.

6. Close the window.

JavaScript Code Editing and Debugging

Throughout this book, you have accomplished tasks in Dreamweaver MX, for which Dreamweaver creates JavaScript code in the HTML document. For example, when you create rollover buttons or navigation bars, Dreamweaver writes JavaScript that loads the images, swaps them when the user rolls over or clicks the buttons, and opens a hyper-linked Web page. Of course you can also write your own script to accomplish customized tasks. Dreamweaver MX provides you with flexibility: it generates scripts for you, and it also provides editing and testing tools to write, modify, and test your own scripts. When you advance to creating Web sites in Dreamweaver MX that connect to a database on a server, you may continue to use the scripts that Dreamweaver MX creates, or you may begin to write your own scripts, either in JavaScript or Visual Basic Script.

This short review describes advanced Dreamweaver MX tools that will help you write and maintain your scripts:

- The JavaScript code in Code view in Figure 11-26 shows how Dreamweaver MX inserts JavaScript within **<script>** tags nested within the **<head>** tags of HTML document. While it is possible to embed JavaScript in other parts of the HTML document, embedding them within the **<head>** tags is better programming practice, because it is easier to locate them.

11

- The Tag Inspector panel in Figure 11-26 locates scripts in the HTML document when you click the `<SCRIPT>` tag in the window.

- The script Property inspector contains an Edit button that opens the script in the Script Properties window for editing, as shown in Figure 11-26.

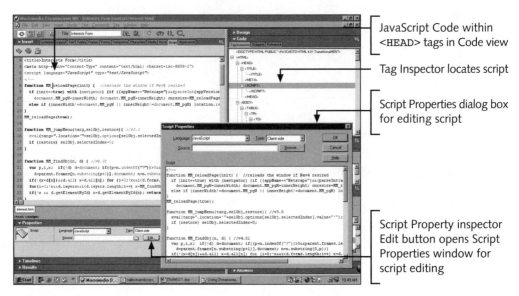

JavaScript Code within `<HEAD>` tags in Code view

Tag Inspector locates script

Script Properties dialog box for editing script

Script Property inspector Edit button opens Script Properties window for script editing

Figure 11-26   JavaScript tab, Script Properties dialog box, and Tag Inspector

The JavaScript debugger is an advanced tool that helps you step through your HTML document to find possible errors. You can run it in the browser by clicking Debug in Browser on the Dreamweaver File menu. Dreamweaver then loads the page in the browser window and opens the debugger window. You can watch and edit variable values, step through and skip over code segments, and set breakpoints that mark spots in the code where you want the program execution to stop. When the program stops executing at that breakpoint, a small arrow appears over the breakpoint, and you can examine the objects and properties that exist at that point. The JavaScript debugger also helps you correct logical errors. It creates and saves debugging documents that show information about the variable contents and the code that helps you figure out what is happening as the page loads and runs in the browser window.

Figure 11-27 shows the contents of the JavaScript Debugger dialog box displayed in front of one of the documents (MM_Debug.js) it creates to analyze the variables and how they change as you move through the document. The debugger creates a second debugging document (MM_DebugIE.js), which analyzes the script functions within the HTML document and what they appear to accomplish. When you develop more advanced HTML documents that connect to a database on a server, the JavaScript debugger will allow you to step through your work and make sure that the scripts accomplish what you intend.

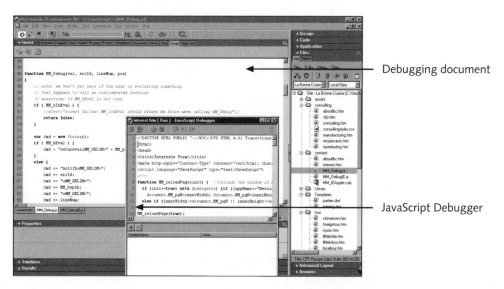

Figure 11-27   JavaScript Debugger dialog box and debugging document

TESTING YOUR WEB SITE

Professional Web site developers test their Web sites locally before they place them into production. You learned about one important command, Check Links Sitewide, in Chapter 4 when you initially set up the La Bonne Cuisine Web site. Dreamweaver MX provides tools as well as a number of tests that you can run on your Web site as you build it. Guidelines you might consider when building and testing your Web site are:

- Making your Web site accessible to individuals with disabilities

- Checking HTML code validation for target browsers and HTML standards

- Checking for target browser compatibility and routing users to compatible code or pages

- Checking for broken links and orphaned files (see Chapter 4 for more information)

- Minimizing file size and HTML document size, and methods to improve the usability of your Web site (see Chapter 8 for more information)

- Running other site reports to test and troubleshoot the Web site

Making Your Web Site Accessible

Accessibility is a big issue in design of all types as we have become sensitized to the problems of people with disabilities that may affect the use of tools and environments. Macromedia Dreamweaver MX lets you set up accessibility preferences that prompt you for additional information when you insert an object, such as an image, multimedia object, or form object, or create a frameset or table. This information may include alternative tags, titles, summaries, captions, shortcut keys, and short descriptions that are available to screen readers. This information makes the Web site accessible to individuals with motor, auditory, visual, and other disabilities. Dreamweaver MX also provides a tool that tests accessibility on a page, part of a page, or an entire Web site and gives you a report that you can use to make it more accessible.

If you set up accessibility preferences in the Preferences dialog box (which you can open by pressing the Ctrl+U key combination), Dreamweaver will prompt you for additional accessibility information as you create objects in HTML documents. Figure 11-28 shows the objects for which accessibility information can be entered: form objects, frames, media, images, and tables. You will be prompted for accessibility information when you create or insert one of these objects, but you are not required to enter information.

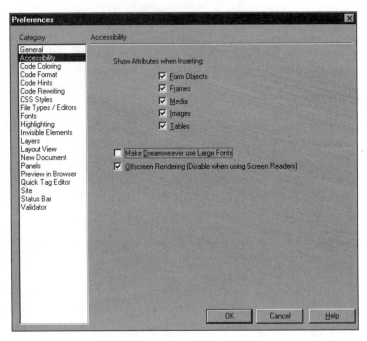

Figure 11-28 Setting up accessibility preferences

HTML Code Validation

Dreamweaver provides a validation utility that allows you to check your HTML code against standards for different Web browsers and document types, including HTML versions and Extended HTML (XHTML). XHTML is the Extensible Markup Language (XML) version of HTML that will probably be widely used in the future. XHTML has very strict tag requirements. All tags must be closed in the order in which they are opened if they are nested. Dreamweaver MX will create XHTML compliant documents if you check the XHTML checkbox when you create a new document.

You set preferences for validation in the Validator category of the Preferences dialog box. You then can run the HTML Validator for a single page or the entire Web site from the Results panel. The Results panel then lists the validation problems. You can save the results in a text document, or click on each line item to jump to the line in the HTML code where it occurs.

To set up validation preferences and validate code:

1. Open **converted.htm** in Dreamweaver Code view. Click the **Window** menu, and then click **Results** to open the Results panel. Expand the Results panel and open the **Validation** tab by clicking on it.

2. Right-click within the Results panel, and click **Settings** on the context menu, which opens the Preferences dialog box. Click **Validator** in the Category list and check HTML 4.0 in the Validate Against window. Deselect other options within this window, if necessary. Click **OK**.

3. Right-click the Results panel again, and select **Validate Current Document** on the pop-up window. Double-click several items to jump to their location in the HTML document. Many of the validation results occur because of style tags or Word HTML code that are not compliant with the HTML 4 standard.

4. Right-click the **Results** list, and then click **Save Results**. Save the results as **ResultsReport.xml** in the ch11practice folder.

Targeting Browsers

Throughout this book, you have learned about problems arising from browser incompatibilities, which are partly the result of rapidly changing browser versions, and partly fallout from the browser wars. During the most heated period in the late 1990s, both Netscape Navigator and Internet Explorer extended HTML standards and introduced new, nonstandard HTML tags to try to influence the direction of HTML standard development. Even though the browser wars have cooled, the mess remains. Dreamweaver MX provides a browser compatibility tab in the Results panel. If you select the Target Browser Check tab and then right-click inside the panel, it will check a single HTML page, a selection of pages, or the entire Web site against the browser version you select for a predefined set of browsers. For example, if you check the chefs.htm page that you created in the previous section of this chapter against the target browser Internet Explorer 6.0 (as shown in Figure 11-29), you receive warning messages about the tags that insert the Flash buttons and text. A warning states the possibility that the <embed> tags vary by plugin type.

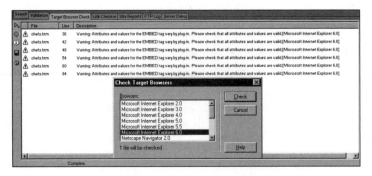

Figure 11-29 Checking browser compatibility

Converting Pages to Work with Target Browsers

Because many older browsers are still in use in the real world, Dreamweaver MX provides methods to deal with potential incompatibilities. You already learned one method for preparing pages that are compatible with older browsers: the Dreamweaver conversion of layers to tables. Only browsers at version 4.0 and above can handle Cascading Style Sheets and layers.

If your HTML page contains CSS and layers (both incompatible with version 3.0 browsers), you can use the Dreamweaver MX conversion command to change layers to tables and convert CSS code to HTML markup language. Figure 11-30 shows two HTML documents. The one on the left contains layers and CSS styles. The one on the right is the result of running the Convert to 3.0 Browser Compatible command and choosing both to Convert Layers to Tables, and to Convert CSS Styles to HTML Markup. Dreamweaver removed the CSS styles that it could not convert to HTML Markup, for example, the blue background for the page heading.

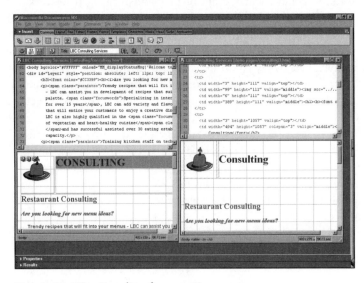

Figure 11-30 Results of converting a page

Redirecting Browsers to Compatible Pages

A Dreamweaver MX behavior can send the viewer to a page that is compatible with the viewer's browser. This behavior is attached to the <body> tag of a page with code that any browser can interpret. Web site designers who provide pages specific to a particular browser's capabilities usually have an initial page that loads quickly, checks the browser, and immediately presents a page compatible with the browser.

First you select the <body> tag selector in the status bar. Next you click the + button on the Behaviors panel, and then choose Check Browser. A dialog box opens. Here you define the URL to which the viewers are directed, depending on whether they use a Netscape version 4.0 or later or an Internet Explorer version 4.0 or later browser. The URL and Alt URL text boxes define the pages to which they are directed. The browser version numbers can also be changed, of course. Browser checking is an onLoad behavior—it occurs as the page loads.

To test for both Netscape Navigator and Internet Explorer, you must have both browsers installed on your computer. If you only see one browser listed in the Preview in Browsers pop-up menu on the File menu and have a second browser installed on your computer, you can add it by choosing Edit Browser List from the Preview in Browsers pop-up menu. Clicking that selection opens Preview in Browsers in the Preferences dialog box, which lets you add browsers to the list.

To set up the check browser behavior:

1. Create a new basic HTML page in Dreamweaver (**Ctrl+N**), and save it as **browsercheck.htm** in the Sites\ch11practice folder. Type **Browser Check Page** in the Title text box, and save the page (**Ctrl+S**). Type **Browser Check Page** at the top of this page, and format it as **Heading 1** in the Property inspector.

2. Repeat Step 1 to create two additional pages, but save the first as **iejump.htm** and the second as **netscapejump.htm** in the Sites\ch11practice folder. Change the title of the first to **Internet Explorer Page** and the second to **Netscape Navigator Page**. Type **Internet Explorer Page!** at the top of the first page and **Netscape Navigator Page!** at the top of the second page, and format the text in **Heading 1** format style for both. Save both pages.

3. Edit **browsercheck.htm**. Click the <body> tag selector in the status bar to select it. Open the **Behaviors** panel (**Shift+F3**), if it is not already open. Click the **+** (plus) button, and select the behavior **Check Browser**.

4. Make these selections on the drop-down lists shown in the dialog box in Figure 11-31: Netscape Navigator: **4.0**; or later, **Go to URL**; otherwise, **Go to Alt URL**; Internet Explorer **4.0**; or later, **Go to Alt URL**; otherwise, **Go to URL**; Other Browsers, **Go to Alt URL**; URL: **netscapejump.htm**; Alt URL **iejump.htm**. Click **OK**.

11

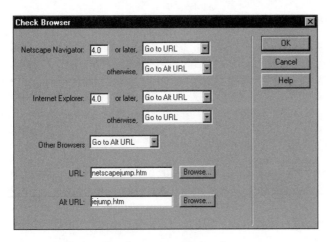

Figure 11-31 Check Browser dialog box

5. Save **checkbrowser.htm** and use the **Preview in Browser** command on the Dreamweaver File menu to test the behavior in both the Netscape Navigator version 4.0 or later and Internet Explorer version 4.0 or later browsers to see if it jumps to the correct page.

6. Close all open windows.

Dreamweaver MX Site Reports

Dreamweaver MX provides a number of reports that you can run against an individual HTML document, a selection of documents, a folder, or your entire Web site. The results of the tests are available in a report that appears in the Results panel. You can go through this list, clicking on each line item, and reviewing its occurrence in the HTML document, or you can save the report and print it out. Many of the line items may not be of consequence to you and the goals for your Web site, but some of the comments may be valuable to you. To run reports, you need to open the Results panel and click the Site Reports tab. If the Results panel is not visible, click Window on the menu bar and then click Results to display it. Then click the green triangle on the left side of the Site Reports panel to open the Reports dialog box. Select the types of reports and their scope (one page, the entire site), as shown in the Reports dialog box in Figure 11-32. The Reports dialog box shows which HTML reports were run against this page.

Figure 11-32 Reports dialog box

CHAPTER SUMMARY

11

❑ Dreamweaver MX libraries enhance productivity by letting you create, store, and maintain library items that you can reuse on many pages. Library items may be graphics, text, plugins, or other objects that you need to reuse. When you change a library item, you can choose to propagate the changes throughout your Web site, or only to selected pages.

❑ Templates are similar to library items in that they store page properties, layout, and content that you can reuse on many pages. You can create templates from scratch or from existing HTML pages. Templates have locked regions that remain the same on all pages that use the template, and editable regions that you can change on individual pages that use the template.

❑ The Dreamweaver MX Assets panel provides access to libraries and templates, as well as other kinds of multimedia objects on your Web site. The Assets panel lets you easily manage assets on your Web pages.

❑ Dreamweaver MX has many tools to help you manage HTML code and JavaScript, including commenting, writing, modifying, cleaning up, validating, and testing HTML code, and debugging JavaScript.

❑ Dreamweaver MX provides commands to test HTML pages for compatibility with specific target browsers. A feedback page indicates problematic tags and code.

❑ Dreamweaver MX also provides tools to convert HTML code on Web pages that contain layers and Cascading Style Sheets to make them compatible with version 3.0 and earlier browsers.

❑ A Dreamweaver MX behavior can check the user's browser version and redirect the browser to Web pages suitable for that browser.

❑ Dreamweaver MX provides tools and reports for testing individual HTML documents or your entire Web site in the Results panel.

REVIEW QUESTIONS

1. Dreamweaver libraries can store all of the following except:

    a. HTML source code that links to an image.

    b. HTML source code that defines a string of text.

    c. HTML source code that links to a Flash Shockwave (SWF) file.

    d. templates.

2. Dreamweaver stores library items in:

    a. a library file.

    b. a library subdirectory or folder within the Web site.

    c. a database.

    d. none of the above.

3. The icon that defines the Library Assets panel looks like:

    a. a folder.

    b. a question mark.

    c. an arrow.

    d. a book.

4. Dreamweaver MX inserts JavaScript that it generates inside `<script>` tags within which tag?

    a. `<div>`

    b. `<head>`

    c. `<css>`

    d. `<body>`

5. Dreamweaver stores templates:

    a. in a Template file.

    b. in a Template subdirectory or folder within the Web site.

    c. in a database.

    d. none of the above.

6. When you first create a template from an existing HTML page, which of the following occurs?

   a. All regions are locked.

   b. All regions are editable.

   c. The regions with existing content are locked.

   d. None of these is true.

7. When you create an HTML page based on a template, you may find that:

   a. the editable region differs from what you expected, depending on the HTML tags that you selected as editable.

   b. you cannot change the page title.

   c. when you select text that is an editable region, you can insert an image in its place on a page based on the template.

   d. the color changes to red.

8. The command that checks for browser compatibility is:

   a. Check Target Browsers.

   b. Fix Target Browsers.

   c. Get Target Browsers.

   d. Find Target Browsers.

9. Ways to make HTML pages compatible with version 3.0 and earlier browsers are:

   a. convert layers to tables.

   b. convert tables to layers.

   c. type Version 3 in a `<head>` tag.

   d. none of the above; it is impossible.

10. If you want to type HTML code into your HTML document in the Document window in Dreamweaver MX, you can use all but which of the following?

    a. Tag Editor

    b. Quick Tag Editor

    c. Assets panel

    d. Code View

11. The Dreamweaver behavior that determines a user's browser version is attached to the:

    a. `<check browser>` tag.

    b. `<meta>` tag.

    c. `<body>` tag.

    d. `<head>` tag.

11

12. Dreamweaver MX has made it much easier to create Web sites that are easy for hearing and visually impaired people to use. It gives you tools that help you configure and test the _____ of your Web site.

13. One of the testing tools that Dreamweaver MX provides allows you to test your Web pages to see whether they are:

    a. bloated with code.

    b. interesting.

    c. compatible with early browsers.

    d. too bright in color.

14. The HTML code for a Word HTML document that you import into Dreamweaver MX and clean up gets longer. True or False?

15. When you save changes to a template in Dreamweaver, which choice can you make?

    a. Propagate the changes to every HTML page on the Web site that uses the template.

    b. Propagate the changes to selected HTML pages that use the template.

    c. Changes do not have to be propagated to any HTML pages that use the template.

    d. all of the above

16. Library items are good to use when:

    a. you have items that appear on many pages in your Web site that you change from time to time.

    b. you want to reuse the same text on many Web pages.

    c. you want to maintain a consistent look and feel on your Web site.

    d. all of the above

17. What is the filename extension for library items?

    a. .dtr

    b. .dwt

    c. .lbi

    d. .lib

18. What is the filename extension for templates?

    a. .dtr

    b. .dwt

    c. .lbi

    d. .lib

19. You can tell an area of an HTML page that uses a template is locked if:

    a. it has a small lock image on it.

    b. it is not within the boundaries of an editable region.

    c. it says "locked" in the Property inspector.

    d. it says "locked" in the Templates Assets panel.

20. You can tell an item on an HTML page is a library item if:

    a. it has a small book image on it.

    b. it is highlighted in yellow.

    c. it says "library item" in the Property inspector.

    d. it says "locked" in the Library Assets panel.

HANDS-ON PROJECTS

Project 11-1

Eats Foods hires you to create a Web site to sell its products and services. The company needs the site in record time, so you decide to use Dreamweaver productivity tools to design and develop it. In Project 11-1 you create a Web site to use in the rest of the Hands-on Projects in this chapter. The templates and library items you develop in the Hands-on Projects should be separate from the La Bonne Cuisine Web site. If you have forgotten how to create a Web site, please review Chapter 4.

1. Use Windows Explorer to create a folder called **eats** inside the Sites\ch11practice folder. Open the **eats** folder. Create a new HTML document named **index.htm**. Create three additional folders called **products**, **services**, and **images** inside the eats folder.

2. Start Dreamweaver, click **Site** on the Dreamweaver menu bar, then click **New Site** to open the Site Definition dialog box. Name the site **Eats**; the location of the Web site directory should be the **Sites\ch11practice\eats** folder. Click the **Refresh Local File List Automatically** checkbox, leave the HTTP Address text box blank, and click the **Cache** checkbox to select it.

3. In the Category list box on the Advanced tab, click **Site Map Layout** to select it, and then click the **File** folder to the right of the Home Page text box. Browse to **index.htm** in the Sites\ch11practice\eats folder, click **index.htm** to select it, and then click **Open** to make it the home page for your Web site.

4. Set the number of columns to **4**, and set column width to **125** pixels. Check **Display Dependent Files**. Click **OK** to finish. If Dreamweaver informs you it is ready to create the cache for the Web site, click **OK**.

11

Project 11-2

The Eats Web site offers food products and services. In this project, you create a template that you will use for pages in the products section of the Web site. You must complete Hands-on Project 11-1 before you begin this project.

1. Copy these images from the Chapter11\images data folder to the Sites\ch11practice\ eats\images folder: **eatsfoods.gif, menus.gif,** and **medtable.jpg.**

2. Open the **Eats** Web site if it is not already open. Press the **F11** key to open the Assets panel, if it is not already open. Click the **Images** icon on the Assets panel and click the **Refresh Site List** button to display the images available in the Eats Web site. Create a new page (**Ctrl+N**). Type **Products** in the Title text box at the top of the workspace. Click **Set Color Scheme** on the Dreamweaver Commands menu, choose **Purple** from the Background list, and choose **Blue, Purple, Green** from the Text and Links list. Click **OK**. Save the page as **products.htm** in the Sites\ch11practice\eats\products folder. Click **Standard View** on the Layout tab of the Insert bar panel, if necessary.

3. Insert a table (**Ctrl+Alt+T**), make it **4** rows and **1** column, **95%** of browser width, and set cell padding and cell spacing to **5** and border to **0**. Select the table and select **Center** in the Align drop-down list in its Property inspector. Click in row 3 and split the row into two columns (**Ctrl+Alt+S**).

4. Click in the top row of the table, select **eatsfoods.gif** in the Images Assets panel, and click **Insert**. Place the insertion point in the row 2 of the table, and follow the same procedure to insert **menus.gif**. Right align this image in the row.

5. Click in the first cell in row 3, and type **30%** in the W text box. Click **Flash button** on the Media tab of the Insert bar. Configure the button as follows: Style, **Soft-Raspberry**; Button Text, **Appetizers**; Font, **Comic Sans MS**; Size, **12**; Link, **appetizers.htm**; Bg Color, **#CCCCFF**; and Save As, **appetizers.swf**. Click **OK**.

6. Press the **Shift+Enter** key combination, and follow the directions in Step 5 to create five more Flash buttons. Type the text for each button: (1) **Salads**, (2) **Pasta**, (3) **Meat & Fish**, (4) **Desserts**, and (5) **Home**. Link to the pages: (1) **salads.htm**, (2) **pasta.htm**, (3) **meat.htm**, (4) **dessert.htm** (which you create in Hands-on Project 11-3) in the Sites\ch11practice\eats\products folder; and (5) **index.htm** in the Sites\ch11practice\eats\folder. You can type the names of the link pages when you create the first four Flash buttons in the Insert Flash Button dialog box since they do not yet exist and since they will be in the same products folder as the Flash buttons. However, you should use the **Browse for File** button to the right of the Link text box to locate the **index.htm** file in the Sites\ ch11practice\eats\folder to ensure that the relative link is correct when Dreamweaver creates the last Flash button SWF file. Save the Flash buttons with these names: (1) **salads.swf**, (2) **pasta.swf**, (3) **meat.swf**, (4) **dessert.swf**, and (5) **home.swf**. Dreamweaver saves the Flash buttons in the same folder (Sites\ch11practice\eats\ products) as the page on which they are created.

7. Click in the second cell of row 3, and insert the image **medtable.jpg** from the Images Assets panel. Select the image, and in its Property inspector, click **Align Center**, then type **15** in the V Space text box and **4** in the Border text box.

8. Click in row 4 and click **Flash Text** on the Media tab of the Insert bar. Click **Comic Sans MS** in the Font drop-down list, type **20** in the Size list box, click the Align **Center** button, type **#0066FF** in the Color text box, and type **#CC6699** in the Rollover Color text box. Type **Contact the Experts at Eats Foods** in the Text text box, **mailto:eatsfoods@LBCuisine.com** in the Link text box, **#CCCCFF** in the Bg Color text box, and **email.swf** in the Save As text box. Center-align the Flash text in the table cell, if necessary. Click **OK** to save.

9. Save the page again as **products.htm**, and then click **Save as Template** on the Dreamweaver File menu to save it as a template named **products** in the Eats Web site. Click in row 2 and select the **<td>** tag selector in the status bar. Define the editable region **titlebar** (**Ctrl+Alt+V**). Select the image in the right column of row 3, and create an editable region, **photo**, that includes the image and its V space and border formatting. Save the template (**Ctrl+S**).

Project 11-3

In this project you create several pages in the products section of the Eats Web site using the template products.dwt. You must complete Project 11-2 before you begin this project.

1. Copy these images from the Chapter11\images data folder to the Sites\ch11practice\eats\images folder: **appetizers.gif, desserts.gif, meat.gif, medappetizers.jpg, medsalad.jpg, medshrimp.jpg, pasta.gif, salads.gif, tartphoto.jpg**, and **tokyonoodles.jpg**.

2. Open the **Eats** Web site in Dreamweaver. Click **File** on the menu bar, click **New**, and then click the **Templates** tab to open the New from Templates dialog box. Create a page based on the products template in the Eats Web site. Check **Update Page when Template Changes**, and click **Create**. Change the page title to **Products: Appetizers**. Save the page as **appetizers.htm** in the Sites\ch11practice \eats\products folder. Click to the right of the image menus.gif in the titlebar editable region, and use the Images Assets panel to insert **appetizers.gif** to the right of menus.gif. Click the image **medtable.jpg** in the photo editable region, and in its Property inspector, click the **Browse for File** button to the right of the Src text box to insert the image **medappetizers.jpg** in place of the image on the template. (If you use the Images Assets panel, you insert a second image rather than replacing the existing image.) Save the page as **appetizers.htm** in the Sites\ch11practice\eats\products folder.

3. Follow the directions in Step 2 to create four pages based on the products template: (1) **salads.htm**, with the title **Products: Salads**, which contains the images **salads.gif** and **medsalad.jpg**; (2) **pasta.htm**, with the title **Products: Pasta**, which contains the images **pasta.gif** and **tokyonoodles.jpg**; (3) **meat.htm**, with the title **Products: Meats & Fish**, which contains the images **meat.gif** and **medshrimp.jpg**; and (4) **dessert.htm**, with the title **Products: Desserts**, which

11

contains the images **desserts.gif** and **tartphoto.jpg**. Save all four pages in the Sites\ch11practice\eats\products folder. Test the pages in the browser to be sure they work correctly.

Project 11-4

In this project you update the products template and then update the pages in the products section that use the template. You must complete Project 11-3 before you begin this project.

1. Open the **Eats** Web site in the Sites\ch11practice\eats folder, if it is not already open. Press the **F11** key to open the Assets panel, if it is not already open. Click the **Templates** icon on the Assets panel to display the template list. Select **products** in the Name list, and click **Edit** on the Templates Assets panel.

2. Click to the right of the Flash text in the fourth row of the table in products.dwt. Press the **Enter** key and type **Visit us at the Foods Show at the Los Angeles Convention Center on June 4!** Highlight this text and in the Property inspector, choose the **Arial** font family, make it **Bold**, and **center align** the text. Save the changes to the template (**Ctrl+S**), and click **Update** in the Update Template Files dialog box. Click **Close** to close the log file and view the changed pages in the browser window.

Project 11-5

In this project you develop the index.htm page of the Eats Web site using the products template and then detach the page from the template so you can modify it. You must complete Project 11-4 before you begin this project.

1. Use Windows Explorer to copy these images from the Chapter11\images data folder to the Sites\ch11practice\eats\images folder: **britishdairy.jpg** and **prodservices.gif**.

2. Open the **Eats** Web site, if it is not already open. Create a placeholder page, **services.htm**, in the services folder.

3. Open the page **index.htm** for editing. Press the **F11** key to open the Assets panel, if it is not already open. Click **Templates** icon on the Assets panel to display the template list. Select **products** in the Name list, and click **Apply** on the Templates Assets panel to apply the template to index.htm.

4. Click **Modify** on the Dreamweaver menu bar, point to **Templates**, and then click **Detach from Template**. Select the image **menus.gif** and replace it with the image **prodservices.gif**. Center the image in the table cell. Change the page title to **Eats Foods**.

5. Delete the Flash buttons and replace them with two new Flash buttons, one with the text **Products** that links to the page **products.htm** in the products folder, and the second with the text **Services** that links to the page **services.htm** in the services folder. Follow the instructions in Project 11-2, Steps 5 and 6, to create a

new set of Flash buttons with the same formatting. Use the **Browse for File** button to the right of the Links text box to create the relative links to the two linked pages. Save these Flash buttons as **products.swf** and **services.swf** at the root directory (Sites\ch11practice\eats), the same location as index.htm.

6. Replace the photo **medtable.jpg** with the photo **britishdairy.jpg**. (Again, if you select the old image and browse to the replacement image, you can maintain the image formatting.)

7. Save the page and test the Flash buttons in the browser.

Project 11-6

In this project you use the products template to create pages in the services section of the Eats Web site, but you detach the pages from the template. Then you create a new set of Flash buttons and make them a library item. You must complete Project 11-2 before you begin this project.

1. Use Windows Explorer to copy the images **beach.jpg, bubbles.jpg, childtitle.gif, entertain.gif, entertain.jpg, medparty.gif, medsalad.jpg, medtable.jpg, picnictitle.gif,** and **services.gif** from the Chapter11\images data folder to the Sites\ch11practice\eats\images folder. If you are asked whether you want to overwrite existing files, click **Yes to All**.

2. Open the **Eats** Web site in the Sites\ch11practice\eats folder, if it is not already open. Open **services.htm** for editing. Press the **F11** key to open the Assets panel, if it is not already open. Select the template **products** in the Templates Assets panel, and click **Apply** to apply the template to **services.htm**. Click **Modify** on the Dreamweaver menu bar, point to **Templates**, and Click **Detach from Template**. Change the page title to **Services**.

3. Delete the Flash buttons. Follow the instructions in Project 11-2, Steps 5 and 6 to create a new set of Flash buttons with the same formatting. Their text should be: (1) **Parties**, (2) **Picnic**, (3) **Mediterranean**, (4) **Children**, and (5) **Home**. Link them to the pages: (1) **parties.htm**, (2) **picnics.htm**, (3) **medparty.htm**, and (4) **kidsparty.htm** in the Sites\ch11practice\eats\services folder, and to (5) **index.htm** in the Sites\ch11practice\eats folder. Use the **Browse for File** button to the right of the Link text box when you create the hyperlinks. Save them as (1) **parties.swf**, (2) **picnics.swf**, (3) **medparty.swf**, (4) **kidsparty.swf**, and (5) **home.swf** in the Sites\ch11practice\eats\services folder.

4. Click the **Library** icon on the Assets panel to switch to the Library Assets panel. Select the set of Flash buttons on the services.htm page, and click the **New Library Item** button on the Library Assets panel. Name the library item **menu**. Select the image **medtable.jpg** and replace it, using the **Browse for File** button in the Property inspector to insert the image **entertain.jpg**. Select the text that begins **Visit us...** at the bottom of the table, and click New Library Item in the Library Assets panel. Name this library item **visit**. If the library item text is not centered, click **Edit** in the Library Assets panel, **center align** the text in

11

its Property inspector, and then save it. If Dreamweaver asks whether you want to update pages that use this library item, click **Update**. Save the page **services.htm** and test it in the browser.

5. Click **File** on the Dreamweaver menu, click **New**, and then click the **Templates** tab to open the New from Templates dialog box. Create a page based on the products template in the Eats Web site. Save the file as **kidsparty.htm** in the Sites\ch11practice\eats\services folder. Follow the directions in Step 2 to detach the page from the template. Type **Children's Parties** in the Title text box at the top of the workspace. Delete the **menus.gif** file from the page, and replace it with the **services.gif** image file. Center align this image. Press the **Shift+Enter** key combination, and insert the **childtitle.gif** image file. Select the image **medtable.jpg** and replace it with the image **bubbles.jpg**, using the Browse for File button in the image Property inspector.

6. Again delete the Flash buttons and any extra blank lines in that table cell. Click inside the table cell. Select **menu** on the Library Assets panel, and click **Insert** to insert the replacement set of Flash buttons in that table cell. Be sure the **Library** Assets panel is visible. Delete the text that begins **Visit us...**, and replace it with the library item **visit**. Save this page as **kidsparty.htm** in the Sites\ch11practice\eats\services folder.

7. Follow the directions in Step 5 to create three more pages in the services folder: **parties.htm**, **picnics.htm**, and **medparty.htm**. Insert the two library items (**menu** and **visit**) to replace the Flash buttons and the text at the bottom of the page, as you did in Step 6. For **parties.htm**, use the page title **Parties**, the graphics **services.gif** and **entertain.gif** at the top of the page, and replace **medtable.jpg** with **entertain.jpg**. For **picnics.htm**, use page title **Picnics**, the graphics **services.gif** and **picnictitle.gif** at the top of the page, and replace **medtable.jpg** with **beach.jpg**. For **medparty.htm**, use the page title **Mediterranean Party**, and the graphics **services.gif** and **medparty.gif** at the top of the page. Save the pages and test them in the browser.

Project 11-7

In this project you change information on all Web pages in the services portion of the Eats Web site by changing a library item and propagating the change to all the pages that use it. You must complete Project 11-6 before you begin this project.

1. Open the **Eats** Web site, if it is not already open. Press the **F11** key to open the Assets panel, if it is not already open. Switch to the **Library Assets** panel. Select the library item **visit**, and click **Edit** in the Library Assets panel.

2. Change the text to read: **Visit us at the Foods Show at the Chicago Convention Center on July 31!**

3. Save the change (**Ctrl+S**) and click **Update** in the Update Library Items dialog box. Check the pages to see the changes.

CASE PROJECTS

Dreamweaver makes templates for and tutorials on Web site design available at *www.macromedia.com/software/dreamweaver/download/templates*. Visit this site and preview at least three templates by clicking on the Preview hyperlink under the template. Download one you like, unzip the tutorial, and browse through the templates tutorial to learn more about available templates.

Browse to the Netmechanic Browser Check page on the ZDNet Web site (*www.netmechanic.com/cobrands/zd_dev*). This page checks a single Web page or the first five pages of a Web site and gives feedback on such items as browser compatibility for tags on the page(s), broken links, and load time. If you have a Web site on the Internet, run a check on one of your pages. Otherwise, run a check on the Dreamweaver Web site (*www.macromedia.com/dreamweaver*). Then complete the following tasks, and write your analysis: (1) Analyze the results of this browser check, and discuss the problems with the HTML tags and page attributes. (2) How could you fix these problems? (3) Should you fix these problems? Try to figure out which problems that the Netmechanic found are worth fixing, based on the likely number of individuals who have browsers that do not understand the items listed as problems.

Write and format a resume for yourself in Microsoft Word. Use formatting such as bullets, indented text, underlined words, and bold text. Use Save as Web page to save it as resumeword.htm in your ch11practice folder. Use the Import command on the File menu in the Dreamweaver workspace to import resumeword.htm into Dreamweaver MX and clean up the Word HTML, when prompted. Save the cleaned up version as resumeclean.htm in the ch11practice folder. View both resumeword.htm and resumeclean.htm in the browser. Which looks better? View the source for both files and compare them to see what Dreamweaver MX removed when it cleaned up the Word HTML.

11

SHORTCUT KEY COMBINATIONS

You can use the information in Table A–1 to help you work more quickly and efficiently in Dreamweaver MX.

Table A-1   Shortcut Key Combinations

Menu Location	Shortcut
File Menu	
New	Ctrl+N
Open	Ctrl+O
Open in Frame	Ctrl+Shift+O
Close	Ctrl+W
Save	Ctrl+S
Save As	Ctrl+Shift+S
Print Code	Ctrl+P
Preview in Browser	F12
Debug in Browser	Alt+F12
Check Links	Shift+F8
Validate Markup	Shift+F6
Exit	Ctrl+Q
Edit Menu	
Undo	Ctrl+Z
Redo	Ctrl+Y
Cut	Ctrl+X
Copy	Ctrl+C
Paste	Ctrl+V
Copy HTML	Ctrl+Shift+C
Paste HTML	Ctrl+Shift+V
Select All	Ctrl+A
Select Parent Tag	Ctrl+[
Select Child	Ctrl+]
Find and Replace	Ctrl+F
Find Next	F3
Go to Link	Ctrl+G
Show Code Hints	Ctrl+Space

Table A-1 Shortcut Key Combinations (continued)

Menu Location	Shortcut
Indent Code	Ctrl+Shift+>
Outdent Code	Ctrl+Shift+<
Balance Braces	Ctrl+'
Set Breakpoint	Ctrl+Alt+B
Preferences	Ctrl+U
View Menu	
Switch Views	Ctrl+'
Refresh Design View	F5
Live Data	Ctrl+Shift+R
Head Content	Ctrl+Shift+W
Standard View	Ctrl+Shift+F6
Layout View	Ctrl+F6
Hide All	Ctrl+Shift+I
Show Rulers	Ctrl+Alt+R
Show Grid	Ctrl+Alt+G
Snap to Grid	Ctrl+Alt+Shift+G
Play	Ctrl+Alt+P
Stop	Ctrl+Alt+X
Play All	Ctrl+Alt+Shift+P
Stop All	Ctrl+Alt+Shift+X
Hide Panels	F4
Insert Menu	
Tag	Ctrl+E
Image	Ctrl+Alt+I
Flash	Ctrl+Alt+F
Shockwave	Ctrl+Alt+D
Table	Ctrl+Alt+T
Editable Region	Ctrl+Alt+V
Named Anchor	Ctrl+Alt+A
Line Break	Shift+Return
Non-Breaking Space	Ctrl+Shift+Space
Modify Menu	
Page Properties	Ctrl+J
Selection Properties	Ctrl+Shift+J
Quick Tag Editor	Ctrl+T
Make Link	Ctrl+L

Table A-1   Shortcut Key Combinations (continued)

Menu Location	Shortcut
Select Table	Ctrl+A
Merge Cells	Ctrl+Alt+M
Split Cells	Ctrl+Alt+S
Insert Row	Ctrl+M
Insert Column	Ctrl+ Shift+A
Delete Row	Ctrl+ Shift+M
Delete Column	Ctrl+ Shift+-
Increase Column Span	Ctrl+ Shift+]
Decrease Column Span	Ctrl+ Shift+[
Align Left	Ctrl+ Shift+1
Align Right	Ctrl+ Shift+3
Align Top	Ctrl+ Shift+4
Align Bottom	Ctrl+ Shift+6
Make Same Width	Ctrl+ Shift+7
Make Same Height	Ctrl+Shift+9
Add Object to Library	Ctrl+Shift+B
Add Object to Timeline	Ctrl+Alt+Shift+T
Add Keyframe	F6
Text Menu	
Indent	Ctrl+Alt+]
Outdent	Ctrl+Alt+[
None	Ctrl+0
Paragraph	Ctrl+Shift+P
Heading 1	Ctrl+1
Heading 2	Ctrl+2
Heading 3	Ctrl+3
Heading 4	Ctrl+4
Heading 5	Ctrl+5
Heading 6	Ctrl+6
Text Align Left	Ctrl+Alt+Shift+L
Text Align Center	Ctrl+Alt+Shift+C
Text Align Right	Ctrl+Alt+Shift+R
Text Align Justify	Ctrl+Alt+Shift+J
Text Style Bold	Ctrl+B
Text Style Italic	Ctrl+I
Edit Style Sheet	Ctrl+Shift+E

Table A-1   Shortcut Key Combinations (continued)

Menu Location	Shortcut
Check Spelling	Shift+F7
Commands Menu	
Start Recording	Ctrl+Shift+X
Site Menu	
Site Files	F8
Site Map	Alt+F8
Get	Ctrl+Shift+D
Check Out	Ctrl+Alt+Shift+D
Put	Ctrl+Shift+U
Check In	Ctrl+Alt+Shift+U
Windows Menu	
Insert	Ctrl+F2
Properties	Ctrl+F3
Answers	Alt+F1
CSS Styles	Shift+F11
HTML Styles	Ctrl+F11
Behaviors	Shift+F3
Tag Inspector	F9
Snippets	Shift+F9
Reference	Shift+F1
Database	Ctrl+Shift+F10
Bindings	Ctrl+F10
Server Behaviors	Ctrl+F9
Components	Ctrl+F7
Site	F8
Assets	F11
Search	Ctrl+Shift+F
Validation	Ctrl+Shift+F7
Target Browser Check	Ctrl+Shift+F8
Link Checker	Ctrl+Shift+F9
Site Reports	Ctrl+Shift+F11
FTP Log	Ctrl+Shift+F12
Server Debug	Ctrl+Shift+F5
Code Inspector	F10
Frames	Shift+F2
History	Shift+F10

Table A-1   Shortcut Key Combinations (continued)

Menu Location	Shortcut
Layers	F2
Sitespring	F7
Timelines	Alt+F9
Hide Panels	F4
Help Menu	
Using Dreamweaver	F1
Using ColdFusion	Ctrl+F1
Reference	Shift+F1

A

Index

489